Contractarianism and Rational Choice

Contractarianism and Rational Choice

Essays on David Gauthier's *Morals by Agreement*

Peter Vallentyne, editor

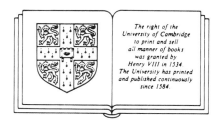

The right of the
University of Cambridge
to print and sell
all manner of books
was granted by
Henry VIII in 1534.
The University has printed
and published continuously
since 1584.

Cambridge University Press

New York

Cambridge   Port Chester   Melbourne   Sydney

Published by the Press Syndicate of the University of Cambridge
The Pitt Building, Trumpington Street, Cambridge CB2 1RP
40 West 20th Street, New York, NY 10011, USA
10 Stamford Road, Oakleigh, Melbourne 3166, Australia

First published 1991

Printed in the United States of America

Library Cataloging in Publication Data
Contractarianism and rational choice : essays on David
    Gauthier's Morals by agreement / Peter Vallentyne, editor.
    p.   cm.
    Includes bibliographical references and index.
    ISBN 0-521-39134-2.—ISBN 0-521-39815-0 (pbk.)
    1. Gauthier, David P. Morals by agreement. 2. Ethics.
3. Contracts. 4. Cooperation. I. Vallentyne, Peter
    BJ1012.038 1991
171—dc20   90-387744
                                                  CIP

British Library Cataloguing in Publication Data
Contractarianism and rational choice : essays on David
    Gauthier's Morals by agreement.
    1. Moral philosophy. Theories of Gauthier, David P. (David Peter)
    I. Vallentyne, Peter
    170.92

    ISBN 0-521-39134-2
    ISBN 0-521-39815-0 pbk

Contents

Preface

This anthology started out as a collection of papers presented at a conference on contemporary contractarian thought that I organized in April 1987 at the University of Western Ontario. Not surprisingly, all but a few of the essays dealt primarily with the work of David Gauthier. In order to increase the focus and coherence of the volume, I decided to drop the pieces that were not specifically on Gauthier's work and to add some pieces on aspects of Gauthier's project not addressed by the other papers.

A great number of thanks are due. To start, the conference from which this volume comes, and some of the prepublication costs, were funded by a grant from the Social Sciences and Humanities Research Council of Canada (#443–87–0012). The conference was also funded by grants from The Faculty of Arts (via the Philosophy Department), The Faculty of Social Sciences, and The Center for Critical Theory at The University of Western Ontario. Terence Moore, Humanities Editor at Cambridge University Press, has been a true delight to work with. He has been extremely supportive and reasonable. David Gauthier kindly agreed to find the time in a tight schedule to write a concluding comment for the volume. David Copp, Jean Hampton, and Chris Morris each provided important advice about getting the volume published. Most of all, however, I owe a deep debt of gratitude to Jules Coleman and Geoff Sayre-McCord. Right from the beginning, Geoff was my main consultant, and without his support and advice, the volume would not have made it to press. Jules Coleman was not involved in the beginning stages, but he was absolutely crucial at the later stages. He very kindly took the time on several occasions to provide specific suggestions on how the volume could be improved in content and organization. Finally, all the contributors have been extremely patient with the slow pace at which the volume has come together.

Notes on the contributors

David Braybrooke is McCullough Professor of Philosophy and Politics at Dalhousie University, where he has taught since 1963. He has published many articles on ethics and political philosophy; and several books, among them *A Strategy of Decision: Policy Evaluation as a Social Process* (with C. E. Lindblom); *Three Tests for Democracy: Personal Rights, Human Welfare, Collective Preference*; and, most recently, *Meeting Needs*.

Jules L. Coleman is Professor of Law and Philosophy at Yale Law School. His most recent book is *Markets, Morals, and the Law* (Cambridge University Press). He is currently completing a book, *Rationality, Risks, and Wrongs*, that is to be published by Cambridge.

David Copp is Professor of Philosophy at the University of California, Davis, where he recently moved from Simon Fraser University and the University of Illinois at Chicago. He has published articles on moral and political philosophy, and coedited *Morality, Reason and Truth* and *Pornography and Censorship*. He is currently writing *Morality, Skepticism, and Society*, a book on the foundations of ethics.

Peter Danielson is Associate Professor of Philosophy at the University of British Columbia, where he teaches political philosophy, ethics, and computer science. He has just completed a book entitled *Artificial Morality*.

Wulf Gaertner studied economics at the University of Bonn, where he received his diploma degree as well as his Ph.D. in economics. He was a lecturer at Bielefeld University and has been a full professor of economics at the University of Osnabrück, West Germany, since 1980. His main areas of research are microeconomic theory, welfare economics, and social choice theory. He is one of the editors of *Social Choice and Welfare*.

Jean Hampton is Associate Professor of Philosophy at the University of California, Davis, and has taught at UCLA and the University of Pittsburgh. She is the author of *Hobbes and the Social Contract Tradition*, and (with Jeffrie Murphy) *Forgiveness and Mercy* (both with Cambridge University Press). Her interests range over topics in political philosophy, ethics, and the philosophy of law.

Donald C. Hubin is an Associate Professor of Philosophy at Ohio State University. His research interests include ethics, practical reasoning, distributive justice, and decision theory.

Marlies Klemisch-Ahlert received her diploma degree and her Ph.D. from the Department of Mathematics of the University of Bielefeld, West Germany. She now is Research Assistant at the Department of Economics of the University of Osnabrück, West Germany. Her main area of research is game theory and its various applications.

Jody S. Kraus received his Ph.D. in Philosophy from the University of Arizona upon completion of a thesis exploring the relationship between game theory and contractarian accounts of political justification. He is now Assistant Professor at the School of Law, University of Virginia.

Mark B. Lambeth is a Ph.D. candidate at Ohio State University, writing his dissertation on Kant's moral philosophy. He is currently working as a developer of computer-based training for Progressive Companies.

Christopher Morris is Associate Professor of Philosophy at Bowling Green State University, Ohio. His interests are in moral and political philosophy, in particular the contractarian tradition and rational-choice theory. He has written essays on a variety of topics on moral and political philosophy, including Gauthier's moral theory, Hobbesian political theory, natural rights, and the ethics of nuclear deterrence. At present he is writing a book on the justification of modern states.

Jan Narveson, B.A. (Chicago), Ph.D. (Harvard), is Professor of Philosophy at the University of Waterloo in Ontario. He is the author of many papers in philosophical periodicals and anthologies, mainly on ethical theory and practice, and of *Morality and Utility*, *The Idea of Libertarianism*, and the editor of *Moral Issues*. He is also on the editorial boards of *Ethics*, *Social Philosophy and Policy*, and several other journals.

Geoffrey Sayre-McCord is Associate Professor of Philosophy at University of North Carolina, Chapel Hill. He has published a number of papers, most of them on moral theory, and has edited a collection of papers on moral realism.

Holly M. Smith is Professor and Head of the Philosophy Department at the University of Arizona. She has written on normative theory, applied ethics, and metaethics, and is presently writing a book entitled *Moral Failings* on the question of how moral theories ought to accommodate cognitive failings that prevent agents from doing what morality requires.

Peter Vallentyne is Associate Professor of Philosophy at the Virginia Commonwealth University. He has written on the teleological/deontological distinction, how teleological theories can be past-regarding, moral dilemmas, deontic logic, moral realism, the theory of social choice, contractarian theory, combining rights and welfare, equal opportunity and the family, and laws of nature. He is currently writing a book on a moral theory that combines rights considerations with welfare considerations.

Biographical note
on David Gauthier

David Gauthier was born in Toronto in 1932 and educated at the University of Toronto (B.A. Hons., 1954), Harvard University (A.M., 1955), and the University of Oxford (B.Phil., 1957; D.Phil., 1961). In 1979, he was elected a Fellow of the Royal Society of Canada (F.R.S.C.).

From 1958 to 1980, he was a member of the Department of Philosophy at the University of Toronto, serving as Chairman from 1974 to 1979. Since 1980, he has been a member of the Department of Philosophy at the University of Pittsburgh, serving as Chairman from 1983 to 1987, and being appointed a Distinguished Service Professor in 1986. He is also a Senior Research Fellow at the Center for Philosophy of Science. He has held visiting appointments at UCLA, UC Berkeley, Princeton, and UC Irvine.

Gauthier is the author of numerous articles and three books, *Practical Reasoning* (Oxford University Press, 1963), *The Logic of Leviathan* (Oxford University Press, 1969), and *Morals by Agreement* (Oxford University Press, 1986). The most recent book is the fruit of two decades of work on developing a contractarian moral theory within the framework of rational choice. A conference on this book was held in April 1987 at the Social Philosophy and Policy Center at Bowling Green State University; the papers have appeared as *The New Social Contract: Essays on Gauthier* (Blackwell, 1988). A second conference on this book took place at the University of East Anglia in March 1989.

In addition to systematic work in moral theory, Gauthier's main philosophical interests are in the history of political philosophy, with special attention to Hobbes and Rousseau, and in the theory of practical rationality, where he begins from an attempt to understand economic rationality, rather than from Kantian or Aristotelian antecedents.

His principal nonphilosophical interest, arising from his observation of trolley cars while still in his pram, is in what is now called light rail transit. When much younger, he was an unsuccessful candidate for election to the Canadian House of Commons, an occasional newspaper columnist, and a writer on public affairs.

1. Gauthier's three projects

Peter Vallentyne

Introduction

Over the last twenty years, and most notably in his recent book *Morals by Agreement*, David Gauthier has been engaged in three distinct, but closely related, projects: (1) defending a contractarian theory of morality, (2) defending a theory of rational choice, and (3) defending the claim that rationality requires that we comply with the dictates of morality.[1] In this introduction, I give a brief overview of Gauthier's work (as it appears in his book) on each of these three projects. We start with his views on morality.

Gauthier's moral methodology

In a world in which the conditions of perfect competition hold – most importantly: there are no externalities, that is, no one is affected by the actions of others except by consent – the unconstrained pursuit of self-interest leads to Pareto optimal results (i.e., results such that no one can be made better off except by making someone else worse off). In such a world, there are, Gauthier holds, no moral constraints on action. In

---

[1] Some of the main articles leading up to Gauthier's book *Morals by Agreement* (Oxford: University Press, 1986) are "Morality and Advantage," *Philosophical Review* 76 (1967): 460–75; "Rational Cooperation," *Noûs* 8 (1974): 53–65; "Reason and Maximization," *Canadian Journal of Philosophy* 4 (1975): 411–33; "The Social Contract as Ideology," *Philosophy and Public Affairs* 6 (1977): 130–64; and "The Social Contract: Individual Decision or Collective Bargain?" in *Foundations and Applications of Decision Theory*, Vol. 2, edited by Cliff Hooker, Jim Leach, and Edward McClennen (Dordrecht, Holland: D. Reidel, 1978), pp. 47–67. Since the publication of the book, a number of journals have devoted volumes to a critical assessment of his work. See, for example, the articles in *Ethics* 97(4) (1987), *Canadian Journal of Philosophy* 18(2) (1988), and *Social Philosophy and Policy* 5(2) (1988).

our world, however, the conditions of perfect competition do not hold. In particular, the world is full of externalities. Consequently, as the familiar Prisoner's Dilemma illustrates, the unconstrained pursuit of self-interest often leads to outcomes that are to the disadvantage of all. The role of morality, in Gauthier's view, is to constrain the pursuit of self-interest so as to ensure Pareto optimal results.

Gauthier explicitly equates moral constraint with rational and impartial constraint on the pursuit of self-interest. Although most people would accept that being a rational and impartial constraint on conduct is a necessary condition for being a moral constraint, many would reject it as a sufficient condition. One might claim, for example, that an element of sympathy for others is also necessary.

Gauthier is not, however, very interested in arguing about the proper conception of morality. His main interest is to give an account of rational and impartial constraints on conduct. If this does not capture the tra-ditional conception of morality, so much the worse for the traditional conception. Rationality – not morality – is the important notion for him.

Gauthier's lack of concern for the traditional conception of morality is apparent in his rejection of any appeal to moral intuitions. He writes:

If the reader is tempted to object to some part of this view, on the ground that his moral intuitions are violated, then he should ask what weight such an objection can have, if morality is to fit within the domain of rational choice. (*Morals by Agreement*, p. 269)

Gauthier rejects not only brute appeal to moral intuition, but also appeal to our considered moral judgments in reflective equilibrium.[2] Consequently, his project is best understood as potentially involving a radically reformist conception of morality. It is not merely that his theory might fail to capture some traditional moral concerns, but rather that its connection with these traditional moral concerns is purely contingent.[3]

Gauthier's concern with rationally acceptable norms of interaction leads him to advocate a contractarian theory quite unlike that of many contractarians, and, in particular, quite unlike that of Rawls. For unlike Gauthier, Rawls' project is not to reduce morality to rationality (and disregard the rest), but rather to use the theory of rational choice to derive moral principles from a *morally loaded* choice situation. Rawls' original position (and his veil of ignorance in particular) is set up to screen *morally irrelevant* features of the status quo (e.g., one's position and capacities). Gauthier, on the other hand, wants to use the theory

---

[2] See Norman Daniels, "Wide Reflective Equilibrium and Theory Acceptance in Ethics," *Journal of Philosophy* 76 (1979): 256–82, for an excellent discussion and elaboration of the method of reflective equilibrium.

[3] In his essay in this volume (chap. 1), Gauthier further elaborates on his moral methodology.

of rational choice to derive moral principles from a *morally neutral* choice situation. For both theories, the relevant agreement is hypothetical, but the relevant circumstances of agreement are grounded, we shall see, much more closely in reality on Gauthier's view than on Rawls'.

Gauthier's contractarian theory

Contractarian moral theories hold that an action, practice, law, or social structure is morally permissible just in case it, or principles to which it conforms, would be (or has been) agreed to by the members of society under certain specified conditions.[4] Like most contemporary contractarian theorists, Gauthier takes the relevant agreement to be hypothetical (i.e., what *would* be agreed to under appropriate circumstances) – not actual agreement.[5]

Gauthier advocates both a contractarian ethical theory and a contractarian political theory.[6] His contractarian ethical theory is *indirect* in that it judges actions permissible if and only if *they conform to principles* that would be chosen under specified conditions. His contractarian political theory, on the other hand, is *direct* in that it judges social structures permissible if and only if *they* (as opposed to principles to which they conform) would be chosen under the specified conditions.[7] Thus, one

---

[4] Contractarian moral theory has been around at least since it was very briefly suggested by Glaucon in Book II of Plato's *Republic*. The main historical works are Thomas Hobbes, *Leviathan* (1651), edited by C. B. Macpherson (New York: Penguin, 1968); John Locke, *The Second Treatise of Government* (1690), edited by Thomas Peardon (Indianapolis: Bobbs-Merrill, 1952); Jean-Jacques Rousseau, *Contrat Social* (1762), in *Political Writings*, edited by C. E. Vaughan (Cambridge: Cambridge University Press, 1915); Immanuel Kant, *Groundwork of the Metaphysics of Morals* (1785), edited by H. J. Patton (New York: Harper, 1958); and Immanuel Kant, *The Metaphysical Elements of Justice* (1797), translated and edited by John Ladd (Indianapolis: Bobbs-Merrill, 1965). The main contemporary work is, of course, John Rawls, *A Theory of Justice* (Cambridge, MA: Belknap Press of Harvard University Press, 1971). In addition to Gauthier's book, some important recent works are James Buchanan, *The Limits of Liberty* (Chicago: The University of Chicago Press, 1975); T. M. Scanlon, "Contractualism and Utilitarianism," in *Utilitarianism and Beyond*, edited by Amartya Sen and Bernard Williams (Cambridge: Cambridge University Press, 1982); Gilbert Harman, "Justice and Moral Bargaining," *Social Philosophy and Policy* 1 (1983): 114–31; Jean Hampton, *Hobbes and the Social Contract Tradition* (New York: Cambridge University Press, 1986); and Gregory Kavka, *Hobbesian Moral and Political Theory* (Princeton: Princeton University Press, 1986).
[5] One of the few authors to advocate actual agreement contractarianism is Gilbert Harman, "Justice and Moral Bargaining," *Social Philosophy and Policy* 1 (1983): 114–31.
[6] That Gauthier advocates a political as well as an ethical contractarian theory is evidenced by his discussion in chap. 8 of choosing social structures. Note that in "Contractualism and Utilitarianism," T. M. Scanlon advocates a contractarian ethical theory, whereas John Rawls, in *A Theory of Justice*, and James Buchanan, in *The Limits of Liberty*, advocate (primarily) contractarian political theories.
[7] The distinction between direct and indirect contractarian theories parallels that between direct and indirect (e.g., act vs. rule) utilitarian theories. The difference lies in whether the object of potential agreement is the object of which the permissibility is being assessed (e.g., an action) or whether it is a set of principles that will assess the object being assessed.

way in which Gauthier's political theory differs from that of Rawls is that he has the parties agreeing on particular social structures, whereas Rawls has them agreeing on principles for assessing social structures.

Gauthier's specification of the conditions under which the agreement takes place is also quite different from that of Rawls. Let us consider his specification of (1) the parties to the agreement, (2) the beliefs of the parties, and (3) the desires of the parties.

The parties to the agreement

Gauthier takes the parties to the agreement for a given society at a given time to include only those currently living members of society whose cooperation would benefit at least some other currently living members of society. Gauthier explicitly takes the hard line that animals, children, the severely disabled, and members of future generations are *not* parties to the agreement, since they offer no benefit to current, nondisabled, adult human beings beyond what the latter can obtain unilaterally.[8] Gauthier's project is to ground morality in rational agreement, and rational agreement, he maintains, requires mutual advantage. Consequently, the protection of those too weak to offer benefits to others is, in Gauthier's view, included in the scope of morality only to the extent that those party to the agreement care about them.

The beliefs of the parties

Unlike Rawls' theory, which imposes a thick veil of ignorance on the parties (allowing them only knowledge of the laws of nature and of some very general features of the state of the world), Gauthier's theory imposes no veil of ignorance at all. Gauthier's social agreement is based on rational negotiation among fully informed, determinate individuals.

Allowing the parties to be fully informed about their capacities and situations allows the parties with more advantageous capacities and positions to bargain for a greater share of the benefits. In Rawls' original position, on the other hand, advantaged parties have no information about their capacities and positions, and, therefore, have no basis for bargaining for a greater share of the benefits. Here again Gauthier's project of reducing morality to rationality leads him to take a tough-minded position regarding the weak. Rationality requires that all available information be used, and since that leads to weaker bargaining

---

[8] In "Contractualism and Utilitarianism," Scanlon, on the other hand, allows children, animals, and future people to be represented in the agreement by a trustee.

positions for the weak, it is unreasonable for the weak to expect the same benefits as the strong.[9]

The desires of the parties

Like Rawls, Gauthier assumes that the parties are mutually unconcerned (do not care how others fare).[10] Since people do, at least to some extent, care – both negatively and positively – about how other people's conceptions of the good are promoted, this assumption is counterfactual. It seems, therefore, to detract from the rational grounding of the resulting agreement. An agreement that would be rational if people had certain sorts of desires need not be (and in general is not) rational, if those people do not have those desires. This is especially problematic for Gauthier, since (unlike Rawls, who could argue that other-regarding desires are morally irrelevant to the choice of principles), Gauthier wants to ground his theory solely in considerations of rational choice. He does not want to rely on any assumptions about what is morally relevant. The rationality of an agreement based on the assumption that people do not have other-regarding desires does not show that such an agreement is rational for people with such desires. So this may be a problematic feature of Gauthier's theory.[11]

These, then, are Gauthier's views on morality. Let us now consider his views on rational choice.

Gauthier's rational-choice framework

Gauthier defends an instrumental conception of practical rationality, according to which a choice is rational if and only if relative to the agent's beliefs it is the most effective means for achieving the agent's goals. Except for certain minimal formal conditions of coherence,[12] the instru-

---

[9] We should note here an alternative approach similar in spirit to Rawls'. Both Thomas Scanlon, "Contractualism and Utilitarianism," and Jürgen Habermas, *Legitimation Crisis,* translated by Thomas McCarthy (Boston: Beacon Press, 1975), have advocated contractarian theories that (like Gauthier's theory) allow the parties full knowledge concerning their situations, capacities, beliefs, and desires, but prevent the parties from simply pursuing their own self-interest, by specifying that the parties are motivated solely by the desire to reach a reasonable agreement. The agreement of these contractarian theories is thus to be understood as that of a consensus rather than a bargain or compromise. Rawls' theory is also consensualist, since the veil is so thick there is no room for conflict and compromise. What Rawls achieves through a veil of ignorance, these authors achieve through a special motivation assumption.

[10] Note that the assumption of mutual unconcern applies only to the parties in the choice situation (in which they come to an agreement). The people whom the chosen principles are to regulate are not assumed to be mutually unconcerned.

[11] I develop this point in chap. 5, "Contractarianism and the Assumption of Mutual Unconcern," in this volume.

[12] Such as being considered, complete, transitive, monotonic in prizes, and continuous.

mental conception of rational choice rejects any attempt to assess the rationality of the goals themselves. Value (utility), Gauthier argues, is subjective (dependent on the affective attitudes of individuals) and relative (not necessarily the same for all individuals). There are no external norms for assessing someone's preferences, Gauthier claims, except the formal coherence properties.

In *parametric choice* – that is, in choice situations in which agents take their environment as fixed – a choice is rational if and only if it maximizes expected utility (i.e., is the most effective means for achieving the agent's goals). In *strategic choice* – that is, in choice situations in which the agent recognizes that the outcome of choice depends in part on the choices of other rational agents – the rationality of a choice depends (in part) on what it would be rational for the agents to agree to. What, then, determines whether an agreement is rational?

The problem of rational agreement is to select a single option (or perhaps a set of options) from a set of feasible options in a way that is rationally acceptable to all the parties to the agreement. On the received view, which Gauthier accepts, rational agreement can be reconstructed as a two-step process. In the first step, an initial bargaining position is determined. This position determines the utility payoff that each person brings to the bargaining table and that is not subject to negotiation. It is only the utility payoff over and above the initial bargaining position payoff that is negotiable. In the second step, an option (or set of options) is chosen on the basis of the initial bargaining position. As we shall now see, Gauthier has a new and interesting account of both steps.

The initial bargaining position

A common specification of the initial bargaining position is as the *non-cooperative outcome*.[13] This is the hypothetical outcome of the unco-ordinated pursuit of self-interest. If agreement is based on the noncooperative outcome, then, although the benefits of cooperation over noncooperation will be distributed among the parties, the distribution of the costs and benefits of noncooperation will be untouched. Agents will end up with the net benefits that they would obtain from non-cooperation and a portion of the benefits of engaging in cooperative behavior.

Gauthier agrees that a rational agreement should make everyone at least as well off as under the noncooperative outcome, but argues nonetheless that the noncooperative outcome should not be treated as the initial bargaining position. A rational agreement, Gauthier claims, must

---

[13] See, for example, James M. Buchanan, *The Limits of Liberty: Between Anarchy and Leviathan* (Chicago: The University of Chicago Press, 1975) for a defense of the noncooperative outcome as the initial bargaining position.

be one with which it is rational for the agents to comply, and agreements based on the noncooperative outcome do not satisfy that condition. In particular, it is irrational, he argues, for those who would be net victims of noncooperative interaction (i.e., those who would be worse off in the presence of the noncooperative activities of others than they would be if left completely alone) to comply with agreements based on the non-cooperative outcome. Such agreements would perpetuate the benefits and costs of coercive activity even though such activity would no longer take place, and therefore be unstable.

Gauthier claims that, in order for there to be a rational basis for all to comply with an agreement, the initial bargaining position must be the hypothetical result of noncooperative interaction *constrained by the Lockean Proviso*, that is, of noncooperative interaction subject to the constraint that no one makes him/herself better off by making someone else worse off.[14] Like the noncooperative outcome, this represents an outcome where all social cooperation ceases. Unlike the noncooperative outcome, however, it is based on the assumption that no one engages in coercive or predatory activity. People neither help nor harm others.

Many will be unconvinced by Gauthier's defense of the relevance of the proviso for the theory of rational choice. The initial bargaining position must, they will argue, reflect how people would fare in the absence of cooperation. And in the absence of cooperation, it is sometimes rational for individuals to better their own position by worsening that of others. The appropriate baseline (the objection continues) is simply the noncooperative outcome – not that outcome constrained by the proviso.

Gauthier's specification of the initial bargaining position for rational agreements is thus both novel and controversial. As we shall now see, his views on the rational allocation of the benefits of cooperation (i.e., the benefits beyond those of the initial bargaining position) are also novel and controversial.

The bargaining solution

The bargaining problem is this: Given a set of feasible options, one of them being the initial bargaining position, which option(s) is it rational

---

[14] On p. 212, Gauthier makes clear that the proviso is weaker than it might seem. It only rules out making someone worse off when worsening the situation of others is *the means* – as opposed to a mere side effect – of bettering one's own situation. Thus, taking without your consent the fish you have caught is prohibited, since I improve my lot *by* worsening your lot; but polluting the river (and thereby killing many of the fish you might otherwise catch) does *not* violate the proviso, since the fact that you are made worse off is purely incidental to the benefit I get from polluting the river (I would still get the benefit, if you did not exist). This raises two questions: Can a clear distinction between means and side effects really be made? If it can, is Gauthier's interpretation of the proviso really rationally more acceptable than a version that prohibits bettering one's situation by worsening – as means or as a side effect – another's situation?

to choose? A bargaining solution is a specification of a procedure for answering this question. The most well-known solution is the Nash solution (also known as the Zeuthen–Nash–Harsanyi solution), according to which rational agreement fixes on an option that maximizes the (mathematical) product of each person's excess utility over the initial bargaining position. Thus, for each feasible option O one calculates the value $[U_1(O) - U_1(O^*)] \times [U_2(O) - U_2(O^*)] \times \cdots \times [U_n(O) - U_n(O^*)]$, where O^* is the initial bargaining position point, and U_i is person i's utility function (where i is $1, 2, \ldots, n$). According to the Nash solution, a rational agreement maximizes this product. For example, if there are two agents and four options, $\langle 0,0 \rangle$, $\langle 100,30 \rangle$, $\langle 50,50 \rangle$, and $\langle 0,100 \rangle$,[15] with $\langle 0,0 \rangle$ being the initial bargaining position, then it is rational to agree upon $\langle 100,30 \rangle$ (since $(100 - 0) \times (30 - 0)$ $[= 3,000]$ is greater, for example, than $(50 - 0) \times (50 - 0)$ $[= 2,500]$).

Gauthier defends a different solution. He claims that rational agents would choose a feasible option that *minimizes the maximum relative concession* that anyone makes. The *relative concession* that a person makes for a given option is the ratio of (a) the excess of (i) the utility for that person of his/her most favorable admissible option over (ii) the utility for that person of the given option to (b) the excess of (i) the utility for that person of his/her most favorable admissible option over (ii) the utility for that person of the initial bargaining position option. An admissible option is one that is both feasible and accords everyone at least as much utility as the initial bargaining position point.[16] In symbols, the relative concession for person i of option O is $[U_i(O_i) - U_i(O)]/[U_i(O_i) - U(O^*)]$, where O^* is the initial bargaining position option, and O_i is i's most favored admissible option (i.e., the admissible option that gives i as at least as much utility as any other admissible option).[17] In the example choice situation of the preceding paragraph, it is rational according to Gauthier to agree upon $\langle 50,50 \rangle$, since its maximum relative concession is 0.5 (50/100), and, for example, the maximum relative concession of $\langle 100,30 \rangle$ is 0.7 (70/100).

According to Gauthier's bargaining solution, then, rational agents would agree to an option for which the highest relative concession is as low as possible. Very roughly, the intuitive idea behind this solution is

---

[15] $\langle n,m \rangle$ represents an option that yields n units of utility to player one and m units to player two.

[16] The minimax relative concession principle is also known as the maximin relative benefit principle, where relative benefit is the proportion received of one's maximum admissible benefit over the initial bargaining position. Minimizing the maximum relative concession is equivalent to maximizing the minimum relative benefit.

[17] Neither Nash's solution nor Gauthier's requires that utility be interpersonally comparable. Because both involve utility differences (e.g., $U_i(O_i) - U_i(O^*)$), they do not require that the zero points of different people's utility scales be comparable. Because (unlike utilitarianism) neither adds one person's utility with that of another, they do not require that the units of different people's scales be comparable.

that, since one's ground of complaint can be measured by one's relative concession, minimizing maximum relative concession minimizes the grounds for complaint.

Both Nash's and Gauthier's solutions have been axiomatized, so the differences between the two can be traced back to differences in which axioms are accepted and are rejected.[18] The difference lies in Nash's acceptance, and Gauthier's rejection, of Condition Alpha:[19] if an option is a rational choice for a given set of feasible options and given initial bargaining position point, then it is also a rational choice for any *subset* of these options with the same initial bargaining position point. The idea is that an option should not cease to be a rational choice simply because some of its competitors are eliminated.

Gauthier rejects Condition Alpha because he holds that what is rational for one to accept depends on how favorable is one's most favorable admissible option. Thus, he holds that an option that is a rational choice for a given initial bargaining position point and a given set of feasible options may not be a rational choice given the same initial bargaining position point and a *subset* of those feasible options. Indeed, Gauthier holds that, in general, such an option will *not* be a rational choice for the subset, if the subset was obtained by eliminating someone's most favorable admissible option.[20]

Given the plausibility of Gauthier's claim about the relevance of options that are someone's most favorable admissible option, his bargaining solution represents an important challenge to the status of Nash's solution as the received solution.

The rationality of complying with rational agreements

The combination of Gauthier's specification of the initial bargaining position (the hypothetical outcome of noncooperative interaction constrained by the Lockean Proviso) and his bargaining solution (minimize the maximum relative concession) specifies what it is rational for agents

---

[18] See, for example, the discussion of the Kalai and Smordinsky solution (solution G) in Alvin Roth, *Axiomatic Models of Bargaining* (New York: Springer-Verlag, 1979). Gauthier's solution is only slightly different from that solution. The two were arrived at independently.

[19] Condition Alpha is also known as the Independence of Irrelevant Alternatives, although it has nothing to do with the condition of the same name introduced by Kenneth Arrow in the theory of social choice.

[20] For example, in the example considered, it is rational to agree to $\langle 50,50 \rangle$ according to Gauthier. In a choice situation in which only $\langle 0,0 \rangle$, $\langle 100,30 \rangle$, and $\langle 50,50 \rangle$ are feasible – but not $\langle 0,100 \rangle$ – then it is rational according to Gauthier to agree to $\langle 100,30 \rangle$ (and not $\langle 50,50 \rangle$). This is because person two's maximum gain drops (from 100) to 50, and, consequently, the maximum relative concession of $\langle 100,30 \rangle$ changes from 0.7 ($= 70/100$) to 0.4 ($= 20/50$), whereas that of $\langle 50,50 \rangle$ remains at 0.5 ($= 50/100$). This violates Condition Alpha, which requires that if $\langle 50,50 \rangle$ is the rational choice in the first case, it must also be the rational choice in the second case (in which $\langle 0,100 \rangle$ is not feasible).

to agree to. There remains, however, a significant problem. It is one thing to agree to cooperate (e.g., to help each other paint our houses), quite another to *comply* with that agreement (e.g., to help you paint your house after you have already helped me paint mine). Although, in general, it may be in one's self-interest to comply with agreements, it seems that, at least sometimes, it is in one's interest not to comply. Why should anyone *comply* with the terms of a rational agreement? More specifically, does rationality *always* require that we comply with rational agreements?

Gauthier thinks so. He argues that under certain broadly characterized conditions, rationality requires that fully informed, rational agents adopt a policy ("choice disposition") of complying with the terms of rational agreements. More specifically, he argues that if there are enough agents disposed to comply with rational agreements, and if our characters are sufficiently translucent (in that other people can have a fairly good idea what we are really like, and likely to do), it is in our self-interest to choose to adopt the policy of *constrained maximization* (maximizing our own utility subject to the constraint that we keep rational agreements with others who are disposed to keep rational agreements) rather than dispose ourselves to be *straightforward maximizers* (maximizing our own utility, even when it involves breaking a rational agreement). For if our characters are sufficiently translucent, and we have not adopted a policy of complying with rational agreements, we will be excluded from beneficial cooperative arrangements, because others will not trust us (they will see that we won't keep the agreements we make). Thus, rationality requires us to adopt a policy of complying.

Furthermore, a choice is rationally permissible, Gauthier claims, if and only if it conforms with a policy that it is rational to adopt. Consequently, under the specified conditions, a choice is rationally permissible only if it complies with rational agreements.

There are thus two main claims in Gauthier's argument. The first is that the policy (choice disposition) of constrained maximization is the most advantageous policy to adopt. Here the issue is whether the policy of straightforward maximization, *or some other policy,* is the most advantageous. The second main claim is that the rational permissibility of a choice is determined by whether it conforms with a policy that it would be rational to adopt. This contradicts the received view that the rationality of a choice is determined by whether *it* (as opposed to some policy to which it conforms) maximizes the agent's utility.

This is an extremely important argument, for it purports to show that there is a rational solution to the problem of compliance. If successful, it follows that no enforcement mechanism (that imposes sanctions on those that do not comply) is needed to ensure compliance among fully rational agents. All we need to do, Gauthier argues, is to properly understand the dictates of rationality.

Gauthier's argument that rationality requires that we comply with our rational agreements is especially important in the context of his contractarian moral theory. According to contractarianism, an action is morally permissible if and only if it conforms to the code of conduct to which it would be rational for the members of society to agree. Thus, if rationality requires compliance with rational agreements, and moral constraints are the object of a rational agreement, then rationality requires that one comply with moral constraints. Gauthier thus has an answer to the age-old question, "Why should one be moral?"

Conclusion

In broad outline, then, Gauthier has three main projects: defending a specific contractarian theory of morality; defending a specific instrumental theory of rationality; and defending the claim that under a broad range of circumstances, rationality requires one to act morally. These are ambitious projects well worth examining carefully. For even if unsuccessful, collectively they represent one of the most carefully articulated and rigorously defended positions on the connection between rationality and morality.[21]

[21] This essay has been drawn largely from my "Gauthier on Rationality and Morality," *Eidos* 5 (1986): 79–95. I have benefitted from the comments of the following people: David Braybrooke, Peter Danielson, Morry Lipson, Chris Morris, Jan Narveson, Geoff Sayre-McCord, and an anonymous referee for Cambridge University Press.

Part I

Gauthier's contractarian moral theory

Overview of the essays

In his essay, Gauthier elaborates on his view that moral judgments require a deliberative justification (i.e., one based on the norms of rational choice). Moral judgments require a deliberative justification, because we no longer believe that there are objective moral values, and because, in any case, deliberative justification is more basic (better reflects our deep sense of self). Morality is not, however, to be rejected. Rather, a place for moral constraint can be found within (but not outside) the framework of deliberative justification. Moral constraints can be identified with those constraints on conduct to which the members of society would agree. Given that deliberative rationality requires that one keep one's rational agreements, it also requires that one comply with the constraints of a contractarian morality. Gauthier also elaborates on his defense of the relevance of hypothetical (rather than actual) agreement in a presocial (rather than a social) context.

In her essay, Jean Hampton contrasts the Hobbesian and the Kantian approaches to contractarian theory. She lays out the core of Hobbes's theory, and then assesses the success of Gauthier's theory as a modern day Hobbesian moral theory. She criticizes Gauthier's use of the Lockean Proviso in the specification of the initial bargaining position. The non-cooperative outcome – not Gauthier's noncoercive (i.e., constrained by the Lockean Proviso) noncooperative outcome – is, she argues, not only more Hobbesian, but also the appropriate baseline for rational agreement. She then argues that Gauthier's recognition of the role of socialization in forming individuals (e.g., their beliefs, desires, and capacities) leads him to abandon the radical individualism of Hobbes. It leads him in particular, she suggests, to view people as intrinsically valuable – not merely instrumentally valuable as on Hobbes's view. And this leads, she claims, to a more Kantian – and more promising – contractarian theory.

David Braybrooke examines some of the implications of Gauthier's theory for moral progress in the selection of social rules. He argues that the implications are mixed. Unlike Rawls' contractarian theory, Gauthier's theory cannot be relied upon to give much protection to civil liberties. Furthermore, Gauthier's assumption that the agents are fully informed precludes a Mill-like defense of liberty as instrumentally valuable for the accommodation of future discoveries about one's preferences. On the other hand, under appropriate circumstances (e.g., imperfect competition in the market, or greater human productivity under a planning mechanism), Gauthier's theory would justify a planned (as opposed to a market) economy, and even justify a revolution to bring it about. But it could just as well justify the abandonment of the week and poor by the strong and rich on the grounds that the former no longer offer benefits in cooperation. Finally, although Braybrooke allows that Gauthier's theory falls in with humane feeling in encouraging moral progress, he argues that Gauthier's agents may not in fact care about advances in legal justice, and may care unduly about other people's private lives. In both respects, Gauthier's contract might revoke recent moral gains.

Peter Vallentyne argues that Gauthier's assumption that the parties to the agreement are mutually unconcerned (take no interest in the interests of others) is incompatible with Gauthier's project of reducing morality to rationality. For if morality is to be *reduced* to rationality, people's actual preference must be taken into account. Since people's actual preferences are not mutually unconcerned, an agreement that would be rational if the parties were mutually unconcerned need not be rational given people's actual preferences.

Chris Morris explores the manner in which contractarian theory in general, and Gauthier's theory in particular, determines what has moral standing, that is, what sorts of things are owed moral consideration. It might seem that only the rational agents participating in the social agreement have moral standing on the contractarian view. Given that, on Gauthier's view, children, the significantly infirm, and animals are not participants in the social agreement (because their cooperation offers no benefit to others), it thus seems they do not have moral standing. Morris argues that this is not so. He distinguishes between primary moral standing (which does not depend on anyone's caring about the entity's interests) and secondary moral standing (which does), and then shows that there is room in Gauthier's theory for infants, the infirm, and animals, for example, to have secondary moral standing, provided that the desires of the parties to the agreement are appropriately other-regarding.

2.   Why contractarianism?*

David Gauthier

I

> As the will to truth thus gains self-consciousness – there can be no doubt of
> that – morality will gradually *perish* now: this is the great spectacle in a hundred
> acts reserved for the next two centuries in Europe – the most terrible, most
> questionable, and perhaps also the most hopeful of all spectacles.
>
> – Nietzsche[1]

Morality faces a foundational crisis. Contractarianism offers the only
plausible resolution of this crisis. These two propositions state my
theme. What follows is elaboration.

Nietzsche may have been the first, but he has not been alone, in
recognizing the crisis to which I refer. Consider these recent statements.
"The hypothesis which I wish to advance is that in the actual world
which we inhabit the language of morality is in . . . [a] state of grave
disorder . . . we have – very largely, if not entirely – lost our comprehension, both theoretical and practical, of morality" (Alasdair Mac-
Intyre).[2] "The resources of most modern moral philosophy are not well
adjusted to the modern world" (Bernard Williams).[3] "There are no ob-

*Two paragraphs of Section II and most of Section IV are taken from "Morality, Rational
Choice, and Semantic Representation – A Reply to My Critics," in E. F. Paul, F. D. Miller,
Jr., and J. Paul (eds.), *The New Social Contract: Essays on Gauthier* (Oxford: Blackwell, 1988),
pp. 173–4, 179–180, 184–5, 188–9 (this volume appears also as *Social Philosophy and Policy*
5 [1988], same pagination). I am grateful to Annette Baier, Paul Hurley, and Geoffrey
Sayre-McCord for comments on an earlier draft. I am also grateful to discussants at Western
Washington University, the University of Arkansas, the University of California at Santa
Cruz, and the University of East Anglia for comments on a related talk.
1 *On the Genealogy of Morals,* trans. by Walter Kaufmann and R. J. Hollingdale (New York:
   Random House, 1967), third essay, sec. 27, p. 161.
2 *After Virtue* (Notre Dame, IN: University of Notre Dame Press, 1981), p. 2.
3 *Ethics and the Limits of Philosophy* (Cambridge, MA: Harvard University Press, 1985),
   p. 197.

jective values. . . . [But] the main tradition of European moral philosophy includes the contrary claim" (J. L. Mackie).[4] "Moral hypotheses do not help explain why people observe what they observe. So ethics is problematic and nihilism must be taken seriously. . . . An extreme version of nihilism holds that morality is simply an illusion. . . . In this version, we should abandon morality, just as an atheist abandons religion after he has decided that religious facts cannot help explain observations" (Gilbert Harman).[5]

I choose these statements to point to features of the crisis that morality faces. They suggest that moral language fits a world view that we have abandoned – a view of the world as purposively ordered. Without this view, we no longer truly understand the moral claims we continue to make. They suggest that there is a lack of fit between what morality presupposes – objective values that help explain our behavior, and the psychological states – desires and beliefs – that, given our present world view, actually provide the best explanation. This lack of fit threatens to undermine the very idea of a morality as more than an anthropological curiosity. But how could this be? How could morality *perish*?

II

To proceed, I must offer a minimal characterization of the morality that faces a foundational crisis. And this is the morality of justified constraint. From the standpoint of the agent, moral considerations present themselves as constraining his choices and actions, in ways independent of his desires, aims, and interests. Later, I shall add to this characterization, but for the moment it will suffice. For it reveals clearly what is in question – the ground of constraint. This ground seems absent from our present world view. And so we ask, what reason can a person have for recognizing and accepting a constraint that is independent of his desires and interests? He may agree that such a constraint would be *morally* justified; he would have a reason for accepting it *if* he had a reason for accepting morality. But what justifies paying attention to morality, rather than dismissing it as an appendage of outworn beliefs? We ask, and seem to find no answer. But before proceeding, we should consider three objections.

The first is to query the idea of constraint. Why should morality be seen as constraining our choices and actions? Why should we not rather say that the moral person chooses most freely, because she chooses in the light of a true conception of herself, rather than in the light of the false conceptions that so often predominate? Why should we not link

---

[4] *Ethics: Inventing Right and Wrong* (Harmondsworth: Penguin, 1977), pp. 15, 30.
[5] *The Nature of Morality* (New York: Oxford University Press, 1977), p. 11.

morality with self-understanding? Plato and Hume might be enlisted to support this view, but Hume would be at best a partial ally, for his representation of "virtue in all her genuine and most engaging charms, . . . talk[ing] not of useless austerities and rigors, suffering and self-denial," but rather making "her votaries . . . , during every instant of their existence, if possible, cheerful and happy," is rather overcast by his admission that "in the case of justice, . . . a man, taking things in a certain light, may often seem to be a loser by his integrity."[6] Plato, to be sure, goes further, insisting that only the just man has a healthy soul, but heroic as Socrates' defense of justice may be, we are all too apt to judge that Glaucon and Adeimantus have been charmed rather than reasoned into agreement, and that the unjust man has not been shown necessarily to be the loser.[7] I do not, in any event, intend to pursue this direction of thought. Morality, as we, heirs to the Christian and Kantian traditions, conceive it, constrains the pursuits to which even our reflective desires would lead us. And this is not simply or entirely a constraint on self-interest; the affections that morality curbs include the social ones of favoritism and partiality, to say nothing of cruelty.

The second objection to the view that moral constraint is insufficiently grounded is to query the claim that it operates independently of, rather than through, our desires, interests, and affections. Morality, some may say, concerns the well-being of all persons, or perhaps of all sentient creatures.[8] And one may then argue, either with Hume, that morality arises in and from our sympathetic identification with our fellows, or that it lies directly in well-being, and that our affections tend to be disposed favorably toward it. But, of course, not all of our affections. And so our sympathetic feelings come into characteristic opposition to other feelings, in relation to which they function as a constraint.

This is a very crude characterization, but it will suffice for the present argument. This view grants that morality, as we understand it, is without purely *rational* foundations, but reminds us that we are not therefore unconcerned about the well-being of our fellows. Morality is founded on the widespread, sympathetic, other-directed concerns that most of us have, and these concerns do curb self-interest, and also the favoritism and partiality with which we often treat others. Nevertheless, if morality depends for its practical relevance and motivational efficacity entirely on our sympathetic feelings, it has no title to the prescriptive grip with which it has been invested in the Christian and Kantian views to which I have referred, and which indeed Glaucon and Adeimantus demanded

---

[6] David Hume, *An Equiry Concerning the Principles of Morals*, 1751, sec. IX, pt. II.
[7] See Plato, *Republic*, esp. books II and IV.
[8] Some would extend morality to the nonsentient, but sympathetic as I am to the rights of trolley cars and steam locomotives, I propose to leave this view quite out of consideration.

that Socrates defend to them in the case of justice. For to be reminded that some of the time we do care about our fellows and are willing to curb other desires in order to exhibit that care tells us nothing that can guide us in those cases in which, on the face of it, we do not care, or do not care enough – nothing that will defend the demands that morality makes on us in the hard cases. That not all situations in which concern for others combats self-concern are hard cases is true, but morality, as we ordinarily understand it, speaks to the hard cases, whereas its Humean or naturalistic replacement does not.

These remarks apply to the most sustained recent positive attempt to create a moral theory – that of John Rawls. For the attempt to describe our moral capacity, or more particularly, for Rawls, our sense of justice, in terms of principles, plausible in the light of our more general psychological theory, and coherent with "our considered judgments in reflective equilibrium,"[9] will not yield any answer to why, in those cases in which we have no, or insufficient, interest in being just, we should nevertheless follow the principles. John Harsanyi, whose moral theory is in some respects a utilitarian variant of Rawls' contractarian construction, recognizes this explicitly: "All we can prove by rational arguments is that anybody who wants to serve our common human interests in a rational manner must obey these commands."[10] But although morality may offer itself in the service of our common human interests, it does not offer itself only to those who want to serve them.

Morality is a constraint that, as Kant recognized, must not be supposed to depend solely on our feelings. And so we may not appeal to feelings to answer the question of its foundation. But the third objection is to dismiss this question directly, rejecting the very idea of a foundational crisis. Nothing justifies morality, for morality needs no justification. We find ourselves, in morality as elsewhere, in mediis rebus. We make, accept and reject, justify and criticize moral judgments. The concern of moral theory is to systematize that practice, and so to give us a deeper understanding of what moral justification is. But there are no extramoral foundations for moral justification, any more than there are extraepistemic foundations for epistemic judgments. In morals as in science, foundationalism is a bankrupt project.

Fortunately, I do not have to defend *normative* foundationalism. One problem with accepting moral justification as part of our ongoing practice is that, as I have suggested, we no longer accept the world view on which it depends. But perhaps a more immediately pressing problem is that we have, ready to hand, an alternative mode for justifying our

---

[9] John Rawls, *A Theory of Justice* (Cambridge, MA: Harvard University Press, 1971), p. 51.
[10] John C. Harsanyi, "Morality and the Theory of Rational Behaviour," in *Utilitarianism and Beyond*, edited by Amartya Sen and Bernard Williams (Cambridge: Cambridge University Press, 1982), p. 62.

choices and actions. In its more austere and, in my view, more defensible form, this is to show that choices and actions maximize the agent's expected utility, where utility is a measure of considered preference. In its less austere version, this is to show that choices and actions satisfy, not a subjectively defined requirement such as utility, but meet the agent's objective interests. Since I do not believe that we have objective interests, I shall ignore this latter. But it will not matter. For the idea is clear; we have a mode of justification that does not require the introduction of moral considerations.[11]

Let me call this alternative nonmoral mode of justification, neutrally, deliberative justification. Now moral and deliberative justification are directed at the same objects – our choices and actions. What if they conflict? And what do we say to the person who offers a deliberative justification of his choices and actions and refuses to offer any other? We can say, of course, that his behavior lacks *moral* justification, but this seems to lack any hold, unless he chooses to enter the moral framework. And such entry, he may insist, lacks any deliberative justification, at least for him.

If morality perishes, the justificatory enterprise, in relation to choice and action, does not perish with it. Rather, one mode of justification perishes, a mode that, it may seem, now hangs unsupported. But not only unsupported, for it is difficult to deny that deliberative justification is more clearly basic, that it cannot be avoided insofar as we are rational agents, so that if moral justification conflicts with it, morality seems not only unsupported but opposed by what is rationally more fundamental.

Deliberative justification relates to our deep sense of self. What distinguishes human beings from other animals, and provides the basis for rationality, is the capacity for semantic representation. You can, as your dog on the whole cannot, represent a state of affairs to yourself, and consider in particular whether or not it is the case, and whether or not you would want it to be the case. You can represent to yourself the contents of your beliefs, and your desires or preferences. But in representing them, you bring them into relation with one another. You represent to yourself that the Blue Jays will win the World Series, and that a National League team will win the World Series, and that the Blue Jays are not a National League team. And in recognizing a conflict among those beliefs, you find rationality thrust upon you. Note that the first two beliefs could be replaced by preferences, with the same effect.

Since in representing our preferences we become aware of conflict among them, the step from representation to choice becomes compli-

---

[11] To be sure, if we think of morality as expressed in certain of our affections and/or interests, it will incorporate moral considerations to the extent that they actually are present in our preferences. But this would be to embrace the naturalism that I have put to one side as inadequate.

cated. We must, somehow, bring our conflicting desires and preferences into some sort of coherence. And there is only one plausible candidate for a principle of coherence – a maximizing principle. We order our preferences, in relation to decision and action, so that we may choose in a way that maximizes our expectation of preference fulfillment. And in so doing, we show ourselves to be rational agents, engaged in deliberation and deliberative justification. There is simply nothing else for practical rationality to be.

The foundational crisis of morality thus cannot be avoided by pointing to the existence of a practice of justification within the moral framework, and denying that any extramoral foundation is relevant. For an extramoral mode of justification is already present, existing not side by side with moral justification, but in a manner tied to the way in which we unify our beliefs and preferences and so acquire our deep sense of self. We need not suppose that this deliberative justification is itself to be understood foundationally. All that we need suppose is that moral justification does not plausibly survive conflict with it.

III

In explaining why we may not dismiss the idea of a foundational crisis in morality as resulting from a misplaced appeal to a philosophically discredited or suspect idea of foundationalism, I have begun to expose the character and dimensions of the crisis. I have claimed that morality faces an alternative, conflicting, deeper mode of justification, related to our deep sense of self, that applies to the entire realm of choice and action, and that evaluates each *action* in terms of the reflectively held concerns of its *agent*. The relevance of the agent's concerns to practical justification does not seem to me in doubt. The relevance of anything else, except insofar as it bears on the agent's concerns, does seem to me very much in doubt. If the agent's reflectively endorsed concerns, his preferences, desires, and aims, are, with his considered beliefs, constitutive of his self-conception, then I can see no remotely plausible way of arguing from their relevance to that of anything else that is not similarly related to his sense of self. And, indeed, I can see no way of introducing anything as relevant to practical justification except through the agent's self-conception. My assertion of this practical individualism is not a conclusive argument, but the burden of proof is surely on those who would maintain a contrary position. Let them provide the arguments – if they can.

Deliberative justification does not refute morality. Indeed, it does not offer morality the courtesy of a refutation. It ignores morality, and seemingly replaces it. It preempts the arena of justification, apparently leaving morality no room to gain purchase. Let me offer a controversial comparison. Religion faces – indeed, has faced – a comparable foundational crisis. Religion demands the worship of a divine being who purposively orders the universe. But it has confronted an alternative mode of explanation. Although the emergence of a cosmological theory based on efficient, rather than teleological, causation provided warning of what was to come, the supplanting of teleology in biology by the success of evolutionary theory in providing a mode of explanation that accounted in efficient-causal terms for the *appearance* of a purposive order among living beings, may seem to toll the death knell for religion as an intellectually respectable enterprise. But evolutionary biology and, more generally, modern science do not refute religion. Rather they ignore it, replacing its explanations by ontologically simpler ones. Religion, understood as affirming the justifiable worship of a divine being, may be unable to survive its foundational crisis. Can morality, understood as affirming justifiable constraints on choice independent of the agent's concerns, survive?

There would seem to be three ways for morality to escape religion's apparent fate. One would be to find, for moral facts or moral properties, an explanatory role that would entrench them prior to any consideration of justification.[12] One could then argue that any mode of justification that ignored moral considerations would be ontologically defective. I mention this possibility only to put it to one side. No doubt there are persons who accept moral constraints on their choices and actions, and it would not be possible to explain those choices and actions were we to ignore this. But our explanation of their behavior need not commit us to their view. Here the comparison with religion should be straightforward and uncontroversial. We could not explain many of the practices of the religious without reference to their beliefs. But to characterize what a religious person is doing as, say, an act of worship, does not commit us to supposing that an object of worship actually exists, though it does commit us to supposing that she believes such an object to exist. Similarly, to characterize what a moral agent is doing as, say, fulfilling a duty does not commit us to supposing that there are any duties, though it does commit us to supposing that he believes that there are duties. The skeptic who accepts neither can treat the apparent role of morality in explanation as similar to that of religion. Of course, I do not consider that the parallel can be ultimately sustained, since I agree with the religious skeptic but not with the moral skeptic. But to establish an explanatory role for morality, one must first demonstrate its justificatory credentials. One may not assume that it has a prior explanatory role.

The second way would be to reinterpret the idea of justification, show-

---

[12] This would meet the challenge to morality found in my previous quotation from Gilbert Harman.

ing that, more fully understood, deliberative justification is incomplete, and must be supplemented in a way that makes room for morality. There is a long tradition in moral philosophy, deriving primarily from Kant, that is committed to this enterprise. This is not the occasion to embark on a critique of what, in the hope again of achieving a neutral characterization, I shall call universalistic justification. But critique may be out of place. The success of deliberative justification may suffice. For theoretical claims about its incompleteness seem to fail before the simple practical recognition that it works. Of course, on the face of it, deliberative justification does not work to provide a place for morality. But to suppose that it must, if it is to be fully adequate or complete as a mode of justification, would be to assume what is in question, whether moral justification is defensible.

If, independent of one's actual desires, and aims, there were objective values, and if, independent of one's actual purposes, one were part of an objectively purposive order, then we might have reason to insist on the inadequacy of the deliberative framework. An objectively purposive order would introduce considerations relevant to practical justification that did not depend on the agent's self-conception. But the supplanting of teleology in our physical and biological explanations closes this possibility, as it closes the possibility of religious explanation.

I turn then to the third way of resolving morality's foundational crisis. The first step is to embrace deliberative justification, and recognize that morality's place must be found within, and not outside, its framework. Now this will immediately raise two problems. First of all, it will seem that the attempt to establish any constraint on choice and action, within the framework of a deliberation that aims at the maximal fulfillment of the agent's considered preferences, must prove impossible. But even if this be doubted, it will seem that the attempt to establish a constraint *independent of the agent's preferences,* within such a framework, verges on lunacy. Nevertheless, this is precisely the task accepted by my third way. And, unlike its predecessors, I believe that it can be successful; indeed, I believe that my recent book, *Morals by Agreement,* shows how it can succeed.[13]

I shall not rehearse at length an argument that is now familiar to at least some readers, and, in any event, can be found in that book. But let me sketch briefly those features of deliberative rationality that enable it to constrain maximizing choice. The key idea is that in many situations, if each person chooses what, given the choices of the others, would maximize her expected utility, then the outcome will be mutually disadvantageous in comparison with some alternative – everyone could do

---

[13] See David Gauthier, *Morals by Agreement* (Oxford: Oxford University Press, 1986), especially chaps. V and VI.

better.[14] Equilibrium, which obtains when each person's action is a best response to the others' actions, is incompatible with (Pareto-)optimality, which obtains when no one could do better without someone else doing worse. Given the ubiquity of such situations, each person can see the benefit, to herself, of participating with her fellows in practices requiring each to refrain from the direct endeavor to maximize her own utility, when such mutual restraint is mutually advantageous. No one, of course, can have reason to accept any unilateral constraint on her maximizing behavior; each benefits from, and only from, the constraint accepted by her fellows. But if one benefits more from a constraint on others than one loses by being constrained oneself, one may have reason to accept a practice requiring everyone, including oneself, to exhibit such a constraint. We may represent such a practice as capable of gaining unanimous agreement among rational persons who were choosing the terms on which they would interact with each other. And this agreement is the basis of morality.

Consider a simple example of a moral practice that would command rational agreement. Suppose each of us were to assist her fellows only when either she could expect to benefit herself from giving assistance, or she took a direct interest in their well-being. Then, in many situations, persons would not give assistance to others, even though the benefit to the recipient would greatly exceed the cost to the giver, because there would be no provision for the giver to share in the benefit. Everyone would then expect to do better were each to give assistance to her fellows, regardless of her own benefit or interest, whenever the cost of assisting was low and the benefit of receiving assistance considerable. Each would thereby accept a constraint on the direct pursuit of her own concerns, not unilaterally, but given a like acceptance by others. Reflection leads us to recognize that those who belong to groups whose members adhere to such a practice of mutual assistance enjoy benefits in interaction that are denied to others. We may then represent such a practice as rationally acceptable to everyone.

This rationale for agreed constraint makes no reference to the content of anyone's preferences. The argument depends simply on the *structure* of interaction, on the way in which each person's endeavor to fulfill her own preferences affects the fulfillment of everyone else. Thus, each person's reason to accept a mutually constraining practice is independent of her particular desires, aims and interests, although not, of course, of the fact that she has such concerns. The idea of a purely rational agent,

[14] The now-classic example of this type of situation is the Prisoner's Dilemma; see *Morals by Agreement*, pp. 79–80. More generally, such situations may be said, in economists' parlance, to exhibit market failure. See, for example, "Market Contractarianism" in Jules Coleman, *Markets, Morals, and the Law* (Cambridge: Cambridge University Press, 1988), chap. 10.

moved to act by reason alone, is not, I think, an intelligible one. Morality is not to be understood as a constraint arising from reason alone on the fulfillment of nonrational preferences. Rather, a rational agent is one who acts to achieve the maximal fulfillment of her preferences, and morality is a constraint on the manner in which she acts, arising from the effects of interaction with other agents.

Hobbes's Foole now makes his familiar entry onto the scene, to insist that however rational it may be for a person to agree with her fellows to practices that hold out the promise of mutual advantage, yet it is rational to follow such practices only when so doing directly conduces to her maximal preference fulfillment.[15] But then such practices impose no real constraint. The effect of agreeing to or accepting them can only be to change the expected payoffs of her possible choices, making it rational for her to choose what in the absence of the practice would not be utility maximizing. The practices would offer only true prudence, not true morality.

The Foole is guilty of a twofold error. First, he fails to understand that real acceptance of such moral practices as assisting one's fellows, or keeping one's promises, or telling the truth is possible only among those who are disposed to comply with them. If my disposition to comply extends only so far as my interests or concerns at the time of performance, then you will be the real fool if you interact with me in ways that demand a more rigorous compliance. If, for example, it is rational to keep promises only when so doing is directly utility maximizing, then among persons whose rationality is common knowledge, only promises that require such limited compliance will be made. And opportunities for mutual advantage will be thereby forgone.

Consider this example of the way in which promises facilitate mutual benefit. Jones and Smith have adjacent farms. Although neighbors, and not hostile, they are also not friends, so that neither gets satisfaction from assisting the other. Nevertheless, they recognize that, if they harvest their crops together, each does better than if each harvests alone. Next week, Jones's crop will be ready for harvesting; a fortnight hence, Smith's crop will be ready. The harvest in, Jones is retiring, selling his farm, and moving to Florida, where he is unlikely to encounter Smith or other members of their community. Jones would like to promise Smith that, if Smith helps him harvest next week, he will help Smith harvest in a fortnight. But Jones and Smith both know that in a fortnight, helping Smith would be a pure cost to Jones. Even if Smith helps him, he has nothing to gain by returning the assistance, since neither care for Smith nor, in the circumstances, concern for his own reputation, moves him. Hence, if Jones and Smith know that Jones acts straightforwardly to

[15] See Hobbes, *Leviathan*, London, 1651, chap. 15.

maximize the fulfillment of his preferences, they know that he will not help Smith. Smith, therefore, will not help Jones even if Jones pretends to promise assistance in return. Nevertheless, Jones would do better could he make and keep such a promise – and so would Smith.

The Foole's second error, following on his first, should be clear; he fails to recognize that in plausible circumstances, persons who are genuinely disposed to a more rigorous compliance with moral practices than would follow from their interests at the time of performance can expect to do better than those who are not so disposed. For the former, constrained maximizers as I call them, will be welcome partners in mutually advantageous cooperation, in which each relies on the voluntary adherence of the others, from which the latter, straightforward maximizers, will be excluded. Constrained maximizers may thus expect more favorable opportunities than their fellows. Although in assisting their fellows, keeping their promises, and complying with other moral practices, they forgo preference fulfillment that they might obtain, yet they do better overall than those who always maximize expected utility, because of their superior opportunities.

In identifying morality with those constraints that would obtain agreement among rational persons who were choosing their terms of interaction, I am engaged in rational reconstruction. I do not suppose that we have actually agreed to existent moral practices and principles. Nor do I suppose that all existent moral practices would secure our agreement, were the question to be raised. Not all existent moral practices need be justifiable – need be ones with which we ought willingly to comply. Indeed, I do not even suppose that the practices with which we ought willingly to comply need be those that would secure our present agreement. I suppose that justifiable moral practices are those that would secure our agreement ex ante, in an appropriate premoral situation. They are those to which we should have agreed as constituting the terms of our future interaction, had we been, per impossible, in a position to decide those terms. Hypothetical agreement thus provides a test of the justifiability of our existent moral practices.

IV

Many questions could be raised about this account, but here I want to consider only one. I have claimed that moral practices are rational, even though they constrain each person's attempt to maximize her own utility, insofar as they would be the objects of unanimous ex ante agreement. But to refute the Foole, I must defend not only the rationality of agreement, but also that of compliance, and the defense of compliance threatens to preempt the case for agreement, so that my title should be "Why Constraint?" and not "Why Contractarianism?" It is rational to dispose oneself to accept certain constraints on direct maximization in choosing and acting, if and only if so disposing oneself maximizes one's expected utility. What then is the relevance of agreement, and especially of hypothetical agreement? Why should it be rational to dispose oneself to accept only those constraints that would be the object of mutual agreement in an appropriate premoral situation, rather than those constraints that are found in our existent moral practices? Surely it is acceptance of the latter that makes a person welcome in interaction with his fellows. For compliance with existing morality will be what they expect, and take into account in choosing partners with whom to cooperate.

I began with a challenge to morality – how can it be rational for us to accept its constraints? It may now seem that what I have shown is that it is indeed rational for us to accept constraints, but to accept them whether or not they might be plausibly considered moral. Morality, it may seem, has nothing to do with my argument; what I have shown is that it is rational to be disposed to comply with whatever constraints are generally accepted and expected, regardless of their nature. But this is not my view.

To show the relevance of agreement to the justification of constraints, let us assume an ongoing society in which individuals more or less acknowledge and comply with a given set of practices that constrain their choices in relation to what they would be did they take only their desires, aims, and interests directly into account. Suppose that a disposition to conform to these existing practices is prima facie advantageous, since persons who are not so disposed may expect to be excluded from desirable opportunities by their fellows. However, the practices themselves have, or at least need have, no basis in agreement. And they need satisfy no intuitive standard of fairness or impartiality, characteristics that we may suppose relevant to the identification of the practices with those of a genuine morality. Although we may speak of the practices as constituting the morality of the society in question, we need not consider them morally justified or acceptable. They are simply practices constraining individual behavior in a way that each finds rational to accept.

Suppose now that our persons, as rational maximizers of individual utility, come to reflect on the practices constituting their morality. They will, of course, assess the practices in relation to their own utility, but with the awareness that their fellows will be doing the same. And one question that must arise is: Why these practices? For they will recognize that the set of actual moral practices is not the only possible set of constraining practices that would yield mutually advantageous, optimal outcomes. They will recognize the possibility of alternative moral orders. At this point it will not be enough to say that, as a matter of fact, each person can expect to benefit from a disposition to comply with existing practices. For persons will also ask themselves: Can I benefit more, not from simply abandoning any morality, and recognizing no constraint, but from a partial rejection of existing constraints in favor of an alternative set? Once this question is asked, the situation is transformed; the existing moral order must be assessed, not only against simple noncompliance, but also against what we may call alternative compliance.

To make this assessment, each will compare her prospects under the existing practices with those she would anticipate from a set that, in the existing circumstances, she would expect to result from bargaining with her fellows. If her prospects would be improved by such negotiation, then she will have a real, although not necessarily sufficient, incentive to demand a change in the established moral order. More generally, if there are persons whose prospects would be improved by renegotiation, then the existing order will be recognizably unstable. No doubt those whose prospects would be worsened by renegotiation will have a clear incentive to resist, to appeal to the status quo. But their appeal will be a weak one, especially among persons who are not taken in by spurious ideological considerations, but focus on individual utility maximization. Thus, although in the real world, we begin with an existing set of moral practices as constraints on our maximizing behavior, yet we are led by reflection to the idea of an amended set that would obtain the agreement of everyone, and this amended set has, and will be recognized to have, a stability lacking in existing morality.

The reflective capacity of rational agents leads them from the given to the agreed, from existing practices and principles requiring constraint to those that would receive each person's assent. The same reflective capacity, I claim, leads from those practices that would be agreed to, in existing social circumstances, to those that would receive ex ante agreement, premoral and presocial. As the status quo proves unstable when it comes into conflict with what would be agreed to, so what would be agreed to proves unstable when it comes into conflict with what would have been agreed to in an appropriate presocial context. For as existing practices must seem arbitrary insofar as they do not correspond to what a rational person would agree to, so what such a person would agree to in existing circumstances must seem arbitrary in relation to what she would accept in a presocial condition.

What a rational person would agree to in existing circumstances depends in large part on her negotiating position vis-à-vis her fellows. But her negotiating position is significantly affected by the existing social institutions, and so by the currently accepted moral practices embodied in those institutions. Thus, although agreement may well yield practices differing from those embodied in existing social institutions, yet it will be influenced by those practices, which are not themselves the product of rational agreement. And this must call the rationality of the agreed practices into question. The arbitrariness of existing practices must infect any agreement whose terms are significantly affected by them. Although rational agreement is in itself a source of stability, yet this stability is undermined by the arbitrariness of the circumstances in which it takes place. To escape this arbitrariness, rational persons will revert from actual to hypothetical agreement, considering what practices they would have agreed to from an initial position not structured by existing institutions and the practices they embody.

The content of a hypothetical agreement is determined by an appeal to the equal rationality of persons. Rational persons will voluntarily accept an agreement only insofar as they perceive it to be equally advantageous to each. To be sure, each would be happy to accept an agreement more advantageous to herself than to her fellows, but since no one will accept an agreement perceived to be less advantageous, agents whose rationality is a matter of common knowledge will recognize the futility of aiming at or holding out for more, and minimize their bargaining costs by coordinating at the point of equal advantage. Now the extent of advantage is determined in a twofold way. First, there is advantage internal to an agreement. In this respect, the expectation of equal advantage is assured by procedural fairness. The step from existing moral practices to those resulting from actual agreement takes rational persons to a procedurally fair situation, in which each perceives the agreed practices to be ones that it is equally rational for all to accept, given the circumstances in which agreement is reached. But those circumstances themselves may be called into question insofar as they are perceived to be arbitrary – the result, in part, of compliance with constraining practices that do not themselves ensure the expectation of equal advantage, and so do not reflect the equal rationality of the complying parties. To neutralize this arbitrary element, moral practices to be fully acceptable must be conceived as constituting a possible outcome of a hypothetical agreement under circumstances that are unaffected by social institutions that themselves lack full acceptability. Equal rationality demands consideration of external circumstances as well as internal procedures.

But what is the practical import of this argument? It would be absurd to claim that mere acquaintance with it, or even acceptance of it, will lead to the replacement of existing moral practices by those that would secure presocial agreement. It would be irrational for anyone to give up the benefits of the existing moral order simply because he comes to realize that it affords him more than he could expect from pure rational agreement with his fellows. And it would be irrational for anyone to accept a long-term utility loss by refusing to comply with the existing moral order, simply because she comes to realize that such compliance affords her less than she could expect from pure rational agreement.

Nevertheless, these realizations do transform, or perhaps bring to the surface, the character of the relationships between persons that are maintained by the existing constraints, so that some of these relationships come to be recognized as coercive. These realizations constitute the elimination of false consciousness, and they result from a process of rational reflection that brings persons into what, in my theory, is the parallel of Jürgen Habermas's ideal speech situation.[16] Without an argument to defend themselves in open dialogue with their fellows, those who are more than equally advantaged can hope to maintain their privileged position only if they can coerce their fellows into accepting it. And this, of course, may be possible. But coercion is not agreement, and it lacks any inherent stability.

Stability plays a key role in linking compliance to agreement. Aware of the benefits to be gained from constraining practices, rational persons will seek those that invite stable compliance. Now compliance is stable if it arises from agreement among persons each of whom considers both that the terms of agreement are sufficiently favorable to herself that it is rational for her to accept them, and that they are not so favorable to others that it would be rational for them to accept terms less favorable to them and more favorable to herself. An agreement affording equally favorable terms to all thus invites, as no other can, stable compliance.

V

In defending the claim that moral practices, to obtain the stable voluntary compliance of rational individuals, must be the objects of an appropriate hypothetical agreement, I have added to the initial minimal characterization of morality. Not only does morality constrain our choices and actions, but it does so in an impartial way, reflecting the equal rationality of the persons subject to constraint. Although it is no part of my argument to show that the requirements of contractarian morality will satisfy the Rawlsian test of cohering with our considered judgments in reflective equilibrium, yet it would be misleading to treat rationally agreed constraints on direct utility maximization as constituting a morality at all, rather than as replacing morality, were there no fit between their content and our pretheoretical moral views. The fit lies, I suggest, in the impartiality required for hypothetical agreement.

The foundational crisis of morality is thus resolved by exhibiting the rationality of our compliance with mutual, rationally agreed constraints on the pursuit of our desires, aims, and interests. Although bereft of a basis in objective values or an objectively purposive order, and con-

---

[16] See Raymond Geuss, *The Idea of a Critical Theory: Habermas and the Frankfurt School* (Cambridge: Cambridge University Press, 1981), p. 65ff.

fronted by a more fundamental mode of justification, morality survives by incorporating itself into that mode. Moral considerations have the same status, and the same role in explaining behavior, as the other reasons acknowledged by a rational deliberator. We are left with a unified account of justification, in which an agent's choices and actions are evaluated in relation to his preferences – to the concerns that are constitutive of his sense of self. But since morality binds the agent independently of the particular content of his preferences, it has the prescriptive grip with which the Christian and Kantian views have invested it.

In incorporating morality into deliberative justification, we recognize a new dimension to the agent's self-conception. For morality requires that a person have the capacity to commit himself, to enter into agreement with his fellows secure in the awareness that he can and will carry out his part of the agreement without regard to many of those considerations that normally and justifiably would enter into his future deliberations. And this is more than the capacity to bring one's desires and interests together with one's beliefs into a single coherent whole. Although this latter unifying capacity must extend its attention to past and future, the unification it achieves may itself be restricted to that extended present within which a person judges and decides. But in committing oneself to future action in accordance with one's agreement, one must fix at least a subset of one's desires and beliefs to hold in that future. The self that agrees and the self that complies must be one. "Man himself must first of all have become *calculable, regular, necessary,* even in his own image of himself, if he is to be able to stand security for *his own future,* which is what one who promises does!"[17]

In developing *"the right to make promises,"*[18] we human beings have found a contractarian bulwark against the perishing of morality.

[17] Nietzsche, *On the Genealogy of Morals,* trans. by Walter Kaufmann and R. J. Hollingdale (New York: Random House, 1967), second essay, sec. 1, p. 58.
[18] Ibid., p. 57.

3. Two faces of contractarian thought

Jean Hampton

" . . . What was I created for, I wonder? Where is my place in the world?"
She mused again.

"Ah! I see," she pursued presently, "that is the question which most old maids are puzzled to solve: other people solve it for them by saying, 'Your place is to do good to others, to be helpful whenever help is wanted.' That is right in some measure, and a very convenient doctrine for the people who hold it; but I perceive that certain sets of human beings are very apt to maintain that other sets should give up their lives to them and their service, and then they requite them by praise: they call them devoted and virtuous. Is this enough? Is it to live? Is there not a terrible hollowness, mockery, want, craving, in that existence which is given away to others, for want of something of your own to bestow it on? I suspect there is. Does virtue lie in abnegation of self? I do not believe it. Undue humility makes tyranny; weak concession creates selfishness. . . . Each human being has his share of rights. I suspect it would conduce to the happiness and welfare of all, if each knew his allotment and held to it as tenaciously as a martyr to his creed. Queer thoughts these, that surge in my mind: are they right thoughts? I am not certain."

– Charlotte Brontë, *Shirley*

The quotation that begins this essay is pertinent to its conclusion. But to launch the discussion, I want to quote from nineteenth-century adventurer Mary Kingsley. Dressed in skirts, she traveled alone into the African interior where no white man or woman had ever been, climbing mountains, navigating rivers, fighting animals – and trading her way because, she explained, "when you first appear among people who have never seen anything like you before, they naturally regard you as a devil; but when you want to buy or sell with them, they recognize there is something human and reasonable about you."[1] The idea that the

---

[1] From Katherine Frank, *A Voyager Out: The Life of Mary Kingsley* (Boston: Houghton Mifflin, 1986), p. 63.

essence of human rationality, and even human morality, is embodied in the notion of a contract is the heart of what is called the "contractarian" approach to moral thinking.

The theory itself goes back hundreds of years.[2] In modern times, Grotius, Suarez, Hobbes, Locke, Rousseau, and Kant used the notion of "what people could agree to" primarily in order to argue for the legitimacy of political institutions with a certain structure and purpose. This explicitly political orientation of the argument is maintained by Robert Nozick in his recent book *Anarchy, State and Utopia*.[3] I call those contractarian theorists who argue for the legitimacy of the state using contract language "state contractarians." Other modern contractarians have not restricted the contractarian form of argument to this one political issue. They are convinced that it can be used to identify and motivate commitment to the best available conception of justice, and perhaps also to other kinds of cooperative behavior that involve constraining one's self-regarding pursuits in ways that benefit the community. I call these sorts of theorists "moral contractarians." John Rawls was one of the first contemporary moral contractarians. Interestingly, Rawls does not even question the state's legitimacy in *A Theory of Justice*,[4] but instead tries to identify the best available conception of justice for the structuring of our political and social institutions by using what he calls a hypothetical contract. Scanlon, Gauthier, Grice, Harman, and Mackie go even further, explicitly endorsing the contractarian argument as a way of understanding not only the duties of justice, but virtually the entire content of morality.

Yet the fact that all of these theorists call their theories "contractarian" is misleading, because that single label masks deep differences among them. The most obvious difference concerns what they take to be the metaethical status of their contractarian moral theories. Consider that two of them – Rawls and Scanlon – have regarded themselves as moral objectivists (although Rawls' thinking has, at least arguably, undergone some change in recent years[5]) and have linked their theorizing in some fashion to Kant, whereas others – for example, Gauthier, Harman, and

---

[2] See J. W. Gough, *The Social Contract: A Critical Study of Its Development* (Oxford: Clarendon Press, 1936), and the Introduction to my *Hobbes and the Social Contract Tradition* (Cambridge: Cambridge University Press, 1986).

[3] Robert Nozick, *Anarchy, State and Utopia* (New York: Basic Books, 1974).

[4] John Rawls, *A Theory of Justice* (Cambridge, MA: Harvard University Press, 1971).

[5] In this essay, the Rawls that is discussed is the Rawls who wrote *A Theory of Justice* and not the Rawls of such recent articles as "Justice as Fairness: Political Not Metaphysical" (in *Philosophy and Public Affairs*, Summer 1985). In the book, Rawls uses the contractarian methodology in a way that is explicitly metaphysical, whereas he is presently inclined to regard metaphysics (and thus the contractarian methodology as I understand it in this essay) as, at the very least, *unnecessary* for the justification of his conception of justice. I am concerned with discussing (only) those contractarian theories that take the idea of a (hypothetical) contract to confer ethical warrant on a moral or political theory.

Mackie – either reject moral objectivism completely or else accept that label for their theories on condition that it be understood in an importantly non-Kantian way. Clearly, there is more than one kind of contractarian moral theory if those who use contract talk in their arguments produce moral theories with such importantly different metaethical foundations.

This essay is interested in critically reflecting on the nature of moral contractarianism. I argue that there are two importantly different kinds of moral contractarian theory in contemporary philosophy, each of which is linked to a different historical figure in the contract tradition, one to Hobbes and the other to Kant. I focus mostly on the Hobbesian variant, recently revived in an exciting form by David Gauthier. I engage in this reflection as one who is deeply attracted to the methodology; I seek to clarify what it is that many of us have found so appealing about the idea that talk of contracts can be a route to understanding the nature of our moral and political obligations.

I

Although Hobbes's masterpiece *Leviathan* is primarily concerned with presenting a contract argument for the institution of a certain kind of state (one with an absolute sovereign), if one looks closely, one also sees a sketch of a certain kind of contractarian approach to morality, which has profoundly influenced contemporary moral theorists such as Gauthier.

Hobbes's approach to morality does not assume there are natural moral laws or natural rights that we discern through the use of our reason or intuition. It is not an approach that assumes there is a naturally good object in the world (such as Aristotle's *Summum Bonum*) that moral action serves and that people ought to pursue. It is not an approach that explains moral action as "natural," for example, as action generated by powerful other-regarding sentiments; Hobbes did not believe that such sentiments were very important or powerful in human life. And it is not an approach that justifies morality as a set of laws commanded by God – although Hobbes believed that his moral imperatives were *also* justified as commands of God.[6] Using his contractarian method, he seeks to define the nature and authority of moral imperatives by reference to the desires and reasoning abilities of human beings, so that regardless

---

[6] Hobbes believed that moral imperatives were commanded by God, but this justification of them is different from the contractarian justification that he also uses to defend them. The contractarian method seeks to define the nature and authority of moral imperatives by reference to the desires and reasoning abilities of human beings, so that regardless of their religious commitments, all people will see that they have reason to act morally.

of their religious commitments, all people will see that they have reason to act morally. So without repudiating the divine origin of the laws, Hobbes invokes contract language in order to develop an entirely *human* justification of morality.

Without going into a lengthy exegesis of Hobbesian texts, which is bound to be controversial among Hobbes scholars, let me simply state here the features of what I take to be the Hobbesian moral theory. Whether or not every detail of the approach was explicitly embraced by Hobbes himself, its overall structure is recognizably Hobbesian:

1. What is valuable is what a person desires, not what he ought to desire (for no such prescriptively powerful object exists); and rational action is action that achieves or maximizes the satisfaction of desire (where it is a fact that the desire for self-preservation is our primary desire, and that human beings are, by and large, mutually unconcerned).

2. Moral action is rational for a person to perform if and only if such action advances his interests.

3. Morality is, in part, a body of causal knowledge about what human actions lead to peace, an end which it is common knowledge people desire and which they can all share, so that such actions are rational for them and "mutually agreeable." (This precept rests on the Hobbesian belief that people are not self-sufficient, and that they are roughly equal in strength and mental ability.)

4. Peace-producing action is only individually rational to perform (hence only moral action) when there is a convention in the community that people perform such action (so that I know that if I behave cooperatively, then others will do so too, and vice versa). These conventions comprise the institution of morality in our society. The rationality of performance is, however, subject to two provisos:

   Proviso 1: In order to be moral, an action must be not only peace producing and performed in the knowledge that others are willing to do so, but also an action that involves no net loss for the agent.[7]

   Proviso 2: Human beings are not, as a group, rational enough to be able to institute moral conventions, and hence must create a sovereign who can use his power to generate them.

---

[7] In his book *Hobbesian Moral and Political Theory* (Princeton: Princeton University Press, 1986), Gregory Kavka denies that Hobbes held this proviso, arguing that Hobbes was a "rule egoist."

5. Defining justice or equitable treatment in situations of conflict is done by considering what principles of justice the people involved "could agree to" or "what they would be unreasonable to reject," where the reasonableness of rejection is determined by a calculation comparing the benefits and costs of accepting an arbitrator's resolution with the benefits and costs of resorting to violence to resolve the conflict. An impartial judge, therefore, arbitrates according to the principle "to each according to his threat advantage in war."

Note that contemporary contractarians have enthusiastically taken on the role of Hobbes's arbitrator, trying to determine the sort of division of goods that could be accorded people in a peaceful way, such that they would perceive the division as fair. Nonetheless, we shall see that most of them, including Gauthier, reject the idea that the "threat advantage" of the parties in this situation is defined by their ability to fight.

Let us reflect, for a moment, on the interesting features and strengths of a moral theory with this structure. Consider, first of all, that the Hobbesian approach relies on a very strong conception of individuality. According to Hobbes, cooperative social interaction is presented neither as inevitable nor as something that people value for its own sake, but rather as something that asocially defined individuals find instrumentally valuable given their primary (nonsocially defined) desires. To think that cooperative behavior needs to be encouraged and justified, so that we must be *persuaded* to behave socially toward one another, is to believe that, even if society has some affect on us, it does not determine our fundamental or "intrinsic" nature as human beings, which is a nature that "dissociates us, and renders us apt to invade and destroy one another" (*Leviathan* 13, 10, 62).

Moreover, notice that there are two quite different ways in which this moral contractarian theory uses the notion of agreement. Features 2 and 3 capture the idea that the behavior enjoined by Hobbes's laws of nature is "agreeable," that is, that such action helps to secure the most-desired objects and/or states of affairs for each individual. Feature 5 captures the idea for which moral contractarians are famous; namely, that certain features of morality (e.g., fair resolution of conflict) can be understood as the *object* of agreement. However, there is a connection, in Hobbes's theory, between the latter way of using agreement and the former. To resolve conflicts via the use of arbitrators and agreement procedures is to resolve them peacefully and with much less cost to the parties than more violent resolution procedures. Hobbes commends the use of arbitrators as individually rational for disputants, and warns the arbitrators that their usefulness to the disputants depends on the extent to which their peaceful resolution is more acceptable than going to war to resolve the dilemma. It is therefore conducive to self-preservation to use a co-operative agreement procedure to resolve conflict, so that defining moral behavior through agreement is itself, for Hobbes, a mutually agreeable – that is, mutually self-preserving – behavior.

But perhaps most important of all, we should appreciate that all five features of Hobbes's moral view fit into a moral theory that is committed to the idea that morality is a *human-made institution*, which is justified only to the extent that it effectively furthers human interests. That is, Hobbes seeks to explain the *existence* of morality in society by appealing to the convention-creating activities of human beings, while arguing that the *justification* of morality in any human society depends upon how well its moral conventions serve individuals' desires.

In fact, there is a connection between Hobbes's contractarian approach to the state and this approach to morality. His decision to justify absolute sovereignty by reference to what people "could agree to" in a prepolitical society is an attempt to explain and legitimate the state's authority by appealing neither to God nor to any natural features of human beings that might be thought to explain the subordination of some to others, but solely to the needs and desires of the people who will be subjects of political realms. In the same manner, he insists that existing moral rules have power over us because they are social conventions for behavior (where Hobbes would also argue that these conventions only exist because of the power of the sovereign).

But Hobbes does not assume that existing conventions are, in and of themselves, justified. By considering "what we *could* agree to" if we had the chance to reappraise and redo the cooperative conventions in our society, we are able to determine the extent to which our present conventions are "mutually agreeable" and so *rational* for us to accept and act on. So Hobbes's moral theory invokes both actual agreements (i.e., conventions) and hypothetical agreements (which involve considering what conventions would be "mutually agreeable") at different points in his theory; the former are what he believes our moral life consists of; the latter are what he believes our moral life *should* consist of – that is, what our actual moral life should model. The contractarian methodology is useful in defining and justifying morality for one who believes that morality is man-made because considering what moral laws "people could agree to" (as well as what laws they have agreed to) is a way of confirming *that* morality is man-made, and a way of appraising how well the present institution serves the powerful self-regarding interests that virtually all of us have.

Note that this way of cashing out the language of hypothetical agreement makes the agreement-talk only a kind of metaphor, and not a device that reveals, in and of itself, the nature of morality or justice. What rational agents could all agree to is the securing of an object and/

or state of affairs, the benefits of which they could all share and for which there is a rational argument using premises that all rational agents would take as a basis for deliberation. Hence, to determine what these agents "could all agree to," one must perform a deduction of practical reason, something that Hobbes believes he has done in Chapters 14 and 15 of *Leviathan*.

Hence, the notion of contract or agreement does not do justificational work *by itself* in the Hobbesian moral theory. What we "could agree to" has moral force for Hobbes not because make-believe promises in hypothetical worlds have any binding force, but because this sort of agreement is a device that *reveals* the way in which the agreed-upon outcome is rational for all of us. The justificational force of this kind of contract theory is therefore carried within, but derived from sources other than, the contract or agreement in the theory.

II

There was enormous interest in this Hobbesian understanding of morality in the seventeenth century by both detractors and supporters alike.[8] The theorist who did most to advance this Hobbesian moral project before the twentieth century in what he took to be the right, and more plausible, direction was David Hume, a philosopher who tends to be incorrectly classed with the Benthamite utilitarians who followed him.[9] Hume was far more willing than Hobbes to credit people with substantial other-regarding desires that he considered to be the (natural) source of many moral virtues, but he also insisted that our self-regarding desires could cause us to invent "artificial" virtues such as being just, respecting others' property rights, keeping one's promises, and being chaste. Hume is so clear in presenting the creation of these virtues as a conventional solution to a coordination problem that David Lewis uses Humean remarks and examples to illustrate what coordination problems are and how conventions work to resolve them.[10]

In the latter half of the twentieth century, we find renewed enthusiasm for this approach and a sustained interest in developing it further. And I suspect that the source of the enthusiasm comes from contemporary

[8] Clearly, Spinoza was influenced by it, but lesser-known theorists found it just as intriguing and some actually sought to "derive" morality from self-interest in Hobbesian fashion even while vociferously denouncing Hobbes's political conclusions and some of his moral laws – for example, Richard Cumberland and Locke's friend James Tyrell. Some unpublished fragments even suggest that Locke himself was intrigued by this project (although the *Second Treatise* assumes that morality is composed of God-made and God-justified natural laws).

[9] See David Gauthier, "David Hume: Contractarian," *Philosophical Review* 88(1) (1979): 3–38, for a discussion of why and how Hume should be understood as a contractarian.

[10] David Lewis, *Convention* (Cambridge, MA: Harvard University Press, 1969).

philosophers' attraction to the most important and fundamental feature of this approach, the presumption that morality is a human creation. For example, James Buchanan insists that

Precepts for living together are not going to be handed down from on high. Men must use their own intelligence in imposing order on chaos, intelligence not in scientific problem-solving but in the more difficult sense of finding and maintaining agreement among themselves.[11]

And J. L. Mackie is especially disparaging of the idea that morality is something objective and "out there" that we find rather than create and that exerts inexplicable prescriptive power over us. Instead, Mackie wants us to understand and *use* the fact that morality is something we generate in order to serve our interests, an idea suggested by the very title of his book, *Ethics: Inventing Right and Wrong*.[12] Declaring in Chapter 5 that "Morality is not to be discovered but to be made: we have to decide what moral views to adopt, what moral stands to take,"[13] Mackie goes on to discuss rather briefly the sorts of game-theoretic situations that can make agreement on moral behavior advisable,[14] and he concludes by insisting that insofar as we make morality because of our interests, we might have to remake it, at least in part, when those interests change. The same rebellious overtones of the social-contract argument welcomed by Locke and Hume in a political context are welcomed by Mackie in a moral context. Given that the contract argument presents the state as a human creation designed to serve human interests, it justifies the people's replacing a ruler who fails to serve those interests. Similarly, given that the argument presents morality as a human invention designed to serve human interests, it justifies replacing a moral virtue that has outlived its usefulness.

The contemporary theory that most completely realizes the Hobbesian approach and that develops it in important ways is presented by David Gauthier in *Morals by Agreement*,[15] where he attempts to "validate the conception of morality as a set of rational, impartial constraints on the pursuit of individual interest."[16] Every one of the features of Hobbes's moral theory is embraced in some fashion by Gauthier. On his view, moral behavior is rational and mutually advantageous behavior (features 1 and 2) that will lead to a cooperative state of affairs that is desired by everyone (feature 3), assuming, of course, that they are equal in rationality and technology, when (and only when) people become disposed

[11] James Buchanan, *The Limits of Liberty: Between Anarchy and Leviathan* (Chicago: The University of Chicago Press, 1975), p. xx.
[12] John Mackie, *Ethics: Inventing Right and Wrong* (New York: Penguin, 1977).
[13] Ibid., p. 106.
[14] Ibid., p. 123ff.
[15] David Gauthier, *Morals by Agreement* (Oxford: Oxford University Press, 1986).
[16] Ibid., p. 6.

to engage in such behavior on a widespread basis (i.e., when a convention to behave cooperatively exists – feature 4). Gauthier also argues that resolution of conflict by such individuals should proceed via principles arrived at by considering the outcome of a hypothetical bargain among equals (feature 5). The people in this theory are quite clearly determinate individuals, who are defined prior to the morality that their contractual agreement is supposed to justify. While Gauthier does not explicitly say, as Mackie does, that the constraints traditionally endorsed as "moral" in human societies are human inventions, that idea, as well as the idea that these constraints can be "reinvented" to better serve human purposes, appears to be the assumption behind his philosophical project, which aims to show what conventions people *would* agree to if they were the sort of perfectly rational people we are all striving to become.[17]

However, what makes Gauthier's moral contractarianism so interesting is the way in which it develops certain features of Hobbes's moral theory to produce not only a more sophisticated moral theory than Hobbes's own, but also one that is more palatable to twentieth-century moral theorists. Consider again feature 4 of Hobbes's theory: that it would only be rational to act cooperatively if others are disposed to do so. In general, Hobbes seems to be right that cooperative situations have a game-theoretic structure such that people are rational to act cooperatively together, but irrational to act cooperatively alone. Yet sometimes cooperation is surely going to have a Prisoner's Dilemma structure, so that even when others are disposed to cooperate, the individual agent is still rational *not* to cooperate. This suggests that the correct moral attitude is one that says, in essence: "I will cooperate with others, when they are willing to do so, except in situations where, by not cooperating, I can gain benefits from them with impunity," but this attitude is hardly what one would call "moral." Hume explicitly worries about this problem when he discusses the "sensible knave" who has exactly the attitude I have just described:

And though it is allowed that, without a regard to property, no society could subsist; yet according to the imperfect way in which human affairs are conducted, a sensible knave, in particular incidents, may think that an act of iniquity or infidelity will make a considerable addition to his fortune, without causing any considerable breach in the social union or confederacy. That *honesty is the best*

[17] For example, see ibid., p. 168: "We do not of course suppose that our actual moral principles derive historically from a bargain, but in so far as the contraints they impose are acceptable to a rational constrained maximizer, we may fit them into the framework of a morality rationalized by the idea of agreement"; or page 231ff., where he says that although unequal possession of technology means that the equality assumption does not hold in our world (so that the conventions he argues for may not be applicable), we are "moving towards" the equal possession of this technology, and so, of equal rationality.

policy, may be a good general rule, but is liable to many exceptions; and he, it may perhaps be thought, conducts himself with most wisdom, who observes the general rule, and takes advantage of all the exceptions.[18]

The knave is essentially saying that he will cooperate if and only if it is utility maximizing for him to do so, and thus will be prepared not to do so in situations, such as the Prisoner's Dilemma, despite the existence of a moral convention to perform the cooperative act in that sort of situation. And what does Hume say to this sensible knave? Essentially nothing. Given the difficulties that Hobbes himself had providing an answer to the same knavish question, we see that it is difficult for anyone who embraces the Hobbesian approach to morality to persuade someone who has no natural sentiments against exploitation of his fellow man not to exploit them when he can do so with impunity. Yet such a person is very far from being moral.

Gauthier attempts, however, to answer the knave, inspired by a line of argumentation that he believes Hobbes suggests (but does not develop adequately) in an attempt to answer the "foole" – who offers roughly the same challenge as Hume's knave.[19] It is rational, says Gauthier, for people to become "disposed" to cooperate in such situations (assuming, however, that a sufficient number of others will become similarly disposed). By doing so, they become "constrained maximizers" rather than knavish "straightforward maximizers," where the former are people who pursue their advantage but who do so respecting a constraint against exploitative noncooperation in Prisoner's Dilemmas, where they have good reason to believe that their partners are inclined to cooperate.[20] Such people are willing to forego benefit in Prisoner's Dilemmas; hence, they are not straightforwardly maximizing utility. Yet they have chosen to be disposed to act in this way because they have determined that they can amass more utility by having this disposition than by not having it. A constrained maximizer refrains from taking advantage of any person who is also disposed to constrain his maximizing behavior because "he is not the sort of person that is disposed to do that sort of thing." That is the "moral" attitude that the sensible knave lacks. But the constrained maximizer has that "moral" attitude because of a prior determination that it is individually utility maximizing to have it. So, true to Hobbesian principles, Gauthier is arguing that moral behavior

---

[18] David Hume, *Enquiry Concerning the Principles of Morals,* edited by L. A. Selby-Bigge, revised by P. H. Nidditch (Oxford: Clarendon Press, 1975), sec. ix, pt. ii, pp. 281–3.

[19] See *Leviathan,* chap. 15. Hobbes's answer to the fool is much discussed in the secondary literature. I give a review of recent interpretations, and one of my own, in *Hobbes and the Social Contract Tradition,* chapters 2 and 3. Gauthier discusses the passage in various parts of chapter 6 of *Morals by Agreement.*

[20] Gauthier, *Morals by Agreement,* p. 170.

is utility maximizing and, in the long run, behavior that involves no net cost.

Contemporary Hobbesians and Humeans would certainly *want* to embrace Gauthier's argument if they could. It offers them a way to explain how collectively rational cooperative action that involves forgoing exploitative opportunities, but which is not dangerous, is also *individually rational* for the agent. But I am not so sure that they can embrace it. First, the idea that one could "will" to be disposed to act as Gauthier describes is dubious if one accepts Hobbesian psychology, and perhaps just as dubious on more plausible contemporary psychological theories. Second, it remains to be seen whether or not Gauthier's argument that it is rational to become disposed to act as a constrained maximizer actually succeeds. If Peter Danielson is right (see his essay, chap. 16 in this volume), it is rational to adopt the more "knavish" cooperative attitude called "reciprocal cooperation," which differs from Gauthier's constrained maximization in that it directs us to exploit (rather than cooperate with) unconditional cooperators. Finally, it might be even more rational only to *pretend* to be disposed to cooperate in either Gauthier's or Danielson's sense, ready to exploit others whenever one can do so with impunity.

The jury is, therefore, still out on the question of whether constrained maximization is rational for individuals to adopt. But other of Gauthier's modifications of Hobbes's project face what seem to be even more serious difficulties. For example, Gauthier argues that Hobbes was wrong to think that we could not establish moral conventions voluntarily, and that we need a sovereign to make their creation possible (although he admits that a limited political power would be needed to handle those among us who are not rational). Not only are most people able to constrain their maximizing tendencies for long-term gain on his view, but they are also able to recognize and act from a principle of acquisition that will provide a rational starting point for further agreement on the terms of cooperation. This principle is what Gauthier calls the "Lockean Proviso" – which directs that one is to acquire goods in a way that leaves no one worse off; and the principle defining fair terms of cooperation that rationally proceeds from a bargain based on this proviso is what Gauthier calls the principle of "minimax relative concession" (hereafter the MRC principle), which essentially directs that the parties are to accept that outcome that is the result of their making equal concessions to one another in the bargaining process.

It may appear that Hobbes has no equivalent of the proviso or the MRC principle since, in his view, there is no way that people could develop a peaceful method of acquiring or dividing goods outside of civil society. But this is not quite so; as we saw, he does consider the kind of principle that an arbitrator (were such a thing possible in the state of nature) would be rational to use in resolving disputes about the acquisition or the division of goods: "to each according to his threat advantage in war." Clearly, there is a big difference between this principle and Gauthier's cooperative rules! Is either theorist's argument for his approach effective?

James Buchanan comes down on the side of Hobbes. Imagine, says Buchanan, a state of nature in which people are competing for some scarce good x:

Each would find it advantageous to invest effort, a "bad," in order to secure the good x. Physical strength, cajolery, stealth – all these and other personal qualities might determine the relative abilities of the individuals to secure and protect for themselves quantities of x . . . as a result of the actual or potential conflict over the relative proportions of x to be finally consumed, some "natural distribution" will come to be established.[21]

It is this "natural distribution" that then becomes the baseline for any further contractual agreements. And it is that distribution that then "defines the individual" for purposes of future bargaining.

This future bargaining should occur, according to Buchanan, because everyone has a motive for resolving disputes and allocating goods peacefully given the substantial costs of predation and defense. Successful resolution of conflict through peaceful means would free up the resources used in warfare, and any agreement reached regarding the distribution of these resources, or any portions of the good x not appropriated, will proceed from the natural distribution. What Buchanan does not notice is that the natural distribution also generates the principle to be used in the peaceful resolution of these sorts of competitive conflicts: it is the principle "to each according to what he would have received in war."[22] Consider the following passage from *Leviathan*:

if *a man be trusted to judge between man and man,* it is a precept of the law of nature, *that he deale Equally between them.* For without that, the controversies of men cannot be determined but by War. He therefore that is partial in judgement, doth what in him lies, to deter men from the use of Judges, and Arbitrators; and consequently (against the fundamental Law of Nature) is the cause of War. (*Leviathan* 15, 23–4, 77)

Hobbes is saying here that an arbitrator in a dispute must beware not to be "partial" in his resolution of the conflict or else the parties will ignore his resolution and go to war to resolve their dispute. But the knowledge that warfare may be deemed rational by the parties if the outcome is not to their liking will affect how the arbitrator resolves

---

[21] Buchanan, *The Limits of Liberty*, p. 23.
[22] I am indebted to a discussion of Hobbes on justice by Brian Barry at the 1986 Pacific Division Meeting of the American Philosophical Association for the kind of strategy I am using to interpret the following passage.

the conflict. He must try, as far as possible, to mimic the distribution of the goods or the resolution of the conflict that the parties believe warfare between them will likely effect (assuming that each would stop short of attempting to kill the other). To do otherwise would be to risk one party deciding, "I won't accept this resolution: I can get more if I go to war." Of course, there are costs to going to war that are not involved in accepting an arbitrator's resolution of the conflict, so that even if the arbitrator got the resolution wrong, he might be close enough to the division each thinks warfare would effect such that no party would feel it was worth the cost of warfare to try to get more. On the other hand, one or both of them may be vainglorious and believe (falsely) that he can win a fight over the other and wrest away everything that he wants, in which case there is no way the arbitator can resolve their dispute that both will find acceptable. But when both are at least fairly realistic in assessing their powers, the arbitrators can peacefully decide conflicts between them using the maxim "To each according to his threat advantage in a conflict between them."

Gauthier argues that the initial bargaining position is misidentified with the noncooperative outcome, and although his argument is directed at Buchanan, it would clearly apply to Hobbes as well. Why, Gauthier asks, should people behave in a way that maintains the effects of predation after it has been banned?

> Were agreement to lapse, then what might I expect? Buchanan depends on the threat implicit in the natural distribution to elicit compliance. But a return to the natural distribution benefits no one. The threat is unreal. What motivates compliance is the absence of coercion rather than the fear of its renewal.[23]

Gauthier is, I believe, trying to make the following point. If people have decided to enter a world in which their interactions are cooperative rather than coercive, then coercive power and the goods that this power has amassed no longer define the parties' bargaining positions; instead, it is their power as cooperators that determines their clout in the bargain, as the MRC principle is meant to represent. If Buchanan and Hobbes reply that past coercers can threaten a return to predation and warfare unless they get them, then Gauthier will counter that such a return is extremely expensive for them, so expensive that it would be a threat they would never feel they could carry out. Not only would they lose the resources that had been freed up by the ban on predation, but they would also give up any productive returns that those freed-up resources may have been able to yield in cooperative investments with others. Gauthier argues that distribution according to predative power should be abandoned, and that initial distribution rationally proceeds according

---

[23] Gauthier, *Morals by Agreement*, p. 196.

to the Lockean Proviso, while the results of further cooperation should be distributed by the market or, when the market fails, according to the MRC principle.[24]

But Buchanan and Hobbes can defend their claim that predative power should still be understood as the foundation of the parties' bargaining on distribution of a cooperative surplus. Imagine a world in which predation has gone on for some time. The predators would certainly prefer to the MRC principle the Hobbesian "warfare threat advantage" principle, which would give every party at least what she would have gotten in the state of war, plus some of the resources that previously went into predation and defense. The predators would point out that no one would lose, and everyone would gain, from this deal, although the weak would not gain as much from this principle as they would from MRC.[25] But why should the weak, who may have considerable cooperative potential, go along with this deal? Doesn't such potential generate a new threat advantage, so that the result of the agreement will be (loosely) "To each according to his production in the cooperative endeavour"? I want to propose that the strong may have a strategy for ensuring that it does not by invoking the very notion of commitment that Gauthier himself thought so powerful in his answer to the knave. The strong would be rational to turn the situation into a two-move game and use what game theorists call a "precommitment strategy," which is essentially just the same as Gauthier's technique of "constraining oneself for gain."[26] On the first move they would perform two actions. They would:

---

[24] I have argued that bargaining clout derived from cooperative power in Gauthier's contractual situation does not result in selection of the MRC principle, but I want to put that argument aside here. See my "Can We Agree On Morals?" *Canadian Journal of Philosophy* 18 (1988): 331–56, reprinted in part in chap. 10 in this volume.

[25] The rational principle of distribution may be slightly more complicated than this. *If* it were possible to determine which resources would have been put to use by individuals for predation and defense, then these resources would not have to be distributed according to the threat-advantage principle on the grounds that *everyone* would benefit from any principle that gave them a portion of these goods (since in the state of nature, they would get none of them). Moreover, the powerful could not threaten to use warfare to force the others to accept the threat-advantage principle, since this would mean losing the very benefits that were being contested. This appears to be the core of truth in Gauthier's argument. However, a large family of principles would be prima facie acceptable to all of the parties in this situation and the threat-advantage principle would be among them and would certainly have the advantage of being *salient*. Nonetheless, if the isolation of goods that otherwise would have gone to predation is difficult or impossible, than the warfare threat-advantage principle is a rational principle of division for all contested goods. I am indebted to conversations with Stephen Munzer, which helped me to clarify this point.

[26] Hence, I am essentially arguing that if Gauthier's kind of constraining device is psychologically possible for human beings, then this may have bad consequences for other elements of his contractarian theory. I am indebted to Christopher Morris for this way of characterizing my argument.

(a) make a threat to reassemble the means of war for as long as it took to persuade the noncompliers to go along with the threat-advantage principle;

and then they would

(b) dispose themselves to keep their threats, no matter how expensive it is to do so.

The second move would be made by the weak. What is their rational response to the first move of the strong? Clearly, they would find it utility maximizing to accept the threat-advantage principle rather than to hold out for a principle more favorable to them. Hence, by transforming the situation into a two-move game and using the first move to make a threat that they would then commit themselves to keep, the strong would be able to insist on ensuring that the structure of future mutual cooperation respects their past predative power.

In response, Gauthier could try to contend that this kind of two-move strategy would be unavailable to the people in his bargaining situation. For example, he might argue that insofar as the weak are perfectly rational, they would know that this strategy would be rational for the strong, and would do their best to block it.[27] But precisely because they *are* weak, blocking this strategy might be difficult. Indeed, it is difficult for Gauthier to *prove* that the weak could block it. His bargaining situation is so sparsely described and highly idealized that we can find nothing in the structure of that situation to rule out this kind of precommitment strategy by the strong, so that it seems possible for both the starting point and the results of a Gauthierian initial contract to be alarmingly Hobbesian.

These remarks make me appear strangely unappreciative of Gauthier's attempt to mount a plausible neo-Hobbesian moral theory. It seems that I am commending to contemporary contractarians the meanest and most unappealing aspects of Hobbes's approach to justice and property. But those mean and unappealing aspects are quite clearly and strongly linked with Hobbes's requirement that moral action involve no net loss to the agent. There are no free giveaways or free rides on Hobbes's theory; you get what it is in your interest to get and what it is in others' interest to let you have. The results of this kind of thinking are not, I think, very attractive. Contemporary Hobbesians like Gauthier try to accept the self-interested underpinnings of the theory but dress up or deny the conclusions that Hobbes claims they force one to draw. I have attempted to suggest in these remarks that Hobbes is right to insist on them. I

---

[27] This response to my argument was made on Gauthier's behalf by Geoffrey Sayre-McCord, who commented on this paper at the conference for which this paper was solicited.

suspect that if Gauthier or other theorists sympathetic to the structure of Hobbesian theory long for "nicer" principles of morality and justice than those that Hobbes develops, they need to find a non-Hobbesian foundation for them. And as I now discuss, there are signs that Gauthier himself suspects this is so.

III

Consider what many have found a particularly ugly side to Hobbesian morality: its radical individualism. Recall that the people in Hobbes's or Gauthier's contracting world are fully developed, asocially defined individuals. But when *Leviathan* was originally published, some readers were shocked by the idea that the nature of our ties to others was interest-based. Aristotelian critics contended that Hobbes's theory goes too far in trying to represent us as radically separate from others. Their worries are also the worries of many twentieth-century critics. Do not our ties to our mothers and fathers, our children and our friends define, at least in part, who we are? Isn't it true that our distinctive tastes, projects, interests, characteristics, and skills are defined by and created within a social context? So how can a moral theory that does not take this into account be an accurate representation of our moral life? It would seem that we *must* bring into our moral theory noninstrumental ties with others that are not based on our affections because it is through such ties that we *become* individuals. This is the kind of criticism that certain feminist writers have made of contractarian theory (e.g., Carole Pateman), and it is part of the reason for its rejection by Marxist thinkers (e.g., Macpherson), who regard the individualism in contractarian thinking as a reflection of the theory's bourgeois, capitalist origins.[28]

Hobbes would either not understand or else resist the claims of our social definition. But Gauthier, a member of our place and time, accepts them, and this has strange consequences for his moral theory. Gauthier is moved by the criticism that it is unfair to use allocation procedures, such as the market, to distribute goods in circumstances where the society permits – even encourages – one class of people to prevent development in another class of people of those talents that allow one to do well in a system using that allocation procedure. Thus, he suggests that we see his contract on the fair terms of cooperation not as an agreement among determinate, already defined, individuals, but as an agreement at a hypothetical "Archimedean Point" among "proto-people" – people who have a certain genetic endowment and who are concerned to select principles that will structure their society such that they will develop well:

---

[28] Gauthier himself has been moved by these kinds of worries, inspired, he says, by Hegel. See his "Social Contract as Ideology," *Philosophy and Public Affairs* 6 (1977): 130–64.

The principles chosen from the Archimedean point must therefore provide that each person's expected share of the fruits of social interaction be related, not just to what he actually contributes, since his actual contribution may reflect the contingent permissions and prohibitions found in any social structure, but *to the contributions he would make* in that social structure most favorable to the actualization of his capacities and character traits, and to the fulfillment of his preferences, provided that this structure is a feasible alternative meeting the other requirements of the Archimedean choice. (My emphasis)[29]

No longer does Gauthier's contract talk presume fully determinate individuals, and no longer is the object of any contract a principle for the resolution of conflict among individuals. Now the contract methodology is used to choose principles that are "for" the structuring of the social system that plays a profound role in structuring individuals. Like Rawls, Gauthier is declaring that the first order of moral business is the definition of social justice.

This is not a benign addition to Gauthier's Hobbesian moral theory: it is an addition that essentially destroys its character as a Hobbesian theory. Of course, it undermines the individualism of the original Hobbesian theory; many will think that this is no great loss. But it was that individualism that much of the rest of the theory presupposed. Consider, for example, that a Hobbesian theory answers the "Why be moral?" question with the response, "Because it is in your interest to be so." But that answer no longer makes sense in a contract theory designed to pursue the nature of social justice using protopeople. Suppose the results of that theory call for a more egalitarian distribution of resources and opportunities open to talents that society will attempt to develop in all its members. If I am a white male in a society that accords white males privileged opportunities to develop talents that will allow them to earn well, then why is it rational for me to pursue a restructuring of social institutions in which this is no longer true?

Indeed, given that their development has already taken place, *why is it even rational for adult minority members or females to support this restructuring?* All of these people are already "made." Restructuring the social world such that it does a fairer job of creating a future generation of individuals is a costly and other-regarding enterprise. Why should these determinate individuals be rational to undertake it, given its cost, unless they just happened to be affected by sympathy for other members of their race or caste or sex, and so enjoyed the struggle? But the nontuistic perspective Gauthier encourages his bargainers to take encourages them to discount any benefits to others from their actions. So assuming the Hobbesian/Gauthierian theory of rationality, what it would be rational

---

[29] Gauthier, *Morals by Agreement*, p. 264.

for "proto-me" to agree to in some extrasocietal bargain seems to have little bearing on what it is rational for "determinate-me" to accept now.[30]

It is because the self-interest of *determinate* individuals does not seem sufficient to explain the commitment to the results of a bargain among *protopeople* that one wonders whether Gauthier's eventual interest in defining fair principles for the development of individual talents in a social system betrays a commitment to the intrinsic value of the individuals themselves. And it is the idea that individuals have intrinsic value that is missing from the Hobbesian approach. It has not been sufficiently appreciated, I believe, that by answering the "Why be moral?" question by invoking self-interest in the way that Hobbes does, one makes not only cooperative action, but the human beings with whom one will cooperate merely of *instrumental value;* and this is an implicit feature of Hobbes's moral theory that is of central importance. Now Hobbes is unembarrassed by the fact that in his view, "The *Value,* or WORTH of a man, is as of all other things, his Price; that is to say, so much as would be given for the use of his Power: and therefore is not absolute; but a thing dependent on the need and judgement of another" (*Leviathan* 10, 16, 42). But this way of viewing people is not something that we, or even Gauthier, can take with equanimity. In the final two chapters of his book, Gauthier openly worries about the fact that the reason why we value moral imperatives on this Hobbesian view is that they are instrumentally valuable to us in our pursuit of what we value. But note *why* they are instrumentally valuable: in virtue of our physical and intellectual weaknesses that make it impossible for us to be self-sufficient, we need the cooperation of others to prosper. If there were some way that we could remedy our weaknesses and become self-sufficient, for example, by becoming a superman or superwoman, or by using a Ring of Gyges to make ourselves invisible and so steal from the stores of others with impunity, then it seems we would no longer value or respect moral constraints because they would no longer be useful to us – unless we happened to like the idea. But in this case sentiment, rather than reason, would motivate kind treatment. And without such sentiment, people would simply be "prey" for us.

Even in a world in which we are not self-sufficient, the Hobbesian moral theory gives us no reason to respect those with whom we have no need of cooperating, or those whom we are strong enough to dominate, such as old people, or the handicapped, or retarded children

---

[30] This point can be made in a slightly different way. If I am a person whose development has in some way been stunted by discriminatory social practices and institutions, I can be the sort of person who will honestly believe that changing the social world such that people of my type receive more and better opportunities is a bad thing for all of us. Moreover, I may be right that given who *I* am, increased opportunities would be a bad thing for *me.* (Consider women who vigorously fight the equal-rights amendment.)

whom we do not want to rear, or people from other societies with whom we have no interest in trading. And I would argue that this shows that Hobbesian moral contractarianism fails in a very serious way to capture the nature of morality. *Regardless* of whether or not one can engage in beneficial cooperative interactions with another, our moral intuitions push us to assent to the idea that one owes that person respectful treatment simply in virtue of the fact that he or she is a *person*. It seems to be a feature of our moral life that we regard a human being, whether or not she is instrumentally valuable, as always intrinsically valuable. Indeed, to the extent that the results of a Hobbesian theory are acceptable, this is because one's concern to cooperate with someone whom one cannot dominate leads one to behave in ways that mimic the respect one ought to show her simply in virtue of her worth as a human being.

Hobbesians themselves are not immune to this moral pressure. Although Gauthier wards it off throughout much of his book, I have argued that he gives way to it when he advocates social justice. I suspect it may also be behind his curious reluctance to admit the legitimacy of using force and coercion in the division of goods despite the fact that the Hobbesian foundations of his theory pressure him to do so. Indeed, signs of respect for persons even break through the surface of the moral theory of that hopeless curmudgeon Hobbes himself! Consider that there is an insistence in *Leviathan* that human beings are *equal;* and it is their equality coupled with their lack of self-sufficiency that make cooperative action instrumentally valuable for them. Yet it is hard to claim that such equality is a *fact;* the world gives us too many counterexamples, and Hobbes himself has difficulty sustaining belief in this "fact." At one point he contends:

If Nature therefore have made men equal, that equality is to be acknowledged; or if Nature have made men unequal, will not enter into conditions of Peace, but upon Equall terms, such equality must be admitted. And therefore for the ninth law of Nature, I put this, *That every man acknowledge others for his Equal by Nature.* The breach of this Precept is *Pride.* (*Leviathan* 15, 21, 77)

This passage is puzzling. If we really *are* equal, then it makes sense to acknowledge it. And if we are not, why must we pretend to be? Hobbes suggests that warfare will result if we do not. But if I am *genuinely* superior to you, then I should be able to win against you in the battlefield, such that it is not in your interest to fight me. And as Buchanan suspected, my superiority in warfare should mean that I may well be able to succeed in getting you to enter into conditions of peace on unequal terms. Moreover, if I am vastly your superior, I need not enter into *any* cooperative agreement to secure your help for me. I can simply coerce it from you; so the cooperative laws of nature are irrelevant to me.

Hobbes persistently refuses to say such things, and his commitment to either the fact of, or the need for the belief in, equality begins to look suspiciously like faith in a premiss that is required if his moral laws are *always* going to be applicable to us. One suspects that like Gauthier, Hobbes does not want to accept the fact that his theory directs us to find others valuable only when we do not have sufficient strength to dominate them or when we find their help necessary to achieve our own plans. Both philosophers feel the pressure of the idea that respect for persons is something we are compelled to pay no matter what their "price" or power.

IV

To abandon the idea that the only value human beings have is instrumental is to abandon the Hobbesian approach to morality. Gauthier drifted toward this abandonment when he started talking about hypothetical contracts among protopeople, whose value at this point in their nonlives could not be instrumental. This way of talking moved Gauthier in the direction of what I call "Kantian contractarianism."

Consider how Kant talks about the "idea" of the "Original Contract" in the context of defining just political policies:

Yet this contract, which we call *contractus originarius* or *pactum sociale*, as the coalition of every particular and private will within a people into a common public will for purposes of purely legal legislation, need by no means be presupposed as a fact. . . . It is rather a *mere idea* of reason, albeit one with indubitable practical reality, obligating every lawmaker to frame his laws so that they *might* have come from the united will of an entire people, and to regard any subject who would be a citizen as if he had joined in voting for such a will. For this is the touchstone of the legitimacy of public law. If a law is so framed that all the people *could not possibly* give their consent – as, for example, a law granting the hereditary *privilege* of *master status* to a certain class of *subjects* – the law is unjust. . . . "[31]

For Kant, asking "what people could agree to" when resolving political issues already *assumes* the intrinsic value of each individual, or, as Kant puts it, the idea that they are "ends-in-themselves." And it is a method for ascertaining the fair or just policy. We are to imagine people equally and fairly placed, and we are to give them a veto power over moral proposals put before them. In this way, we represent their value as ends-in-themselves amongst other such ends. So in Kant's view, the contract methodology is a *way of reasoning about how persons with such value ought to be treated.*

[31] Immanuel Kant, "On the Common Saying: 'This May be True in Theory, But It Doesn't Apply In Practice,' " in *Kant's Political Writings,* edited by Hans Reiss (Cambridge: Cambridge University Press, 1970), p. 63.

Kant's use of the social-contract method is picked up by Rawls in *A Theory of Justice,* and used to pursue the nature of social justice that the *fact* of our social nature makes the first item of moral business. Scanlon also makes this kind of use of the contract methodology, seeing it not so much as a tool for social justice, as a general procedure for defining a variety of moral obligations toward others. For these theorists, morality is not so much "invented" as it is "constructed," where the latter term is meant to suggest that specific moral laws and conceptions are not self-interested inventions of human beings, but theorems derived from human reason. For example, Rawls explicitly compares his original position procedure to Kant's categorical imperative procedure,[32] and Scanlon suggests that the contractarian form of argument is a kind of proof procedure for ethics, analogous to proof procedures in mathematics, having its basis in human reason and which we use to construct moral laws in a way that gives them objectivity.[33]

But Hobbesians such as Gauthier would be highly suspicious of the claim that this sort of approach to morality offers a justification of moral behavior. If the method works by *assuming* that human beings have equal, objective, and intrinsic value, they would ask how one could presuppose something as controversial, unsupported, and ill-defined as this. And even if one could make sense of the idea that we are valuable as "ends-in-ourselves" and establish that it was true that we had such value, they would wonder why any of us should *care* about respecting that value in others.

Kantians might reply by maintaining that our nature as ends-in-ourselves is a fact that has enormous prescriptive force. Or they might try to argue that this value should itself have the status of a human invention, a creation of civilized human culture that has instrumental value for its members. This last answer may have some appeal for Hobbesians, but is unlikely to be "objective" enough for those Kantians who want to see our intrinsic value as something more than a useful pretense.

Alternatively, the Kantian might give up the idea that the contract method assumes our value, and argue instead that the method generates the concept of treating human beings as ends. In this view, the method (and its placement of human beings relative to one another) would be taken to be foundational (e.g., as identical to reason in its practical form), and the use of that method to determine how to act in the world with regard to others would, indirectly, be the way one would construct and give content to the concept of treating someone as an end. (So I am treating you as an end if I behave toward you in such and such a way,

---

[32] Rawls, *Theory of Justice,* sec. 40.
[33] Thomas Scanlon, "Contractualism and Utilitarianism," in *Utilitarianism and Beyond,* edited by A. Sen and B. Williams (Cambridge: Cambridge University Press, 1982).

as mandated by the contract method.[34]) But even assuming that the contract method can be understood as conceptually prior to determinations of the value of human beings, the reply seems only to push the problem back a step, for now the Hobbesians will certainly challenge either the existence or the authority (or both) of this supposedly foundational method, and will be poised to attack any account of our motivation to follow it which insists (e.g., as Kant's would) on the motivational force of moral reasoning.[35]

Any of the justificational accounts just presented finds the justificational force of the contract method in sources *other* than the actual contract used in the method, and this was also true (as we discussed) of the Hobbesians' approach to the justificational force of their contract method. However, even if theorists such as Gauthier didn't directly use the contract to provide endorsement of the agreed-upon results, they did use it as a device to reveal the actual justification of those results, that is, their instrumental value. So the contract has a definite use in their theory. But Gauthier would question whether the Kantian's contract talk has any use at all. It is not just that he would question the force of make-believe promises in hypothetical worlds. The problem is more serious. Given that the Kantians traditionally structure the reasoning and information of the bargainers in the hypothetical contract in great detail, it appears they present us with not so much a *bargain* as a theorem in rational-choice theory based on certain supposedly weak and readily acceptable axioms (which generally turn out to by anything but weak and readily acceptable) involving the equality and "fair placement" of the parties relative to one another in a way that represents their equal intrinsic value.

Perhaps Kantians could answer this challenge by resisting any move to make determinate the reasoning of the parties in their arguments. Their hypothetical contract might be best understood not as a theorem in rational choice theory, but as a model that contains ethical intuitions that are too complex and nuanced to be successfully axiomatized, but which are present and alive to us in the right kinds of ways when we attempt to determine an answer to a moral quandary by asking, "What could people agree to – what would they be unreasonable to reject?" Still, such indeterminacy makes the contractarian "proof procedure" a messy, ill-defined business, and so reliant on intuitions as to make it

---

[34] This reply is suggested by Kant's own characterization of his categorical imperative procedure in a passage of his "Paradox of Method," in the *Critique of Practical Reason*, trans. by Lewis Beck (Indianapolis, IN: Bobbs-Merrill, 1956), p. 65–7.

[35] They would not, presumably, challenge Scanlon's approach to this motivational issue, which involves positing a desire in us to act so as to receive others' endorsement/agreement. But they would probably claim such a desire was not very widespread, or else not very strong, in most of the population.

appear only a more sophisticated variant of traditional ethical intuitionism.

It remains to be seen whether or not Kantian contractarianism can be
developed to answer these sorts of problems. I confess to being (perhaps
unreasonably) optimistic that it can. However, there is a third kind of
criticism that critics of *all* kinds of contractarian theory would want to
make of this Kantian variant. Is not the Kantian variant still too individualistic? The Kantian's persistent use of Hobbes's premise that the
parties to the contract are "mutually unconcerned" seems to show that
even these contractarians are still heavily in the grip of outmoded and
distorting individualistic thinking (indicative of the fact that this kind of
theory was developed by capitalists and by males).

However, I have concluded after reflecting on certain remarks of Gauthier that Kantian contractarianism is right headed precisely because it
preserves this remnant of Hobbesian moral theory, and that its Hobbesian side is what makes it a theory to which feminists (if not Marxists)
should be attracted.

Hobbes's central insight about ethics was that it should not be understood to require that we make ourselves a prey for others. It is this
insight that both varieties of contractarianism respect. Consider a relationship between two human beings that exists for reasons of either love
or duty; let us also suppose that it is a relationship that can be instrumentally valuable to both parties. In order for that relationship to receive
our full moral endorsement, we must ask whether either party uses the
duty or the love connecting them in a way that affects the other party's
ability to realize the instrumental value from that relationship. To be
sure, good marriages and good friendships ought not to be centrally
concerned with the question of justice, but they must also be, at the
very least, relationships in which love or duty are not manipulated by
either party in order to use the other party to her detriment. In Gauthier's
words, our sociality

> becomes a source of exploitation if it induces persons to acquiesce in institutions
> and practices that but for their fellow-feeling would be costly to them. Feminist
> thought has surely made this, perhaps the core form of exploitation, clear to
> us. Thus the contractarian insists that a society could not command the willing
> allegiance of a rational person if, without appealing to her feelings for others,
> it afforded her no expectation of benefit.[36]

The contractarian should insist that this be true for *any* social relationship, not just that of the polis.

Of course, no contractarian would want to deny that love can lead
one to willingly give up one's benefits. It can also lead one to serve
others who cannot, for various reasons, reciprocate; for example, infants,

[36] Gauthier, *Morals by Agreement*, p. 11.

or the impoverished, or the aged. Gauthier's remarks suggest not that one should never give gifts out of love or duty without insisting on being paid for them, but rather that one's propensity to give gifts out of love or duty *should not become the lever that another party uses to get one to maintain a relationship to one's cost.*

Perhaps this is most deeply true within the family. Consider a woman whose devotion to her family causes her to serve them despite the fact that they fail to reciprocate; in this case, they are exploiting her love and sense of duty, which cause her to maintain a relationship with them and to serve them. Of course, infants cannot assume any of her burdens; fairness cannot exist between such radically unequal persons. (Note that this relationship is not unfair either; the infant does not use the mother's love in order to exploit her.) But older children can. Indeed, as children grow into the equality they will eventually attain as adults, it is increasingly alarming to see them treating Mom as the maid. Unless they are encouraged to benefit her as they become able to do so, they are being allowed to exploit another human being by taking advantage of her love for them.

Gauthier's remarks suggest that contractarianism of either variety is a moral theory that insists that relationships among equals can only prosper against a backdrop of reciprocity. Our ties to those who are able to reciprocate what we give to them (as opposed to victims of serious diseases, impoverished people, infants) are morally acceptable, healthy, and worthy of praise only insofar as they do not involve, on either side, the infliction of costs or the confiscation of benefits over a significant period of time. What kind of costs and benefits are we talking about here? Not the costs and benefits that come from the affection itself – for among other things, these cannot be distributed and are outside the province of justice, but rather the nonaffective costs and benefits that the relationship itself creates or makes possible.

A person who would inflict such costs on another without compensating him for them or who would take such benefits without benefitting him in turn is failing to respect that person's value and importance as a human being. And the person who would *allow* this exploitation in the name of love or duty is failing to respect his own value and importance. Indeed, if the two of them are supposed to be in a loving relationship (e.g., a marriage), then the exploiter is failing to love the other in virtue of what she does. So love and justice are not opposing responses, for the latter, in the form of reciprocity, is built into the former.

Hence, the Kantian contractarians' insistence on each party's self-concern in his method is not an embarrassment. They need not say (as Hobbes very nearly does) that we are *only* self-interested. Instead, they can be interpreted as saying that in the process of determining whether any loving or duty-based relationship among equals is exploitative, one must leave aside these connections and ask, from the standpoint of each party, "Is the present distribution of the possible nonaffective costs and benefits of the relationship one which I would be unreasonable to reject?" The Kantian contractarians' insistence that each party to a relationship take such a self-concerned perspective is really the insistence that each of us is right to value ourselves, our interests, and our projects, and right to insist that we not become the "prey" of other parties in the pursuit of their projects. So the contractarian method is valuable in my view not merely because of the way in which it forces us to take into account the well-being of others, but also because it is a method that grants us what Charlotte Brontë in the quotation at the beginning of this essay seems to want, namely, a way to be tenacious advocates of ourselves.[37] What has attracted so many to the contractarian form of argument and what makes it worthy of further pursuit is precisely the fact that by granting to each individual the ability to be her own advocate, this method enables us to conceive of both public and private relationships without exploitative servitude.[38]

---

[37] Remember that it was because of Rawls' conviction that the utilitarian calculation, which does not incorporate such claims, thereby allowed for the exploitation of some by others that he turned to a contractarian mode of reasoning to get a better understanding of justice. A utilitarian might respond by maintaining that he allows each of us to count equally in the utilitarian calculation. But this way of "counting" still isn't good enough for the contractarian, who would note that each person appears in the utilitarian calculation as a number representing how much he contributes to the total good. This means that it is not really the individual so much as the summable units of good that he or she contributes (and, in the final analysis, represents in the calculation) that the utilitarian takes seriously. Each individual is, therefore, rewarded (and valued) by that theory (only) to the extent that he or she responds to any resources by contributing units of good to the total.

[38] I wish to thank Carl Cranor, David Dolinko, Alan Donagan, David Gauthier, Christopher Morris, Stephen Munzer, Geoffrey Sayre-McCord, an anonymous referee for Cambridge University Press, and members of the Saturday Afternoon Discussion Group in Los Angeles during the Spring of 1987 for their comments on, and help during the writing of, this paper. Portions of the paper were read at the 1988 Pacific Division Meeting of the American Philosophical Association.

4. Gauthier's foundations for ethics under the test of application

David Braybrooke

Gauthier's program for refounding ethics on a contract among rational agents seeking through cooperation to obtain public goods will not be completed until the contract embraces the public goods involved in having a market or in having measures against force and fraud, which make a market possible. Gauthier faces some difficulty in distinguishing the benefits from these public goods from the benefits of having the private goods obtained in the market. However he puts the distinction through, moreover, the amount of information required to give any application to his theory will increase. But the amount of information required is already so much, extending as it does to a survey by the agents of the returns to them of all feasible arrangements for producing public goods, as to defy any application of the theory, even as a guide to the direction of social policy. Can they be suitable foundations if the edifice erected upon them has no possible use? This may well seem too troubling a question to waive even for a moment. I have, however, treated it elsewhere (along with the problem of completing the program by embracing the public-goods aspects of the market)[1]; and waiving it, as I propose to do in this essay, will enable us to see how further questions about the foundations that Gauthier proposes come up independently of the problem about information. If we consider how the theory might be given application over the full range of in-principle possible variations in information, we shall be troubled, I think, by what we shall see: that

---

[1] "Social Contract Theory's Fanciest Flight," *Ethics* 97 (1987): 750–64, the fanciest flight being Gauthier's in *Morals by Agreement* (Oxford: Oxford University Press, 1986). I hope that in that paper as well as in this my admiration for Gauthier's work comes through clearly. I think the program that culminates in his book has taught us more about the relations between self-interest and morality than the program of any other philosopher, though it is not quite the lesson that he meant to teach.

the foundations give no guarantee of upholding such things as civil liberties and due process of law; that they may lend support to the expulsion of part of the population of an established society; that here, and in other connections as well, they may establish an ethics that top and bottom is at odds with humane feeling. It is true, as we should fairly allow, that within the range of in-principle variations in information, Gauthier's theory may elsewhere turn out to favor humane feeling and progressive causes; but his foundations fall far short of giving us assurance of such favor everywhere.

Even if we assume – a breathtaking assumption – that the information required to apply a sophisticated social contract theory like Gauthier's will be forthcoming, a residue of realism may persuade us that ordinary people in everyday life will not have to refer their choices of actions directly to the standard offered by the theory. This is not just because it is unrealistic to suppose that they would go through the calculations called for by the standard whenever they acted in all the variety of ways in which they are acting, or even whenever they had to act in ways new to them in their own lives. The implications of the standard as to the optimum mix of private and public goods will vary over time, as technology brings in new goods and tastes change.[2] The optimum determined by the theory will be changing with the changes in the profile of personal utility functions of which the optimum itself is a function. But it will be inefficient (because confusing) and impractical (to the point of being counterproductive) to change the pattern of production and distribution from moment to moment. It will be realistic to persist with rules implying any given pattern for some time after it ceases to be in principle optimal, precisely, for that period of time that corresponds to an optimal periodization of change, allowing for the revision of human habits and for the efficiency in formulation and comprehension of various intermediate rules for coordinating the actions of the people affected.

Thus, the contract itself will imply the use of intermediate rules. Some will derive from the conditions laid down by the theory for the contracting process; some, from the contract itself. Thus, under Gauthier's theory, on the one hand, people will act by the rules associated with the right of private property (when these rules cannot be improved upon)[3]; on the other hand, by the rule requiring economic rent to be redistributed so that every member of the society has an equal share[4] (or by even more specific rules that combine to have this effect). But

---

[2] Gauthier, *Morals by Agreement*, p. 340: "We may think of the essentially just society . . . under the impact of changing utility and production functions, as continually adjusting to make possible maximum relative benefit."
[3] Ibid., p. 217.
[4] Ibid., p. 274.

these rules are themselves liable to change. Moreover, in real life, they will be just a few instances of rules amid a great variety, the whole manifold of rules that people live by; and in our experience, these rules are not only liable to change; they are continually changing, though perhaps not changing so fast as the optimum mix of private and public goods.

We may therefore ask of any social contract theory, as I shall ask with particular attention to Gauthier's, how well does it consort with familiar processes for arriving at social rules? Would it assist them, or obstruct them, and to what effect? How far is it relevant at all, even under the breathtaking assumption that the theory can be applied? Would we want it to play a leading part in the processes even if it could?

Deliberation

Deliberating changes of rules under Gauthier's theory might, in principle, efficiently replace politics as we know it (as might any form of utilitarianism commanding equally specific information). The sole subject of discussion would be whether circumstances and tastes had so changed that the new pattern of maximin relative benefit required a certain change in the intermediate social rules. This, at any rate, is the way things would go if Gauthier's theory were comprehensive. But it does not seem to be comprehensive, or if it is, it leaves a lot of morally important matters to be determined, subject to the principle of maximin relative benefit, by the happenstance of the given profile of personal utility functions. How does Gauthier's contract provide for freedom of expression, for freedom of association, for the right to participate in political decisions, for natural justice and due process? Other contractarians, most notably Rawls, have made careful explicit provision for most of these things[5]; and they have all been cherished by the political side of the liberal tradition. I expect Gauthier cherishes them, too; and the mood in which he dilates, in *Morals by Agreement*, on the virtues of "the liberal individual" may be taken as a sign of his affection for them.[6] But is the affection firmly entrenched anywhere in Gauthier's foundations – in the framework for bargaining or in the contract? Is it something that the theory requires people deliberating about changes in received social rules (like those guaranteeing civil liberties) to take into account?

Gauthier tells us that the liberal individual will value participating in the cooperative activities of her society.[7] But this may go no further than valuing participation in the production of the public goods that the

---

[5] Compare the first principle of justice, the principle of equal liberty, as set forth in John Rawls, *A Theory of Justice* (Cambridge, MA: Harvard University Press, 1971), pp. 60–1.
[6] Gauthier, *Morals by Agreement*, pp. 330–55 (chap. XI).
[7] Ibid., pp. 337–9.

contract, given the agents' utility functions over the whole range of feasible social arrangements, includes in the optimal mix. Neither as such public goods nor otherwise may the rules characteristic of political liberalism figure in the arrangements selected. If the agents' utility functions are just those assignable to (say) General Pinochet and his supporters, the deliverances of Gauthier's contract and hence of this theory will be quite hostile to civil liberties. As externalities, they will not strike everyone as goods. They certainly do not strike General Pinochet as goods. They may strike a number of people (say, those positioned to do especially well out of the market and rejoicing in Gauthier's strong advocacy thereof) as evils; and when all the utilities and disutilities have been taken into account in the social contract, little or no provision for these things may emerge.

It is not open to Gauthier to argue with Mill that the agents will be unwise not to make such provisions, for by doing so they will cut themselves from discoveries of more alluring life plans under novel social arrangements.[8] Gauthier, it is true, holds that every party to the contract "begins with a fundamental freedom to fulfill his preferences or advance his interests,"[9] and it may be allowed that everyone must have this freedom in order to discover what her considered preferences are, and hence her personal utility function, over all feasible social arrangements. But this has already been discovered before the bargaining begins. Gauthier's agents already have, under the assumption about full information that we are granting him, all the information about the delights open to them under all feasible social arrangements; and they bargain, referring each of them to her own personal utility function, to make the most of those delights.

Unlike Rawls' agents behind the veil of ignorance, they have no incentive to hold open the possibilities of following life plans that none of them happen to favor; or hold open the freedom to explore life plans with at least the resources given them by the social minimum.[10] It is true that we can find reasons in *Morals by Agreement* to think that their bargain is more complicated than I just allowed. Gauthier says, "Rational choice must be directed to the maximal fulfillment of our present considered preferences, where consideration extends to all future effects in so far as we may now foresee them."[11] How far ahead do we try to look? Although Gauthier is not explicit on this point, I think that his agents are must plausibly supposed to look ahead over their whole lifetimes, or at least over the whole of the lifetimes remaining to them. Otherwise,

---

[8] John Stuart Mill, *Utilitarianism, Liberty, and Representative Government* (London: Dent, 1910). All three works are relevant.
[9] Gauthier, *Morals by Agreement*, pp. 257–8.
[10] Rawls, *Theory of Justice*, pp. 92–3.
[11] Gauthier, *Morals by Agreement*, p. 37.

it would be difficult to make sense of Gauthier's provision for bargaining between members of different generations.[12] They need not work from personal utility functions corrected to allow for changes in their considered preferences.[13] If they did, they face a difficult problem, for how are they to compare the utilities corresponding to preferences at one time with the utilities corresponding to different preferences at another? Either way, the present considered preferences that they bring to bargaining would not necessarily call for much in the way of civil liberties; the optimal paths of change for the various agents once they have identified what changes will occur (and, perhaps, what changes they most want to occur) may be quite narrow and require little freedom for exploration. In real life, they might need the freedom to hit upon the changes; but under the assumption of full information, they do not, or do not henceforth; they are even in a position to eliminate the costs of the wrong turnings in real life paths.

Alternatively, they may wish to give some weight to their present preferences for having opportunities to change preferences in the rest of their lifetimes. But these present preferences may not be very strong. Moreover, it is far from clear that even if they were strong, they would call for much in the way of civil liberties. Even those changes that might ensue upon innovations in technology could come about under an authoritarian regime, as could the innovations themselves. In practice, no doubt, one could not trust an authoritarian regime to remain true to Gauthier's theory – to adjust the optimal mix of private and public goods, once preferences had changed, or to reopen the bargaining. But this observation brings into play contingent political considerations that Gauthier's theory does not assume; and he cannot lightly appropriate their favorable consequences for civil liberties.

Moreover, many people's personal utility functions may happen to ascribe to their own comfortable arrangements under an authoritarian regime more utility than to civil liberties as safeguards against the regime's turning against them. The functions may ascribe so much more utility to comfort that they bring the maximin relative benefits solution down on the side of that regime – an authoritarian capitalism, perhaps, with a robust market, such as General Pinochet's Chile at one time seemed to be setting out to be.

This is not to say that deliberation about the implications of Gauthier's

---

[12] Ibid., pp. 298–303, 343. In the latter passage, responding to points discussed by Derek Parfit, Gauthier writes as if one's possible future selves could be parties to the virtual bargain envisaged in the Archimedean choice. If the bargain is to be determinate, the Archimedean choice will presuppose full information about these selves and some way of relating their maximum claims – and actual returns – to those of present agents; or presuppose present values for future opportunities to change preferences. I take up both of these possibilities, both of them ways of bargaining for lifetimes.

[13] Ibid., pp. 31, 342.

social contract for changes in received intermediate rules would always lead away from civil liberties and toward more privilege for private property with more room for the market. On the contrary. Gauthier does allow that rights (except insofar as they enter under the Lockean Proviso into the determination of the agents' minimum claims on the cooperative surplus in public goods)[14] may have to be changed to keep the regulative ideal of maximin relative benefit current.[15] Nor do these rights seem to be sacrosanct respecting received resources for entering the market; inheritance may be limited or abolished. Gauthier is also well aware that what his theory holds for the ideal market may not hold for markets in the real world. His Archimedean actor, he tells us, is not "an ideal socialist."[16] Her ideal is the market for private goods and for public goods cooperation under the principle of maximin relative benefit. In the real world, she may have to accept various interferences with the market, perhaps enough to create, in effect, the welfare state.

Gauthier says at one point,

Karl Marx paid capitalist society its highest compliment in supposing it to have overcome scarcity through the creation of productive forces. For Marx, communism had become possible only because humankind could pass from a condition of scarcity to one of plenitude. Marx was mistaken.[17]

What is Marx supposed to have been mistaken about? The ensuing passage in *Morals by Agreement* shows that what Gauthier chiefly has in mind is the contention that scarcity has been overcome or ever could be.

Even if we suppose material scarcity entirely overcome, there would remain scarcity in the forms of human fulfillment. No human being is capable of realizing in herself all of of the possible modes of human activity.[18]

Gauthier does not pause to consider that, granting this point, Marx might still have been correct in claiming that after capitalism had reached a certain stage in the development of the productive forces, communism (a society relying on planning rather than the market) would fulfill the principle of maximin relative benefit better than the combination of market with public-goods provision that Gauthier himself has centrally in view. Or if Marx is mistaken about this, it is a mistake about the facts. It does not imply any restriction of the logical scope of Gauthier's contract and principle.

[14] Ibid., pp. 213–14, on the "initial positions" of the bargainers as determined by the Proviso.
[15] Ibid., pp. 272–4 (on economic rent); pp. 300–02 (on inheritance); p. 340 (on maximin relative benefit as a regulative ideal). I supply the assumption that changes in technology will affect economic rents and the incentives relating to inheritance.
[16] Ibid., pp. 261–2.
[17] Ibid., p. 333.
[18] Ibid., p. 334.

Circumstances may have so changed that everyone could, in a planned economy, have more in private goods in a lifetime and at the same time realize more in utility from public goods. Marx thought that the recurrence under capitalism of periods of economic standstill, ever more comprehensive, ever longer lasting, had come to imply such a change in circumstances.[19] One might postulate, in addition, improved institutional facilities for planning, such as the organizations already developed by some large firms for carrying on production.[20] In this case, Gauthier's theory, even taken narrowly, supports changing to a planned economy (and, I presume, bringing private goods within the embrace of the principle of maximin relative benefit along with public ones). I do not suppose that the theory means to hold out for a market if markets fail on the Pareto welfare criterion by comparison with other arrangements.

I could rest the case for this possibility upon the difference between a real-world market, subject to periodic breakdowns, and a planned industrial economy started up (as the real-world experiments have not been) with consensus and commitment in an economy with advanced industry. But even the ideal market may not compare favorably with an ideal planned economy over time. Suppose, for example, that in a planned economy to which workers were genuinely committed (among other things, because of propitious arrangements for participation in the planning), the productivity of labor will be greater than it could be induced to be under a market regime. Is this backwardness in motivation under a market regime something to be counted as an imperfection, so that the market is not ideal after all? But why should people be wholehearted about the market? They may be perfectly rational if they are wholehearted only about working alongside other people under a common plan, whether this is just because they like the company of other, like-minded people, or because acting straightforwardly to meet the needs of other people is an important source of utility to them.

People deliberating about changing intermediate rules – the rules of the market society in favor of the rules of a planned economy – may come upon another ground for changing to a planned economy. (Again, this ground may tell against a society with an ideal market as well as against a society with an imperfect one, though I shall not again spell out this implication.) Suppose – something that does not seem entirely implausible – that a different assortment of abilities (or, at least, of people) would take the lead in productivity under planning and that as a consequence overall output would rise. Then the possibility arises that whether or not these people gain higher rewards than others, the person-by-person pattern for the distribution of private goods might everywhere

[19] For instance, in the *Communist Manifesto*, and in the *Critique of the Gotha Program*.
[20] See Friedrich Engels, *Socialism Utopian and Scientific*, trans. by E. Aveling (Chicago: Charles H. Kerr, 1908), pp. 121–5.

give more private goods under planning, though the positions of the persons in the pattern differ; and, again, that everyone would realize more in utility from public goods. That is the second way in which deliberation about the application of Gauthier's theory may end up favoring a change away from a market society.

It is true, I am here taking a certain liberty with Gauthier's theory (as well as in this abstract in-principle discussion running clean against the actual evidence in this century from the most thorough-going attempts at planned economies). I am not giving full credit to the possibility that the distribution of the agents' maximum claims is such that the relative concessions for some of them (the.most competitive) are less under the market than the minimax relative concession (the mirror image of maximin relative benefit) under planning, even though the person worst off under planning gains more by her personal utility function than the person worst off in the market society. I am assuming that either this is not the case or that Gauthier would generously amend his theory so as not to let it stand in the way of a change to a pattern that as such seems more attractive. (It is, of course, a pattern that Rawls' contract would call for[21]; and it may be noted that there is no implication of free riding on the part of the person worst off under planning.[22])

Oskar Lange, the Polish economist, once suggested that socialists should erect, "in the great hall . . . of the Central Planning Board of the socialist state," a statue of Ludwig von Mises, to commemorate the contribution that Mises made by insisting that socialism would not be feasible without "an adequate system of economic accounting to guide the allocation of resources."[23]

Next to that prophet, more ancient even than the prophet Hayek, of the economic creed that the University of Chicago shares with the Bible colleges, should there not be a statue of Gauthier? He has revised social contract theory so that its support of private property and free enterprise is unlike Locke's contingent on circumstances[24]; and if circumstances turn out to be as Marx described them, which in an age of intractable high unemployment we should not lightly rule out, Gauthier's theory shows the way from the social contract to communism.

---

[21] In the Difference Principle. See Rawls, *Theory of Justice*, pp. 75–83.

[22] Cf. Gauthier, *Morals by Agreement*, p. 220, where Gauthier charges that, in general, "For Rawls morality demands the giving of free rides."

[23] Oscar Lange, "On the Economic Theory of Socialism," in *On the Economic Theory of Socialism*, edited by Benjamin E. Lippincott (Minneapolis: University of Minnesota Press, 1938), pp. 57–143, at pp. 57–8.

[24] John Locke, *Second Treatise of Government* (Indianapolis, IN: Hackett, 1980), p. 66: "The great and *chief end* . . . of men's uniting into commonwealths, and putting themselves under government, *is the preservation of their property*," to which they have rights under natural law that do not presuppose government (chap. V, "Of Property").

Revolution

Going through Gauthier's contract to communism would work out quite peacefully, to a conclusion from calm deliberation, if all the agents concerned were rational and regardless of their personal prospects (once due account had been taken of their personal prospects) adhered to the maximin relative benefit solution. Indeed, the first way, which improves everybody's position in the distribution of goods, private and public, would fail to be peaceful only if there were some agents who failed to appreciate this fact – for example, some property owners who did not recognize that they, too, will be better off when private property in the means of production disappears. But we are assuming agents who in arriving at the solution to the contract problem are fully informed on this and other points.

The other way puts more strain on the agents' conscientious adherence to the principle of maximin relative benefit. There will be a set of people who will lose personally by the change by losing their advantage over others under market arrangements. If they were formerly convinced by Gauthier's theory, will they not waver now? Indeed, with as much force as they can command, may they not resist carrying out the change that the theory recommends? By Gauthier's lights, they will be wrong to do so. If their resistance is too great for peaceful political processes (like a series of deliberations) to overcome, Gauthier's theory will justify revolution to seize power from them. For justifying the revolution by showing that justice requires revolution, the statue subsequently erected may well not just show Gauthier pushing a pen with one hand; he will be wielding a sword with the other.

There is another sort of revolution – many would think, a much uglier sort, though in some quarters it will perhaps be found a more plausible sort – that Gauthier's approach to the social contract might favor (depending on circumstances within the range of in-principle variations in information). Here it is not only the way in which his theory works out, given the whole body of his assumptions; we can identify some specific assumptions, features of the foundations of his theory, that come into question. One is the assumption (which he shares with other social contract theorists, including Hobbes, Locke, and Rawls) that the society formed by the contract will be "a society for mutual advantage."[25] Another is the position (explicit only with him and maybe peculiar to him) that abstaining from predatory force does not count as a contribution to mutual advantage.[26]

---

[25] Gauthier, *Morals by Agreement*, p.10. Gauthier takes from Rawls the assumption that society is "a cooperative venture for mutual advantage" among "persons conceived as not taking an interest in one another's interests."

[26] Gauthier allows that when they are not fully free to bargain rational agents may "ac-

The sort of revolution that I now have in mind falls into a class of cases that Gauthier himself worried about in an article that preceded his book[27]; he set it aside there, without repressing his worries; but no trace of the worries seems to have survived in the book. It is a class of cases to which Gregory Kavka (who cites Gauthier's article) gives the name "the secession problem."[28] The sort of case that I have in mind has a better claim to that name, however, than any that Gauthier or Kavka have considered; for it does not just raise a problem about circumscribing the original contracting group so that "there is no sub-group, each of whom prefers agreement only with other members of the sub-group" (other exceptionally productive people, or at least other people who are able to earn their keep in private goods) "to agreement with all."[29]

Suppose in a society formerly embracing everyone with every other in a relation of mutual advantage (let us say, specifically, earning their keep in private goods and making a net contribution to the production of public goods), developments occur that make a substantial part of the population redundant, so far as contributing anything of value to the remaining part goes. On the contrary, the redundant part, who inhabit the North, drain away goods from the South to support them in idleness. What would the people in the South make of that? The interdependence of utilities that along with free affectivity once united them with their now redundant fellow contractors would no longer have a foundation.

Would it not be rational for them, and in accordance with Gauthier's assumptions, to form a coalition and secede from the larger society? Perhaps they would make some provision for a partial exchange of populations: The aged poor of the South would be moved North: the Rt. Hon. Christopher Smoothe, made famous by Michael Frayn as Minister of Chance and Speculation, would tour the North to invite youths capable of training in public relations, stock broking, and currency trading to move South. Perhaps there would have, in justice (somebody's conception of justice), to be some sort of settlement under which people

---

quiesce" in arrangements that give them less in advantages than justice would (*Morals by Agreement*, pp. 220–1). But bargainers, when bargaining is fully voluntary, do not use threats (ibid., pp. 155–6). "Threats are compatible with rationality, but not in the context of co-operation. In effect, threat behavior would be proscribed by the constraint on the individual bargaining position" expressed in the Lockean Proviso (ibid., p. 156, footnote, referring to pp. 186–7). Distinguishing his position from Hobbes's, Gauthier says, "If interaction is to be mutually beneficial, then it must preclude the unilateral imposition of costs by one person on another" (ibid., p. 258).

27 David Gauthier, "The Social Contract: Individual Decision or Collective Bargain?" in *Foundations and Applications of Decision Theory*, Vol. 2, edited by C. A. Hooker, Jim Leach, and Edward McClennen (Dordrecht, Holland: D. Reidel, 1978), pp. 47–67, at pp. 62–3.

28 Gregory S. Kavka, *Hobbesian Moral and Political Theory* (Princeton: Princeton University Press, 1986), p. 240.

29 Gauthier, "The Social Contract," p. 62.

in the North, now to be left to their own devices, are compensated for any residual claims that they might have, based on their past contributions, to the facilities enjoyed by people in the South. But once this has been sorted out, would not threats of aggression from the North be justifiably ignored, so far as it was safe to do so? And if it was not safe, would not these threats raise difficulties that fall outside the assumption that predatory force is not to be used either in the bargaining itself or in establishing the initial bargaining positions of the several parties? Not even Margaret Thatcher has contemplated such secession publicly; if Gauthier is to have (to match his statue in the socialist state) a Tory-sponsored statue at Westminster, it will have to be kept from public view.

Will bargaining for lifetime returns prevent this result? If the contract theory and the principle of maximin relative benefit are invoked now as the standards for achieving justice in England's green and pleasant land, the people living in the South may insist on bargaining just for the remainders of lifetimes; and the people of the North have (I am assuming) nothing to offer during the remainders of theirs and the Southerners' lives. Not to insist would for the Southerners jeopardize the identification, on which Gauthier lays so much weight, of their interests with the interests of particular parties to the bargain.[30] Moreover, if the Southerners do relent, and agree to bargain on the basis of whole lifetimes all around, this may not help the Northerners; their net contribution to mutual advantage over the whole of their lifetimes, when everything is reckoned in – social services, subsidies to regional industry – may be zero or negative.

Accumulation of exceptions

There is a third process for changing rules that should be considered, not because its results will be less varied, or any less capable in various instances, troubling or not, of winning the approval of Gauthier's theory, but because it enables us, more easily than deliberation and revolution, to compare with the motivations that Gauthier's theory discards the motivations that we may suppose to be normally at work in moral progress.

Even people prepared to believe that it makes sense to speak of genuine moral progress and to believe further that such progress actually occurs will hesitate to say that it has made uniform headway in the century of the two world wars; of the famine deliberately fostered to kill off the kulaks; of the Holocaust; of Hiroshima; of Dresden; of the genosuicide of Kampuchea. However, in what are now considered the liberal

---

[30] Gauthier, *Morals by Agreement*, pp. 220–1, 251.

democracies, some instances of what champions of moral progress regard as successes can be cited even during this period and in the century preceding. Slavery has come to an end. The death penalty has given way to penalties more favorable to rehabilitation. A more refined conception of the legal rights of persons accused of crime has come to prevail. Entering matrimony and leaving it approach being free choices for both partners, given income and economic opportunities widely available. Sexual activity in and out of marriage goes on in wider variety for greater proportions of people, more generally approved than disapproved, except when intimidation and violence (and now the threat of AIDS) enter. Educational and vocational opportunities once closed to Jews, blacks, and women now unfold for them. Ethnocentricism has diminished – especially among educated people in easy circumstances – to the point of becoming disreputable, not only in respect to domestic policies, public and private, but also in respect to policies affecting peoples and cultures abroad.

How has this come about? It has had the assistance of deliberated legislation, rulings by the courts, and government edicts. In large part, however, it has come about by the accumulation in private actions and forbearances, inspired by a lot of agitation, literary and oratorical, of exceptions to what were once (in some cases as recently as a quarter of a century ago) established moral rules. Sometimes, perhaps, the exceptions have accumulated into simple reversals; they have become the norm and the old norm has retired to the field of exceptions. The examples that I just cited suggest that often the changes have been more radical: exceptions contrary, not just to the letter of the older rules, but to their spirit, have been safeguarded against interference. The police are no longer permitted to burst into married people's homes and arrest them for having sexual congress not in the missionary position.[31] Or things once permitted have step by step been decried, and the safeguards of those former permissions undermined. White employers cannot in good conscience refuse to consider aborigine applicants, much less shoot stray aborigines out of hand.

The changes that I have cited have led to wider demographic scope for the benefits of the rules; or have led to people within the same demographic scope being treated more sensitively. In both cases, the effect of the changes is the effect that would have come from a broadly distributed increase in humane feeling, with a concomitant reduction of the associated threshold of sensitivity. In fact, the changes may have come about without there having been much change in the distribution or intensity of humane feeling. The proportion of people who feel in-

---

[31] Not much more than twenty years ago, there was a report in the Canadian newspapers of police coming upon a Winnipeg housewife "giving head" (as our present tolerant phrase has it) to her husband in their kitchen; both were arrested.

tensely enough to make little of differences in race, culture, and tastes may be much the same. What has happened is that the rest of the population, less desperately competitive than they once had to be, comfortably preoccupied now with their own private lives, have stood aside and let the projects of the intensely humane reach fruition. Humane feeling will still have counted decisively in bringing about moral progress even in the latter case. What does Gauthier's theory make of humane feeling?

Again, we shall be led to mixed results. In some respects, the theory falls in nicely with what humane feeling demands. First, like other social-contract theories, it sets its face against fanaticism. Moralists have often been so horrified by the absence in Hobbes, for example, of any reference to love or friendship, that they have failed to allow with Hobbes that there are worse things than cool self-interest. Racism, chauvinism, and sectarian zeal are worse things. Gauthier's agents, at their coolest, would be readier than people afflicted by these things to extend the benefits of democratic scope to outsiders (when the outsiders are potentially productive) and to refrain from inhumane practices (when these have been shown to be counterproductive; or just useless).

Second, like other contract theories (whether these seek to establish principles of justice in the first place or just give effect to principles already known), Gauthier's theory offers a precaution of the sort called for by the injustice-disaffecting hypothesis, that is to say, the hypothesis that if people are being treated unjustly in comparison with their associates, they are likely to become disaffected. The way to prevent this disaffection is to examine their relationships by a standard that does do justice to their own several interests; and to modify the relationships accordingly, even if for the time being, perhaps because of ignorance to the degree to which they are being exploited, the people treated unjustly are happy enough to make the sacrifices. Gauthier says, in effect, that the people concerned should strike a new bargain; and given (among other things) the amount of unhappiness generally caused by such exploitation, humane feeling could not help but agree. Whether people can ever have enough information to reach Gauthier's own solution to the bargaining is problematic, though we have been assuming that they can; even if they could not, they could perhaps use his solution concept as a metaphor, asking themselves, for example, "Would any of us do better outside the present relationships altogether? Or better in them if we all took into account how they would be arranged if they most suited us?"

Asking such questions, they are exhibiting a degree of sensitivity to each other's fates that concurs to some extent with humane feeling. But Gauthier's theory does more than this. The third way in which it falls in with humane feeling is to assume a truly extraordinary sensitivity on the part of all agents to one another's personal utility functions. The agents are not, of course, going to concede one another's maximum claims[32]; but they are going to respect the measurements of one another's concessions relative to those claims, even when this leads to disadvantages to themselves, in the mix of public goods or in the amount of their taxes. They would get a mix that they preferred or lower taxes not only if their maximum claims were honored but if some other solution concept were used, say, equality of money income and choice of public goods by majority vote. Nevertheless, they feel so much for one another's stakes in personal utility that they accept arrangements less congenial to them.

I do not take this implication as a sign that after all Gauthier's theory is imbued as much with affective morality as with rational concern for self-interest. I take it as an anomaly in his theory: Where did that degree of sensitivity come from? Like other people who have taken up decision theory in reflections upon ethics, Gauthier wants to have it both ways – to allow for people's having lots of utility at stake in their concern for others, but to make no use of this allowance in theorizing about the decisions that they will make.[33] And in his theorizing, leaving the anomaly aside, Gauthier dispenses with that feeling, at least until after the bargain has been struck and the ground laid for the germination of free affectivity.

Whether the rational agent required for the theory to go through cares tuppence about the legal rights of persons accused of crime may depend solely upon the probability that he thinks he himself faces of being so accused or so penalized. In respect to marriage and sex, Gauthier's theory leaves agents free to consider liberal practices in these matters, as in the civil liberties proper, more public evils than public goods. They will then bargain for a good deal more systematic repression. This is the effect of Gauthier's not taking the precaution following other writers (for instance, Barry and Fishkin) of setting aside wants that are other-regarding in an objectionable way.[34]

Could we say that it is in the spirit of Gauthier's approach to add this precaution? The agents are supposed each to be taking care of her-

---

[32] Each agent's maximum claim is for the utility that he would receive under the feasible social arrangement most favorable to him were all the other agents to receive just enough utility from cooperation to make cooperation worth their while, and he were to receive in return for his own contribution all the rest of the gain from cooperation that might figure in his utility function. Gauthier, *Morals by Agreement*, pp. 133–4, 154, 264.

[33] Ibid., p. 7; cf. p. 87 on the independence of the agents' utility functions and their "non-tuism"; also p. 128 on the same attitude in bargaining for cooperation.

[34] James S. Fishkin, *Tyranny and Legitimacy* (Baltimore: Johns Hopkins University Press), pp. 26–9; Fishkin's term is "public-regarding wants," which he takes from Brian Barry, *Political Argument* (London: Routledge, 1965), p. 63. The "other-regarding wants" that cause the difficulty that I have in mind are a subclass in which N wants for M something that M does not want.

self – of her own affairs – and allowing each other full freedom to do this (subject to the Proviso) in taking up bargaining positions. Does it not run contrary to the allowance of full freedom as well as unduly complicate the bargaining to let other-regarding wants have any weight? People should be more reasonable. Gauthier's invitation to behave rationally might in practice encourage agents to remodel their self-interests; to stop worrying about what other people are doing in other bedrooms; to renounce (as Hobbes would join Gauthier in advising) the vindictive pleasure of seeing people prospectively harmless beheaded.

Does the theory itself bring about this remodeling, however? The sense of being "reasonable" that might back such remodeling "in the spirit" of the theory begs some questions about moral attitudes[35] that the rationality strictly invoked in the theory does not imply (at least once the maximum claims are identified and accepted as such all around). In upshot, Gauthier's theory may run against humane feeling as much as it runs with it; and, therefore, the theory offers only mixed assistance to moral progress. In the accumulation of exceptions and in other processes for changing social rules, the main action for moral progress lies elsewhere, in activity prompted more by sentiment than by theory. Contract theory, the new wave of rationalism in ethical theory, does not seem to have learned the chief lesson of emotivism, which I always took to be, "If you want people to respond to moral appeals, you had better make sure that they have receptive sentiments." Contract theory may teach us how to guard against sentiment licensing sloppy results; but contract theory cannot do the moral work for which, in the foundations and in the applications of ethics, sentiment has been appointed.[36]

[35] As Virginia Held is en route to begging (quite sensibly, in my view) with her distinction between "rational" and "reasonable: see Held, "Rationality and Reasonable Cooperation," *Social Research* 44 (1977), pp. 708–44, at p. 736. But for present purposes, she does not go far enough; she goes no further than Gauthier himself in describing an agent who "accepts the proviso as a constraint" (Gauthier, *Morals by Agreement*, p. 206).

[36] I read an earlier version of this essay to the weekly colloquium of the Department of Philosophy at Dalhousie University and benefited from criticisms raised then, especially those voiced by Neera Badhwar, Nathan Brett, Robert Bright, and Richmond Campbell. Upon deliverance at the University of Western Ontario, and subsequently, I have received further criticisms and made grateful use of them.

5. Contractarianism and the assumption of mutual unconcern*

Peter Vallentyne

A contractarian moral theory states that an action (practice, social structure, etc.) is morally permissible if and only if it (or rules to which it conforms) would be agreed to by the members of society under certain circumstances. What people will agree to depends on what their desires are like. Most contractarian theories – for example, those of Rawls[1] and Gauthier[2] – specify that parties to the agreement are mutually unconcerned (take no interest in each other's interests). Contractarian theorists do not, of course, believe that this is true of real people, but they insist (with Kant) that the basic moral constraints on conduct (if there are any) apply independently of whether individuals care about each other.

I argue against the appropriateness of the assumption of mutual unconcern for contractarian theories, such as Gauthier's, that are supposed to ground morality solely in rationality.

Gauthier's project is to "generate, strictly rational principles for choice, ... without introducing prior moral assumptions" (p. 6). Unlike Rawls, Gauthier does not merely want to apply the principles of rational choice to some morally privileged choice situation (i.e., a choice situation, such as Rawls' original position, in which morally irrelevant features of reality have been screened off). He wants to apply the principles of rational choice to real-life choice situations. Consequently, in Gauthier's theory,

*Reprinted with minor modifications by the author by permission of *Philosophical Studies* from "Contractarianism and the Assumption of Mutual Unconcern," by Peter Vallentyne, in *Philosophical Studies* 56 (1989): 187–92. Copyright © 1989 by Kluwer Academic Publishers. I have benefited from suggestions from Grant Brown, Morry Lipson, and an anonymous referee for *Philosophical Studies*.
[1] John Rawls, *A Theory of Justice* (Cambridge, MA: Harvard University Press, 1971).
[2] David Gauthier, *Morals by Agreement* (London: Oxford University Press, 1986). All page and chapter references are to this book.

"the parties to agreement are real, determinate individuals, distinguished by their capacities, situations, and concerns" (p. 9). In particular, no veil of ignorance is imposed on the parties.

Gauthier assumes, however, that the parties are mutually unconcerned (take no interest in each other's interests) (pp. 10–11, 102–3). Note that there are two different places that assumptions about people's preferences (desires, utility functions) may enter in contractarian theory. One place is in the specification of the features of the people whom the agreed-upon norms are to regulate. More specifically, it concerns assumptions relevant for determining the outcome of adopting a given set of norms. What will happen if a given set of norms is adopted depends on how people will act if it is adopted, and that depends in part on what their preferences are. Clearly, for these purposes, realistic assumptions about people's preferences must be used. Given that people have at least a limited sympathy for others, it would be inappropriate to assess norms on the basis of what their outcome would be if people had no sympathy for others. Rationality requires that one use realistic assumptions.

The other role for an assumption about people's preferences concerns their motivation *at the bargaining table*. This is relevant for determining which option(s) the parties would agree to, given the information available to them (including the expected outcomes of each option). It is here (and only here, I think) that Gauthier and Rawls assume that individuals are mutually unconcerned.

But why not use people's true preferences here, too? Both Rawls and Gauthier defend this assumption by saying that the goal is to show that – no matter what our preferences are like – there are rationally acceptable constraints on conduct. Gauthier, for example, writes: "For we agree with Kant that moral constraints must apply in the absence of other-directed interests, indeed they must apply whatever preferences individuals may happen to have" (p. 100).[3] We must be careful here, however, with the order of the quantifiers. On the strong view (the one held by Kant), the existential quantifier over constraints comes first: there are (particular) rational constraints on conduct that apply no matter what people's desires are like. On the weak view, the universal quantifier over preferences comes first: no matter what people's preferences are like, there are (some sort or other of) rational constraints on conduct. The weak view, but not the strong view, allows the content of the constraints to vary depending on people's preferences.

Because Gauthier accepts the instrumental conception of rationality (which Kant rejected), he cannot hold the strong view. For the strong view says that there are rational constraints on conduct, the content of

---

[3] See also Gauthier, *Morals by Agreement*, p. 104, and Rawls, *Theory of Justice*, pp. 129, 254.

which does not depend on what people's preferences are like, and that entails that the rationality of conduct does *not* depend solely on how well one's preferences are satisfied – as claimed by the instrumental conception of rationality. Thus, because Gauthier accepts the instrumental conception of rationality, he must accept only the weaker reading of the "Kantian" dictum.

But on the weaker reading, there is no need to *assume* that we are mutually unconcerned. On the weak reading, the important point to make is that *the existence* of constraints on conduct does not depend on the nature of our preferences (and, in particular, it does not on the presence of altruistic preferences).[4] One need not establish that the *content* of these constraints is independent of what our actual preferences are like. Indeed, if these constraints are to be rationally grounded, and if one accepts (as Gauthier does) the instrumental conception of rationality, then the exact content of the constraints (determining which actions satisfy the constraints) must depend on people's actual (reflective) preferences. The counterfactual assumption of mutual unconcern, therefore, undermines the rationality of the constraints that would be agreed upon.

To restate this point: there are two contractarian projects at issue here. One is the theoretical project of showing that the *existence* of rational constraints on the pursuit of self-interest does not depend on any sympathetic concern for others. For this purpose, contractarians should make *no assumption* concerning the nature of people's preferences. Contractarians can then argue that no matter what people's preferences are like (even if they are purely self-interested, for example), it is rational for them to agree and conform with principles constraining their pursuit of self-interest. Here Gauthier does not need the assumption of mutual unconcern. Indeed, to be successful, he must not make any assumption about people's preferences.

The second project is to defend particular constraints as rationally justified. On the contractarian view, a set of norms is rationally justified just in case it would be rationally chosen by the members of society. If one assumes, as Gauthier does (chap. 2), an instrumental conception of rationality, according to which a choice is rational if and only if it best satisfies one's considered preferences, then it is inappropriate for a contractarian theory to ignore any of one's considered preferences. Although, if I were purely self-interested, it might be rational for me to

---

[4] For simplicity, I have ignored one assumption that contractarians must make about people's preferences for their argument for rational contraint to succeed. This is the assumption that mutual benefit from cooperation is possible. This rules out zero-sum game situations, that is, situations in which people's preferences are strictly conflicting (one's person's gain is always another person's loss). So, strictly speaking, the contractarian argument must be: if mutual benefit from cooperation is possible, then there are rational constraints on conduct. (Gauthier's argument has exactly this form.)

agree to norms that are favorable for me, but extremely unfavorable for my friends and family, it need not (and in general is not) rational for me to agree to such norms *given that I care about how my friends and family fare*. By making the legitimacy of norms depend on what we would agree to if we had preferences that we do not in fact have, Gauthier undermines the rationality of the agreed-upon norms.[5]

Of course, a contractarian theory need not maintain the tight connection between the *actual* preferences, capacities, and circumstances of agents and those assumed for the social contract. Such a theory might assume mutual unconcern on the grounds that a *negative* concern for others (such as that stemming from envy or hatred) is (for obvious reasons) *morally irrelevant* to the social contract; and assume that *positive* concern for others is morally irrelevant for reasons of symmetry, or because it allows someone's welfare to be counted more than once (if several people care about it).

Although Rawls does not defend the assumption of mutual unconcern along the above lines (at least not in his book), such a defense is open to him. This is because he does not reject the use of assumptions about what is morally relevant to the social contract. Indeed, his imposition of the veil of ignorance is defended precisely on the grounds that the knowledge that is blocked (of one's capacities, social position, etc.) is morally irrelevant to the selection of principles of justice.

The above defense of the assumption of mutual unconcern is not, however, open to Gauthier. This is because, unlike Rawls, he wants to base the social contract solely on real life, rational considerations without any moral assumptions (e.g., about what is relevant). On his theory, the correct principles of justice for a given community are those that it would be rational for those members to choose in full knowledge of their positions, capacities, and concerns. No feature of reality is to be deemed morally irrelevant. This aspect of Gauthier's theory, which makes the theory so interesting, makes it inappropriate to use counterfactual assumptions in general, and about people's preferences in particular.

It might be objected that I have misunderstood the role of the assumption of mutual concern. Its role, it may be suggested, is simply that of a worst-case scenario. Gauthier uses the assumption to show, the suggestion goes, what sorts of constraints (in terms of their content)

---

[5] On p. 11, Gauthier suggests another reason for the assumption of mutual unconcern, and that is that "it becomes a source of exploitation if it [sociability, concern for others] induces persons to acquiesce in institutions and practices that but for their fellow-feelings would be costly to them." He cites the oppression of women as an example of such exploitation. This is a possible defense of the assumption of mutual concern, but it is incompatible with an instrumental conception of rationality, which takes people's considered preferences as they are. Since Gauthier assumes the instrumental conception, this defense is not open to him.

would apply in the worst case. It is highly doubtful that Gauthier does use the assumption in this way,[6] but in any case, it is not an appropriate use of the assumption of mutual unconcern. For that assumption does not represent the worst-case scenario. Far worse is the case where people are highly *negatively* concerned for others. In such a case, people actually desire that others be poorly off (either in absolute terms or relative themselves). So, if the purpose is to identify what sorts of constraints would be justified in the worst-case scenario, the assumption of mutual unconcern is not the right one.[7]

Another role the assumption might have is as a simplifying assumption. People are, we may grant, predominately unconcerned for others. They care for their friends and family, but are often largely unconcerned for others outside this limited sphere.[8] Thus, the assumption of mutual unconcern may be approximately correct. So, the assumption may very well be appropriate as a simplifying device, but it must be kept in mind that: (1) it is an empirical assumption – not a commitment of the moral theory, and (2) a more careful application of the theory would recognize that we are not mutually unconcerned.

If Gauthier is to generate rational principles of interaction, he must drop the assumption of mutual unconcern – except perhaps as a simplifying assumption for the application of the theory.[9]

[6] Certain passages do suggest this reading of Gauthier. See, for example, the bottom of p. 101.

[7] I owe this point to Grant Brown.

[8] Gauthier does write sometimes as if the role of the assumption is as a simplifying assumption, for example, on pp. 100–1.

[9] For further discussion of the role of the assumption of mutual unconcern, see Christopher Morris, "The Relation Between Self-Interest and Justice in Contractarian Ethics"; Laurence Thomas, "Rationality and Affectivity: The Metaphysics of the Moral Self"; and David Gauthier, "Morality, Rational Choice, and Semantic Representation: A Reply to My Critics"; all are in *Social Philosophy and Policy* 5(2) (Spring 1988). See also L. W. Sumner, "Justice Contracted," *Dialogue* 26 (1987): 523–48. These articles, which I read only after this essay was originally written, make many of the same points.

6. Moral standing and rational-choice contractarianism*

Christopher W. Morris

One of the issues raised by the contemporary debate about abortion concerns the *scope* of our moral principles: to what extent, if any, are human fetuses protected by moral prohibitions of killing and harming? Similarly, there is considerable controversy about the moral status of, for example, humans in irreversible comas, the mentally handicapped, nonhuman animals: to what extent, if any, are they owed moral consideration? Scope questions, or issues about the moral status of particular creatures, are familiar to all conversant with the philosophical literature concerning contemporary moral problems.

In the past, controversies about the scope of moral principles or norms were different. Our ancestors debated the moral status of members of other races and of foreigners or barbarians. These no longer are our concerns, and presumably those of our descendants will differ from ours. The theoretical considerations, however, are the same: namely, what is the moral status of different sorts of creatures or entities? Who, or what, counts? Let us say that to be owed (some) moral consideration is to possess (some) *moral standing.*[1] Then the question is, what has moral standing?

The manner in which this question is usually addressed in the literature is worth noting. It is asked in virtue of what features do entities acquire moral standing. And, typically, the features are held to be certain natural or nonconventional attributes or properties of the entity in question. So, for instance, inquiries are made concerning the rationality, self-

*For comments on an earlier draft, I am grateful to Peter Danielson, Edward McClennen, Wayne Sumner, and Peter Vallentyne.
[1] The notion of moral standing I borrow and adapt from L. W. Sumner, *Abortion and Moral Theory* (Princeton: Princeton University Press, 1981), p. 26ff.

consciousness, species membership, or sentience of some creature; and it is usually concluded that some feature (e.g., rationality, sentience, humanity) is either necessary or sufficient (or both) for moral standing. Moral standing is, in this manner, typically ascribed or denied to fetuses, the retarded, nonhuman animals, landscapes, art objects, monuments, and the like.

There are two theoretically significant features of this approach to criteria of moral standing that it is important to highlight, and that contrasts with the approach that I examine in this essay. The first is it is normally assumed that the conditions that contribute to something's possessing moral standing are nonconventional, nonrelational properties or attributes of the creature in question. For instance, rationality, species membership, sentience, and the like are attributes of individuals that are possessed independently of relations to others.[2] And it is the attribute, or cluster of attributes, itself that generates moral standing.

The second significant feature of this approach to criteria of moral standing is that it is implicitly assumed that such standing is universal in a particular way: if something has moral standing, it has it in relation to all moral agents. That is, it is usually assumed that there is one morality that binds all moral agents to accord moral considerations to all who possess moral standing.

Utilitarians thus accord moral standing to all, and only, sentient beings,[3] and members of the natural law and Kantian traditions tend to focus on rationality as the decisive property. By contrast, some moral theories – namely, certain contractarian theories – do not regard the possession of any natural or independent properties as sufficient for moral standing. For such theories, moral standing requires in addition that individuals be related to one another in certain ways. Further, some of these theories even impose certain conditions regarding the *will* of individuals with moral standing; to have moral standing requires that one act toward others in certain ways. Thus, many of these moral theories may deny moral standing to, for example, some rational, sentient humans who do not stand in the appropriate relations to other agents or behave in prescribed ways. Additionally, these theories will tend to be relativist in the sense that they deny that there is a single morality that binds all moral agents to all who possess moral standing. For these theories, moral standing will typically be possessed only in relation to

---

[2] Or at least of *particular* others. For some philosophers claim that our rationality and self-consciousness are developed, or even constituted, by our relations with others. As will be clear presently, even views of moral standing that employ such "social" accounts of rationality and the like contrast with the view that is examined in this essay.

[3] A utilitarian defense of a sentience criterion is defended by Sumner in *Abortion and Moral Theory*.

proper subsets of moral agents. For these theories, possession of moral standing is a more complicated matter than for the more familiar theories mentioned before.

It is the different and complicated manner in which such contractarian theories accord individuals moral standing that I shall explore in this essay. In particular, I shall focus on the particular account of moral standing implicit in David Gauthier's neo-Hobbesian theory, "morals by agreement." Many find the implications of Gauthier's theory regarding moral standing implausible or at least unsettling. It is important to determine both to what extent these implications do follow from the theory and to determine exactly what assumptions are therefor responsible. Further, it is important to determine to what extent such implications are an unavoidable feature of such moral theories. I shall not, however, do more than determine the account of moral standing implicit in morals by agreement. For many critics, this will suffice, given the counterintuitive nature of some of the implications. This suffices as well for those convinced that contractarianism is the most plausible approach to moral theory, or at least to the theory of justice.

Rational-choice contractarianism

There is a long western tradition, dating back to Glaucon, developed by Hobbes, Hume, and Rousseau, and continued by K. Baier, Rawls, Mackie, Harman, Scanlon, Gauthier, and others[4] that understands morality, or at least justice, to be conventional and, in some sense, the product of agreement. According to this tradition, the norms of morality or justice are conventions that ideally serve to advance the goals of all in certain situations. This tradition is dubbed "contractarian" as it often understands the terms of justice to be the outcome of a hypothetical bargain or "social contract." We may, perhaps less misleadingly, think of contemporary versions of the tradition – especially Gauthier's – as offering a "rational-choice" conception of morality after John Rawls' remark, "The theory of justice is a part, perhaps the most significant part, of the theory of rational choice."[5] We focus on David Gauthier's "morals by agreement."

---

[4] For the latter, see Kurt Baier, *The Moral Point of View*, abridged edition (New York: Random House, 1958, 1965); John Rawls, *A Theory of Justice* (Cambridge, MA: Harvard University Press, 1971); J. L. Mackie, *Ethics: Inventing Right and Wrong* (Harmondsworth: Penguin, 1977); Gilbert Harman, *The Nature of Morality* (New York: Oxford University Press, 1977); T. M. Scanlon, "Contractualism and Utilitarianism," in *Utilitarianism and Beyond*, edited by A. Sen and B. Williams (Cambridge: Cambridge University Press, 1982), pp. 103–28; and David Gauthier, *Morals by Agreement* (Oxford: Oxford University Press, 1986). See also Gregory S. Kavka, *Hobbesian Moral and Political Philosophy* (Princeton: Princeton University Press, 1986).
[5] Rawls, *Theory of Justice*, p. 16. Rawls no longer accepts the view expressed in this quote.

David Gauthier's theory of morals by agreement is an account of the constraints that agents have reason to accept to bring about the mutually advantageous outcomes not attainable by independent, rational action. These constraints Gauthier identifies with the requirements of morality. Thus, he says, "moral theory is essentially the theory of optimizing constraints on utility-maximization" (*MbA*, p. 78).[6]

Starting with a maximizing account of rationality and a subjective account of value, Gauthier provides an analysis of the problems that rational individuals face in interaction, problems typified by the well-known Prisoners' Dilemma. The core of his theory consists in arguing that, under certain conditions, (1) rational agents faced with such problems will accept constraints on their individual actions, (2) they will rationally comply with these constraints, even in the absence of government or collective enforcement, and (3) these constraints are those of morality, albeit an ideal, as opposed to a common sense, morality. In addition, (4) Gauthier argues for two particular sets of constraints on interaction: (a) a principle that determines the division of the fruits of rational cooperation (the principle of "minimax relative concession") and (b) a "Lockean Proviso" and a consequent set of basic moral rights and duties that define the starting point or baseline for cooperative interaction.

Morals by agreement is what I call, after Rawls' remark, a rational-choice theory of morality or justice.[7] Rational-choice theory is the theory of rationality for individual and social choice, whether in context of independent or of interdependent choice. The conception of rationality invoked and developed is that of utility maximization, where an individual is rational insofar as he or she maximizes the satisfaction of his or her preferences.[8] Rationality and justice are related thus. Rational individuals may often find themselves in situations where cooperative, nonmaximizing behavior is mutually beneficial, given their preferences; these are "the circumstances of justice."[9] Yet in the absence of constraints

See "Justice as Fairness: Political not Metaphysical," *Philosophy and Public Affairs* 14 (1985): 237n.

[6] References to *Morals by Agreement* (*MbA*) are made parenthetically.

[7] Justice is traditionally understood to be one of many moral virtues. Gauthier's theory focuses on justice, suggesting that for morals by agreement, it is the main, if not the sole, moral virtue. Henceforth, I talk about justice, leaving it open whether there are other contractarian moral virtues.

[8] "Preferences," in this technical sense, are rankings of outcomes. To have an ordering that can be maximized, preferences must be represented by a function that satisfies certain conditions or axioms (e.g., completeness, transitivity). Such preferences, we say, are *coherent*. In addition, for the purposes of moral theory, Gauthier requires that preferences be *considered* (*MbA*, p. 29ff.).

[9] The main conditions are relative but variable scarcity and self-bias (*MbA*, pp. 113–14). The phrase is from Rawls; for his account of these conditions, see *A Theory of Justice*, p. 126ff. See also H. L. A. Hart, *The Concept of Law* (Oxford: Oxford University Press,

on individually rational behavior, such cooperation may not be possible, for such individuals will act in maximizing ways that disadvantage others. Justice imposes the constraints necessary to make mutually beneficial cooperation possible, thereby stabilizing Pareto-efficient outcomes in situations analogous to n-person Prisoners' Dilemmas.

Several cooperative outcomes may each be Pareto-efficient. Given that rational individuals will not be indifferent as to which is selected by the norms of justice, we may imagine the specific constraints of justice to be determined by a mutually advantageous agreement to select (principles for the selection of) particular Pareto-efficient outcomes. Cooperation is advantageous to all, but there may be different cooperative arrangements, each distributing the benefits of cooperation differently. We may think of the agreement to select particular forms of cooperation as a type of bargain: each individual presses for the cooperative arrangement most beneficial to him or her, and all agree to some mutually acceptable cooperative arrangement. The theory of justice thus makes use of a particular part of the theory of rational choice, namely, bargaining theory.

How are we to conceive of this bargain, or more importantly – for this will determine what is necessary to possesses moral standing – how are we to conceive of these bargainers? First, they are rational, that is, utility maximizers. Second, they are maximizers of subjective value, for Gauthier takes utility to be a measure of preference and value to be determined solely by (coherent and considered) preference.[10] This has the important consequence that values are relative to individual perspectives, that is, agent-relative.

For the purposes at hand, this may be thought to suffice as a characterization of rational bargainers. For such individuals, whatever their preferences, may find themselves in Prisoners' Dilemmalike situations. All that is needed for such dilemmas is that the preferences of individuals have a certain structure; it is not necessary that they be self-regarding. And agent relativity suffices for preferences to have the requisite structure.[11] It is important, then, to note that the introduction of a utility-

---

1961), pp. 189–95. The classical accounts are to be found in Hobbes and Hume. For the latter, see esp. *An Enquiry Concerning the Principles of Morals*, sec. III, pt. I, p. 149.

[10] "Value is then not an inherent characteristic of things or states of affairs, not something existing as part of the ontological furniture of the universe in a manner quite independent of persons and their activities. Rather, value is created or determined through preference. Values are products of our affections" (*MbA*, p. 47; see also pp. 24–6).

[11] Gauthier writes:

> For the basic contractarian argument, that it is advantageous for each person to comply with constraints that it would be rational for all to agree to, provided others may be expected to be generally similarly compliant, does not depend in any way on supposing that persons have nontuistic preferences. Rather, it depends only on the Prisoner's Dilemma-creating structural features of interaction.

maximization conception of rationality does not, by itself, bring in self-interestedness. As Gauthier puts it, such a conception of rationality introduces a purely formal, not a material, selfishness (*MbA*, p. 73).[12]

Gauthier, however, adds a third condition to the characterization of the bargaining agents of morals by agreement, namely, a type of self-interestedness. More precisely, he wishes to assume that their values are independent in another sense than that of agent relativity. Utility functions are to be defined independently of one another (*MbA*, p. 86). That is, the preferences of the rational bargainers do not range over the preferences of others. Gauthier thus assumes that individuals do not take an interest in the interests of others,[13] or weaker yet, they do not take an interest in the interests of those with whom they interact. The latter condition is that of Wicksteed's "nontuism," the former that of mutual unconcern.[14]

Gauthier believes that "this conception, of persons as taking no interest in one another's interests, is fundamental not only to economics, but also to moral theory" (*MbA*, p. 100). Mutual unconcern and non-tuism here, we should note, are merely assumptions, albeit important ones. They are not meant literally to characterize humans.[15]

In morals by agreement, then, agents maximize the satisfaction of their mutually indifferent, or nontuist, (considered) preferences. Justice is to be identified with the principles to which such agents would agree, given the situation in which they find themselves.

Moral standing

To have *moral standing* is to be owed moral consideration. Depending on the particular account we adopt of moral consideration (e.g., natural duty theory, utilitarianism), depending on the particular moral virtue in question (e.g., justice, benevolence), or depending simply on the duties in question, moral standing admits of degrees. Thus, something that is owed more moral considerations than another may be understood

---

Gauthier, "Morality, Rational Choice, and Semantic Representation: A Reply to My Critics," *Social Philosophy and Policy* 5 (1988): 215.

[12] See also Gauthier, "The Incompleat Egoist," *The Tanner Lectures on Human Values*, Stanford University, May 10, 1983, p. 73.

[13] The phrase is from Rawls, *Theory of Justice*, p. 13.

[14] I simplify matters by focusing on mutual unconcern and on nontuism, but the story is actually more complicated than this. Some of the complications are discussed in my "The Relation between Self-Interest and Justice in Contractarian Ethics," *Social Philosophy and Policy* 5 (1988): 119–53, esp. 123–5. See also Peter Vallentyne, "Contractarianism and the Assumption of Mutual Unconcern" (chap. 5 in this volume).

[15] "Throughout our argument, non-tuism has served as an assumption . . ." (*MbA*, p. 329).

to possess greater moral standing. These matters of degree aside, there is an important distinction to be made between inclusion in the exclusion from the scope of (a) morality, and it is this distinction that is drawn by the concept of moral standing.

To make clearer the notion of moral standing, I introduce some additional notions. A *moral object*, I say, is something that is an object of moral consideration. A *direct* moral object is something to which (or to whom) that consideration is paid; an *indirect* moral object is something *about* or *concerning* which moral consideration is paid. The latter is a *beneficiary* of the moral consideration. Typically, direct moral objects are beneficiaries of moral considerations owed to them; thus they typically are also indirect moral objects. But this need not be. The different objects of moral duties can be determined by asking *to* whom/what and *regarding* whom/what are they owed. Suppose that Albert promises Beatrice to care for Calvin. Albert's duties would be owed to Beatrice *regarding* Calvin; the latter would be an indirect moral object of those duties. Were Albert not to care for Calvin in the requisite manner, he would fail in his duties toward Beatrice; though Calvin would fail to be benefited, he would not be wronged by Albert's delinquency.

In terms of this distinction, people typically are direct moral objects, or so we normally believe. Protected natural sites, national monuments, significant works of art might be examples of indirect moral objects. When we destroy the latter, we may be understood to fail in our duties to other people. Animists and others could use this distinction to give a different account of whom we fail to respect when we defile nature.

To have moral standing, then, is to be a direct moral object. Something that is merely an indirect moral object – for instance, a sculpture or a relic – would lack moral standing. It is important to note that the category of *moral value* is broader than that of moral standing. For an inanimate object such as a sculpture could have moral value without having moral standing, as it would in the case that it is a mere indirect moral object. Presumably, this is the account that most will want to offer of the moral status of the environment; Yosemite and the Grand Canyon would thus have moral value, without having moral standing.[16]

To have moral standing, then, is to be owed moral consideration, that is, to be a direct moral object.[17] It is important to note that moral standing

---

[16] The concept of a moral object is not to be confused with that of a moral *subject*. The latter is something that has moral duties or may be expected to give moral consideration to direct moral objects. Presumably, young infants can be direct moral objects without being moral subjects. Also, being a moral subject is not necessarily to have moral standing, for owing moral considerations to others does not entail that the latter owe one similar consideration.

[17] A worry about this characterization of moral standing, which is meant to be as neutral as possible between competing moral theories, is that it may not be applicable to utilitarian and other theories that do not make essential use of deontic notions. For, as I

is a *relation*: something has moral standing to the extent that something else owes it moral consideration. So something could not have moral standing if there were no other thing that owed it moral consideration. Further, and most importantly, we should note that it should not be supposed that moral standing must be *universal*. It would beg the question this essay addresses to suppose that all beings of a certain sort (e.g., rational agents) possess moral standing. But that is not the sort of universality that I have in mind. Rather, I want to note that we should not suppose that if some individual has moral standing, then it has standing in relation to all other individuals or moral subjects. The relations of moral standing may be particular (or even, in the extreme, pairwise). That is, it may be that Albert has moral standing in relation to Beatrice and Calvin but not in relation to Daphne; whereas Beatrice and Calvin owe Albert moral consideration, Daphne does not.[18] Moral standing, then, is a relation between classes of moral objects and moral subjects, and we may not suppose that membership in either of these classes is universal.

The question, then, is to determine what has moral standing (in relation to what). Or rather, the question is to determine how to determine what has moral standing (in relation to what).

Moral standing in rational-choice contractarian morality

In virtue of what, then, do entities have moral standing in morals by agreement?

One might think that contractarian justice accords moral standing to all and only agents who are members of the (hypothetical) "social contract." In this view, only agents capable of so contracting could acquire moral standing; though presumably not all of these will, in fact, acquire it (as I argue later). Participation in the social contract would thus be necessary for moral standing. But such a view depends on understanding contractarian ethics as involving contracting, whether actual or hypothetical, and that, I argue, is to take the metaphor of a social contract too literally.

---

have explicated these notions, moral standing involves being *owed* certain considerations, being that to which (rather than *regarding* which) consideration is due. These deontic notions may introduce an individualist or agent-relative perspective and consequently bias the discussion against certain theories. At the same time, utilitarian theories do distinguish between those things that count morally, to which the principle of utility is applied, and those that do not. So my characterization of moral standing should be sufficiently neutral so as not to beg any important question.

18 Indeed, this is precisely the implication of Gilbert Harman's relativist conventionalism. Peter Danielson suggests metaphors of firms and partnerships for our cooperative (i.e., moral) relations. The latter may be as complex as relations between employees, employers, partners, suppliers, business competitors, government agents, and foreign counterparts.

The metaphor of the social contract serves to express this particular conception of justice as an ideal convention, the terms of which may be thought of as the outcome of a rational bargain. The metaphor of the social contract is extremely misleading if it is taken, as it often is, in any other way. For agreement (or "contracting") here has only a heuristic value.[19] As I understand Gauthier's contractarianism, justice and related parts of morality are conventions, and the purpose of a hypothetical social "contract" is to determine the terms of the best (i.e., most rational) convention, at least for particular places and times. Hypothetical agreement determines maximal advantage.[20]

Why then is hypothetical agreement necessary for the determination of rational moral principles in morals by agreement? If the nonmoral world that constitutes the starting point for morals by agreement satisfies, for some set of individuals, the circumstances of justice, it is Pareto-inefficient. Suppose that in some such world there is only one outcome that is Pareto-superior and that it is in fact strongly Pareto-superior – that is, it is unanimously preferred to the status quo. Then this outcome would be uniquely mutually advantageous and would be selected by rational principles of distributive justice. Morals by agreement would not, for such a world, require hypothetical agreement to determine the content of principles of justice; mutual advantage would be both necessary and sufficient for such principles. This shows that hypothetical agreement is necessary only because of a feature of our world, namely, that there are many Pareto-superior outcomes and that we must choose among these. The function of hypothetical agreement, then, is to make this choice.

One may argue that contract or agreement has another role in morals by agreement. Its first role, it may be admitted, is that of a heuristic device to determine the content of acceptable moral principles. Its additional role may be to bind individuals to these principles. A contract of this type cannot *morally* bind contractors, for independently of agreement, there are no moral constraints.[21] How might such a contract bind?

---

[19] In conversation, the author of *Morals by Agreement* has expressed doubts about my claim that hypothetical agreement has *only* heuristic value.

[20] "Theories of hypothetical consent discuss not consent but cognitive agreement." Joseph Raz, *The Morality of Freedom* (Oxford: Clarendon Press, 1986), p. 81, n. 1.
    Criticisms of contractarianism, to the effect that a hypothetical contract is no contract at all or that a nonmoral agreement does not bind, are consequently misplaced. For instance, see Ronald Dworkin, "The Original Position," in *Reading Rawls*, edited by Norman Daniels (New York: Basic Books, 1976), pp. 16–53.

[21] Note that I say that there can be no moral constraints *independently of* agreement. This is not to say that there cannot be moral constraints *prior to* agreement, for, in effect, Gauthier argues that there are some such constraints, namely, the proviso and the initial rights (*MbA*, chapter VII). "Although a part of morals by agreement, it [the proviso] is not a product of rational agreement. Rather, it is a condition that must be accepted by each person for such agreement to be possible" (*MbA*, p. 16).

Elsewhere, Gauthier "distinguish[es] contracts from other agreements by characterizing the former as exchanges of intentions to act that introduce incentives, whether internal or external, moral or other, to supplement or replace each party's motivation to attain the true objective of the agreement."[22] Contracts, so understood, are distinguished from purely coordinative agreements. While in both, all prefer the outcome of agreement to that of no agreement; in coordinative agreements, all prefer compliance with the agreement to noncompliance, given compliance by the others. Further, in coordinative agreements, each expects the others to comply, and intends to do so himself or herself. Contract, then, could play an additional role and thus would be instrumental in determining who has moral standing. Contract, as characterized before, might serve additionally to bind agents to the principles generated by agreement; thus, only agents who were members to the contract would have moral standing.

This does not follow, however. That is, the necessity of introducing contract to guarantee rational compliance does not require membership in a contract as a condition for moral standing. First, note that such a notion of contract is a substantive normative device, albeit not necessarily a moral one. Granting that such contracts introduce additional incentives, how are they available to individuals who find themselves in the circumstances of justice? Simply to postulate the availability of such contracts, without providing an account of their source, would be to beg the question. The problem is not that such contracts are moral and that their assumption would thus be question begging. Rather, the problem is that such contracts provide additional incentives (and consequently are normative), and an account of how they do this is needed. Now Gauthier does provide such an account when he tries to show that rational utility maximizers have a reason, in certain circumstances, to cease being "straightforward" maximizers and to become "constrained" maximizers.[23] His account, however, makes no essential reference to contract or agreement, or even to collective choice or action.

Requiring participation in a contract or agreement for moral standing is to understand contractarian theory as a type of consent theory. On

---

[22] "Hobbes's Social Contract," *Noûs* 22 (1988): 73.

[23] *MbA*, chap. VI. Roughly, a straightforward maximizer chooses the utility-maximizing act at each decision node, whereas a constrained maximizer acts on a utility-maximizing policy, one which may require acts that are themselves nonmaximizing. Thus, for instance, in some one-play and finitely iterated Prisoners' Dilemmas, the former "defects" no matter what the others do, while the constrained maximizers "cooperate" when they believe that the others are similarly disposed. The success of Gauthier's argument is, of course, a subject of great controversy. Critical assessment of this part of Gauthier's theory is provided by the essays in Part III of this collection.

such an understanding, a particular act of *will* – participation in an agreement – is necessary for moral standing. Thus, someone who had not consented in the requisite manner, would lack moral standing. If the requisite act of will is taken to be participation in an actual agreement, then this understanding of morals by agreement as a consent theory is obviously mistaken. If, however, we understand consent differently, then there may be a sense in which morals by agreement is a consent theory. Joseph Raz suggests that:

[c]onsent is given by any behavior (action or omission) undertaken in the be-lief that

1. it will change the normative situation of another;
2. it will do so because it is undertaken with such a belief;
3. it will be understood by its observers to be of this character.[24]

Rational-choice contractarianism does require, as a condition of pos-sessing moral standing, a particular act of will that will constitute consent in Raz's sense. To this we now turn.

One of the conditions giving rise to the need for justice is the possibility of mutual benefit. Others are the capacity and willingness of rational beings to impose constraints on their behavior. In the absence of such conditions, it would appear, one has no reason to abide by the constraints of justice in one's conduct toward others.[25] This is impor-tant, for it effectively means that in the absence of (1) mutual bene-fit or of (2) the capacity or of (3) the willingness of others to be just, an individual is not constrained by justice in his or her behavior toward others.[26]

Supposing that the circumstances of justice be satisfied, morals by agreement understands rational humans, capable and willing to impose moral constraints on their conduct toward others, as moral subjects and direct moral objects (in relation to specified others). Thus, for this theory, as for most others, in normal circumstances, adult humans have moral obligations and are owed certain moral considerations. According to morals by agreement, then, some individual *A* has moral standing in relation to some person *B* if and only if

---

[24] Joseph Raz, *Morality of Freedom*, p. 81.
[25] As Hume noted:

> Suppose, likewise, that it should be a virtuous man's fate to fall into the society of ruffians, remote from the protection of laws and government . . . his particular regard to justice being no longer of use to his own safety or that of others, he must consult the dictates of self-preservation alone, without concern for those who no longer merit his care and attention. (*An Enquiry Concerning the Principles of Morals*, sec. III, pt. I, p. 148)

[26] "This is plainly the situation of men, with regard to animals . . . ," ibid., p. 152.

(1) *A* and *B* are in the circumstances of justice,
(2) *A* and *B* are capable of imposing constraints on their behavior toward one another, and
(3) *A* so constrains his or her behavior toward *B*.

If and, it would seem, only if these three conditions are satisfied, then *B* owes *A* (some) moral considerations.

In this view, it sometimes may be the case that a rational agent lacks moral standing in relation to another. For instance, if some of the circumstances of justice are not satisfied (condition 1), then some agents will lack moral standing.[27] Or an individual – for instance, an infant – who lacks the capacities required for constraint (condition 2, which I call the agency requirement) may lack moral standing with regard to others. (I shall discuss exceptions presently.) Lastly, suppose that someone is unwilling to constrain his or her action toward another (condition 3). Then that individual lacks moral standing in his or her relations with others.

This last implication especially will strike many people as counterintuitive. Now ordinary moral intuitions, as Gauthier emphasizes, have no weight in fundamental contractarian moral theory (*MbA*, p. 269). However, note that this implication does not mean that one is permitted – or rather, not forbidden – from treating such creatures as one pleases. For they may still have moral value in the technical sense characterized earlier; that is, they may be – and presumably would be in the case of human infants – indirect moral objects. Thus, we would not be morally allowed to mistreat them.[28]

Still, infants and others about whom we care would lack moral standing on this view. And leaving aside the matter of the counterintuitive nature of this implication, consider the more serious problem of the possible incoherence of such implications and the conception of value that Gauthier invokes.[29]

Consider the case of Emil, Frederica, and Gerhardt. Emil, although rational, exploits Frederica. He does this because he is able to do so and it is to his advantage. Emil and Frederica do not find themselves in the circumstances of justice, perhaps due to the former's superior strength.[30]

---

[27] See *MbA*, p. 17.
[28] This essentially is the strategy Mary Ann Warren takes, perhaps unwittingly, to avoid justifying infanticide. "The needless destruction of a viable infant inevitably deprives some person or persons of a source of great pleasure and satisfaction. . . . " "Postscript on Infanticide" appended to "On the Moral and Legal Status of Abortion," in *The Problem of Abortion*, 2nd ed., edited by Joel Feinberg (Belmont, CA: Wadsworth, 1984), p. 117.
[29] What follows is a modification of a case I discuss in "The Relation between Self-Interest and Justice in Contractarian Ethics," pp. 146–8.
[30] This case is explicitly considered by Hume:

> Were there a species of creatures intermingled with men, which, though rational, were possessed of such inferior strength, both of body and mind, that they were

While Gerhardt does not find himself in the circumstances of justice with regard to Frederica, he does with regard to Emil. According to morals by agreement, poor Frederica stands outside of the protection of justice. She finds herself in a Hobbesian state of nature, where she and others are at liberty to do as they please with one another. Emil and Gerhardt, however, are in a different situation. They are morally bound to one another insofar as rational cooperation is mutually advantageous.

While Emil is a purely self-interested fellow, Gerhardt is not. Indeed, the latter is most upset by the former's treatment of Frederica. Gerhardt does not consider Frederica's virtual slavery to be unjust, for it is neither just nor unjust according to morals by agreement. It is rather that he simply takes an interest in her interests. He would like to liberate Frederica from her plight, by force if necessary. However, morals by agreement does not permit him to do so. For Gerhardt is morally obliged to respect Emil's life, liberty, and possessions, as well as to accord him the distribution of the social surplus afforded him by the principle of minimax relative concession.

Suppose Gerhardt were to consider himself in a Hobbesian state of nature with regard to Emil and thus be able to liberate Frederica? This would be irrational, according to Gauthier's account of morals by agreement, for he is not in such a state of nature given his self-interested preferences, that is, given the assumption of mutual unconcern. Indeed, it would actually be unjust for Gerhardt to come to Frederica's aid!

Note that the objection here is not the standard sort of criticism made of morals by agreement, that it violates one of our intuitive moral judgments. I do not deny that this is the case; the implications are morally unintuitive. But that is not the objection. (Nor is it an objection, given the rational-choice methodology.) Rather it is that rational, other-regarding individuals, with utility functions like ours, are not moved by justice in cases such as these. The problem is not (merely) one of compliance; it is not that we would refuse to comply with norms that we would otherwise endorse. It is that we would find the norms themselves unacceptable in such situations.

Does morals by agreement have such implications? Recall the two motivational assumptions used by Gauthier to characterize the rational bargainers of morals by agreement: Rawls' mutual disinterest or unconcern and Wicksteed's nontuism. This case presupposes the first form of self-interestedness. If parties are disinterested in the manner postulated

incapable of all resistance, and could never, upon the highest provocation, make us feel the effects of their resentment; the necessary consequence, I think, is that we should not, properly speaking, lie under any restraint of justice with regard to them, nor could they possess any right or property. . . . (*An Enquiry Concerning the Principles of Morals*, sec. III, pt. I, p. 152)

by Rawls in his theory of justice, then the previous objection goes through. If, however, the type of self-interestedness assumed is that of nontuism – taking no interest in the interests of those with whom one interacts – then the objection, it may be argued, fails.[31] For the assumption of nontuism does not rule out Gerhardt's concern for Frederica in the determination of the principles governing the relations between Gerhardt and Emil.

Suppose that Gerhardt's tuistic preferences are such that in the hypothetical bargaining situation, he would insist that Frederica be given moral standing. He cares about her to such a degree that it would not be rational for him to interact with others except on the condition that she be accorded moral standing. An intermediate case would be one where Frederica would be given the status of an indirect moral object. But such a case is not theoretically interesting. More important is the previous case, where Gerhardt's preferences are such that Frederica would have to be given the status of a direct moral object.

Were agents to care in this manner for (some) others and were morals by agreement to take this into account, then there would be a second way in which individuals could acquire moral standing – namely, by being the object of the preferences of an agent who finds himself or herself in the circumstances of justice. Thus, Frederica might acquire moral standing in her relations with Emil through being the object of Gerhardt's preferences. And, similarly, children and others who do not meet the conditions for agency would presumably be accorded moral standing.

In addition, then, to the straightforward way in which agents can acquire moral standing, discussed earlier, there is a second, indirect manner to acquire such standing. An individual who is not an agent or who is not in the circumstances of justice can acquire moral standing by being the object of the preferences of others. We distinguish, then, the two ways in which individuals can acquire moral standing in morals by agreement:

> *Primary moral standing: A* has moral standing in relation to *B* if
> (1) *A* and *B* are in the circumstances of justice, (2) *A* and *B*
> are capable of imposing constraints on their behavior toward

---

[31] Gauthier so argues in response to my original case:

> In terms of his interaction with Adolf, Charles's concern with Bécassine is nontuistic. In any interaction, concerns with the interests of a third party are nontuistic. . . . Nontuism thus does not have the implications for contractarian moral theory that the assumption that all preferences are self-interested or self-directed would have.

Gauthier, "Morality," p. 215. In the text of *Morals by Agreement*, however, it is not always clear which motivational assumption – mutual unconcern or nontuism – is being made.

one another, and (3) *A* so constrains his or her behavior toward *B*.

Secondary moral standing: A has moral standing in relation to *B*
if (1) *B* and *C* are in the circumstances of justice, (2) *B* and *C*
are capable of constrained action, (3) *C* constrains his or her
acts toward *B*, and (4) *A* is the object of *C's* preferences, that
is, *C* cares sufficiently about *A* that it would not be rational
for *C* to cooperate with *B* unless *A* were accorded moral standing in his or her relations with *B*.

"Secondary moral standing," it should be emphasized, is merely a manner in which moral standing can be acquired. Someone who acquires
moral standing in this way has genuine moral standing. It is secondary
only in the sense that were no one to have primary moral standing, no
one could have secondary moral standing.[32]

Morals by agreement, then, may accord moral standing to infants, the
infirm, and others in the second way indicated before. Presumably, even
nonhuman animals may be accorded some moral standing in this manner.[33] What creatures are recognized as direct moral objects depend
heavily on the particular other-regarding preferences of the nontuistic
agents of morals by agreement.[34]

Self-interest and moral standing

We have determined two ways in which something can acquire moral
standing according to morals by agreement. It is difficult to see how
there might be other ways. What I wish now to explore is the manner
in which the particular implications of morals by agreement, regarding

---

[32] In *Persons, Rights, and the Moral Community* (New York: Oxford University Press, 1987),
pp. 152–3, Loren E. Lomasky argues that

> all those who are characterized by property F (project pursuit) have property G
> (possession of basic rights). . . . That there must be F's in order for there to be
> G's does not entail that *only* F's are G's. Some beings who lack F can yet be G's
> by piggybacking on those who are F's.

[33] Whether nonsentient things could acquire moral standing in this secondary way would
depend on whether the notion of owing moral considerations requires that the object
have interests. One would suppose that it would, but insufficient content has been
given to the notion to permit an exploration of this question. Some of my remarks about
justice and benevolence that follow have bearing on this question.

[34] Wayne Sumner has argued that the range of beings accorded moral standing by contractarian theory is determined largely by the range of the concerns of the agents. I
failed to understand his point at the time, but it now seems correct to me. See Morris,
"Value Subjectivism, Individualism, and Moral Standing: A Reply to Sumner," and
Sumner, "A Response to Morris," in *Values and Moral Standing, Bowling Green Studies
in Applied Philosophy* VIII, edited by Wayne Sumner, Donald Callen, and Thomas Attig
(Bowling Green, OH: Bowling Green State University, 1987), pp. 16–21, 22–3.

the moral standing of individuals, are dependent on particular assumptions about preference and value. Gauthier assumes that value is determined by (coherent and considered) preference and that the latter, for the purposes of fundamental moral theory, are nontuistic. What if we drop either of these two assumptions? I explore the matter of nontuism, leaving to another occasion that of subjective value.[35]

Recall the interactions between Emil, Frederica, and Gerhardt. Suppose that the relevant assumption is that of mutual unconcern. Then Frederica lacks moral standing. If we replace this assumption with nontuism, then the conclusion no longer follows; should Gerhardt care sufficiently for Frederica, then she will acquire moral standing in the second, indirect manner.

Let us distinguish between several motivational assumptions that appear in *Morals by Agreement*. I enumerate them in order of weakness.[36] *Nontuism* requires that agents not take an interest in the preferences of those with whom they interact. *Mutual unconcern,* Rawls' mutual disinterest, requires that agents not take an interest in the preferences of others. *Egoism* I characterized earlier as requiring that all of an agent's preferences be self-regarding. Egoism, thus characterized, conflates rationality and prudence. Egoism is stronger than mutual unconcern; mutually disinterested agents need not be egoists as they may take nonagents or nonhumans to be the object of their concern.

Further, there is the general condition of asocial motivation or *asociality,* which Gauthier introduces late in the book (*MbA,* p. 311), requiring that descriptions of the preferences of individuals not make mention of other individuals. This condition is stronger yet than egoism, as asocial agents cannot have the concerns with, for example, relative status possible for egoists. Lastly, there is what I shall call the assumption of *private consumerism,* for want of a better label. This is the motivational assumption, often made in the theory of perfectly competitive markets, that requires that agents' utilities are functions only of "commodities," none of which are public goods.[37] We might make more determinate the character of "economic man" by characterizing his preferences in this way.[38] The assumption of private consumerism is thus the assumption that agents are "economic men."

---

[35] In "Agent-Relative Value, Justice, and the Compliance Problem" (manuscript), I argue that Gauthier's subjectivist account of value is stronger than is required by most of his substantive conclusions and that these would not be affected were it to be replaced by any of several nonsubjectivist accounts.

[36] Where by "weakness" I mean that a strong assumption entails a weaker one, but not vice versa.

[37] That is, commodities are private goods, divisible and excludable.

[38] This would accord with much of what Gauthier says about economic man in Chapters X–XI of *MbA,* as well as in his earlier "The Social Contract as Ideology," *Philosophy and Public Affairs* 6 (1977): 130–64. It would not, however, be consistent with his character-

I have distinguished, in order of weakness, various motivational assumptions that are invoked or otherwise mentioned in *Morals by Agreement*: nontuism, mutual unconcern, egoism, asociality, and private consumerism. In the case of Emil et al., only the condition of nontuism allows Frederica (secondary) moral standing.

Weaker yet than nontuism is simply to allow preferences to range over the interests of anyone, whether one is interacting with them or not.[39] To do this, however, allows the possibility of "double counting." Suppose that

> I, considering us equally fond of cake, prefer that each of us get half, not only to your having a larger share but also to my having it, and if you prefer more cake for yourself to less, whatever I get, then it seems implausible to suppose that a rational and fair division gives you three-quarters of the cake and me one-quarter.[40]

Your preferences in this example are counted twice, that is, weighted more heavily than mine. Double counting, at least in the formulation of principle of distributive justice, is thought by many to be counterintuitive.[41]

Double counting might be inefficient, however, and rational agents may find it mutually agreeable to bargain without referring to their tuistic preferences. Or so Gauthier argues in a recent defense of nontuism:

> As I now see it, social institutions and practices should be justified by an appeal to a hypothetical agreement based largely on the nontuistic preferences of the parties concerned, because each person expects ex ante to benefit if she forgoes the inclusion of her tuistic preferences in determining social arrangements provided others do the same. Double-counting will be ruled out, as, of course, will preferences directed at the frustration of other's [sic] preferences. . . . Positive, but not negative, regard for others will then be furthered.[42]

ization of "economic rationality" in "Economic Rationality and Moral Constraints," *Midwest Studies in Philosophy* 3 (1978): 75–96.

[39] This is the strategy of Loren Lomasky in his conventionalist theory of rights, where he assumes that agents come to take an interest in the interests of those with whom they interact. See Lomasky, *Persons*, p. 65ff.

[40] Gauthier, "Morality," p. 214. See also Morris, "The Relation," pp. 137ff.

[41] See the reviews by Gregory S. Kavka, *Mind* XVCI (January 1987): 117–21, and by Loren Lomasky, *Critical Review* 2 (Spring/Summer 1988): 36–49. Kavka and Lomasky, however, are mistaken in attributing these counterintuitive implications to Gauthier's morals by agreement, as they are blocked by the assumption of nontuism.

[42] "Given this revision [from the account offered in *Morals by Agreement*], the exclusion of tuism from the justification of social institutions and practices and so from the public realm rests simply on an empirical fact, if, as I suppose, it is one, about the role that tuistic and nontuistic preferences play in our concerns." Gauthier, "Morality," p. 216.

Robert Goodin similarly argues that social-choice theory can exclude certain preferences without having recourse to nonutility information; thus, social-choice theory need not be "welfarist." See his essay, "Laundering Preferences," in *Foundations of Social Choice Theory*, edited by Jon Elster and Aanund Hylland (Cambridge: Cambridge University Press, 1986),.pp. 109–21.

I shall not pursue the matter of a plausible defense of nontuism. Instead, let us return to the suggestion that we not restrict the range of concerns to be considered and that we allow preferences to range over the interests of anyone, whether one is interacting with them or not. To do this would be to be make an assumption yet weaker than nontuism. What implications would this have for questions of moral standing?

The implications are interesting, although explaining them is a rather complicated matter. Suppose that Henrietta and Ivan are interacting in a situation that meets some but not all of the circumstances of justice. While both are rational agents, Ivan is weak, and Henrietta is sufficiently strong that she can gain more from coercive interaction with Ivan than from cooperation. Assuming nontuism, or any of the stronger assumptions, it follows that Henrietta is not bound by justice toward Ivan – unless, what I am assuming not to be the case, that Ivan has secondary moral standing.

The fact that Henrietta is *not obligated* by justice to accord certain treatment to Ivan – for example, to respect his life, liberty, and possessions – does not, of course, entail that she is *forbidden* from doing so. Morals by agreement determines what requirements morality imposes on Henrietta; she clearly is permitted to do that which she is not required to do. Still, she is not required, by morals by agreement, to respect Ivan's moral rights – for he has none (in his relations with Henrietta). The assumption of nontuism prevents Ivan's acquisition of moral standing.

Suppose that Henrietta refrains from exploiting and otherwise harming Ivan because the satisfaction of his preferences are one of the values of her utility function. I phrase the matter in a technical way, so as to leave open, for the moment, the nature of Henrietta's concern. Let me now introduce some distinctions that do not appear in *Morals by Agreement*.

It is traditional to distinguish the moral virtue of justice from those of friendship, courage, moderation, and the like. These virtues are not mentioned in the pages of *Morals by Agreement*.[43] Nor is that of benevolence. Henrietta may care about Ivan, and for that reason refrain from harming him. But she may also be moved by considerations of benevolence, that is, by *moral* considerations over and above her (nonmoral) sympathies for him. Can morals by agreement make sense of, that is, generate obligations of benevolence? The answer is unclear, at least to me. We may interpret Hume as a contractarian about justice (and prop-

---

[43] Modern moral theories, especially social theories such as contractarianism, tend to classify such virtues as largely nonmoral. And David Gauthier suggested, after a lecture at UCLA in 1983, that he would relegate these to the domain of psychology.

erty)[44] and note that he counts benevolence as a moral virtue, and an important one at that. Hume's account of benevolence, however, is distinctively not contractarian or even conventionalist. Rather, he offers a moral sense account.[45] So his approach is foreign to that of Gauthier's morals by agreement.[46]

Let us distinguish between being the (direct) object of considerations of justice and of considerations of benevolence. We could say that a being that is a direct moral object both of considerations of justice and of considerations of benevolence has *full moral standing*. Something that is a direct moral object only of justice or only of benevolence (but not both) has *partial moral standing*. Something that is neither the proper direct object of considerations of justice nor of benevolence is said to have *no moral standing*.[47] Thus, mere indirect moral objects, although the (indirect) object of moral consideration, will lack moral standing. The American flag, Yosemite Park, the Louvre, for instance, will be protected by morality by being indirect moral objects of our duties to each other; they will lack moral standing, however, since *they* are neither owed considerations of justice or of benevolence. Hume, then, generates partial moral standing – being the direct object of considerations of benevolence – by reference to sentiments widely, if not universally, possessed by humans; what I have called full moral standing requires his more complete, contractarian account.

Suppose, then, that we drop nontuism and related assumptions. Morals by agreement might then accord Ivan partial moral standing in his relations with Henrietta; the former, it might be argued, is a suitable object of the latter's benevolence. A more interesting possibility is that of extending full moral standing to him. Recall that Ivan is an agent, that is, that he is capable of acting intentionally and imposing constraints on his behavior. He is, I am supposing, also willing to do so. His problem, however, is that he does not find himself in the circumstances of

---

[44] See Gauthier, "David Hume, Contractarian," *Philosophical Review* 88 (1979): 3–38. See also J. L. Mackie, *Hume's Moral Theory* (London: Routledge and Kegan Paul, 1980), chap. VI, and Rawls, *Theory of Justice*, pp. 32–3.

[45] Hume, *An Enquiry Concerning the Principles of Morals*, sec. II.

[46] In addition, note Gauthier's antisentimentalism:

> Hume believed the source of morality to lie in the sympathetic transmission of our feelings from one person to another. But Kant, rightly, insisted that morality cannot depend on such particular psychological phenomena, however benevolent and humane their effect, and however universally they may be found. (*MbA*, p. 103. See also pp. 309, 326–9, 338–9.)

[47] This crude, tripartite classification of degrees of moral standing assumes that justice and benevolence are the only moral considerations that can be owed to entities. Note that this assumption restricts moral standing to entities that can be owed considerations of justice or benevolence, which presumably will be creatures with a welfare. See footnote 32.

justice in his relations with Henrietta, given her superior strength. Now if we drop the assumption of nontuism and factor in the latter's concern for Ivan, then it is possible that the circumstances of justice will be satisfied. That is, it is possible that Ivan and Henrietta might be in the circumstances of justice *given the latter's other-regarding preferences*, an effect of the "double counting" of Ivan's preferences.[48]

This manner of extending full moral standing may not, however, work for those incapable of cooperating, that is, for nonagents. Thus, infants do not acquire moral standing in this way.[49] Their moral standing has to be secondary. We should note, however, that typically it is the moral standing of infants *in relation to nonparents* that is secondary. It is not clear how it is that infants acquire moral standing *in relation to their parents*. Consider the case of Johann, the son of Katherine and Luigi. Suppose that Johann's parents are the only people (with primary moral standing) who care about him, or at least care about him sufficiently for him to be accorded secondary moral standing in his relations with others. Then, in light of the conclusions drawn before, it is not clear how Johann can acquire moral standing in his relations with his parents. Presumably such a case, where the only people (with primary standing) who care about an infant are his or her parents, is rare. Still, it is an interesting (and bizarre) implication that such infants lack moral standing in their relations to their parents, though not necessarily in their relations to others. It appears that someone need not have moral standing in relation to the agent(s) who is the vehicle for one's secondary moral standing.[50]

I have explored the complicated manner in which morals by agreement accords individuals moral standing. I have also discussed the ways in which some of the substantive implications of Gauthier's theory depend on certain motivational assumptions that he makes. Some of these implications may be avoided by weakening or otherwise altering these assumptions. This fact may not fully satisfy critics, but it advances nonetheless our understanding and appreciation of the theory.

[48] Additionally, it may also be, as is the case with many human relations, that the benefits to Henrietta from interacting with Ivan can be obtained only noncoercively. And the relation that Henrietta desires to have with Ivan may be one that presupposes the minimal equality of justice.

[49] The moral status of infants, it seems to me, is determined in part by their *potential* agency. I do not know how potential agency determines standing, so what follows ignores this aspect of the matter. The considerations mentioned in footnote 47 are also important in this regard.

[50] Suppose that Luigi becomes abusive of Johann and is opposed by Katherine. Given the latter's concern for Johann and given that Luigi and she remain in the circumstances of justice, then Johann may acquire secondary moral standing in his relations with his father.

Part II

Minimax relative concession and the Lockean Proviso

Overview of the essays

Peter Danielson argues that Gauthier is mistaken to take the initial bargaining position to be that of noncooperation constrained by the proviso. For rational bargainers will only be concerned with improving upon their prebargain positions. Since their prebargain positions are *not* based on any constraint from the proviso, Gauthier is mistaken in his claim that rational bargains must be based on the proviso. Furthermore, Danielson argues that rational agents would treat property rights as one of the issues that will be settled by the bargain – and not as something that is built into their initial bargaining positions.

Don Hubin and Mark Lambeth argue that Gauthier's use of the proviso is inappropriate as a foundation for moral rights on the following grounds: (1) The proviso permits one to worsen the situation of others very significantly, when doing so is necessary to prevent one's own situation from being worsened only slightly. (2) The proviso permits one to kill, beat, or rob others when someone else would do so if one didn't. (3) The proviso permits one to use people in all sorts of horrible ways as long as one also helps them in various ways so that the *net effect* on them is positive. (4) Because worsening is understood in terms of people's subjective preferences, the proviso can (under appropriate circumstances) prohibit all sorts of activities (such as going for a walk) simply because someone else prefers that one doesn't engage in that activity.

In his essay, Jan Narveson starts by considering Gauthier's minimax relative concession-bargaining solution. After briefly questioning one of the assumptions on which Gauthier's solutions rests, Narveson argues, against Gauthier, that bargaining theory makes sense only in a context in which the parties already have rights. And if that is so, then the (moral?, rational?) requirement to respect such rights does not depend on conformity with any bargaining solution. Narveson then goes on to discuss Gauthier's use of the Lockean Proviso. Although he agrees with Gauthier that the appropriate initial bargaining position is the hypothetical outcome of noncooperation constrained by the Lockean Proviso, he argues that the proviso is relevant only for determining the distribution of the benefits of cooperation (after agreement) – not for (re)distributing the benefits of coercion that took place prior to agreement.

Jean Hampton criticizes Gauthier's bargaining solution by arguing that it is more plausible that rational agreement would be based on a principle that allocates benefits in proportion to contribution to the social surplus (and not – as Gauthier claims – so as to minimize the maximum relative concession).

Wulf Gaertner and Marlies Klemisch-Ahlert discuss Gauthier's minimax relative concession-bargaining solution. They start by discussing Nash's solution and the Kalai–Smordinsky solution. They finish by giving an axiomatization of Gauthier's solution (the first that has ever been given) that clearly isolates the differences between his solution and the others.

A caveat: Gauthier defends the view that the *rational* permissibility of strategic choices is determined by the application of the minimax relative concession principle to the Lockean-Proviso-constrained noncooperative outcome. He also holds that a strategic choice is *morally* permissible if and only if it is rationally permissible. Consequently, he holds that the *moral* permissibility of strategic choices is also determined by the application of the minimax relative concession principle to the Lockean-Proviso-constrained noncooperative outcome. There are two issues here: (1) Are minimax relative concession and/or the proviso relevant for rational choice? (2) Are they relevant for moral choice? In Gauthier's contractarian theory, these two issues are coextensive, but conceptually they are distinct. Since authors do not always clearly distinguish these two issues, readers should be careful to determine exactly which claim is being assessed.

7.   The Lockean Proviso*

Peter Danielson

There are numerous ways to divide the fruits of beneficial social cooperation, which satisfy differentially the competing interests of the would-
be cooperators. Selecting one of these principles of distributive justice
is what we will call the contract problem. In spite of sharp disagreement
over the solution of this problem, there is wide agreement over how to
picture it, so we focus on a diagram (see Fig. 7-1).

In this simple example, the problem is to divide the social product
between two groups, the masters and the slaves. The utility of a distribution to the masters is represented along the horizontal axis; the utility
to the slaves along the vertical axis. There are two important sets of
points in this space. First, the set of possible optimal distributions ranges
from almost all to the slaves in the upper left to almost all to the masters
in the lower right. (It is concave to the origin, reflecting the greater utility
of equal distributions.) Second, there is a set of alternatives to full social
cooperation. Since they fall short of full cooperation, these states of
nature (labeled with I's for initial positions) are clustered in the southwest. For example, there is the natural distribution, I_N, where the masters coerce the slaves. In contrast, there is the noncoercive I_B, where
only what we call personal rights are respected. Note that here the slaves
do better and the masters worse than at I_N. There is also the Lockean
state of nature, I_C, where property rights are respected as well as rights
against coercion. I_C is northeast of I_N and I_B as everyone does better
here, although, as we shall see, the masters do better than the (ex)slaves.

*Excerpted by permission of the *Canadian Journal of Philosophy* from "The Visible Hand of
Morality," by Peter Danielson, in *Canadian Journal of Philosophy* 18 (1988): 357–84. Copyright
© 1988 by *Canadian Journal of Philosophy*.

SLAVES

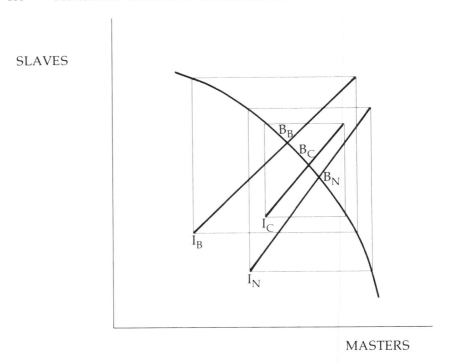

MASTERS

Figure 7-1.   After Gauthier, figure 9, p. 228, showing bargaining beginning from three initial positions (I) to three optimal results (B).

We can categorize the major contending theories of distributive justice by the way they use these two sets of points. Rawls and the utilitarians emphasize the irrelevance of alternatives to cooperation and ignore the I set. Nozick takes the contrary position that one morally framed alternative, namely, the point resulting from individual acquisition (I_C), precludes any collective decision on social cooperation. Gauthier uses both sets, because he uses bargaining to select a unique distribution.[1]

Simplifying greatly, bargaining theory selects an end point by triangulation on an initial point and the possibility curve. The diagonal lines show how our three I's project to B_B, B_C, and B_N in Fig. 7-1. It is clear that this form of argument for a unique distributive end point requires that one first identify a unique starting point. This seems to invite regress: How does one avoid having a similar problem of disagreement among starting points? (Indeed, Chapter VII describes several candidates for the initial bargaining position.) Gauthier is well aware of this problem. He argues for a moral constraint, the proviso on appropriation,

---

[1] David Gauthier, *Morals by Agreement* (Oxford: Oxford University Press, 1986), p. 14. All page and chapter references are to this book.

that singles out a unique initial position, I_C, for both cooperation and the market.

> We are led to constrain the initial bargaining position through a proviso that prohibits bettering one's position through interactions worsening the position of another. . . . [The proviso] induces a structure of personal and property rights, which are basic to rationally and morally acceptable social arrangements (p. 16).

Yet he does not – and cannot, given his rational-choice framework – argue from the *morality* of the proviso: "[w]ithout the prospect of agreement . . . there would be no morality, and the proviso would have no rationale" (p. 193).

The deep disagreement between Rawls and Nozick reminds us of the tension between contractarian and natural rights theories. If agents are to decide on moral constraints, why should they be constrained by natural – that is, at least precontractual – rights? This suggests the difficulty that confronts Gauthier's innovative attempt to combine these two approaches. He builds his social contract on a set of precontractual constraints that prohibit coercion and permit appropriation of property. Why should rational contractors admit such constraints not of their choosing? Moreover, unlike Nozick's, Gauthier's precontractual rights are not natural in a second sense. They have no independent moral appeal for rational agents; they are defended merely as necessary preconditions for the social contract. This makes it more difficult to protect them from the contractors' wills. We argue that Gauthier fails to defend a bundle of precontractual rights that include the proviso. We show that only a subset of the precontractual rights would attract some of the contractors; therefore, Gauthier's proviso is not necessary for agreement. Our purpose is not to defend an alternative solution to the contract problem, but to suggest that it has no unique rational solution.

Moralities and starting points

Recall that solving the contract problem requires specifying the distribution of the benefits of social cooperation. Since we are accepting Gauthier's bargaining method (which selects a unique distribution given a unique starting point), the problem becomes one of arguing for the most appropriate initial position. Because there is little basis to choose between I_N, I_B, and I_C as uninterpreted points in utility space, the argument proceeds by interpreting these in terms of compliance with three different moralities (see Fig. 7-1). Personal rights, prohibiting coercion, keep us from I_N and get us to I_B. I_B can be improved by two kinds of activity: trade and cooperation. Each requires moral constraint additional to the prohibition on coercion. Trade requires that we respect others' property; initial property rights are identified by the proviso that regulates appropriation. Cooperation (in Gauthier's technical sense; cf. p. 166) requires that we keep agreements, in particular the agreements that secure various public goods insufficiently supplied by the market. The link to public goods suggests the label: public morality. Summarizing, we can divide moral constraint into three stages, protecting persons, property, and public goods, respectively.

Gauthier proposes that property rights be included with personal rights against coercion, together determining the initial position for bargaining (at I_C). We will propose that bargaining begin at I_B, presupposing only personal rights and treating both property and public goods as subject to the bargain. The question that separates us then is the type of justification appropriate to the proviso, which permits acquisition of property. Gauthier claims that the proviso must be accepted prior to agreement and therefore receives the same sort of precontractual transcendental justification as rights against coercion. We shall argue that the proviso need not be accepted prior to agreement. Indeed, we shall show that the proviso conflicts with Gauthier's basic argument for precontractual personal rights. We begin with the latter criticism.

Slaves, servants, and serfs

Although the initial positions for bargaining admit of moral interpretations, Gauthier cannot, given his rational-choice methodology, argue from the morality of the proviso. The only rationale for constraint is "the prospect of agreement and society" (cf. p. 193); the justification of the proviso must be forward-looking. The argument is transcendental (an unfortunate term); the proviso is defended as a necessary precondition to a rational subgoal, namely, the social contract. We begin with a case where Gauthier's justificatory strategy works well before turning to criticism.

Consider James Buchanan's proposed initial position, the coercive no-agreement point, I_N. There is much to be said in favor of this natural baseline, which grounds bargaining in a positive, nonmoral account of stability. Gauthier allows that agreements based on I_N may be beneficial. For example, B_N is unequivocably better – that is, northeast – of any of the initial positions; an unfair cooperative arrangement may be better for all than any state of nature. Nonetheless, he contends that it would be irrational to be disposed to comply with unfair agreements. Why? Because this disposition would "invite others to engage in predatory and coercive activities as a prelude to bargaining" (p. 195). Hence, the slaves that Gauthier discusses in Section VII.1 rationally reject a bargain based on their coercive condition. The advantages the masters receive at B_N reflect the coercive situation that no longer obtains. "As one of the ex-slaves explained . . . there wasn't any reason to expect voluntary compliance – we weren't about to become willing servants" (p. 191).

We accept this argument; we allow that "it is rational to comply with a bargain, only if its initial position is non-coercive" (p. 192). We further allow that this is a moral constraint, required by the process of agreement, but not chosen by agreement. However, we will argue that rational contractors might stop here, making personal rights the only precondition of bargaining, while Gauthier insists we go on, to the proviso:

> The initial position must be noncoercive. But must we go further in constraining natural interaction, in so far as it determines the basis of market or cooperative interaction? We shall argue that the terms of fully rational cooperation include the requirement that each individual's endowment . . . must be considered to have been initially acquired by him without taking advantage of any other . . . cooperator (p. 200f.).

We reply to Gauthier by embellishing his tale of the slaves. The slaves are freed and soon get to witness an enormous land rush, whereby the exmasters appropriate almost everything available, limited, of course, by the proviso. They announce to the exslaves that they are now ready to bargain and offer secure serfdom at B_C as an improvement on initial position I_C. Not surprisingly, the would-be serfs reject this offer; indeed, they reject the exmasters' claim to property rights. Their rejection is similar to Gauthier's of I_N. It would be irrational, they say, to invite others to engage in appropriative activities prior to bargaining, since the inequalities thus generated will determine the cooperative optimum (at B_C). The would-be serfs therefore reject the appeal to the proviso that moves the initial position from I_B to I_C because it moves the social result from B_B to B_C.

Gauthier can reply to this tu quoque challenge by pointing to the moral and rational differences between proviso-constrained appropriation and coercion:

> The proviso, forbidding the taking of advantage, represents the weakest constraint rationally acceptable to persons who would avoid costly interaction with others [i.e., interaction that leaves them worse off than I_C], and the strongest constraint rationally acceptable to persons who would be free to benefit themselves. Thus the proviso reflects the equal rationality of persons who must constrain their natural interaction in order to enter into mutually beneficial social relationships (p. 227).

The crux of this justification is the claim that appropriation under the proviso leaves no one worse off due to interaction. However, the would-be serfs are unimpressed. They note that I_C is determined by a moral constraint, proviso-based property rights. They recall that "the prospect of agreement" provides the only rationale for moral constraint. Therefore, they conclude, the *only* feature relevant to accepting a starting point is its effect on the resulting bargain. Since beginning with I_B would get the would-be serfs to their preferred optimum, B_B, the masters' appropriation, although limited by the proviso, *does* make the serfs worse off, at B_C. It worsens their social bargaining position and the social agreement is the only context of interaction that matters to rational bargainers.

Two examples illustrate their point. Jim's building a house may satisfy the proviso and leave homeless Bob no worse off until private home ownership acts as a constraint on cooperative interaction, perhaps preventing a socialized housing policy. In the prospect of cooperative agreement, Bob is worse off. Some criticisms of private provision of schooling or medical services often make a similar point. They focus not on the immediate detraction from the public services, but on the shift in the initial position for bargaining that may block improvements to the public services.

Thus, there is an incoherence in Gauthier's main defense of the proviso. It leaves one no worse off only if the effect of appropriation is taken to be localized to the preagreement situation. However, the only reason we are supposed to accept the constraint of the proviso is with regard to the "prospect of mutual benefit." In other terms, Gauthier's argument is path-dependent. But maximizing agents do not care about the path, or history, that got them to B_B or B_C; they care about the benefits. Since they can see how constraints on the initial position affect their benefits, they have no reason to restrict their attention to the local features of some history. We contend that they will globally maximize. On the contrary, Gauthier assumes that rational agents do care about the precontractual history, so we must consider this in detail, which will take us to our second criticism, which focuses on Gauthier's appeal to the market.

The market as moral anarchy

First, a particular hypothetical history is implicit in the way Gauthier develops his argument. We begin in the state of nature, with coercive interaction. We constrain ourselves with the proviso. Given this morality (which we have distinguished into two stages, protecting persons and property, respectively), the market takes off; we all benefit further thereby. But the market sometimes fails; it does not provide public goods optimally. Correcting this requires cooperation involving further constraint of the public morality. Thus

each person acts rationally . . . subject to two levels of constraint. First, each is constrained by the right of her fellows, as determined by the proviso. . . . Second, each is constrained by the requirements of minimax concession, within cooperative institutions and practices ... the compatibility of the two levels of constraint ... is a theme basic to the idea of morals by agreement (p. 222f.).

No doubt if the contractors accept this view, they will see cooperation built on the gains assured by personal rights, property rights, and the market. But why should they accept this particular hypothetical history? There is at least one respect in which it could be changed. We can allow Gauthier's separation of moral constraint into two parts, with only the second the subject of agreement, and still differ about the dividing line. Gauthier proposes to include the proviso-based property rights with rights against coercion as precontractual. We propose to include property rights with the public morality as subject to the contract. According to our alternative account, individual gains from appropriation and trade are not assured before the bargain. Since in Gauthier's framework, all gains from moral constraint ultimately depend on social agreement, our account, which makes them part of the social surplus to be explicitly bargained about, would seem prima facie more suitable.

Gauthier reinforces his positioning of the market prior to agreement with some misleading rhetoric: "The first conception central to our theory is ... that of a morally free zone, a context in which the constraints of morality would have no place. The free zone proves to be ... the perfectly competitive market" (p. 13). "Morality arises from market failure" (p. 84). It is true that the market does not require what we have called the public morality of cooperation, which is designed to correct market failure. But as Gauthier acknowledges, the market requires moral constraint. "In understanding the perfect market as a morally free zone we shall be led back to its underlying, antecedent morality" (p. 85). This antecedent morality protects persons and property. On Gauthier's account, these are *noncontractual* constraints, but they are still moral constraints. The slogans "morally free zone" and "moral anarchy" may mislead us into forgetting that all gains from market interaction are due to others' moral restraint, which is (for Gauthier) ultimately dependent on social agreement. Strictly speaking, the market is (at most) *cooperation-free*. This revised slogan does not suggest that the gains from market interaction must be respected while agreeing on morality.

We turn from rhetoric to Gauthier's explicit argument for moving from noncoercion to the proviso:

The initial bargaining position must be noncoercive. But must we go further in constraining natural interaction, in so far as it determines the basis of market or cooperative interaction? We shall argue that the terms of fully rational cooperation include the requirement that each individual's endowment, affording him a base utility not included in the the cooperative surplus, must be considered to have been initially acquired by him without taking advantage of any other person. . . . Otherwise those who consider themselves taken advantage of in initial acquisition will perceive society as unfair, in demanding payments from them without offering a compensating return, and will lack sufficient reason to accept market arrangements or to comply voluntarily with cooperative joint strategies (p. 200f.).

Let us accept that the proviso ensures that no advantage is taken and that rational contractors would find this moral consideration salient. Still the argument has limited force. It works against any principle allowing appropriation that is not equivalent to the proviso; such appropriation involves the taking of advantage. However, it says nothing against ignoring appropriation altogether. One cannot be taken advantage of in initial appropriation if appropriation is not permitted to influence the social bargain. Or, to put the antecedent more precisely: any advantage taken in appropriation is open to rectification in the social bargain, where the morality of appropriation is ultimately settled. As Gauthier reminds us, "no one suffers injustice simply because [the market] is absent" (p. 321). To subordinate appropriation in this way is the alternative we proposed earlier that proved so attractive to the would-be serfs. They would treat property claims as subject to the social agreement. This is not an original suggestion; Hal Varian's theory of fairness shows how one can make use of markets for allocation without relying on appropriation to determine an initial distribution of property rights.[2]

Prerequisites for social agreement

The difference between us lies in Gauthier's insistence that personal and property rights be justified together, by the proviso, while we separate their justifications. We conjecture that Gauthier identifies personal and property rights through overestimating the endowment required to define agents for social contracting.

His specification of the agents' endowment can be seen as a rejoinder to our primary objection to his historical argument. The rejoinder notes that although rational agents may not care about the path to agreement, they do care about agreement, and, therefore, about any necessary prerequisites thereto. One of these prerequisites, in any contractarian theory, is that agents be defined sufficiently to reach a determinate and stable agreement. However, there is a limit to the justificatory weight transcendental arguments will bear. We must remember that the exis-

---

[2] Hal R. Varian, "Distributive Justice, Welfare Economics, and the Theory of Fairness," *Philosophy and Public Affairs* 4 (1975): 223–47; reprinted in *Philosophy and Economic Theory*, edited by F. Hahn and M. Hollis (Oxford: Oxford University Press, 1979). Varian's criticism that property rights are not necessary to achieving an efficient market outcome is directed against Robert Nozick, *Anarchy, State, and Utopia* (New York: Basic Books, 1974), chap. 7. It is stronger against Gauthier, who does not claim that property rights or the proviso have independent moral status.

tence of a determinate agreement is precisely what is at issue. We cannot assume that there is a contractarian solution without begging the question. A fortiori, we cannot assume that there is a bargaining solution based on an initial position that also enables market interaction. For example, Gauthier writes, "the application of [minimax relative concession], or more generally, the emergence of either cooperative or market interaction, demands an initial definition of the actors in terms of their factor endowments" (p. 222). But while this is true of the way Gauthier applies his principle (after market interaction), he has not shown it to be the case for agreeing to cooperate generally. To assume that contracting agents must follow Gauthier's procedure would beg the question.

Therefore, we are forced back to the more general prerequisite. Are proviso-based property rights necessary to define a contracting agent per se? In the context of Locke's use of the proviso, Gauthier suggests that they are. He writes, " . . . the actor obtains the material endowment in the factors of production that is required fully to define him for the purposes of market and cooperative interaction" (p. 208). Note how *fully* these agents are defined. The proviso's "effect is to afford each person a sphere of exclusive control. . . . This exclusive sphere constitutes a moral space, which defines the individual in his market and cooperative relationships" (pp. 201–2).

We submit that such full definition is only required for market relationships. We allow that agents must have exclusive control of commodities to attain the perfect market relations Gauthier discusses in Chapter IV. But it does not follow that cooperative relations require the same full definition. Indeed, what makes market and cooperative arrangements *complementary* is that the latter do not require parsing a situation into a set of exclusive property rights before they can be brought to bear on it. For example, we may cooperatively solve the externality of air pollution without first deciding who owns how much air. Thus, it is difficult to see why Gauthier identifies the definitions of the agents needed for cooperation and the market. Indeed, we should distinguish *three* levels of specification: cooperation, agreement, and bargaining. We are claiming that certainly the first and likely the second and third are possible without fully defined property rights. Cooperation may be agreed to – even *bargained* to – as long as agents are defined in any number of less definite ways, including appeals to equality and non-coercion. The contractors need some precontractual individual rights, but they do not need fully developed property rights. (We suggest a more constructive approach to the problem of defining the agents in the next section.)

Summing up, our criticism rebuts Gauthier's assumption that the precontractual rights necessary for social agreement include property rights.

We rebut the claim of necessity by showing that an alternative is possible within Gauthier's contractarian framework. We do not wish to defend our proposal as an alternative contractarian proposal for distributive justice. Indeed, our aim is to criticize the contractarian aspect of Gauthier's framework by showing how open it is to rival distributive proposals. Nonetheless, it would give a false impression of the resources of Gauthier's theory were we to neglect how he might respond to our proposed alternative.

Three rejoinders

We turn to three rejoinders Gauthier might deploy against our inclusion of property claims with public morality. First, our argument may appear too Hobbesian in the sense of focusing on the zero-sum aspect of conflict at the contract locus, thereby ignoring the possibility of joint gains the market allows (cf. sec. X.3.2). However, we do not give up the advantages of the market (any more than Gauthier gives up the advantages of cooperation). We subject them to the terms of the agreement.

This suggests a second objection: in attempting to control the market to serve collectively defined goals, does not one run afoul of Gauthier's two criticisms of the utilitarian justification of property? First, "In order to minimize inefficiency in a manner compatible with maximizing welfare, it is necessary to change factor endowments – to reallocate rights. But this undermines the fixity that rights must have" (p. 108). We can blunt this criticism by limiting reallocations to lifetimes.[3] (Those attracted to rule utilitarianism might reply otherwise.) Gauthier's second criticism is that "utilitarianism denies to individuals in society the freedom enjoyed by Robinson Crusoe.... For the utilitarian supposes that even a person's natural attributes ... are vested in her only in so far as this proves socially convenient." We avoid this criticism by accepting the precontractual constraint on coercion, which guarantees basic endowments.

Third and finally, to the extent that we put market gains into the surplus to be cooperatively distributed, we must face Gauthier's criticisms of Rawls' similar attempt:

One's natural capacities are what one brings to society, to market and cooperative interaction. Why should they not determine, or contribute to determining, what one gets in society? How could a principle determine impartially how persons are to benefit in interaction, except by taking into account how they would or could benefit apart from their interaction? (p. 220)

---

[3] Compare the concept of wealth fairness, Varian, p. 247.

Again, we are less exposed to this argument because, unlike Rawls, we allow some natural inequalities into the initial position governed by personal rights. Still, Gauthier's first question remains: Why not allow the effects of appropriation a determining role as well? There are two reasons. The first recalls our argument in the second section. Gauthier rejects the effects of coercive interaction as irrelevant to setting the initial position. The point of agreement is to *replace* coercive interaction with constrained interaction; there is no prima facie reason why the former should influence the latter. On the contrary, this provides a reason to ignore the premoral, preagreement situation as irrelevant. Nonetheless, recalling that for Gauthier impartiality is the cardinal feature of morality, his final open question is important: If we ignore what goes before agreement, how can the agreement be impartial?

We propose a rather speculative answer to this question that will allow us to say something new on the issue of identifying the contracting agents. So far, we have not had reason to focus on the range of entities that count as agents for Gauthier's theory. We suppose that a more general theory is to be preferred. One would like to know if moral constraint can be justified for any entity capable of rational choice and then, as a subsidiary (although for many, most important) question, whether the proposed justification applies to us humans. A general functionalist theory of rational morality, one that quantifies over kinds of agents as well as over situations, should be able to specify what it is about an entity that makes it a moral agent. (It will not do to fall back on barely disguised theology or speciesist naturalism; the general theory must be able to distinguish Sony Ltd. from Fly-by-Night Electronics Ltd.) Since Gauthier mainly identifies rational agents with human beings, saying little about this general functional approach, a review is not the place to develop this sense in which ethics may be artificial.[4] (See my *Artificial Morality*, in progress.)

The general functional approach to rational morality is relevant to the issue at hand, that is, identifying an impartial initial position. In particular, we note that for Gauthier moral constraint requires special dispositions and skills. (We discuss these dispositions in our other article in this collection, Chapter 16.) This has the consequence that we can rank agents with respect to how well they embody these dispositions and skills. Here is a standard for determining benefit that is *internally* relevant to morality: to each according to his contribution to morality as such. Notice first that this sort of principle is not available to those, like Rawls, who take an ideal approach to morality. It is available to us

---

[4] In "Deterrence, Rationality, and Rationality," Gauthier writes, "[O]ur analysis of deterrence is intended to apply generally. . . . I am particularly concerned with the rationality of deterrent policies in the context of relations among . . . nations" (*Ethics* 94 [1984]: 478).

because we are working within Gauthier's nonideal approach, where morality is something some agents may work – likely with varying motivation, skill, and success – to achieve and uphold. What Gauthier does not see is that his account of moral constraint allows a standard that treats agents in a way that is relevant to distributing the gains from morally supported trade and cooperation. This standard is arguably more relevant than either the proviso or even egalitarian personal rights. After all, one's natural talents and ability to appropriate and to trade are not themselves necessary conditions to having a morality. Indeed, they often run counter to morality. But self-constraint and the ability to discriminate moral from nonmoral agents are – according to Gauthier – necessary to any rational morality. Therefore, we propose that these dispositions and skills could be used to determine shares from social cooperation. This could be done in either of two ways. Indirectly, they could form the basis for specifying endowments in the initial position. More directly, they could enter into a principle of distributive justice. In either case, these morally necessary dispositions and skills would provide a basis for impartial distribution, obviating the need to appeal to morally irrelevant gains from appropriation and trade. This echos our first reason for disagreeing with Gauthier's claim that appropriation ought to influence the social bargain: appropriation looks as morally irrelevant as the coercive nonagreement point. More generally, it presses the account of distributive justice in the methodologically satisfying direction, where the contracting parties (if not the principles) are determined by the functional prerequisites of the device of moral constraint.

To conclude our criticism, we contend that Gauthier's *contractarian* defense of the proviso is not compelling. We emphasize "contractarian" because as moral casuistry, Gauthier's defense of the proviso's impartiality is superb. But the problem remains that from the point of view of would-be contractors, this particular account of impartiality will not command universal rational assent. There is (at least) one popular alternative to a precontractual proviso. Personal rights need not be identified with property rights; the market can be regulated by the social contract. Therefore, proviso-based property rights are not a necessary precondition to bargaining. They are, at most, sufficient and salient, not necessary. Thus, Gauthier's attempt to replace Nozick's natural right to property with a transcendental contractarian justification of property rights fails. Morality is more subject to agreement – and disagreement – than Gauthier allows. The contractarian method leaves more to convention than one would like.

We set out to test Gauthier's claim to "generate [morality] from nonmoral premises of rational choice" (p. 4). We have argued that as a derivation, Gauthier's argument fails. The proviso does not follow from the premises. We agree with Gauthier's broad conclusion that rational agents would choose to constrain their choices by a morality. But our criticism shows that the constraint of property rights is not necessary to agreement. Therefore, matters of distributive justice are more conventional than Gauthier allows and there is more room for disagreement about them.

Consider Gauthier's intriguing metaphor of morality as a visible hand, which he uses to stress how morality complements the market: "We may then think of cooperative interaction as a visible hand which supplants the invisible hand, in order to realize the same ideal as the market provides under conditions of perfect competition" (p. 128). The metaphor also reminds us that Gauthier's method is inspired by Hobbes; his solution is internal, moral – not external, coercive – constraint. Thus, Hobbes's "sovereign acts as a very visible foot." This "very costly solution" (p. 164f.) contrasts with the less costly visible hand of morality.

Our criticism showed that the market is more visible than Gauthier allows. From the point of view of the would-be contractors, various moral constraints that permit the market to function are available as alternatives. In the context of a social contract between rational agents with partially opposed interests, this leads to disagreement. Thus, this criticism weakens Gauthier's theory, taken as a contractarian theory of distributive justice. He illegitimately tries to constrain the contractors to take as fixed property rights that we argue they can see to be open to their decision. The crucial structures of distributive justice are, in this sense, conventional, not necessary.

8.   Providing for rights*

Donald C. Hubin
and Mark B. Lambeth

Hypothetical contractarians hold that justice is defined by a contract that would (rationally) be made in some specified situation. The characterization of this situation is a matter of great controversy. If it is taken to be our real-life situation, obvious counterexamples arise. Previous acts of predation may make rational an agreement that could hardly be called "just." Various alternative characterizations have been offered with a variety of justifications. Still, this is a difficult point in contractarian theory.

In his book, *Morals by Agreement*,[1] David Gauthier finds footing for the contractarian in an unlikely place – natural rights theory. The initial bargaining situation is the situation that would occur if those bargaining had never violated each other's rights. This restriction prevents the outcome of the bargain from being tainted by the effects of predation and freeloading. The obvious counterexamples are avoided and the resulting outline of a theory is highly attractive, blending the insights of Locke and Nozick with those of Hobbes and Gauthier.

There are those who would find fault with the footing, however, for the name of natural rights has too often been invoked in lieu of argument – as if to call something a natural right exempted it from further justification.

This is not always done, of course. Locke offers a lovely (though flawed) defense of property rights in external objects. Since it is an improved and extended version of this very argument that Gauthier offers as the foundation of natural rights, this is where we begin. In the

*Reprinted with minor modifications by the authors by permission of *Dialogue* from "Providing for Rights," by Don Hubin and Mark Lambeth, in *Dialogue* 27(3) (Autumn 1988). Copyright © 1988 by *Dialogue*.
[1] David Gauthier, *Morals by Agreement* (Oxford: Oxford University Press, 1986).

following section, we present Gauthier's justification of natural rights. In subsequent sections, we criticize it on several different grounds. Finally, we consider the effects of these criticisms on Gauthier's larger enterprise.

I

John Locke begins his defense of property rights by assuming that one has an exclusive right to one's body and powers. He then argues that since one has a right to one's labor, one acquires a right to that with which one has mixed one's labor as long as there is "enough and as good left" for others. This condition is known as "the sufficiency condition" or "the Lockean Proviso." Robert Nozick correctly identifies the motivation for the proviso: it "is meant to ensure that the situation of others is not worsened" by one's acquisitions.[2] Henceforth, we refer to this underlying rationale as the Lockean Proviso. It states that "[a] process normally giving rise to a permanent bequeathable property right in a previously unowned thing will not do so if the position of others no longer at liberty to use the thing is thereby worsened."[3]

Gauthier defends a modified version of the proviso and attempts to base all natural rights on it. The basic strategy is to assume that, in the absence of market or cooperative relations, one may permissibly do whatever one wills as long as it does not violate the proviso. One then has a liberty right to use something as long as such use is permissible. One has an exclusive right to use something when one's use is permissible and the use of the object by others is impermissible (because it violates the proviso). To evaluate the plausibility of Gauthier's foundation for natural rights, we must look first at the modification Gauthier makes to the proviso and then at the way he extends the application of his modified version of the proviso.

Gauthier is looking for a general constraint on action, not simply a constraint on acquisitive behavior. He wants a version of the proviso that will prohibit freeloading and parasitism. Nozick's version of the proviso is too strong for Gauthier's purposes because of what it forces us to say in cases where someone's ass has to be gored and your only choice is whether it is yours or someone else's. According to one statement of Gauthier's modified version of the proviso, it "prohibits wors-

---

[2] Robert Nozick, *Anarchy, State, and Utopia* (New York: Basic Books, 1974), p. 175. That this is what Locke has in mind seems clear from his comments in Section 33 of Locke's *Second Treatise of Government* (John Locke, *Two Treatises of Government* [New York: Mentor Books, 1963]).

[3] Robert Nozick, *Anarchy, State, and Utopia*, p. 178.

ening the situation of others except where this is necessary to avoid worsening one's own position."[4]

In light of the sorts of cases he has in mind, Gauthier seems right in claiming that Nozick's version of the proviso is too strong – at least as a general constraint on action.[5] But surely Gauthier's version is too weak. For in the sort of situations we are considering (let us call them "tough situations"), it allows us to worsen the position of others to an arbitrarily large degree to avoid worsening our own only slightly. We believe that an adequate statement of the proviso would include some sort of proportionality requirement for tough situations, but we shall not pursue this here.

Gauthier employs his version of the proviso to a more ambitious end than either Locke or Nozick do theirs. Locke, of course, defends the assumption that people have property in their bodies and the labor of their bodies only by appeal to a theological argument. By invoking his version of the proviso as a general constraint on action, Gauthier intends to place the assumption on firmer footing. That is, he will base *all* rights, including the right to one's body and one's powers, on the proviso. Whatever natural rights theorists think of the contractarian aspects of Gauthier's theory, his defense of rights represents a significant contribution to natural rights theory.

Let us begin our discussion of Gauthier's theory by examining more closely what his version of the proviso allows and what it prohibits, for the statement of it cited earlier is misleading in light of further comments Gauthier makes. Not all worsening of the positions of others is prohibited even where such worsening is not required to avoid worsening one's own position. Consider an example offered by Gauthier:

> Suppose that we live as fisherfolk along the banks of a river . . . [I]f you, living upstream from me, . . . use the river for the disposal of your wastes, then even though you thereby kill many of the fish in my part of the stream, you do not violate the proviso.[6]

Such a claim might shock Locke, but Gauthier's real concern is not with getting Locke right, but with explicating the notion of taking advantage of another. Gauthier's version of the proviso is intended to ensure that

---

[4] David Gauthier, *Morals by Agreement*, p. 203. As one would expect given the deontological or side-constraint nature of the proviso, Gauthier makes much of the distinction between actions and omissions – between worsening someone's position and allowing someone's position to be worsened. In light of this, his statement of the proviso may be stronger than he intends. For as stated, it only allows the worsening of the position of others to prevent *worsening* your situation. Gauthier may intend to allow worsening the position of others whenever it is necessary to prevent your situation from *being worsened*.

[5] It appears that Gauthier's weakening of the proviso winds up permitting actions that fit his intuitive characterization of freeloading and parasitism. Such actions will be allowed by his proviso when the only alternative requires worsening one's own position.

[6] David Gauthier, *Morals by Agreement*, p. 211.

people not take advantage. Since the upstream fisherman is no better off polluting the stream in the presence of the downstream fisherman than in his absence, his pollution does not count as taking advantage.

Perhaps the clearest statement Gauthier offers of his version of the proviso is this: "the proviso prohibits bettering one's situation through interaction that worsens the situation of another."[7] To give a fuller understanding of what Gauthier has in mind, we must look at his account of "bettering one's situation through interaction that worsens the situation of another." The notions of better and worse are taken to be unproblematic; they are defined in terms of an increase or decrease in one's subjective expected utility. The problem then becomes one of determining how one's actions affect oneself and others. Gauthier says, "the base point for determining how I affect you, in terms of bettering or worsening your situation, is determined by the outcome that you would expect in my absence."[8] So, A's doing x worsens B's position *iff.* B would be better off in A's absence than with A's doing x.[9]

Clearly, the notion of bettering (or worsening) one's own position cannot be given a parallel treatment. (Whatever sense could be made of being better off in your own absence than you are given that you perform an action would be the wrong sense.) But since we are only interested in the notion of bettering (or worsening) oneself *through interaction with another,* we can use as a baseline the situation that would exist in the *other's* absence. A betters his position through interacting with B *iff.* A prefers the outcome he gets to what he would have gotten in B's absence.

In the fishing case, the upstream fisherman undeniably worsens the

---

[7] Ibid., p. 205.

[8] Ibid., p. 204.

[9] This account is problematic. It is unclear how long an absence we are to imagine when we determine whether B would be better off in A's absence. If we are to imagine that A never existed, parents would have to harm their children very badly before it would count as worsening the situation of the children. The father who gains momentary sexual gratification by raping his minor daughter and thereby causing her great psychological trauma is clearly worsening her position even if she would not be better off if she had never existed. (We assume that one would not exist if either of one's parents did not exist.) *And* it seems that this bettering of his position through worsening hers is just the sort of thing Gauthier wants the proviso to rule out. If, on the other hand, we imagine the absence to be only for the moment, then the proviso seems to be too strong. Suppose that we have often acted so as to benefit each other in the past, but on a particular occasion we find ourselves in competition over some object. It might well be true that the loser in this competition would have been better off in the absence of the winner *and* that the winner is better off than she would be in the absence of the loser. The reason the loser might be better off in the temporary absence of the winner is obvious – she would have obtained the object. And the winner might be better off by having bested the other in competition because of the effect on her self-esteem, her security, or her reputation. As Hobbes notes, people are driven to competition not only for gain, but for diffidence and glory. These later goals may be better attained by having beaten someone to achieve your goal than by having achieved it without competition.

position of the downstream fisherman in the relevant sense, but he does not do so through interaction that betters his own position. It is for this reason that Gauthier's version of the proviso does not rule out such behavior.

We believe that these accounts of "bettering" and "worsening" are unsatisfactory in light of cases of causal (pseudo-)overdetermination. Typical cases of slavery are paradigmatic of the sort of parasitism that Gauthier wishes to rule out by the proviso. But it is not clear that his account of "bettering" and "worsening" has this effect. Suppose that I am one of only two slave owners in an area. Though I am horribly cruel and abusive, the other slave owner is even worse. Suppose that, were I not around, all of my slaves would be owned by him. Now, though I better my own position through interaction with my slaves, it cannot, on Gauthier's account, be said that I worsen their situation. For they are better off than they would be in my absence. Parasites who protect their hosts from worse parasites do not violate the proviso as stated.[10]

This problem is not unique to Gauthier (similar problems arise for Nozick) and it has little to do with the problems on which we shall focus. We will suppose that some adequate account of "bettering one's situation through interaction that worsens the situation of another" can be given. Even assuming that the proviso can be strengthened so as to avoid this problem, we argue in the next section that it is unacceptable as a universal account of natural rights because it is already too strong in other respects. In the third section, we discuss and evaluate Gauthier's attempt to base all rights, and in particular the right to one's body and powers, on his version of the proviso.

II

We have already criticized Gauthier's proviso for being too weak in two respects: first, in omitting a proportionality test; and, second, in allowing one to take advantage of another provided that had he not done so, someone else would have. Of course, many would take the fishing case presented by Gauthier to show that the proviso is too weak; though presumably Gauthier is not troubled by this case. (In the third section, we discuss other respects in which the proviso is too weak.) But Gauthier's proviso is also too strong, at least as a *general* constraint on action. It requires refraining from actions that are morally permissible and thus fails to justify all the rights one would have in a Lockean state of nature. Suppose that you are a bounty hunter, hired to find me by a party I have injured. By returning me to my victim for punishment, you violate

---

[10] The issue raised here is the very difficult one of when an action can be justified by showing that if the agent were not performing the action, someone else would be producing a similar effect.

the proviso. You have bettered your position over what it would have been in my absence, we may suppose, because your cost of finding and returning me was less than your fee. But you have worsened my position because, let us imagine, if you had not found me, no one would have. Yet, of course, your action seems perfectly permissible.

Consider another example. You seek to punish me for some grievous injury I have done you. Quite plausibly, the harm legitimately inflicted on me as punishment exceeds the benefit I received, if any, from the injury I inflicted on you. So, we may suppose, your act of punishment worsens my position – I would have been better off had you not existed. It is not so clear that the punishment has bettered your position. Of course, if it has the effect of reducing the likelihood that I will wrong you in the future, you may be better off having punished me than you would had you not punished me for this injury. But this is not the appropriate baseline. The question is: How would you fare in my absence? (We shall interpret this to mean "had I never existed.") Could the punishment you justifiably inflict on me make you better off than you would have been in my absence? Quite possibly. For it may be that by punishing me, you deter others from harming you – others who in the absence of evidence of your retaliatory dispositions might not have been deterred.

These counterexamples could be avoided by treating the proviso as a portion of an ideal theory of justice – that is, a theory of what justice requires given that everyone complies with the theory. But then, of course, we cannot treat the proviso as a *general* constraint on action in a state of nature, for it only applies in situations in which no injustice has been done. Nor can it serve as the basis for many of the rights that natural rights theorists proclaim. In particular, one cannot say that a person has a right of retribution for an injury only if such retribution does not violate the proviso.

We assume that Gauthier means his proviso to be a principle of an ideal theory of justice. Despite the fact that this limits its interest in other respects, such an interpretation is consistent with his ultimate theoretical goal – to define a suitable initial bargaining position for a hypothetical social-contract theory. But even restricting the application of the proviso to ideal theory, we do not avoid the problem of excessive strength. For as will become clear in the next section, the proviso unjustifiably restricts a person's bodily rights.

III

That one has a right to one's body and one's powers has, for many, been a starting point for a theory of justice in holdings. As starting points go, it is not bad. It is at least nominally endorsed by theorists with otherwise antagonistic political views, and few feel an inclination to disagree with the abstract statement of the proposition when they are first asked to consider it.

Still, if one could show that this proposition can be justified by appeal to some more basic moral commitment we make, this would constitute a major theoretical achievement. Such a result would be of practical importance as well. If the justification were successful, not only in the sense that the more basic commitment *entailed* a right to one's body and powers, but also in the sense that we came to believe that this really was the *foundation* of our belief in such a right, significant progress could be made in clarifying the nature of that right. For while there is great agreement on the statement that one has a right to one's body and powers, there is still significant disagreement on the implications of such a right.

Gauthier proposes to ground the exclusive right to one's body and powers on his version of the proviso. Doing so requires showing both that one has a right to the use of one's body and powers and that others do not. Gauthier argues, then, that my use of my body and powers does not violate the proviso, whereas someone else's nonconsensual use of my body and powers does:

Each person, in the absence of his fellows, may expect to use his own powers but not theirs. . . . Continued use of one's own powers in the presence of others does not in itself better one's situation; use of their powers does better one's own situation. Refraining from the use of one's own powers worsens one's situation; refraining from the use of other's powers fails to better one's situation but does not worsen it. Continued use of one's own powers may fail to better the situation of others but does not in itself worsen their situation; use of other's powers, in interfering with their own use, does worsen their situation. Thus the proviso . . . affords to each the exclusive use of his own [powers].[11]

The right to one's body and powers is, then, based on the proviso and a set of empirical facts, including facts about one's special connection to one's body and powers. We could test the philosophical adequacy of Gauthier's thesis by imagining outlandish empirical hypotheses and considering whether Gauthier's thesis gives us the right answer about bodily rights in such situations. The problem with such an approach is that our moral "intuitions" are often infused with empirical assumptions and they serve us ill when we apply them to situations that violate those assumptions. Because of this, we shall, while engaging in some modest science fiction, avoid truly bizarre situations. We believe that the cases we offer are ones about which we have pretty reliable convictions. And, in any event, we progress from somewhat fanciful cases to completely

[11] David Gauthier, *Morals by Agreement*, p. 209.

commonplace ones so that, at least by the end, we have not forced the imagination to stretch beyond reasonable limits.

The defense of bodily rights Gauthier offers depends on the assumption, which he makes explicit twice, that my use of the body or powers of another must interfere with his own use of them. This certainly need not be so. Consider Dr. Demento, who has discovered a drug that will put people into a trance for eight hours and rejuvenate their bodies so that they need no sleep. The fiendish doctor realizes that he has a way to use the bodies of others without making them any worse off than they would be in his absence. Demento is, as the reader will have guessed, demented. In addition to making his temporary zombies work in his lab at night, he engages in vile and disgusting sex acts with them, which he videotapes. He then sells the tapes at great profit in foreign countries. He is becoming a wealthy and thoroughly satiated person. Clearly, he betters his position relative to what it would be in the absence of those whose services he enlists. But, a critic might claim, his action does not violate the proviso because he does not worsen the situation of others.

This last claim might sound outrageous. But, we must remember that, by assumption, the lives of Dr. Demento's victims seem no different to them than the lives of the nonvictims. They suffer no ill effects on their health, have no painful memories, and never find out what has been done to them nor have any dealings with those who have viewed the videotapes. In this sense, their lives are not worsened.

However, as Nozick argues,[12] we care about things outside our experience. If this is so and utility is a measure of the subjective desirability of certain states of the world, then Gauthier would probably offer the following reply. Presumably Demento's victims prefer that their bodies and powers not be used in this way. (If they do not, it is not *so* clear that Demento is doing anything wrong in using them in this way.) Thus, a situation in which their bodies and powers are used in this way has less utility for them than one in which no such use takes place. For the utility of an outcome for an individual need not depend on how that individual is affected by the outcome. But then Dr. Demento is violating the proviso because he is making his victims worse off than they would be in his absence.

This would seem to put the Demento case to rest. However, the bump appears elsewhere in the carpet. For if utility is simply a measure of the degree to which a person's desires are satisfied, two problems arise. First, the manipulation of people's preferences can lead to very counterintuitive consequences. Second, the existence of people with unusual desires can unjustifiably undermine one's claim to one's body as well

---

[12] Robert Nozick, *Anarchy, State, and Utopia*, pp. 42–5.

as to external objects. The first problem suggests that the proviso, so understood, is too weak; the second that it is too strong.

As an illustration of the first point, consider the following case. Imagine a father, let us call him Manny, who loves his children – after a fashion. At least, he would never do anything to make himself better off by making his children worse off. Of course, he understands "bettering" and "worsening" in terms of preference satisfaction. So, while he would never violate the proviso with respect to his children, he sees nothing wrong with raising them like a gardener raises a Bonsai tree. While his children are young, he stunts their intellectual and social development and, using sophisticated psychological and neurophysiological techniques, he leads them to desire only to serve him. He leads a life of utter dependency, while his children play the willing role of slaves. With his death, they have nothing left to live for and pass away in ennui.

Manny's manipulations do not violate the proviso because though he is better off in his children's presence than he would be in their absence, they are not worse off in his presence than they would be in his absence. This is because their preferences are more fully satisfied in his presence than in his absence. Despite the fact that Manny is not violating the proviso, he certainly seems to be taking advantage of his children; he seems to be a parasite; and, we believe, he is violating the rights of his children and doing wrong. If we are correct, then this understanding of the proviso is too weak because it treats the manipulating parasite as a symbiote.

As an example of the second problem, consider first the case of an external physical object. Suppose that I find a piece of obsidian that I wish to use for an arrow tip. I discover that there once existed a strange religious sect the members of which believed in the divinity of the magma of the Earth. As God's expectorate, obsidian is sacred – never to be used to further the worldly ends of mortal men. Though there are now no adherents to this view, those who did exist strongly preferred that obsidian never be used as I propose to use it. I, being deeply sacrilegious, take great delight in flouting the religious customs of any sect – even a dead one. In making my arrow tip, I better myself through interaction with the members of the religious sect that worsens their position. Yet it does not seem wrong to make it.

One might be inclined to protest that there is no interaction here. The now dead members of the now defunct sect are not affected one way or another by my action. But this reply is not available if we follow Gauthier in defining "better" and "worse" in terms of subjective expected utility (at least if that phrase is given its usual meaning).[13] If we

---

[13] This problem is common to theories that take the satisfaction of preferences to be of intrinsic moral relevance without regard to when those preferences exist. Thus, utilitarian theories that take the *summum bonum* to be the satisfaction of any desires or

choose to give up this account and insist that what is relevant is how our actions affect the lives of others, then we seem stuck with the Dr. Demento case.

One initially attractive response to the problem raised by the obsidian arrow tip case would be to modify the proviso so that one need consider only the utility of those alive when or after the act is performed. But such a restriction is inadequate to avoid other troublesome cases. (It may well be too strong in other respects – a possibility we do not explore.) We illustrate this with an example about bodily rights. Suppose that Ellen is toying with the idea of working out so that she can win female body-building contests. She mentions this to her covivant, Todd, who disapproves of it in such strong terms and expresses such a proprietary attitude about her body that he quickly becomes an *ex*covivant. After the separation, she finds that he still abhors the idea of her becoming a body builder, perhaps because he fears that others will think less of him for having been involved with a woman who would want to develop "that sort of body." Ellen's inclination to take up body building may have passed quickly had she not heard of Todd's continued concern. Knowing of it, she has a strong preference to work out. Indeed, being somewhat spiteful, she looks forward to thwarting the desires of her former lover. She wants this even though she will not be able thereby to cause him any unhappiness, for, unfortunately, he has just taken off on Earth's first interstellar probe (never to return) and the only messages that can be sent to him must concern official business.

Even if her motive is just to spite Todd and she gains utility from doing so, Ellen has a right to become a body builder if she chooses. This is so despite the fact that she achieves a higher utility for herself by decreasing Todd's utility. (And, of course, if Todd prefers that she not become a body builder, her doing so decreases his utility regardless of whether it affects *him* at all.) Perhaps we usually ought to seek to satisfy others' preferences, but, even when we ought to do so, we often have a right not to. This is especially clear in Ellen's case.

Again, it appears that focusing on how an act affects others rather than on how it affects their subjective utility (i.e., the satisfaction of their preferences) may avoid this problem case. But it is unclear how to avoid both this case and the case of Dr. Demento. Furthermore, this last case

---

preferences allow past desires a seemingly undeserved moral weight. If everyone who existed up until the midtwentieth century had fervently desired that we never explore space, would that give us a weighty moral reason for not doing so? For Gauthier, preferences of others do not in themselves have moral weight, but if we better ourselves by thwarting such preferences, we violate moral constraints (provided we are not in a "tough" situation).

suggests ones that cannot be avoided even by shifting our focus to effects on persons.

Imagine two pioneer farmers: Old McDonald and Young McDougal. Old McDonald has been using his powers and abilities to work his end of a valley with great success for some time. Young McDougal moves into the other end of the valley to try his hand at farming. As it happens, he is not very good at it. So Old McDonald does well and Young McDougal does poorly, but it does not seem that McDonald is doing well at McDougal's expense.

McDonald and McDougal are, though, very competitive. Each would prefer to be the best farmer in the valley by being better than others in the valley to being the best farmer in the valley because he is the only farmer in the valley. But each would prefer to be the only farmer in the valley to being shown up by another farmer. And, since each knows whether the other is there and how the two of them are faring, let us suppose that their well-being varies according to the degree to which their preferences are satisfied.

Now it appears that McDonald's use of his powers and abilities to better himself violates the proviso. For he prefers the outcome he gets to that he would get in McDougal's absence and McDougal prefers the outcome he would get in McDonald's absence to that which he actually gets. Thus, McDonald's use of his powers and abilities betters his own position and worsens the position of McDougal. Nor is the worsening of McDougal's position incidental to the bettering of McDonald's. We have chosen the correct baseline; McDonald is better off than he would be in McDougal's absence.

Yet it seems that McDonald has a right to use his abilities to their fullest and his doing so certainly does not constitute taking advantage of McDougal. So something has gone awry – something quite independent of whether we concern ourselves with the effect of our actions on others or on their utility. The problem is that just as rights function as claims against general utility, so they function as claims against the proviso; just as we sometimes have a right to advance our own interests even when this conflicts with promoting the general interest, so we sometimes have a right to increase our own utility by decreasing the utility of others.

One might object to any of these last three examples (as well as to ones yet to come) on the grounds that they depend crucially on individuals taking an interest in one another's interest – on them having so-called "tuistic" desires. The obsidian hunter delights in thwarting the desires of the dead religious sect as Ellen delights in thwarting those of Todd, and McDonald and McDougal are concerned with how they fare vis-à-vis each other. Gauthier specifically assumes that "the proviso is intended to apply to interaction under the assumptions of individual utility maximization and mutual unconcern."[14] Thus, these examples are irrelevant.

Such a restrictive assumption as mutual unconcern, though, is both undesirable and unjustifiable. It is worth noting that such an assumption is certainly not in the spirit of Hobbes, who tells us that there are three sources of conflict in the state of nature: competition, diffidence and glory.[15] To assume mutual unconcern is clearly to ignore diffidence and glory, which depend typically on one's *relative* power. Of course, there are limits to Gauthier's adherence to Hobbes; perhaps this is one of them.

But this is not a good place to depart from Hobbes, for even if individuals in the state of nature are intrinsically concerned only with gain, they ought to be instrumentally concerned with relative power. Having more wealth, strength, or intelligence than others with whom you interact increases your probability of gain. A rational utility maximizer, concerned with his absolute share of nonpositional goods, will be required to be concerned about his position vis-à-vis others.

Furthermore, even if one could justify setting aside desires for *positional* goods, people clearly have other intrinsic desires that violate the mutual unconcern restriction.[16] Benevolent and malevolent desires are, perhaps, the most obvious examples. Setting such desires aside in determining when a person is better off or worse off in order to set the baseline for a social bargain has clearly unacceptable consequences. I may, for example, take delight in enslaving you only because I want to thwart your ability to satisfy your own desires; I may gain no other advantage from your enslavement. Now, once we enforce the requirement of mutual unconcern (nontuism) on people's preferences in order to determine when they are bettering their position at the expense of others, we find that I am not violating the proviso. Although you are worse off than you would be in my absence, I am no better off *in terms of my nontuistic desires* than I would be in your absence. Hence, the existing condition of enslavement satisfies the proviso and may be, for all we know about it, an appropriate situation from which to strike the social bargain.

Perhaps most importantly for Gauthier's ultimate concern, insofar as he aims at "rationalizing" social institutions, it is a mistake to make artificial assumptions about people's concerns. If people, in fact, are concerned that others fare well (or ill) or are concerned with how they fare vis-à-vis others and the initial bargaining point assumes this away,

---

[14] David Gauthier, *Morals by Agreement*, p. 205.

[15] The version of this paper that was published in *Dialogue* mislabeled Hobbes' three sources of conflict. We are indebted to Jan Narveson for pointing this out.

[16] The cases of the obsidian hunter and of Todd and Ellen involve tuistic, but nonpositional, desires.

then it is unclear how the rationality of the bargain rationally justifies the outcome to the participants.[17]

IV

The real test of Gauthier's theory of natural rights is not whether it accounts for all of the rights that we believe ourselves to have. Many of those rights may be the result of market or cooperative structures and not be founded directly on the proviso. In our examples, we have tried to appeal to convictions about what rights a person would have in the absence of such structures. Since we find the examples persuasive, we think that Gauthier's proviso will not serve as a foundation even for natural rights. But Gauthier is not a natural rights theorist, and his ultimate goal is not to provide a foundation for rights but a basis for bargaining. The question of whether the proviso will serve this function remains open (temporarily). For all we have said, it may still be that the agreement people would make from the situation they would be in were no one to violate the proviso accurately and nonaccidentally captures the rules of justice. It is to this issue that we finally turn.[18]

Consider again the case of Old McDonald and Young McDougal. We have claimed that McDonald has a right to use his powers to their fullest and that such use does not constitute taking advantage of McDougal even if Gauthier's proviso is thereby violated. But suppose that McDonald refrains from violating the proviso, believing himself to have a right only to those advantages he can secure without violating it. Hoping

---

[17] Thus, while we agree with Narveson ("Gauthier on Distributive Justice and the Natural Baseline," Chapter 9 in this volume) that Gauthier will have difficulty establishing his claims for the rationality of compliance with the bargain if he begins with unrealistic assumptions, we disagree with his claim that the vast majority of us are not concerned with positional goods. Indeed, from a casual observation of behavior, it seems reasonable to conclude that most people are intrinsically concerned with positional goods.

[18] Our primary concern here is not with whether the proviso is rationally acceptable, not with whether it is rational to comply with the terms of a bargain that would be made given strict compliance with the proviso. Rather, we engage in an excercise in reflective equilibrium. Does the agreement that rational agents would arrive at from the situation in which the proviso is satisfied necessarily coincide with our considered judgments concerning justice? (This project is very different, then, from those undertaken by Jan Narveson and Peter Danielson in their essays in this volume.) Gauthier, himself, may be tempted to dismiss the counterexamples offered, for he, "trusting theory rather than intuition" (p. 269), rejects appeals to moral intuitions as a test of moral theories. But we believe that these are the sort of counterexamples that should trouble Gauthier. We do not present instances in which Gauthier's theory merely diverges from "the supposedly 'plain duties' of conventional morality" (p. 269), but instances that also cast doubt on the claim that rational individuals would bind themselves to the principles Gauthier's theory endorses. This is the sort of criticism that he may escape but cannot reasonably ignore. In effect, we are suggesting that he has misunderstood (or not fully understood) the implications of his own position. And this is a form of criticism he explicitly allows (p. 269).

to do better through cooperation, McDonald opens negotiations with McDougal. Though both bargain rationally and in good faith, McDonald gets the short end of the stick. This is because in order to secure the right to use his powers fully, he must compensate McDougal. Such an agreement is, we assume, better for him than continuing to abide by the proviso in McDougal's presence or else McDonald would never have consented to it. But it is, we suppose, not as good for him as using his powers fully in McDougal's presence. More troublingly, it may not be as good for him as using his powers fully in McDougal's absence. If, as we believe, McDonald is within his rights to employ his powers to the fullest without compensation (in the scenario suggested), it is difficult to see why justice would require compensation from him. Adherence to the proviso skews the outcome because it awards McDougal unwarranted bargaining power.

Some may disagree with our claim that the outcome of such a bargain is skewed inappropriately. In his fascinating and entertaining book, *Choosing the Right Pond*,[19] Robert Frank defends (among other things) the thesis that justice requires the transfer of wealth from the better off to the worse off because the latter provides a service to the former that is not reflected in the marketplace (i.e., is a market externality). The service is the provision of someone to whom they can feel superior. One might argue, based on such a view, that McDonald does owe McDougal a share of his wealth.

There are, though, problems with such an approach. In the first place, it has implications that would be difficult to accept. Frank supposes that we are especially concerned to "get position" with respect to those with whom we come into contact and deal with frequently. But, if true, this is surely not a necessary truth. To illustrate, let us consider an example used by Gauthier – the sixteen Robinson Crusoes.[20] Actually, we need consider only two. Imagine two strong, clever Robinson Crusoes living on well-supplied islands. They differ only in this: one is energetic and the other is lazy. Suppose that, as in Gauthier's case, they are able to communicate with each other, but supplies can be sent only from the energetic Crusoe's island to the lazy Crusoe's island. We add to Gauthier's example only the supposition that these two have the desire for positional advantage. Now the energetic Crusoe by using his abilities to the fullest makes himself better off than he would be in the lazy Crusoe's absence and he makes that Crusoe worse off than *he* would be in the absence of the energetic Crusoe. The proviso is violated and the hard-working Crusoe is now justified in using his abilities to the fullest

---

[19] Robert Frank, *Choosing the Right Pond* (New York: Oxford University Press, 1985).
[20] David Gauthier, *Morals by Agreement*, p. 218ff.

only if he compensates the other. But, absent our additional assumption, Gauthier does not believe that justice requires any such compensation. He says:

If . . . [the] Robinson Crusoes lived, each on a separate island, and if each used his capacities to provide for himself from the resources of the island, then the outcome, whatever it might be, could not be unjustified.[21]

It seems implausible that desire for positional advantage should alter the situation so drastically in the Robinson Crusoes case.

Now, of course, this case is just a variant of the McDonald/McDougal example. But perhaps the variation makes clear what is at issue. At least for many, the conviction that those with the positional advantages ought *as a matter of justice* to compensate those with less seems to depend on the existence of social relations. McDonald and McDougal were individuals set in a situation in which there typically is social interaction. Although we did not assume any such interaction, still one's convictions about the case may be influenced by the setting. In the Robinson Crusoes example, such extraneous influences are not present.

The situation is worse if we remind ourselves that in order to avoid the problems with Dr. Demento, Gauthier must be concerned not with an action's effect on people, but with its effect on people's utility. Given this, we can imagine that the two Robinson Crusoes lack the ability to communicate with each other and neither ever learns of the existence of the other. Let us suppose that their desires remain the same (i.e., that each would prefer to be better off than someone else to being the lone person in existence and that each would prefer this latter situation to being worse off than someone else). It turns out that for the energetic Crusoe to use his abilities to the fullest is a violation of the proviso (even in their ignorance of one another's existence) – an excusable violation, no doubt, but a violation just the same. This seems wrong.

*   *   *

What these cases suggest is that the problem in Gauthier's theory is not with the attempt to describe the initial situation for a contractarian theory of justice in terms of a state of nature in which there have been no rights violations. Indeed, although others have criticized this approach, we find it to be a major attraction of his theory.[22] The problem is that even Gauthier's version of the proviso is not an adequate foundation for rights.[23]

[21] Ibid., p. 221.
[22] See, for example, "The Lockean Proviso" by Peter Danielson and "Gauthier on Distributive Justice and the Natural Baseline" by Jan Narveson, both in this volume, Chapters 7 and 9, respectively.
[23] We are indebted to Daniel Farrell, David Gauthier, and an anonymous referee for *Dialogue* for providing helpful comments on an earlier draft of this paper.

9. Gauthier on distributive justice and the natural baseline

Jan Narveson

Introduction: Gauthier's contractarianism

Contractarians hold that the fundamental principles of morals are the objects of something very like an "agreement," which in turn is the outcome of what is in some sense a "bargain." Just what sort of an agreement, "made" how and in what circumstances, is a matter on which different theorists in the contractarian tradition have given very differing accounts.

Gauthier's *Morals by Agreement* is the latest, the most sophisticated, and, in my view, by far the most compelling and perceptive effort in this great tradition. Let me briefly summarize what I take to be the distinctive points in his account. Gauthier sides with Hobbes and against Rawls, for instance, on the amount of idealization that goes into the construction of the appropriate "starting point" of the Social Contract. We do not reason from behind Rawls' Veil of Ignorance, but instead in full view of our assorted individual characteristics – but also, of course, in full view of our fellows. And, as with Hobbes, we begin with no moral presuppositions. Morality is to be the set of interpersonally applicable rules on which reason, driven by our actual (though considered) preferences, tells us to agree, and it tells us to agree on them despite the lack of any assumption of fellow feeling, love, or charity, or even of such philosophically popular constraints as universalizability, impartiality, or equality. We accept only such of these as can be seen to fall out of our fundamental project, which is to make the best life we can for ourselves in view of our actual situations vis-à-vis our fellows who, like us, are also rational pursuers of interests. Lacking moral constraints, we do worse; possessing them, we do better. Gauthier, however, also eschews the Hobbesian Sovereign. Rational people will internalize an assortment of constraints on their pursuit of advantage, even though they reason from advantage in adopting the constraints. Yet once adopted, rational individuals adhere to them.

The theory comprises three subtheories: (1) a theory of bargaining, minimax relative concession (MRC), (2) a theory of compliance, constrained maximization, and (3) a theory of the appropriate natural baseline for the social contract, (his version of) the Lockean Proviso on acquisition. In this inquiry, I query the first and third of these in some respects. These are queries rather than major dissents, both in the sense that I am in very broad agreement with Gauthier on most matters, and in the sense that I have considerably less than total confidence in both of the modest dissents put forward here. Both, however, could make some, perhaps appreciable, difference to the practical implications of his theory.

My queries are motivated by the concerns implied in the preceding thumbnail sketch. Gauthier's project is to supply fully nonquestion-begging foundations for what are recognizably moral outcomes. Thus, his version cannot require the participants to take up unreal positions, positions they could not occupy in real life. Nor can it assume that the participants are impartial or natively equipped with respect for their fellows or for reason, either in some disputable version or even in the thin and hopefully less controversial version employed in the theory. If we are to emerge with a morality that is impartial, as Gauthier insists, then a rationale for this impartiality must be found. The rationale that the results agree with our pretheoretical intuitions is rejected: we wish to convince the previously unconverted, not just those previously disposed to agree.

As I see it, to motivate this impartiality, we need merely remind ourselves that we seek intersubjectively valid rules, rather than arbitrary personal edicts. Moral constraints are administered, fundamentally, from within. They must have the support of all reasonable persons – there is no one else but ourselves to do the job. But unless all support them, the support of any one individual becomes less rational. Now, we assume that each person naturally appraises situations from the perspective of her own values, which are likely to be highly biased: she is anything but impartial by nature. Why, then, must the rules we agree on be unbiased in relation to all actual participants? Because if they were not, then some would be called on to sign into an agreement that is either *suboptimal* – she could do better with no one doing worse – or *unfair*. In either case, Gauthier supposes, those individuals would have reason to refrain from accepting the proposed rules. But lacking their support, we would find ourselves on the skids back to the horrors (a.k.a. "suboptimalities") of the State of Nature. Self-interested choosers, if they know what they're doing, choose rules for the containment of externalities because this yields a greater benefit for each, provided that all comply, than they would be able to attain in the absence of such rules. Similarly, they choose impartial rules for the distribution of *co-operative* benefits because each wants as much as possible and has no reason to settle for less than an equal share.

That suboptimality would yield the desired adherance is, in my view, plausible, and is not questioned here. Unfairness, however, brings up other and trickier issues. "Unfair" rules may be said to disproportionately reflect the distribution of relevant claims. When what we are negotiating for is distributive shares, then the outcome must reflect our prior claims, if we have any. And here we enter the vexed area of assertions concerning "equality." One way for the Social Contract to be unfair would be for it to provide unequal benefits for some when the prior claims of all are equal. Another would be for it to provide equal benefits when claims are in fact unequal. We must steer between these opposite errors.

This brings us to the two problems in Gauthier's theory that I wish to focus on in the remainder of this essay: (1) the status of his proposed principle of distributive justice, minimax relative concession, and (2) the status of his Lockean Proviso, specifically as it related to the status of preagreement gains in the postagreement situation. We discuss each in turn.

Gauthier on distributive justice

In Gauthier's view, justice is "the disposition not to take advantage of one's fellows, not to seek free goods or to impose uncompensated costs, provided that one supposes others similarly disposed" (p. 113).[1] He introduces his discussion of bargaining by distinguishing two domains of justice: on the one hand, it prohibits taking advantage, gaining at others' expense. Here the rules avoid "mutually destructive conflict" (p. 115). On the other, it is concerned with "the cooperative provision of mutual benefits" (p. 114) made possible by the fact of variable supply, which can be positively affected by cooperation. In cooperative production, there will be a cooperative surplus, not available without the participation of each cooperator. The question is how these surplus goods are to be divided among those participants.

The general bargaining problem is the problem of what principle of distribution is rational for such cases. Gauthier's project is to arrive at the appropriate principles, calling for the right constraints on the part of those concerned. These principles, setting the constraints required

---

[1] David P. Gauthier, *Morals by Agreement* (Oxford: Oxford University Press, 1986). Page references to this book are made in unattributed parentheses in the remainder of this essay. All other references are footnoted.

for rational cooperation, are arrived at *through* bargaining, but "are no part of the bargaining process" (p. 129). The bargainer is simply trying to maximize his utility: "each person's behaviour must be a utility-maximizing response to her expectation of others' behaviour. . . ." (p. 129).

How to proceed? To begin with, it is axiomatic that the outcome of the bargain for each bargainer, what she carries *from* the table, must, if bargaining is to be rational, be an improvement for her relative to the status quo: she must leave with more than she had when she came.[2] (Call this "condition A.") Each person then puts in an initial *"claim"* for some portion of the surplus in question. This corresponds to the opening round in haggling between buyer and seller in, say, an Arab market. How big is the opening claim? Since the first condition is satisfied by any distribution that leaves everyone at all better off, the prima facie answer is supplied in the first of Gauthier's four "conditions on rational bargaining," (i) that one claims *all*, or more precisely, just short of all, of this surplus (subject to one further restriction: what one claims is only the nearly-all of "that part of the surplus to the production of which he would contribute. Each person's claim is bounded by the extent of his participation in cooperative interaction" (p. 134). For, obviously, one is otherwise taking advantage, by free-riding on those who did the producing.) Then the bargaining problem is the problem of where, rationally, to settle among the infinitude of possible but mutually incompatible distributions determined by each person's maximal claim, giving to each of the others the minimum that would make it rational for them to participate at all; and so on through all the other distributions, each giving a portion to each participant that continues to satisfy condition A. Here enters Gauthier's ingenious and attractive solution.

We identify the cooperative surplus itself by finding, first, what each person could get without participating. As seen above, condition A requires giving that person at least as much as his or her next-best available option from outside. This, therefore, can be subtracted from the surplus available for bargaining. Next, we must be able to characterize each person's claim in a way that makes that claim *comparable* to the claims of others. The utilitarian idea of cardinal, interpersonally comparable utility is rejected as the appropriate unit, for good reasons that we can't go further into here (pp. 126–9). Gauthier chooses as the appropriate measure that *relative fraction* of the bundle of goods which is the potential surplus in question going to each person. We assume that each wants as much as possible of that surplus – it might be money, for instance – and that each would find it rational to participate for any part of that surplus; fractions of it, then, make a plausible

---

[2] Our second problem, discussed in what follows, concerns one aspect of this requirement.

choice for comparison: "... the rationale turns on an interpersonal comparison of the proportion of each person's potential gain that he must concede ...," (p. 139) – remembering, of course, that what each person gains, above his minimum, is an exact inverse of what he loses, below his maximum, through concession – the gainer of 350 out of a potential 500 has foregone 150, whereas her counterpart, who has gained only 35, has foregone only 15 (pp. 138–9).

The argument then proceeds as follows. For each person, (ii) there must *be* a point at which he would be prepared to settle if need be; for otherwise, there can be no distribution of the surplus. (We can envisage the problem facing a set of potential cooperators deciding in advance on how to divide the gains, so that if there is no conclusion, then there is also no cooperation and hence no surplus to divide.) Each bargainer, being rational, knows this about each other bargainer. Then comes the crucial move. In Gauthier's words, "(iii) ... Each ... must be willing to entertain a concession in relation to a feasible concession point if its relative magnitude is no greater than that of the greatest concession that he supposes some rational person is willing to entertain (in relation to a feasible concession point)" (p. 143). But being rational, (iv) he will therefore settle for nothing *less* than that either. For that point is by definition one that it is possible for all to settle at, so it is feasible; yet anything less would be irrational, since one doesn't have to settle below it.

Interesting, and plausible. But we must ask what makes condition (iii) plausible? What Gauthier says is that it "expresses the equal rationality of the bargainers. Since each person, as a utility-maximizer, seeks to minimize his concession, then no one can expect any other rational person to be willing to make a concession if he would not be willing to make a similar concession." (pp. 143–4). This sounds good. But there is a problem. The argument talks of the "equal rationality" of the bargainers. How is that to be understood? Gauthier's theory of rationality is the maximizing theory (cum Constrained). Now presumably either one is a maximizer or one isn't: it's not a matter of degree, like wit or intelligence. How, then, can what is not a matter of degree at all be invoked to account for a disposition to accept an equal division in what necessarily are matters of degree? For the equal divisions claimed to be generated by MRC are genuine cases of equality: that is, we have divisible magnitudes of which each gets an equal share.[3]

That it is unreasonable to expect any other rational person to be willing to make a concession if one would not be willing to make a *similar*

---

[3] The distinction, which Gauthier points out is necessary, between cases of equal division and cases of unequal division which dominate the equal division in question is irrelevant here. See his discussion of Roth (p. 140, top).

concession is interesting, but on reflection invites the question, "Why?" After all, in bargaining contexts, we are arguing over how to cut up a piece of pie. More for you is less for me; but all we are given is that each wants *as much as possible*. If we say, "Yes, but how much *is* possible under the circumstances?" then the answer would seem in principle to vary depending on the propensities of the other bargainers. Given – as seems obvious – that anything *is* possible, within the range of just long of nothing (leaving almost all for the others) to just short of everything (leaving almost nothing for the others) for bargainer B_1, then the question of why we should be settling in the middle rather than somewhere else, as a supposed matter of "reason," becomes acute. The appeal to "equal reason" seems inappropriate.

What are the alternatives? One thought is this: if our bargainers are both recognizably human, then the fact that there is no inherent reason, in the nature of the case, why one division should be any better than another may be appealed to on the ground that disputes which cannot be settled by reason are likely to be settled by force; but the application of force in human affairs violates the Hobbesian equality principle. Hobbes, as we know, argues for equality in the "natural condition of man." He qualifies this almost immediately, noting that "there bee found one man sometimes manifestly stronger in body, or of quicker mind than another . . . "; but his conclusion is equalitarian nevertheless: ". . . when all is reckoned together, the difference between man, and man, is not so considerable as that one man can thereupon claim to himselfe any benefit, to which another may not pretend, as well as he."[4] The fact that you would win in a fair fight today may give you a temporary edge; but what about the unfair fight that will follow that one? And what about the fight in which my friends back me up? (And/or yours you?) And what about the question whether I should ever deal with you again, if I can possibly help it?

A further thought: we bargain, in the real world, against a time budget. Neither of us can wait forever, both can wait quite awhile, and all of the time spent waiting is time wasted, in principle. Assuming that our patience and, in general, our budgetary constraints in terms of time to spend bargaining are pretty equal, we would again get equality as a plausible operating assumption. The equality of this budgetary constraint is by no means axiomatic, though, and it is noteworthy that sometimes a bargain will be concluded unequally due to the superior patience of one party. Is Gauthier to claim that in these cases there has been injustice? But my man in the Arab market *owns* the carpet in question: he doesn't have to sell on *any* terms if he doesn't want to. And I

---

[4] Hobbes, *Leviathan* (New York: Dutton, 1950), p. 101.

own the money, which I don't have to part with if I don't want to. There is no right answer to the question: What is the *correct* price of the carpet?[5]

Moreover, we should recall that ordinarily the cooperation in question involves effort; and where there is a cooperative surplus, it is plausible to invoke the principle that one's share of the product should be proportional to one's share of the production cost, such as effort. To be sure, this intuitively plausible suggestion, which may be taken to be the root idea underlying the Labor Theory of Value of Marxist fame, runs into horrendous conceptual problems which can be resolved only by leaving the determination of what constitutes "equal effort," and the like, to the market.[6] Even so, it will often be possible to make a rough comparison of our respective efforts in relation to production, and then one can appeal to equal contributions as a basis for equal shares.

Perhaps, then, the principle of MRC is slightly misstated, or at any rate, Gauthier's account of it is misleading. In his account, it is not the disposition of minimax relative concession *itself* that makes for an equal outcome, but rather the assumption of "equal claims for equal rationality." It is *not* true, just like that, in the case where "a single transferable good, produced in fixed quantity and divisible in any way among the cooperators" is one such that "maximum concession is minimized if and only if each person receives an equal share of the good" (p. 153). What is true is only that my (or anyone's) maximum concession is minimized *relatively to the others* – and that only on the assumption of a linear utility function for the rational agent in question against quantities of the good in question – if and only if it is equally divided. "MERC" would be a better name for it.

However, let us put aside these quibbles, especially since the principle Gauthier proposes is so beautiful and so intuitively right. Instead let us address a very different and extremely important issue: What, in fact, are its implications? Now, some have evidently thought them considerable. David Braybrooke, for example, supposes that MRC would apply to a whole society, in which case we would have to try to figure out what the maximal and minimal claims of each individual would be – "making fantastic demands on information, which no contracting parties and no current critics of government could ever meet."[7] But, as I have complained elsewhere,[8] it is by no means evident that MRC applies at

---

[5] The relevant formal principle here is, I suppose, Zeuthen's, discussed by Gauthier on pp. 71–5. This principle says that the person whose ratio between cost of concession and cost of deadlock is less must rationally concede to the other. The empirical surmise is that considerations of human time budgets make it generally implausible to suppose that differences in this respect will make concession rational.

[6] Among many recent destructive discussions of the Marxian notions of value, I would mention my own in "Marxism: Hollow at the Core," *Free Inquiry* (Spring 1983): 31–2.

[7] David Braybrooke, "Social Contract Theory's Fanciest Flight," *Ethics* (July 1987): 760.

[8] Jan Narveson, *The Libertarian Idea* (Philadelphia: Temple University Press, 1989), p. 195.

this level, despite Gauthier's suggestion that "Society may be viewed as a single cooperative enterprise" (p. 274). For one thing, as Gauthier himself observes, when there are more than two persons, each receives "only that part of the surplus to the production of which he would contribute" (p. 134). And it is simply not plausible to suppose that everyone contributes to the production of everything in our or any society. Or if we say so, then the "contribution" in almost every case will consist merely of that person's refraining from upsetting the productive applecarts of those actually engaged in cooperative productive activities. And to regard *that* as a "productive contribution" is to bring us to our other subject, pursued in the following.

Meanwhile, there is one further point, possibly of fundamental importance. Gauthier contrasts two interesting cases: (1) that of Ms. Macquarrie, the pharmaceutical chemist, versus her lab assistant, Mr. O'Rourke, and (2) that of Sam McGee, the Yukon prospector, versus Grasp, the banker. Ms. M. discovers a wonder drug that makes her a millionaire, but does not divide her royalties equally with O'Rourke. Sam, on the other hand, forced to borrow a measly $100 from Grasp in order to register his claim to the richest vein of gold in the Yukon, "will (rationally) have to offer Grasp a half-share in the claim" (p. 153). The difference seems striking.

Why the disparity? Because Ms. M., it seems, did not carry on her experiments *as* a cooperative venture with O'Rourke. "Although she required an assistant, she did not require O'Rourke. Her relationship with him was strictly a market transaction; she hired him at (presumably) the going rate for laboratory assistants" (p. 153). Sam, on the other hand, enters into full cooperation with Grasp, without whom his venture will not succeed at all. And one thinks here of resourceful marketers who reap the major share of profits on inventions technically far beyond their capabilities, gleaned from cooperative ventures with the computer innovators, chemists, and so on whose ingenuity provides them with the goods they sell.

If the difference in the two cases seems fundamental, we must also admit that it is fortuitous. In another possible world, O'Rourke would be the only lab assistant available and without him Ms. Macquarrie could do nothing, and Sam could choose among a half-dozen sources for the loan he needs, as Gauthier agrees (pp. 153–4). Now consider ordinary business deals or the activities among any cooperating set of business people. How do they proceed? In general, by someone having an idea, getting in touch with others, making an offer, and so on. People to help are either hired on a wage/salary basis or taken on as partners at some level or other, or both; perhaps market shares are sold, and so on. People have a sense of when they have made a good deal and when not; and sometimes a deal is made in bad faith, as a result of deception, or under some subtle or not so subtle type of coercion, in which case its effect is rejected or disputed. But when a deal is not defective in such ways, where does MRC, or anything like it, come into it?

Gauthier's characterization of MRC as a principle of "justice" puts it on the same level as, say, the principles of promise keeping, truth telling, or fair dealing. In fact, he suggests that all of them "are to be defended by showing that adherence to them permits persons to cooperate in ways that may be expected to equalize, at least roughly, the relative benefits afforded by interaction. These are among the core practices of the morality that we may commend to each individual by showing that it commands his rational agreement" (p. 156). Can we accept this? I think not. The validity of a promise is surely not due to its approximating an equal division of anything. If the background conditions are properly observed, and everything is on the up-and-up, then promises and contracts are valid by virtue of their form, of the fact of agreement itself, and not in virtue of the resulting distributions exemplifying some or other proportions. That does come into the parties' estimation of how satisfactory a deal they have struck: if it doesn't look promising, they don't make the deal. But it does *not* affect their sense of whether it was a valid agreement at all. If I later discover that Mohammed would have settled for $20 less had I but known, or if I decide to settle – gullible tourist that I am – on his opening price, then he doesn't owe me a dime. Should the product be not as advertised, or subtly defective, that's another matter. He is then guilty of deceit. But deceit isn't a matter of failing to approximate MRC in any sense I can readily think of.

It must also be evident that MRC makes sense only against the background of independent rights of the parties concerned: rights to their own persons in the way of abilities and other resources, and rights to assorted items of external property. If we don't already have those rights, no intelligible sense of bargaining can get off the ground.[9] Yet if we do have them, then the validity of the transactions we make concerning them is due simply to the continued operation of those rights themselves. You can give me an X because it is yours; I can give you a Y in exchange because it's mine. What makes Y yours when I do give it to you is simply the fact that I have done so, and not any supposed fact that the resulting distribution of some set of benefits

---

[9] See the important passage on p. 222: ". . . the emergence of either cooperative or market interaction, demands an initial definition of the actors in terms of their factor endowments, and we have identified individual rights with these endowments. Rights provide the starting point for, and not the outcome of, agreement. They are what each person brings to the bargaining table, not what she takes from it." Obviously, however, if this viewpoint is pressed too hard, then there is an end to the contractarian project as I have described it at the outset of this essay. See my brief discussion in Narveson, *The Libertarian Idea*, p. 190.

would approximate an equal proportion of our maximal preagreement claims.

In fact, given broadly Lockean rights in ourselves and in external items of property, it would seem that MRC is a subordinate and largely dispensable principle, best not regarded as a principle of *justice*, strictly speaking, at all. The moral force of actual bargains is transferred to the results of those bargains directly from the antecedent rights of the parties concerned to the goods or services being exchanged, rather than from their "claims" via Gauthier's interpretation of MRC.

And for good reason. For the principle we *really* need, once property rights are in place, is not MRC, but constrained maximization (CM). CM ensures that we both benefit from exchanges, by ensuring that we both actually get what we have agreed upon. It does not go into the question how *much* we benefit, leaving deliberations on that matter to the antecedently operating practical reasoning of each. MRC serves as a plausible guide here, to be sure; but that seems to be all.

Gauthier on predatory gains and the Lockean Proviso

Gauthier's version of the Lockean Proviso on acquisition forbids the pursuit of advantage by imposing disadvantage on others. The proposed baseline for assessing my advantage and disadvantage in interacting with person P is how things would be for me in P's absence. If my action is such that I would do as well or better if P weren't around at all, then I am not taking unfair advantage of his presence. If, on the other hand, my action will lead to my benefit only if P *is* around, yet renders P worse off than if I had not been around, then I *am* taking unfair advantage of P.

The present question concerns what we should take as the baseline for our negotiations regarding future arrangements of society. Would we accept a status quo incorporating differential predatory gains of some parties due to past interaction? Or should we, as Gauthier insists, "purify" our starting point for this fundamental purpose by invoking the Lockean Proviso retroactively?

Gauthier had previously adverted to the matter with this thought: "We may agree that each person must take from the bargain the expectation of a utility at least equal to what she would expect from noncooperative interaction, if she is to find it rational to cooperate. It does not follow that she must bring such a utility to the bargain, as determining her share of the base point from which bargaining proceeds" (p. 133). The question to be pursued here is: Why not?

For analytical purposes, at least, let us make a distinction between two sorts of "powers" that might conceivably be relevant to distributive questions: what we will call "productive" and "predatory" powers.[10] Of course acts of predation are all, in their way, productive: if A makes his living by stealing from B, then he is, if successful, producing something, namely, what he takes to be a better overall situation for himself, or whoever is the recipient of the ill-gotten gains in question. However, those gains had originally to be "produced" in a more fundamental sense of that term. When A gets on by predation on B, what A does is to redistribute wealth, whereas B, let us assume, was the actual originator of it.

It is obvious, I take it, that contributions to production, in this latter sense, *are* a relevant basis for distribution. Possession of unusually great productive powers, then, is a likely basis for some sort of distributive recognition.[11] It is less obvious that predatory powers are so. One might simply insist that they are no basis whatever for just distributive claims, and indeed, both Hobbes and Locke would agree with this in one way or another.

Hobbes, familiarly, imagines a prepolitical and premoral "State of Nature" in which distributions of goods are determined by the total array of powers, predatory as well as productive, available to each party. But Hobbes claims that the distribution of predatory powers is such as to render the overall distribution in the State of Nature equal, as we have already noted before: ". . . when all is reckoned together, the difference between man, and man, is not so considerable as that one man can thereupon claim to himselfe any benefit, to which another may not pretend, as well as he."[12] In Hobbes' view, the plausible outcome is to forbid predation across the board, leaving the question of how to distribute the produce from productive powers to the Sovereign to decide.[13]

But if it is plausible to accept Hobbes on the rough equality of predatory powers, the distribution of creative or productive powers is another matter. These, surely, are very unequal. In Locke's view, in contrast to Hobbes', the proper principle regarding the distribution of goods flowing from the exercise of these productive powers is, in effect, to leave them to the market, constrained by property rights.[14] This is the Libertarian's view, and the one to which I am inclined.[15]

---

[10] This should not be confused with C. B. Macpherson's distinction between "extractive" and "developmental" powers, which is, I believe, essentially confused. See *Democratic Theory* (Oxford: Clarendon Press, 1973), pp. 40–52.

[11] There are social philosophers who apparently deny this, and Rawls may be among them. I will not discuss their arguments in this treatment.

[12] Hobbes, *Leviathan*, ch. XIII, p. 101.

[13] "Seventhly, is annexed to the Soveraigntie, the whole power of prescribing the Rules, whereby every man may know, what Goods he may enjoy . . . without being molested by any of his fellow Subjects: And this is it men call *Propriety*." Hobbes, *Leviathan*, chap. XVII, p. 149.

[14] Locke, *Second Treatise of Civil Government* (New York: Dutton, 1966), chap. v, pp. 129–

But a question arises about the relevant principles here. Suppose that predatory powers are *not* equal: then what? Gauthier introduces his deliberations on this matter with a tale about a society of masters and slaves, the latter serving the former through coercion (p. 190 ff.). Only force, rather than any sense of moral obligation or ideology, preserves the situation. However, we are to suppose that the masters currently have the whip hand: the coercive apparatus by which the masters remain masters is essentially permanent, the slaves being incapable of unilaterally dismantling it. Still, the costs of maintaining the apparatus are considerable to the masters. They therefore propose a deal: "You slaves will continue to serve, but *voluntarily*; in return, we masters will refrain from beating you, and even give you better living conditions into the bargain. What do you say?" According to Gauthier, this offer is one that cannot be rationally accepted, because its outcome could not be rationally complied with. He puts the following speech into the mouth of the new Prime Minister, elected by the Ex-Slaves: "It was only because of the power they held over us that it seemed a rational deal. Once that power was taken away, it became obvious that the fruits of cooperation weren't being divided up in accordance with that fancy principle of minimax relative concession. And so there wasn't any reason to expect voluntary compliance . . . " (p. 191).

If this is the correct reasoning, then Gauthier has served up a lesson for all masters: since you can't expect stable optimal bargains from slaves, don't bother to try to treat them better in hopes of improving your own situation through cooperation! But is the PM's reasoning correct? Or is there, instead, hope for slaves, short of chancy resort to violent revolution? Let us consider.

Gauthier points out that "fair procedures yield an impartial outcome only from an impartial initial position" (p. 191). True. But he has also made it clear that *impartiality* does not imply *equality*. The division of profits between me and Robert Redford from my movie, in which he gets six million while I settle for two hundred thousand, is fair and impartial and sanctioned by MRC, though of course not equal.[16] The question, then, is whether the particular inequalities of the initial situation prior to the acceptance of the Social Contract, in which many of those who are better off are so by virtue of having exerted coercive force on those worse off, are capable of being incorporated properly in a baseline for fair bargaining.

---

40. To further complicate matters, the realization of benefits from the exercise of these powers is due largely to cooperation. Consequently, important issues arise concerning the distribution of those benefits. The discussion in the fifth section of this essay is concerned with that issue.

[15] See Narveson, *The Libertarian Idea*, esp. chaps. 6–8 and 15.

[16] Except, as we have seen, in the peculiar way that minimax relative concession reckons.

As Gauthier correctly observes, predatory activity is suboptimal. (We must distinguish between the situations under discussion here and, for example, those of sadistic masters who simply enjoy coercing their (non-masochistic) slaves; the latter will not be considered here.) The efforts of the coercers must be unproductive so far as they go: they stimulate productive activity on the part of the slaves, but, we assume, the slaves would be capable of equal or superior production in the absence of force, if they could be sufficiently motivated by other means (such as the prospect of a reasonable share in the product). The time now spent in beating the slaves could be spent more pleasantly by both parties: playing chess, perhaps, or taking a nap. Why, then, shouldn't both parties accept, and keep, an agreement in which the same productive/service activities as before are carried out, but the time formerly devoted to the exertion of force by the masters over the slaves is now devoted to these more desirable activities? It would be better for both parties, we are assuming. So why not?

It is important to bear in mind that in our contractarian deliberations, we follow Hobbes in assuming that the State of Nature is a *totally amoral* state – a condition in which *nothing* is wrong, nothing forbidden. Contrary to the assumptions of our story, Hobbes also believed that this initial state was one of equality of coercive powers. We are in part here exploring the implications of the non-Hobbesian assumption. If we make the Hobbesian assumption of equality of coercive powers in the State of Nature, then it is plausible enough, I take it, that we can get from Hobbes to Locke: the use of force to pursue one's ends, in all cases when a cooperative arrangement could have yielded a greater benefit, will be unequivocally and universally forbidden. But it is less obvious, at least, that this will be so if our starting point is one of *unequal* predatory powers.

Many may find it not so clear that we can get, as I put it, from Hobbes to Locke. However, I am here exploring the situation if we are given the Hobbesian assumption of roughly equal predatory powers in the status quo ante. Still, it might be argued that the flat prohibition on force might well be less plausible than various alternative formats in which *some* ends could be pursued using coercion, at least if it were employed by a public agency under fair rules. This is not the place to pursue this important subject. For the present, let us assume that there is a flat prohibition on privately wielded force for private ends other than self-protection, leaving the more difficult question for another time.[17]

Specifically, let us consider the case where A is greatly superior to B in predatory capabilities, while B is greatly superior in productive powers. A is accustomed to making his living by raiding B, who understand-

---

[17] I explore this matter, if not as satisfactorily as I would have liked, in Norveson, *The Libertarian Idea*, chap. 14, pp. 154–84.

ably finds this a nuisance. Against this background, *A* proposes a deal: *B* will simply transfer to *A* a fixed percentage of the fruits of *B*'s highly effective labors, and *A* will thenceforth renounce the use of force in his dealings with *B*.

There are two cases to distinguish. In case 1, *A* puts his weapons in a convenient place, to be taken out instantly in case *B* should fail to live up to his part of the bargain. In case 2, however, *A* melts his swords into ploughshares, which he cheerfully supplies to *B*, whose productivity is thereby increased the more. Since *A* gets a percentage of *B*'s product, he naturally expects to share in the benefits.

If Gauthier is right, case 2 is one in which *A* is in for a nasty shock. *B*, if rational, will cease to deliver as soon as the last sword is duly converted into the last ploughshare. Obviously there is a complication in the example in that the *technology* of warfare presumably has not been melted down along with the hardware. In a real-life situation, there would be the likelihood that *A* would be able to resume full-scale predation in fairly short order. I therefore wish to rule this out for present purposes, admittedly at the expense of making the example still more artificial than it already is: my swords-to-ploughshares conversion is irreversible. My question now concerns the justice of *B*'s Gauthier-sanctioned action, given Gauthier-sanctioned premises (which I in general share).

The situation is made yet more interesting if we suppose that negotiations are carried on between *A* and *B* in which the distinction between cases 1 and 2 is very clearly and explicitly recognized by the parties. Importantly, we want the move from 1 to 2 to constitute, in the abstract, an optimal strategy: both parties are better off in 2 than in 1. But at the time of the negotiation, *A* is in a position to choose between them, and *B* is aware of this. Why wouldn't this agreement be binding?

As I understand it, Gauthier's reason for thinking that it would not be rational for *B* to carry out this agreement is that at the time at which it is to be carried out, the coercive apparatus by means of which *A* was able to exact agreement in the first place has been dismantled. In his fable, the newly elected Prime Minister, an ex-slave, says, "Once that power was taken away, it became obvious that the fruits of cooperation weren't being divided up in accordance with that fancy principle of minimax relative concession. And so there wasn't any reason to expect voluntary compliance – we weren't about to become willing servants." To which Gauthier adds, "clearly an individual would be irrational if she were to dispose herself to comply, voluntarily, with an agreement reached in this way. Someone disposed to comply with agreements that left untouched the fruits of predation would simply invite others to engage in predatory and coercive activities as a prelude to bargaining.

She would permit the successful predators to reap where they had ceased to sow . . . " (p. 191).

But if party A (the masters, in Gauthier's example) foresees that party B (the slaves) would use this reasoning, then of course they will not make the deal. For we are supposing that they would be worse off under noncompliance by the (ex-)slaves than under the status quo, and Gauthier agrees that where that is so, the rational masters will not move voluntarily to the new situation.

Gauthier's example is clouded by the Prime Minister's further remark that the Masters had probably "saved themselves a revolution" in trying their deal, despite its outcome having been very contrary to expectations (p. 191). But let us assume that a revolution mounted against the Masters with their current coercive technology intact would be futile, whereas a revolution mounted after the agreement would, indeed, be successful – but only because the Masters had *voluntarily dismantled* the technology in question.

Now, one would think that they *would* move voluntarily to a situation which, after all, dominates the status quo – would, that is, if this new situation is possible. Its possibility, however, is contingent on compliance. And if the argument is that compliance is impossible, then there is bad news awaiting us. For consider the principle of constrained maximization itself, which calls upon us to forgo noncooperative gains in Prisoner's Dilemma situations. If we look at agreements generally, this attitude would seem to land us in Hobbes' "easie truth," that "Covenants are but words, and breath, having no force to oblige, contain, constrain, or protect any man, but what it has from the publique Sword."[18] The person who carries out her part of a bargain first, lays herself open to noncompliance from the second party, who has now got what he wants. Why shouldn't he take the money and run? Yet that is precisely the attitude that constrained maximization rules out. Why should things be any different when the Pareto superior situation is a move up from an arrangement originally secured by superior force alone? Why, that is, when the situation ex ante was one in which the agreement in which "Morals by Agreement" consists is *not* as yet in place. Doesn't that make it out of order to object to the initial depredations as "unfair"?

Gauthier does not, as he cannot, in general disavow the use of predatory force in interpersonal relations. Consider the rather significant subject of our dealing with animals, for instance. We do not make a Social Contract with those individuals. One reason, no doubt, is that we can't: animals are not in general capable of entering into contracts

---

[18] Hobbes, *Leviathan*, chap. XVIII, pp. 146–7.

at any very high level of sophistication, we suppose. But that isn't the only thing blocking the way to a General Mammalian Contract. The fact is that we (or at least, we carnivores) regard our present situations as preferable to those we might be in were we to constrain our behavior toward them by invoking the Lockean Proviso. The benefits are not mutual. Were the Lockean Priviso a categorical imperative, we would have to resort to the implausible move of the likes of Kant and Descartes, holding that non-human animals are "irrational," in order to justify our rather predatory behavior toward them. But we don't need to do any such thing, nor does Gauthier. We simply say, "Tough!" And we do not think we are thereby violating any duties we have toward them. In the view of us contractarians, there simply are no such duties. The foundation of duty is mutual advantage, and in the case of the animals, a contract, were one possible given current animal capabilities, would not be advantageous to us. But why is not mutual advantage a sufficient, rather than merely a necessary, condition of the rational assumption of duties? And is not the relation of slaves to masters precisely one where mutual advantage is an obvious possibility? Consider the workhorse, broken to the harness in manifest opposition to its native instincts. Still, the horse may reason that it is better off if it simply obeys orders and collects its daily allowance of oats and water than by kicking against the pricks and retaining the disposition to run off whenever its master isn't around.[19]

Second: we identify predation with the use of force. However, I wonder whether we might not also consider the case of superior powers generally as instructively akin to it, though of course not identical. Suppose that I am extremely fond of piano music, and that a certain individual, Vladimir, can supply my demand far better than I can myself (I'm a hopeless pianist). Suppose too that Vladimir is a born pianist, and I am not. We have labored equally, or perhaps he far less than I, but, owing to inborn ability, Vladimir has become a great pianist, whereas I am somewhere around the write-off level. There is nevertheless no objection whatever to his entering into exchanges with me that are, at least in some points of view, greatly to his advantage. Like Wilt Chamberlain, Vladimir cheerfully collects a modest fee from thousands of admiring music-lovers, thus accumulating wealth beyond the wilder dreams of mere professors. Now along come certain social philosophers who object to this accumulation based, for present purposes, on the

---

[19] As Gauthier points out in connection with workhorses, for instance, on p. 17. For further defense of this point of view, see Jan Narveson, "Animal Rights Revisited," in *Ethics and Animals*, edited by Harlan Miller and William Williams (Clifton, NJ: Humana Press, 1983), pp. 19–45. An important commentary, in a considerably different vein, is in the essay following mine in that collection, Annette Baier's "Knowing Our Place in the Animal World," pp. 61–78.

accidents of fortune. Why, they say, isn't Vladimir unfairly exploiting my lack of powers (and, of course, my inordinate passion for his wares)? Why shouldn't a Lockean Proviso forbid inequalities of all sorts that are due to the mere accidental distribution of powers, be they predatory or benign?

The reply is simple and convincing. Vladimir's "exploitation" of me, if that is what anyone wishes to term it, is to my advantage, whereas predatory exploitation – that is to say, exploitation properly speaking – normally is not. In exerting his superior powers, Vladimir contributes to my overall level of satisfaction, whereas the predator, in exerting his, detracts from it. It is a good answer, and the right answer. But there is a problem. In the hypothetical Hobbesian State of Nature, neither of us cares anything about the other, and if you, due to superior predatory powers, are predatorily exploiting me, that's just too bad for me. But then, that may also be the background for a bargain: you cease your predatory violence and I make it worth your while. If we then develop cooperative relations still more to our mutual advantage, as well we may, then bully for both of us! Do these incorporate in some unfair way your initial predatory gains? Must the Social Contract begin by requiring compensation from you to me for all those gains exacted by superior force? I am inclined to be dubious about this.[20]

Perhaps some suppose that these gains hang around, infecting all future transactions in an unsatisfactory manner. I think this unlikely, but in any case it doesn't clearly prove anything. Short-term consumption gains would, of course, not "hang around." So what about capital gains, so to speak? They might indeed continue into the indefinite future. But it is unclear whether this matters. For one thing, once we have respect for property rights in place, then if I am ingenious, my gain could be greater than yours in any case, for I may convert my initially lesser resources into a capital greater than yours in the process. More importantly, however, there is the fact that as time goes by, both of us are better off. Not only are we better off than we would have been had we remained in the State of Nature, but if all goes well, each of us is better off at any given time than we were in the preceding time. Even if you, who had the superior starting point by virtue of your superior predation in the status quo ante, remain ahead of me, I remain ahead of where I would otherwise have been.

We must also remember that capital is only capital. In order to derive continuing rewards from it, there must be some whose labors are rendered more efficient by its use, and normally most of them are persons other than ourselves. Our profit from ownership, therefore, will derive

---

[20] As Gauthier has noted, James Buchanan, in *The Limits of Liberty* (Chicago: The University of Chicago Press, 1975), takes a contrary view to his. See esp. pp. 23–5.

from a *further* agreement with those others regarding their remuneration for this labor. The minimum claim of the laborers will be set by the condition they would have been in had we remained in a predatory condition. But their maximum claim is quite another matter. If our labor makes you, the erstwhile predator, much better off than you were in the predatory condition, then it is also rational for you to agree to a division of it enabling us to share in these further gains. Otherwise we would have no incentive to provide this greater gain; and yet, since it is above the level you would have been in had you remained in the State of Nature, it is not rational for you to threaten a return to it (as Gauthier rightly observes).

Once the Lockean Proviso sets in, our benefits from cooperative activity follows the rule To Each His Marginal Product, and in all probability, the effects over time of initial inequalities due to previous predatory gains become trivial. (Peter Berger observes that the upward social diffusion of the bourgeoisie in Europe following the industrial revolution was "probably affected above all by the intermarriage of aristocratic men and bourgeois women (the typical bargain by which the latter obtained a title for themselves and their children, while the former were rescued from bankruptcy by the dowry bestowed on daughters by doting bourgeois fathers)."[21]).

Thus, we should not accept the argument that in settling on a beginning point that incorporates predatory gains, we are necessarily setting a bad precedent for the future. That future will, indeed, contain no predation, because we will accept as part of the initial bargain the Lockean Proviso for the future. Our predator dismantles his predatory apparatus permanently, for he realizes that in inducing me to arm myself against his predation both he and I are wasting efforts which could instead be converted into mutual gains. The initial predatory gains, however, were exacted *prior* to the onset of our Social Contract. At the time they were exacted, to exact them was not wrong, because nothing was wrong. To take the view that we must retroactively extend the Lockean Proviso to cover all past history is to suppose that morality is natural in a stronger sense of "natural" than Gauthier can accept. For he is, after all, advancing the thesis that morals are "by agreement."

On the Hobbesian starting point

When the Social Contract view is advanced as a set of propositions in abstract decision theory, as it is by Gauthier, then there is a temptation to argue that the "State of Nature" is purely an abstraction, with no possible real-world instances to concern ourselves about. But this had

---

[21] Peter Berger, *The Capitalist Revolution* (New York: Basic Books, 1986), p. 99.

better not be true. The contract is not, indeed, historical in the sense of a universal meeting of all persons at some given time. But if it is to have any real-world significance, it must be something that can happen in particular minds at particular times. And it is possible that there could be encounters between individuals neither of whom had internalized the principle of constrained maximization. A sequence of such encounters could lead to a mutual appreciation of the advantages of peace, and thus to a real bargain between those erstwhile warring parties, followed by a real-world instantiation of the very problems I have just been discussing in the slightly fanciful terminology of classical social contract theory.

Hobbes may have thought that there was actually a time when people had no morality at all. But he also thought that morality presupposes government, and the absence of government is at least more obviously a possibility, one might suppose, than the absence of morality, the lack of operative social rules of any kind at all.[22] Nevertheless, let us try to imagine a circumstance in which people regard human predation upon fellow humans with roughly the same indifference that they so regard animals' predation upon fellow animals. When A kills B, depriving B of B's hard-won goods, C merely looks on curiously, or in turn sets about attempting to get it away from A. In general, the situation would be that no one applies any sort of reinforcing epithets, nor engages generally in any other recognizable moral reinforcement. The baseline for morality in such a condition must, surely, be wherever the parties are at the time they began to appreciate the advantages of moral restraint.

All of this reflection has been on the assumption that what we have regarded as "gains" are not measured in terms of what Hobbes calls "Glory." If this happens, of course, we get into a zero-sum game (your greater glory is necessarily my lesser and vice versa), and then all bets – all hope of a mutually beneficial Social Contract – are off. In this respect, perhaps, we may accept the charge that all contractarian speculations are infected with "bourgeois values." If the overriding passion of our lives is not simply to get ahead of where we were before, but rather to get ahead *of the others*, no matter where those others or we ourselves may currently be, then gains from cooperation are impossible. That vast majority of us who (I suppose) share in the "bourgeois" orientation which settles for a good life, reckoned in terms of values that require no such comparisons, have a great interest in pointing out to any who

---

[22] R. E. Ewin, in his important though little noted book *Cooperation and Human Values* (New York: St. Martin's Press, 1981), points to the overwhelmingly fundamental role that certain kinds of cooperation play in human life, observing that it must be questionable whether there could even be language without cooperation, since discourse depends on mutual understandings that are examples of cooperation. See pp. 10–13.

suppose themselves to be otherwise in this respect that their predilections for glory will in all likelihood lead to familiar bad ends.

In the State of Nature, those who invade for gain are engaging in activities that are as "legitimate" as any others one might attempt. But in the civilized state in which we realize the gains of cooperation, invasion for gain is not legitimate, and when it occurs, it is strictly *unfair*. Those who live by plundering in the civil state have taken advantage of their fellows, who have extended, throughout the lives of the predators, their protection and forbearance – which would *not* be true in a genuinely Hobbesian State of Nature. Had they any reason to suppose that certain persons would take to plunder, they could have quickly rendered nugatory any threat of force from those quarters. The predator under the social contract, therefore, has no leg to stand on. He cannot maintain that he is entitled to his predatory gains, because there would have been no possibility of such gains had there never been any contract, and a reasonable contract would forbid predatory activities from the start. There is, therefore, no reason to worry about setting a bad precedent were there any initial predatory gains to recognize. The future is different from the past, and bygones when things were very different should be let bygones.

Relations between states

I have pointed to one area in which this theoretical discussion is more than merely theoretical, namely, our relations to the lower animals. Possibly another, and much more potentially important if so, is that of mutual relations among nation-states. There we have many complications – far too many to permit a conclusive discussion here. Moreover, we should surely reject the claim that nation-states are simply in a State of Nature. All or nearly all states have made gains because of the willing cooperation of other states – at the very least the cooperation constituted by forbearance from exploitative activities, but usually a good deal more as well. In general, that is, states have *not* been in an antecedently amoral mutual condition. Nor do modern states claim to have been.

Besides, the very existence of states is surely suspect on the contractarian view. Once we see that the Sovereign is not the answer to the initial problems posed by the Hobbesian State of Nature, we may also see that it is not the answer to those posed by civilized society, either. If all individuals deal with all other individuals *as* individuals, then the supposition that aggressive war can be waged to advantage quickly reduces to an absurdity. That is an important conclusion, surely. Still, it remains that the history of the modern world has been characterized by the emergence of groupings of states founded on military alliance and mutual noninterference pacts, the object being "collective security"

– against other similar alliances or against individually formidable states. It is hardly to be doubted that these have often been characterized by inequalities due to prior predation. And global peace was thought to be contingent on a rough equality, especially military equality, between the major coalitions. The system was (is?), of course, unstable and not very effective. But what interests us here is that its subordinate members, while very keen indeed on obtaining political independence, did not always press for the reimbursement of gains made by the coalition leaders in the process of putting together their empires. Mexico has not insisted on the return of Texas; and so on. Sometimes, to be sure, they do so insist, and sometimes an uneasy or "cold" peace ensues when hostilities cease, but issues about land claims are not really settled.

The point here is that insofar as wars and other international disagreements are instances of unilateral abrogation of reasonable moral constraints, it is not clear that Gauthier's rule is going to make for peace. Certainly it will not in the short run; in the longer run, the question is more difficult. One can argue that if we insist always on the Lockean rule, the message conveyed will be that war is futile, since no long-run gains from it are possible. But the alternative message is that any nation that does make such gains is going to have to remain indefinitely on a war footing in order to hang onto them, since as soon as it disarms it will be forced to divest itself of those gains. Can there be any doubt at all that at least in material terms (and numbers of lives lost), the Middle East Arabs would be better off today had they simply made peace with Israel at the start, despite the latter's arguably wrongful incursions into their territory? Material benefits aren't everything, of course. But it should surely be matter for doubt whether the particular kind of "nonmaterial" values that reinforce bloody and intractable conflicts are all that terrific.

But that gets us into areas lying beyond the confines of this investigation. As said before, the discussion here does not pretend to be conclusive, but only to cast some doubt on an interesting and important feature of Gauthier's work.

Summary

The persuasiveness of the contractarian theory lies in the fact that it secures the weight of our nonmoral reasons on behalf of moral constraints. Only thus can it claim that *any* rational person will be bound by these considerations. In order for this crucial aspect of the theory to be effective, we must show that the envisaged "starting points" for the theory are ones about which we must be concerned. We must be sure that the contractarian machinery incorporates no spurious normative inputs in the process of generating moral results. This concern motivates queries about Gauthier's arguments for minimax relative concession, on the ground that the basis appealed to – "equal rationality" – appears to be in principle spurious, though some nonspurious (but uncertain) reasons are suggested. I have also queried Gauthier's condition for the retroactive application of his fundamental principle against the use of force and fraud, the Lockean Proviso. Though fully accepting the proviso itself, doubts arise concerning its application, which denies continued possession of their gains to those who previously gained from predation. This would seem to preclude benefits to some parties under some conceivable conditions. I then asked how this argument would apply to real-world situations of war and peace. My argument here is that extending civilized protections to all depends on taking Hobbes seriously, in particular on the point that we are all essentially equal in our capacity for predation. That assumption, plausible at the level of one individual against another, is not obviously so at the group level. I do not claim to have resolved this issue, which may appreciably effect our understanding of the contractarian theory.

10. Equalizing concessions in the pursuit of justice: A discussion of Gauthier's bargaining solution*

Jean Hampton

In *Morals by Agreement*, David Gauthier embraces the Hobbesian thought that morality is authoritative for us only insofar as it advances our interests. But this thesis on authority has implications for the content of morality: if morality is to further our interests, then, says Gauthier, it must be possible to generate it "as a rational constraint from the non-moral premises of rational choice." But how can this be done? Gauthier's problem is to explain, first, how unattached, mutually unconcerned utility-maximizing individuals whose interests frequently conflict can come to agree on the *terms* upon which it would be rational for each of them to cooperate with one another; second, how they could be trusted to comply with these terms; and third, how to define the initial position from which cooperation should proceed in order for the resulting distribution of cooperative benefits to be fair. His solutions to all three problems are controversial, but here I want to evaluate his attempt to solve the first problem by defining terms of cooperation using what he calls the principle of minimax relative concession (hereafter called the MRC principle).[1]

Gauthier elaborates on and defends this principle in Chapter V of *Morals by Agreement*. Consider, he says, that in the first stage of a bargaining process, each party advances a claim. If (as is likely) these claims are incompatible, there is a second stage in which each party offers concessions to the others by withdrawing some portion of his original

*Excerpted with minor additions by the author by permission of the *Canadian Journal of Philosophy* from "Can We Agree on Morals?" by Jean Hampton, in *Canadian Journal of Philosophy* 18 (1988): 331–56. Copyright © 1988 by *Canadian Journal of Philosophy*.
[1] I say something about his solution to the second and third problems in "Two Faces of Contractarian Thought," Chapter 3 in this volume, and focus on his solution to the second problem in "Constrained Maximization and the Nature of Reason," unpublished manuscript.

claim and proposing an alternative outcome. Concession making continues until a set of mutually compatible claims is reached, or until the parties are deadlocked.

How much is it rational for an individual to concede? We suppose that cooperation is better for each person than noncooperation, so that each person must not concede so little as to deadlock the group, or so much as to be excluded from the benefits of cooperation. Where is the happy medium for each? Gauthier argues that it is reached when each party makes concessions that are (as nearly as possible) *equal* to the concessions of the others.

But how does one measure and compare concessions? Starting from the assumption that a cardinal measure of intrapersonal utility is possible using the von Neumann-Morgenstern method, Gauthier defines the concept of *relative concession*: if the initial bargaining position affords some person utility u^* and he claims an outcome affording him $u\#$, then if he concedes an outcome affording him utility u, the absolute magnitude of his concessions is $u\# - u$, and of complete concession $u\# - u^*$, so that the relative magnitude of his concession is $(u\# - u)/(u\# - u^*)$. Notice that because relative concession, so defined, is invariant with respect to positive linear transformation of utility functions, it is possible to make interpersonal comparisons with the measure. Gauthier's claim is that "an outcome should be selected only if the greatest or maximum relative concession it requires is as small as possible, or a minimum, that is, no greater than the maximum relative concession required by every other outcome" (p. 137).

The principle of minimax relative concession only seems plausible as a definition of *distributive* justice, and not what might be called justice in treatment (e.g., the sort of justice that is supposed to exist in procedures for criminal trials, or in hiring procedures), or justice in conflict resolution.[2] But Gauthier does not intend this principle to govern distributions from all joint ventures. Normally, he argues, the market is the appropriate distributive tool in a society. But there are interactive situations in which the market "fails" and the parties will perceive the distribution of costs and benefits as "inappropriate." When does the market fail and why does it do so? Gauthier's answers to these questions are unclear. Certainly he believes the market fails when the presence of externalities means either that people can benefit from a nonexcludable good without paying for it or that they are forced to pay costs associated with a good's production without receiving any benefits from it. Presumably what it means to say that the market fails in these situations is that it does not motivate people to engage in activity that will be both

---

[2] See Gregory Kavka's review of Gauthier's book "Morals by Agreement," *Mind* 96: 117–21, which essentially makes this point.

collectively and individually rational. Hence, one might formulate on Gauthier's behalf the following definition of market failure: the market fails whenever the rational exchange activities of rational persons are unable to move the parties to the Pareto-efficient outcome. As we discuss (and question) in what follows, Gauthier believes markets fail in this way in the production of private goods involving rent (understood in the economist's sense) and in the production of private goods in circumstances where each party is essential to the cooperative surplus, that is, no other person is available who can substitute for him and his contribution is necessary for the good's production (at least at a certain level).

Whenever the market fails, Gauthier argues that people need to engage in "a new mode of interacting" (p. 117), which he calls "cooperation." Pure market interaction is *not* really cooperative interaction in his view; it is only exchange in pursuit of individual goals. Genuine cooperation exists when people, in order to exclude free riding and parasitism, ignore the market and agree to use a mutually advantageous principle to determine the distribution of benefits from their interactions. The MRC principle is supposed to be this mutually advantageous principle.

In examining the principle's operation, I follow Gauthier's practice of considering only examples in which it is supposed that utilities are linear with monetary values, so that the MRC's distribution of utility is identical to its distribution of money. This supposition is meant merely to facilitate ease of discussion. But note that by using it, Gauthier suggests that there is a way to make cardinal interpersonal comparisons of utility, which many believe is impossible. Even more worryingly, the supposition causes him to run roughshod over the issue of whether justice involves the distribution of resources or of welfare. Because the MRC principle distributes utility, it is a welfarist conception of justice, but by using this supposition, Gauthier may be constructing examples that really appeal to us only because they involve what we intuitively take to be correct distributions of resources. I will not pursue this issue further, but the reader should remember that the following discussion of the operation of the MRC principle using Gauthier's supposition is importantly problematic for a resource theorist.[3]

Would we approve of the MRC principle's operation in practice? Gauthier shows (pp. 152–3) that a division of utility according to this principle

---

[3] For more on the issue whether or not justice involves resources or welfare, see Ronald Dworkin's two articles: "What is Equality? Part I: Equality of Welfare," *Philosophy and Public Affairs* 10(3) (Summer 1981): 185–246; "What is Equality? Part II: Equality of Resources," *Philosophy and Public Affairs* 10(4) (Fall 1981): 283–345. See also John Roemer's response to Dworkin, "Equality of Talent," *Economics and Philosophy* 1 (1985): 151–87. I am indebted to Edward Green for discussions of this point.

results in each person getting what he would have made on his own, plus an equal share of the cooperative surplus if it comes in a fixed, fully divisible form (such as money). So, consider Abel and Mabel, each of whom can make 5% a year on their money in a passbook savings account, but reap 10% a year if they pool their money and invest it in a money market account. I will presume that no other person could invest instead of either one of them (so that each is necessary to realize the cooperative surplus) and that utilities are linear with monetary values. Suppose that at least $700 is needed to establish the fund, and that Abel has $400 and Mabel $600. If each invests separately in the bank, Abel will earn $20, and Mabel $30. But if their money is jointly invested in the money market account, they would receive – as such accounts *now* operate – $40 and $60, respectively. I will call the present principle of distribution in these acounts the *Principle of Proportionality* in distribution, which is that *in a cooperative endeavor, each person receives that portion of the total benefit that is proportionate to her contribution to it.* Notice that this principle can *only* be used in situations where the contributions of each party to the cooperative surplus can be determined, and in the money market case this is clearly so.

However, according to the MRC principle, Abel has conceded too much if he accepts only $40:

For Abel:
$u\#$ = 470 [i.e., 400 + 20 (the amount he could make on his own) + 50 (the entire cooperative surplus)]
u = 440 [i.e., 400 + 40 (the amount we are supposing Abel to concede)]
u^* = 420 [i.e., 400 + 20 (the amount he could make on his own)]
Therefore:
$$\frac{470 - 440}{470 - 420} = \frac{3}{5}$$

For Mabel:
$u\#$ = 680 [i.e., 600 + 30 (the amount she could make on her own) + 50 (the entire cooperative surplus)]
u = 660 [i.e., 600 + 60 (the amount Mabel would get if Abel accepted $40)]
u^* = 630 [i.e., 600 + 30 (the amount Mabel could make on her own)]
Therefore:
$$\frac{680 - 660}{680 - 630} = \frac{2}{5}$$

Their concessions are equal (½ and ½) when Abel gets $5 more ($445) and Mabel $5 less ($655). So Mabel, the bigger investor, prefers the proportionality principle to the MRC principle, whereas Abel's preference is the reverse.

The MRC division would certainly unsettle contemporary bankers, but should it worry us? Let us start by evaluating it from a moral point of view. In Chapter III on the market, Gauthier argues for a conception of morality as "an impartial constraint on the direct pursuit of individual utility" (p. 95). Impartiality in the context of market interactions is defined more precisely as follows: each person "has a sufficient reason to consider interaction with his fellows to be impartial only in so far as it affords him a return equal to the services he contributes through the use of his capacities" (p. 100). Hence, a division of goods produced by a cooperative interaction is partial to some, and thus in conflict with morality, when they are able to reap rewards from *others'* services.[4] Gauthier gives a sustained argument that market distributions are impartial in this sense (see p. 95ff.). So when the market fails and unfair distributions result, he supports the use of a principle that will effect the impartial distribution.

But doesn't the MRC principle violate rather than realize this concept of impartiality? If Abel receives $445 rather than $440, isn't the extra $5 taken from what rightfully ought to be Mabel's share? Gauthier would deny this; in the example, the cooperative surplus is only possible if *both* of them contribute. Therefore, "since neither can gain any part of the cooperative surplus without the other, then each is equally responsible for making it available, and so is entitled to an equal share of it" (pp. 152–3). But this argument is dubious. Suppose Mabel had only invested the same amount ($400) as Abel; in this case, the total yield from their investment is $80, and the MRC principle gives them $40 each (exactly what the proportionality principle would give them). So in this case, each dollar invested by Abel and Mabel earns him or her $0.10. Now suppose that Abel's contribution remains the same, but that Mabel invests $200 more, for a total of $600. That extra $200 invested (over and above the original $400 investment) yields $20 in interest by itself, but on the MRC principle, Mabel receives only $15 of it. This means that each of her additional 200 dollars invested only earns her $0.075; the other $0.025 goes to Abel *despite the fact that he has done nothing for it.* So Abel is being allowed to benefit from *her* contribution in exactly the way Gauthier said was a sign of a partial system of distribution.[5]

---

[4] I would argue that this notion of partiality is not an exclusively capitalist idea; it is at the heart of Marx's argument using the labor theory of value that the laborer is exploited by the capitalist.

[5] David Copp has suggested an interesting response to this argument: Consider that Mabel couldn't earn the $20 without Abel's help, but could only earn $10. This means the

Table 10–1

Abel's contri- bution	Mabel's contri- bution	Payoff from MRC to Abel	Payoff from MRC to Mabel	Rate of return per dollar invested		Mabel's share of investment profits
				For Abel	For Mabel	
400	400	40	40	0.10	0.10	0.5
400	600	45	55	0.112	0.091	0.55
400	800	50	70	0.125	0.087	0.583
400	1000	55	85	0.138	0.082	0.607

Table 10–1 shows how, on the MRC division, Mabel's investment dollars earn less as she contributes more, whereas Abel's investment dollars earn more despite making no increase in his contributions. Moreover, in the last column, we see that although Mabel's share of the profits goes up, the rate at which it goes up decreases despite a constant rate of increase in her contributions, revealing once again that Abel is able to enjoy some of the increased profits made possible by Mabel without doing any work for them.

Mabel, therefore, seems right to conclude that whenever a contributor invests more in a cooperative venture than her partner(s), the MRC principle will allow some of the proceeds of the extra investment to be filched by the lower investor, thus allowing him to have a partial "free ride" on the back of the higher investor. Indeed, one might even argue that the MRC principle allows Abel to charge rent for his contribution to the cooperative venture. The notion of economic rent, to use Gauthier's definition, is "the premium certain factor services command, over and above full cost of supply, because there is no alternative to meet the demand" (p. 272). If there were someone competing with Abel to cooperate with Mabel, then he should offer to split profits using the proportionality principle, thereby making it rational for her to drop Abel and cooperate with him. When there is no such competitor, Abel can

cooperative surplus is $10. Isn't it fair to split it, so that her fair share is $15 and his is $5 – exactly the MRC division? This way of looking at the example is revealing. Abel is trying to argue that his $400 should be "counted" in determining his share of the profits *more than once* if his partner contributes more than he does. Abel is saying to Mabel that his $400 not only allowed her to reap high profits from her $400, but that it also allowed her to reap profit from her $200. Whenever Mabel increases her investment share, Abel smugly points to his initial contribution to argue that it played a role in the return that this share was able to make. But while it is true that Mabel could not have earned the $20 without Abel's help, it is equally true that she could not have earned it without the help of her own $400 contribution. So why does Abel's $400 investment entitle him to claim a portion of the profit from her additional $200, whereas her own $400 investment yields no such entitlement?

use the MRC principle to derive profits from his cooperative venture with Mabel that are greater than the cost of supplying his contribution, because as that contribution remains constant, his profits go up.

The argument just made attempts to show that the divisions effected by the MRC principle are not in accordance with what we (and Gauthier) intuitively think of as "impartial" or "fair." But intuitive appeals are notorious for not decisively singling out one principle of justice. As we have just seen, both the MRC principle and the proportionality rule can be made to appear intuitively plausible; but there are other principles that can be made to seem just as intuitively appealing.[6]

The "mushiness" of our intuitions on these matters gives us good reason to turn to a contractarian methodology in the hopes that it will persuasively single out a unique distributive principle. Gauthier insists that this methodology singles out the MRC principle, but my argument against the MRC principle suggests that his contract language only disguises an implicit appeal to our intuitions about fairness. Why, after all, should contractors agree that concessions must be equal in the bargain? Why wouldn't they insist on equality of reward for contribution (which is what the proportionality principle respects) or (as another critic has wondered)[7] equality of utility in outcomes? Depending on what intuitions one has, one will prefer a certain method of reward, and it is easy to imagine (and define) contractors in a hypothetical contract situation who share these intuitions and preferences. But such imagining hardly counts as proof.

Whether or not contractarianism is a moral theory that is genuinely different from ethical intuitionism depends upon whether we can develop a way of using contract talk that is not simply a cover for an appeal to our ethical intuitions. In what follows, I want to outline a new contractarian procedure that has the promise of being more than such a cover, and that, as it happens, does not yield the MRC principle as the agreed-upon solution. Moreover, if one accepts, with Gauthier, that market distributions normally exemplify impartiality, then one needs a

[6] Consider the following argument by Mabel for yet another principle dividing cooperative profits: "While it is true," she could say, "that from an investment of $400 from Abel and $600 from me, $50 is the cooperative surplus, and while it is true that both of us are equally necessary to securing this surplus, we do not play equal roles in securing the *amount* of this cooperative surplus. My contribution yields ⅔ of that surplus and Abel's yields ⅓. Hence, of that cooperative surplus, I should get $33.33 (⅔ of $50) + $30 (what I could have made on my own), and he should get $16.66 (⅓ of $50) + $20 (what he could have made on his own), or $63.33 for me and $36.66 for him." Note that on this way of determining profits, Abel receives *less* and Mabel *more* than they would receive from either the MRC principle *or* the proportionality rule. So now we have a third rule of distributive justice, which is defended by an argument that has the same "ring of fairness" as the arguments for the other two principles.
[7] See David Braybrooke, "The Maximum Claims of Gauthier's Bargaining: Are The Fixed Social Inequalities Acceptable?" and "Inequalities Not Conceded Yet: A Rejoinder To Gauthier's Reply (*Dialogue: Canadian Philosophical Review* 21 [1982]: 411–30, 445–8).

contract argument that can identify a principle that reproduces the market outcome in situations of market failure. The argument I present was also developed in order to allow us to make such an identification.

But before presenting the argument, a brief digression on the concept of economic rent is necessary. As an example of someone whose salary includes rent, Gauthier gives us Wayne Gretzky, who prefers playing hockey with the Edmonton Oilers to some other occupation as long as he gets a certain minimal salary, but who is paid a far higher salary given his unique and remarkable talents as a hockey player. Gretzky is a monopolist, whose earnings are supposed to be greater than the true cost to him of supplying his talents to the team. Thus, Gauthier supposes that taxation of the rent in Gretzky's salary would not affect efficiency or natural freedom in the market (p. 273).

But does Gretzky's high salary really include rent? Consider the best explanation of why he is paid so much – he gets outside offers. Suppose Gretzky began his hockey career with a salary that was a shade more than the amount that would leave him indifferent between playing hockey with Edmonton and (let's say) being a bartender at a local club. Then suppose the New York Rangers come along and offer him much more, knowing that it will take a higher salary to lure him to New York. They offer him a shade more than the amount that leaves him indifferent between playing hockey in New York and playing hockey in Edmonton. Let's suppose that the Los Angeles Kings also want Gretzky and know they must outbid New York if they will succeed in getting him to their city; so they offer him a shade more than the amount that leaves him indifferent between playing in New York and playing in Los Angeles. Now Edmonton hear of these offers, and what do they do? In order to ensure that Gretzky is not rational to go to L.A., their offer must be a shade higher than the amount that leaves him indifferent between playing in L.A. and playing with them. Suppose they make such an offer and he accepts it. Is there rent in his salary? No, because the salary is covering his *opportunity* costs, that is, costs defined by economists in terms of opportunities forgone.[8] If Edmonton paid him anything less, Wayne would be losing money by supplying his services to them rather than to Los Angeles or New York.

Gauthier seems confused about how to compute costs in the Gretzky case. The only opportunity costs he takes seriously are the costs of the nonhockey alternatives for Wayne; but clearly the example shows that Wayne has hockey-related opportunity costs. Note also that if he were taxed on a salary that barely covered these costs, there would be profound implications for economic efficiency and market freedom (as Noz-

---

[8] For example, see Jack Hirshleifer, *Price Theory and Applications,* third edition (Englewood Cliffs, NJ: Prentice-Hall, 1984), pp. 176–7.

ick originally realized in his "Wilt Chamberlain" example). For example, if Wayne knew that he could not receive all of the salary offered to him by Los Angeles insofar as that was judged to include rent, he would not find it rational to leave Edmonton. The tax would interfere with his market choices and benefit the small number of Edmonton fans at the expense of the large number of Gretzky fans in Los Angeles.

With this understanding of the way in which markets set salary, we return to the construction of a new style of contract argument identifying a principle applicable to market-failure situations. Let us start with Gauthier's assumption that in the contract situation, people are determinate individuals for whom it is common knowledge what each person's factor endowments are. However, departing from Gauthier's model, imagine that in this situation each individual has the option of cooperating or not cooperating with one or more of the others in something that I will call a "cooperative company." These are not groups of people established to produce any particular good, but rather coalitions of people who agree to cooperate with one another in the production of goods in market-failure situations. Accordingly, each individual thinks of herself as "up for sale" in just the way Wayne Gretzky does; she offers herself (and thus her factor endowments) to any prospective company "buyer" and what it will pay her for her work in producing a good along with others will be her "cut" of the cooperative surplus that she helped to create. But if she does not like the salary offered her by any prospective company buyer, she is free either to offer her services to other buyers who are prepared to pay her more, or else to form a new societal coalition with others in which the cooperative surplus will be split in a way that is more advantageous for her. Those companies who wish to hire her must strive to cover her opportunity costs in just the way that Wayne's hockey teams must do.

The competition among "societal employment agencies" is very much like the competition between Nozick's competing protection agencies. A market emerges among cooperative companies as they compete for employee-cooperators. What will be the results of the competition? Employees will tend to converge on *one* cooperative company, insofar as the more employees a company has, the more substantial the good they can produce and thus the greater the cooperative benefits that the company can make possible for them. But which company will everyone decide to join? Answer: the group that is prepared to give each individual her marginal product. No group that pays anybody *more* than her marginal product will survive because it will not be able to cover its costs by doing so. But no group that pays anyone less than her marginal product seems likely to survive either, because by doing so it makes it rational for that individual to realign herself with others who are prepared to offer her more.

It has been shown that in situations of perfect competition, individuals will receive their marginal product.[9] So a perfectly competitive market will naturally reward people in the way that any contractor in the previous situation would prefer. But there is a problem determining exactly what any individual's marginal product is in one of the "market-failure" situations about which Gauthier is most concerned. Whenever there is a "collective step good," that is, a cooperative venture that requires a certain level of contribution before *any* of the good can be produced, each individual who participates in the good's production can justifiably claim that the entire surplus is his marginal product since, but for him, there would be no surplus. But clearly you cannot give everyone the entire profit! Gauthier's MRC principle essentially proposes that the profit be divided up equally. But rather than be content with this answer, which has (as I have argued before) only the appearance of fairness, we should return to the contract situation and ask, "What would people who were considering whether or not to enter a cooperative venture with others be able to demand as 'pay' for their cooperation in these special circumstances?"

Suppose a cooperative company offered an individual the MRC division. She might be happy with this if she were a small investor, but if she were a large investor, she would prefer any higher offer, and for her, the proportionality principle would be a better offer. Moreover, if the large investors were to form their own society, it seems they would be rational to offer one another distribution according to this principle rather than the MRC principle, because the latter would make it rational for those large investors contributing more than the others to pull out of this cooperative company and pursue alternative investment possibilities. Small investors could ill afford alienating large investors, and large investors could ill afford alienating one another. So the proportionality principle appears to be a better candidate than the MRC principle for offering the equivalent of the marginal product in these situations.

I am reluctant to say that this principle *is* the solution, because I suspect that a more complicated economic analysis, probably using a richer specification of the contract situation and relying on theories of the core[10]

---

[9] See Joseph M. Ostroy, "The No-Surplus Condition as a Characterization of Perfectly Competitive Equilibrium," *Journal of Economic Theory* 22 (1980): 183–207; and Louis Makowsky and Joseph M. Ostroy, "Vickrey-Clarke-Groves Mechanisms and Perfect Competition," *Journal of Economic Theory* 24 (1987): 244–61.

[10] The core is a notion in game theory defined as a set of agreements among players that (1) is Pareto-optimal; (2) cannot be bettered, from the point of view of any one player, by going it alone; and (3) cannot be bettered, from the point of view of some proper subset of players, by leaving the agreement set and forming an independent coalition. Note, therefore, that in the core, each individual player and each coalition must receive its noncooperative maximin payoff. For a more complete discussion, see Michael Bachrach, *Economics and the Theory of Games* (London: Macmillan, 1976), p. 124ff. One might

might be necessary to prove it. But the advantage of this way of defining the contract problem is that *proof* for the outcome may be possible. Moreover the approach is interestingly similar to market-style contract arguments developed by Nozick and me[11] to argue for certain governmental structures. Its market orientation would seem to make it an attractive approach for market enthusiasts such as Gauthier.[12] It may well be the implementation of Edgeworth's idea that with a sufficiently large number of agents, the only core solutions are those that mimic the workings of the market.[13]

diagnose Gauthier's mistake in his contractarian methodology as one of ignoring (3) above; the rational solution to a bargain depends not only upon how much each could get by herself, but also upon how much each could get if she joined alternative coalitions.

[11] See Nozick's *Anarchy, State and Utopia* (New York: Basic Books, 1974), chapter 2; and my *Hobbes and the Social Contract Tradition* (Cambridge: Cambridge University Press, 1986), chapter 6.

[12] However, despite its market orientation, Gauthier may dislike my reinterpretation of the contract problem, since in his book he restricts his analysis to the situation in which an individual only has the option of joining *one* society (although he admits the possibility of having more than one option in "The Social Contract: Individual Decision or Collective Bargain?" in *Foundations and Applications of Decision Theory,* vol. II, edited by Cliff Hooker, Jim Leach, and Edward McClennen [Dordrecht, Holland: D. Reidel [1978], p. 47–67). In terms of my discussion, this would mean that individuals would be prevented from forming alternative coalitions of cooperators, with the result that there could be only one societal investment opportunity for each individual. But why should we restrict the contract problem in this way? *To do so is to disallow the possibility of an obvious market solution to the problem of division in cooperative situations.* Nonetheless, suppose we accept Gauthier's unargued-for restriction. It is still the case that the MRC division is in trouble, because even within *one* society, people have multiple cooperative opportunities, and are thus in a market. To see this, suppose Mabel is irritated by the Gauthier division and hears about another person, called Gable, who has $400 and who wishes to invest it with the help of a partner in another money market fund that also requires at least $700 to be established. (Again, suppose for the sake of argument that Able and Gable are prevented from pooling their resources, and no person other than Mabel can or will invest with either of them.) She reasons: I can invest $300 with Abel and $300 with Gable, and receive more interest in total than I would receive had I invested all $600 with Abel. (She receives $10 more.) She receives more because she is now the lower investor relative to each of them and is thus able to enjoy some of the benefits produced by their higher investments. Given the advantages that the MRC principle gives to lower contributors, people will find it rational, whenever possible, to distribute their investments such that contributions to cooperative endeavors are equal. And to the extent that people succeed in this strategy, *they will be mimicking the distribution according to the proportionality principle* because whenever people invest with others on equal terms, distribution according to the MRC principle and distribution according to the principle of proportionality are the same!

So if people in Gauthier's contract situation believe that they will have competing opportunities to engage in cooperative endeavors (as he defines them) in the only society that they are allowed to join, then a market for cooperators in nonmarket situations exists for them, and the large investors, in virtue of their resources, will be highly valued in this market. The large investors can use this fact to gain bargaining clout. Specifically, they can say to the lower contributors: "look, you might as well accept our proportionality principle because, given the existence of this market, we have a strategy for ensuring that we get (at least) what it would distribute to us (and maybe more) even if the MRC principle is selected."

[13] This idea grew out of correspondence with Robert Sugden.

But the market orientation of this method would trouble those who are hostile toward markets (e.g., Marxists). Wouldn't one have to use moral notions or morally loaded concepts to argue for it? And will not moral reasons need to be given for assuming that the people in the contract procedure are fully determinate individuals rather than people whose identities are pared down in some fashion by a veil of ignorance? Finally, if a richer specification of the contract situation is necessary in order to get a proof of the results of the bargaining, will not these additional specifications be potentially morally loaded? In my view, it is probably correct to answer "yes" to all of these questions. However, the need to provide moral grounding for this style of contract argument raises no special difficulties for it as opposed to its contractarian competitors. Those contractarians who understand the social contract as specifying how much any individual ought to *get* of the available social resources subject to certain restrictions and constraints such as the veil of ignorance must argue why that approach, with those restrictions and constraints, is preferable to an approach that regards the contract as specifying how much an individual is *worth* (assuming that she is fully defined as an individual). Contemporary contractarians have been too ready to follow Rawls in assuming that only the former statement of the contract problem is possible. But once the latter possibility is raised, an advocate of either approach is under pressure to give reasons for preferring his favorite. I cannot see how moral considerations can fail to be relevant in providing these reasons, so that it seems impossible for contractarians such as Gauthier to claim that this methodology can generate morality *entirely* out of nonmoral components, but the hope (raised by Rawls) that it could provide such a justification is probably a pipe dream.

So getting rid of the appeal to ethical intuitions *within* the argument does not rule out the fact that support for the argument itself may require such an appeal. However, the "market" approach to the contract problem avoids having such appeals play such a large role in the functioning of the contract method as to make it doubtful whether or not contracting is doing any work at all in the argument.

Nonetheless, I do not think this style of contractarian argument can be ultimately successful in defining justice. As with Gauthier's argument, it still starts from an inadequate understanding of the problem bargainers must solve if their solution is to illuminate the nature of justice. If we ask, along with Gauthier, which conception of justice determinate individuals would agree upon in a hypothetical choice situation, we have probably already admitted injustice into the bargaining situation since the skills, characteristics, and relationships of determinate people – that is, real people – are created in ways that reflect the injustices and inequalities of real societies. Justice, as Rawls has said, is not only concerned with the relationships that prevail among human beings, but also with the forms of socialization that help to create these individuals. Hence, a contract situation adequate to the task of defining justice has to be more Rawlsian: individual bargainers must be concerned not merely with how much they will get, but also with how well they will develop in societies governed by alternative conceptions of justice.

I have argued elsewhere that this Rawlsian perspective creeps into Gauthier's thinking late in *Morals by Agreement*.[14] Those who are attracted to contractarian forms of argument should not forget what Gauthier very nearly does, namely, that in view of the profound impact of social institutions on our individual identity as determinate persons, political justice must be the first (albeit certainly not the only) concern of moral theorists.

[14] See "Two Faces of Contractarian Thought," Chapter 3 in this volume.

11. Gauthier's approach to distributive justice and other bargaining solutions

Wulf Gaertner and Marlies Klemisch-Ahlert

Adam Smith asserted that by pursuing his own interest, the individual "frequently promotes that of the society more effectually than when he really intends to promote it."[1] Smith used the metaphor that the individual is "led by an invisible hand to promote an end which was no part of his intention." Economists in modern times have refined and reformulated this ingenious idea and have cast it into the following theorem: Given a number of (ideal) conditions, optimizing behavior on the part of individuals and firms yields an efficient (Pareto-optimal) outcome for society. The ideal competitive system presupposes that the agents' behavior is mutually independent, noncooperative, fully rational, and instrumental. Via a system of prices, the market mechanism takes decisions for the whole of society. However, Pareto-efficiency no longer holds if externalities arise. Then the pursuit of self-interest in a competitive environment may result in suboptimal outcomes. "When the market fails, each person, seeking to maximize her utility given the strategies she expects others to choose, fails to maximize her utility given the utilities those others receive. The equilibrium outcome of mutually utility-maximizing responses is not optimal."[2]

Gauthier considers cooperation as the rational response to market failure. In his view, cooperative bargaining is a mode of conduct that allows each individual to rationally participate in the production of a societal surplus. "Where the invisible hand fails to direct each person, mindful only of her own gain, to promote the benefit of all, cooperation provides a visible hand."[3] In his bargaining approach, Gauthier attempts

[1] Adam Smith, *An Inquiry into the Nature and Causes of the Wealth of Nations* (London: Home University Library, 1776), chap. II, bk. IV.
[2] David Gauthier, *Morals by Agreement* (Oxford: Oxford University Press, 1986), p. 116.
[3] Ibid., p. 113.

to link distributive concerns and moral decisions to a conception of rational interaction that lets individually rational bargainers reach an agreement where everyone forgoes part of his (her) potential gain. More precisely, the individuals agree on a principle that guarantees that the maximal relative concession is minimized. Gauthier finds his own approach preferable to the Nash bargaining model, which, in his view, proposes the maximization of some aggregate quantity of utilities, a concern the individual bargainer cannot be assumed to care about. As we point out in this essay, the Nash solution can, however, be interpreted as the end point of a sequence of mutual concessions among the bargainers so that for us at least, this proposal appears to lend itself to an individually maximizing interpretation.

The structure of the essay is as follows. In the first section, we present Nash's much discussed bargaining solution. We briefly refer to Kaneko and Nakamura's Nash Social Welfare Function in this context. The following section is devoted to an approach proposed by Kalai and Smorodinski. The third section starts out from a bargaining scheme suggested by Zeuthen and then discusses Gauthier's resolution mechanism. We end with some concluding remarks.

Nash's bargaining solution

Nash[4] formulated his approach to bargaining for a two-person situation; a generalization to an n-person society is, however, straightforward. The economic situations Nash himself had in mind were the bilateral monopoly, the trade relationship between two countries, and the negotiations between entrepreneurs and trade unions. Nash carefully pointed out that the bargaining problem he was analyzing had to be viewed as an idealization. Why? Because it was assumed that "the two individuals are highly rational, that each can accurately compare his desires for various things, that they are equal in bargaining skill, and that each has full knowledge of the tastes and preferences of the other."[5] Nash described a bargaining situation as a situation in which the individuals involved "have the opportunity to collaborate for mutual benefit in more than one way." For Nash, a bargaining solution determines "the amount of satisfaction each individual should expect to get from the situation"[6] on the basis of rational behavior.

Before going into more details, let us introduce some notation and definitions. A nonempty set of alternatives, denoted by X, is given consisting of all logically possible results (or outcomes) of the bargaining process. X is assumed to include lotteries between finite numbers of

[4] J. F. Nash, "The Bargaining Problem," *Econometrica* 18 (1950): 155–62.
[5] Ibid., p. 155.
[6] Ibid.

results. Furthermore, it is assumed that there exists an alternative x_o in X resulting from disagreement. The social state x_o is often called the status quo. It is postulated that each individual expresses his preferences over alternatives in X in terms of numerical utilities, more precisely, in terms of a von Neumann-Morgenstern utility function that is determined up to positive affine transformations of the utility scale. The von Neumann-Morgenstern type of utility function is cardinal so that the consideration of utility differences becomes meaningful. An interpersonal comparison of utilities is, however, excluded since each individual is allowed to transform his (her) utility in an arbitrary way, as long as this transformation is positive affine.

A bargaining problem is solved, if an alternative is found to which all individuals agree. If the individuals do not come to an agreement, the chosen alternative is the status quo. In order to develop the determination of a bargaining solution in X, the standard approach is to consider the image of the pair (X, x_o) under the utility functions of the n individuals in an n-dimensional utility space and to define a bargaining situation in that space. In other words, the bargaining problem is mapped from some economic environment to its corresponding utility possibility set.

Let $S \subset IR^n$ be a compact and convex set of feasible utility vectors, and let $d \in S, d = (d_1, d_2, \ldots, d_n)$ be the status quo point (or disagreement point), with $N = \{1, 2, \ldots, n\}$ being the set of individuals or players. The pair (S, d) is called a bargaining situation if there is at least one $s \in S$ such that $d < s$. A bargaining solution is a function f that defines for each bargaining situation (S, d) a point $f(S, d) \in S$. In other words, a solution is a scheme that assigns to each bargaining situation a feasible utility vector. Solutions in the commodity space are those alternatives in X, which are mapped by the utility functions of the n individuals onto the utility vector $f(S, d)$. Nash wanted a solution to satisfy a particular set of axioms. This set has been reduced by Luce and Raiffa, and others, to the following four conditions:

Condition 1. The bargaining solution is invariant with respect to positive affine transformations of the individual utility functions.

   The players can transform their utility scales independently, that is, without considering the transformation(s) other players are using. The utility payoffs that are assigned to the players will then, of course, change. The underlying allocations in the commodity space, however, remain the same.

Condition 2. A bargaining solution always chooses a Pareto-efficient outcome.

   If $x \in S$ and there exists another point $y \in S$ such that $y > x$, then $x \neq f(S, d)$.

Condition 3. If the bargaining situation is symmetric, then $x_1 = x_2 = \cdots = x_n$ for $f(S, d) = (x_1, x_2, \ldots, x_n)$.

   A bargaining situation (S, d) is called symmetric if $d_1 = d_2 = \cdots = d_n$

and for all $s = (s_1, s_2, \ldots, s_n) \in S$ and bijections $\pi : \mathbb{R}^n \mapsto \mathbb{R}^n$, $s_\pi = (s_{\pi(1)}, s_{\pi(2)}, \ldots, s_{\pi(n)}) \in S$.

Condition 4. For every two bargaining situations (S,d) and (T,d) with $S \subset T$, if $f(T,d) \in S$, then $f(S,d) = f(T,d)$.

If $x = f(T,d)$ and the feasible set is reduced in size to S, then it is required that x remains the solution in the smaller set if x is still feasible. Unfortunately, the name tag "independence of irrelevant alternatives" for this condition has caused a lot of confusion because of Arrow's well-known condition of the same name.[7] Nash's requirement can be interpreted as a rationality condition under set contraction. In the social-choice literature this requirement is known as Property α or the Chernoff condition. Kalai remarks that the condition can also be viewed in a different way.[8] Starting from the set S with its solution $f(S,d)$, one considers an enlargement of this set to T. The condition then requires that one does not pick a different alternative among the old ones because of the addition of new elements.

Consider any two utility payoff vectors $x, y \in S$, $y \neq x$, with $x > d$ and $y > d$. For both x and y, we now form the n-fold product of utility increments or gains with respect to the status quo point. We obtain $\Pi_{i=1}^n (x_i - d_i)$ and $\Pi_{i=1}^n (y_i - d_i)$, respectively. The Nash bargaining solution picks that utility vector in S where the product of utility increments with respect to $(d_1, d_2, \ldots, d_n)$ is maximal. Nash's remarkable result says that this solution point is unique.

Theorem 1. There is a unique solution satisfying conditions 1–4.

For a two-person society, the Nash solution can be illustrated in a straightforward manner. Compare the areas of all rectangles that have as their common "southwest" corner point d and each of them has as its "northeast" corner a point on the boundary of S. Look for that point on the boundary of S where the area of the corresponding rectangle is maximal. The coordinates of that point represent the Nash bargaining solution.

Roth has shown that it is essentially unnecessary to require Pareto-efficiency in order to derive Nash's solution.[9] Roth has shown that there are precisely two solutions $f(S,d)$ that satisfy condition 1, conditions 3–4, and a property requiring individual rationality (this property is implicit in Nash's original approach), viz. the Nash solution and the disagree-

---

[7] K. J. Arrow, *Social Choice and Individual Values* (New York: Wiley, 1951, 1963).
[8] E. Kalai, "Solutions to the Bargaining Problem," in *Social Goods and Social Organization, Essays in Memory of Elisha Pazner*, edited by L. Hurwicz, D. Schmeidler, and H. Sonnenschein (Cambridge: Cambridge University Press, 1985), pp. 77–105.
[9] A. E. Roth, "Individual Rationality and Nash's Solution to the Bargaining Problem," *Mathematics of Operations Research* 2 (1977): 64–5.

ment solution $f(S,d) = (d_1,d_2, \ldots, d_n)$ for all bargaining situations (S,d). The uniqueness of the Nash solution is then regained if one requires that the solution always selects a point that strictly dominates the status quo.

Various criticisms have been brought forward against Nash's axioms. One is that Nash's approach does not allow for interpersonal comparisons of utility. On issues of distributive justice it seems quite difficult to imagine that sensible judgments can be made without comparing values, vaguely perhaps, between and among persons. One should, however, keep in mind that it was not Nash himself who proposed his bargaining approach as a model to solve distributive issues. But also in other contexts, an abstraction that totally omits interpersonal comparisons may depart too far from real-life bargaining situations.[10]

Strong objections have been raised against Nash's independence condition. Imagine 2 two-person bargaining situations having the same status quo point. Let the difference between the two situations be that by going from the first to the second, the potentialities of person 2 are increasing in terms of additional utility payoffs while no changes occur for person 1. Let us suppose that the individuals have agreed on a solution to situation 1. Then they are informed that the real situation is situation 2. Should individual 2 now deserve a better outcome? If the answer is "yes," the independence condition is violated. Luce and Raiffa, who no longer find this argument against assuming independence appealing, give an explanation why one might wish to consider potentialities of the individual players: "The levels of aspiration of the players" are "certainly one of the psychological factors often involved in bargaining temperaments."[11] However, since in bargaining problems there always is the possibility that the players end up in the status quo, "certain aspirations are merely empty dreams." The argument to consider irrelevant alternatives should be viewed against this threat.

Considering bargaining problems as primarily distributive problems, Gauthier rejects the independence condition as a property of a bargaining solution. Gauthier argues that this axiom leads to a solution that maximizes a certain quantity, namely, the product of the gains of the individuals. "But [joint] maximizing is not a direct concern in bargaining. Each bargainer has a maximizing concern – a concern with maximizing his own payoff – but there is no ground for the supposition that these unite into a single maximizing concern to be resolved in bargaining."[12]

As already mentioned, we next discuss a model by Kalai and Smo-

[10] See, for example, R. D. Luce and H. Raiffa, *Games and Decisions* (New York: Wiley, 1957), pp. 131–2.

[11] Ibid., p. 133.

[12] David Gauthier, "Bargaining and Justice," in *Ethics and Economics*, edited by E. Frankel Paul, J. Paul, and F. D. Miller, Jr. (Oxford: Clarendon Press, 1985), pp. 29–47.

rodinski that replaces the independence condition by a monotonicity axiom that reflects changes in potentialities. And in the third section, we represent the conclusions Gauthier draws from his objection against Nash's independence condition.

Nash's solution crucially depends on the status quo point. Since the status quo point indicates the threat potentials of the different players involved in the bargaining procedure, the question arises whether the Nash approach yields an ethically appealing solution. Coming back to a bargaining situation that Nash had envisaged himself, Sen argues: "In a labour market with unemployment, workers may be agreeable to accept subhuman wages and poor terms of employment, since in the absence of a contract they may starve, but this does not make that solution a desirable outcome in any sense."[13] Sen actually shows that there is no bargaining solution that satisfies the four Nash conditions and a fifth axiom requiring the solution to be independent of the status quo point.[14]

Welfarism is a particular way of evaluating alternative outcomes. Welfarism asserts that states of affairs are to be judged entirely in terms of personal utility information relating to the alternative states, the use of nonutility information being ruled out. Nash's bargaining theory as well as the other two solution concepts already mentioned clearly are welfarist approaches. Any two economic environments that yield the same utility possibility set are treated identically in all three approaches. The Rawlsian theory of justice,[15] which uses the notion of "primary social goods" and not the utility concept, is definitely nonwelfarist. In Rawls' theory, two principles of justice are the object of a collective agreement or social contract that is made under a "veil of ignorance." The agreement is unanimous since people do not know their particular features and positions in the actual world. "The aim is to rule out those principles that it would be rational to propose for acceptance, however little the chance of success, only if one knew certain things that are irrelevant from the standpoint of justice."[16] Rawls deliberately prevents certain types of information (such as information on the position of a threat point) to enter his theory; "to each according to his threat advantage" was an unacceptable principle of justice for him.

Diametrically opposed to Sen and Rawls is Gauthier, who claims that social decisions on alternative states should indeed be based on bargaining. Gauthier continues: "Someone might say that natural differences are arbitrary; society should redress them. But to call natural differences arbitrary is to treat them as if they were, not natural differ-

---

[13] A. K. Sen, *Collective Choice and Social Welfare* (San Francisco: Holden-Day, 1970), p. 121.
[14] Ibid., p. 128.
[15] J. Rawls, *A Theory of Justice* (Cambridge, MA: Harvard University Press, 1971).
[16] Ibid., p. 16.

ences, but the result of a distribution made without any basis. . . . Why should society seek to undo natural differences?"[17]

The last two quotations from Rawls and Gauthier show that even among philosophers, there by no means appears to be an agreement on the role that the status quo should play in the formation of social choices. We resume the arguments for the different ways of treating the status quo in the third section.

Kaneko and Nakamura[18] have proposed a solution concept that is very close to Nash's. The main difference is that Kaneko and Nakamura do not choose the status quo as the solution point in the case of disagreement among the players. They select instead a so-called worst point that is different from the status quo. The worst point is added to the set of feasible alternatives. The authors then introduce the Nash Social Welfare Function, which is defined to be the sum of logarithms of individual utility gains as calculated from society's worst point. As the worst point, the authors suggest an alternative "which represents one of the worst states for all individuals that we may imagine."[19] But if there were a discussion in the society as to where the worst point should lie and there were several proposals, also in this approach, the position of the worst point would matter (i.e., the welfare-maximizing solution is not independent of the worst point). However, if the worst point is very far away from the feasible set, changes in its position do not affect the solution as much as changes in the status quo do in Nash's own model.

The Kalai–Smorodinski solution

The Kalai–Smorodinski solution considers the status quo, the set $S^+ \subset S$ of feasible utility vectors that are individually rational in (S,d), that is, $S^+ = \{x \in S \mid x > d\}$, and the ideal point $\bar{x}(S)$, which in the case of two players is defined by $\bar{x}(S) = (\bar{x}_1, \bar{x}_2)$, where $\bar{x}_i = \sup\{s_i \mid (s_1, s_2) \in S^+\}$, $i \in \{1,2\}$. For each person i, $\bar{x}_i$ gives the maximally attainable utility payoff.

The Kalai–Smorodinski approach uses conditions 1–3 of Nash, but rejects the independence condition since, as we have outlined before, it does not adequately reflect changes in a player's maximum feasible utility level. The authors formulate a monotonicity requirement instead. We present the following weak version:

Condition 5. If (S,d) and (T,d) are bargaining situations such that $S \subset T$ and $\bar{x}(S) = \bar{x}(T)$, then $f(T,d) \geq f(S,d)$.

[17] David Gauthier, "Social Choice and Distributive Justice," *Philosophia* 7 (1978): 245.
[18] M. Kaneko and K. Nakamura, "The Nash Social Welfare Function," *Econometrica* 47 (1979): 423–35.
[19] Ibid., p. 423.

This axiom says that if the set of feasible utility payoffs is increased from S to T, and the ideal point is left unchanged, the solution point after the change is such that each player's payoff is at least as large as it was in the old situation. The Kalai–Smorodinski solution chooses $x = (x_1,x_2)$ as the maximal point in S such that

$$\frac{x_1 - d_1}{\overline{x}_1 - d_1} = \frac{x_2 - d_2}{\overline{x}_2 - d_2}$$

Raiffa[20] already discussed this solution and showed that it fulfills conditions 1–3. The complete axiomatic characterization is given by Kalai and Smorodinski.[21]

Theorem 2. For two players, there is a unique solution satisfying conditions 1, 2, 3, and 5.

This solution lends itself to a straightforward interpretation. For each player i, $\overline{x}_i - d_i$ is the maximal possible utility gain that he (she) can obtain as seen from the status quo. Normally, $(\overline{x}_1,\overline{x}_2)$ is not achievable since it lies outside S^+. The ratio $(x_i - d_i)/(\overline{x}_i - d_i)$ reflects the "degree of success" that player i has had in trying to achieve the maximal possible utility gain. The Kalai–Smorodinski solution selects a unique point x, where the previous ratio is equal for both persons. Futhermore, at x, this ratio is maximal with respect to the individually rational set S^+. In order to find the Kalai–Smorodinski solution graphically, one has to construct a rectangle whose "southwest" corner is point d and that is minimal with respect to S^+ (the smallest rectangle that envelops S^+). The northeast corner of the rectangle is the ideal point $\overline{x}$. All points x on the diagonal between the two points d and $\overline{x}$ have the property that

$$\frac{x_1 - d_1}{\overline{x}_1 - d_1} = \frac{x_2 - d_2}{\overline{x}_2 - d_2}$$

The Kalai–Smorodinski solution is that point from the intersection of the diagonal and S^+ that has a maximal distance from d. This point is unique. Clearly, the solution is not independent of the status quo point either.

At this point, we should like to mention that every individually rational n-person bargaining solution depends on the status quo. It can be shown for all cases in which X does not exclusively consist of two pure alternatives and all lotteries between them, that there exists no n-

[20] H. Raiffa, "Arbitration Schemes for Generalized Two-Person Games," *Annals of Mathematics Studies* 28 (1953): 361–87.
[21] E. Kalai and M. Smorodinski, "Other Solutions to Nash's Bargaining Problem," *Econometrica* 43 (1975): 513–18.

person bargaining solution fulfilling the condition of invariance with respect to positive affine transformations of the utility functions, the requirement of individual rationality, and the axiom of independence formulated by Sen.[22] In order to obtain this result, it suffices to require a weak version of individual rationality (i.e., for every individual, the utility value of the bargaining solution is not smaller than his (her) utility value at the status quo point), which is a basic property of each bargaining solution.

The Kalai–Smorodinski solution is well-defined for games with any number of participants. However, this solution does not necessarily satisfy the Pareto-efficiency condition for bargaining situations with more than two players. Actually, Roth[23] has shown that for bargaining situations with three or more participants, no solution exists that fulfills the conditions of Pareto-efficiency and symmetry, and the monotonicity requirement in condition 5.

However, this difficulty vanishes if one is willing to accept the assumption of free disposal of utility. Then the Kalai–Smorodinski solution is the unique weakly Pareto-optimal point with equal relative utility gains for all individuals, but it is not always strongly Pareto-optimal. If one additionally accepts the availability of small utility transfers, then this problem disappears, too. One of the approaches that generalizes the axiomatic characterization of the solution to the case of n persons is due to Imai.[24] He replaces the fourth condition by two axioms, an axiom of individual monotonicity together with an axiom of independence of irrelevant alternatives other than the ideal point. The latter is a version of condition 4, where situations that are being compared have identical status quo points and identical ideal points. Imai's set of axioms uniquely characterizes a lexicographic maximin solution in relative utility gains.

Gauthier's maximin solution

Zeuthen[25] has proposed a bargaining solution for negotiations about wage rates between employers' and workers' organizations that uses the notion of concession. In order to define the value of a concession, the point of disagreement has to be known, which in Zeuthen's model is determined by the expected costs that the parties incur if there is a wage fight. Imagine a bargaining situation with two players; let the point of disagreement be $d = (0,0)$. Each player now proposes an outcome for this game. Let person 1 suggest (x_1, x_2) and person 2 propose (y_1, y_2),

[22] Sen, p. 128.
[23] A. E. Roth, *Axiomatic Models of Bargaining* (Berlin and Heidelberg: Springer-Verlag, 1979).
[24] H. Imai, "Individual Monotonicity and Lexicographic Maximin Solution," *Econometrica* 51 (1983): 389–401.
[25] F. Zeuthen, *Problems of Monopoly and Economic Warfare* (London: Routledge, 1930).

both suggestions being Pareto-efficient. Consider $(x_1 - y_1)/x_1$. The numerator describes the amount of gain that person 1 would forgo if he (she) agreed to person 2's proposal. The denominator gives person 1's gain in relation to disagreement if his (her) own proposal were accepted $(x_1 - 0)$. Zeuthen's formula for measuring the concession of person 1 (the argument is analogous for person 2) is $(x_1 - y_1)/x_1$, and according to the author, player 1 should make a concession if and only if

$$\frac{x_1 - y_1}{x_1} \leq \frac{y_2 - x_2}{y_2}$$

with the inequality reversed for the case that person 2 should make a concession. We should mention parenthetically that the inequality is equivalent to $x_1 x_2 \leq y_1 y_2$, so that from a formal point of view, Zeuthen's approach turns out to be equivalent to Nash's product-maximization solution.[26] Zeuthen argues that according to the inequality, the person with the smaller relative concession will offer a revised proposal that must be such that the next concession has to be made by the other player. Clearly, this procedure makes the product of the players' utilities increase in each round, and an agreement is reached when the product is maximal (Nash's solution).

Gauthier's approach uses Zeuthen's idea of a sequence of successive concessions among the players. However, Gauthier's theory is, from a conceptual point of view, much broader than Zeuthen's proposal. Gauthier's theory has to be viewed as a bargaining model of moral choice where social values are to be distributed.

Let each bargainer i propose that the ideal payoff $\bar{x}_i$ is allocated to him (her). Under normal circumstances, the vector of ideal payoffs is no solution since it lies outside of S^+. Consider any outcome $x \in S^+$. The concession required by person i if he (she) agrees to x is, according to the Zeuthen formula, $(\bar{x}_i - x_i)/(\bar{x}_i - d_i)$. As explained before, this expression determines the proportion of gain over the disagreement payoff forgone by person i. Notice that Gauthier applies Zeuthen's formula to utility differences between ideal utility values and the status quo or between utility values of proposed points and the status quo. Gauthier argues, "Each bargainer looks upon the utility, to him, of the status quo as a minimum, and evaluates other social states in relation to that minimum."[27] The second modification of Zeuthen's procedure is that every concession of player i during the bargaining process is measured in relation to $\bar{x}_i - d_i$, whereas in Zeuthen's formula the de-

[26] See J. C. Harsanyi, "Approaches to the Bargaining Problem Before and After the Theory of Games: A Critical Discussion of Zeuthen's, Hick's, and Nash's Theories," *Econometrica* 24 (1956): 144–57.
[27] Gauthier, "Social Choice and Distributive Justice," p. 246.

nominator changes. This underlines the importance of the ideal point not only for the first proposals of the bargainers, but also for the whole procedure. Otherwise the Nash solution in utility gains with respect to the status quo would be achieved.

Naturally, a person is less willing to make a concession the larger this concession is. Therefore, consider the largest concession required for each of the possible bargaining outcomes. For any $x \in S^+$, the maximum concession is $\max_i(\bar{x}_i - x_i)/(\bar{x}_i - d_i)$. Since the maximum concession will obviously elicit the maximum degree of resistance to agreement, we are looking for an outcome with the least maximum degree of resistance to agreement. Following Zeuthen, such an outcome must be accepted. "The person required to make the maximum concession needed to yield this outcome is more willing to concede than any person required to make the maximum concession needed to yield any other outcome."[28] Thus, the bargaining solution is the outcome with the least maximum concession. Therefore, the solution of Gauthier's bargaining process does not depend on the sequence of proposals made by the bargainers. It shares this property with Zeuthen's solution. However, as Gauthier shows, the requirement that the maximum concession be minimized is equivalent to the demand that the minimum proportion of possible gain be maximized. The minimum proportion of possible utility gain is, of course, $\min_i(x_i - d_i)/(\bar{x}_i - d_i)$, so that according to Gauthier, given an n-person bargaining situation (S,d), $x \in S$ is the solution if and only if

$$\min_i \frac{x_i - d_i}{\bar{x}_i - d_i} > \min_j \frac{y_j - d_j}{\bar{x}_j - d_j} \quad \forall\, y \in S^+, y \neq x$$

It is obvious that the Gauthier solution satisfies condition 1. Also, the comparisons that are made with respect to proportionate gains or concessions do not presuppose any degree of interpersonal comparability of individual utilities. The Gauthier solution shares this characteristic with all the other solutions we have discussed in this essay. Actually, for only two individuals, the Gauthier solution and the solution à la Kalai–Smorodinski are identical. There is, however, a problem with Gauthier's solution proposal. It is not well-defined in games of more than two players. In the general case of $n \geq 2$ persons, the solution has to be defined by the unique element in S^+ that is maximal with respect to the lexicographical maximin ordering on the set of n-tupels of relative utility gains. Furthermore, the following question arises: Which set of axioms fully characterizes the Gauthier solution? The author himself has made no attempt to provide an answer for the case of more than two individuals.

---

[28] Gauthier, "Bargaining and Justice," p. 37.

Klemisch-Ahlert[29] has shown that Gauthier's solution can be uniquely characterized by condition 1, a condition of strong Pareto-efficiency (condition 2') and a third requirement to be explained in what follows. Gauthier's solution can be given a lexicographic maximin interpretation.

Condition 2'. If (S,d) is a bargaining situation and $x \in S$ such that $x \geq f(S,d)$, then $x = f(S,d)$.

In the formal representation of the third requirement, a sufficient condition is formulated for individually rational points not to be the solution. Suppose a point $y \in S^+$ is proposed as the solution for the bargaining situation (S,d) with ideal point $\bar{x}$. Suppose, furthermore, that there is a person j and a set M of one or more than one person not including j such that the relative utility gain $\dfrac{(y_j - d_j)/}{/(\bar{x}_j - d_j)}$ of person j is lower than the relative utility gain any person $i \in M$ would receive in y. If it is now possible to find a point x in $\bar{S}^+$, the individually rational subset of the comprehensive closure of S, such that person j's relative gain is improved upon while the relative gain of every person $i \in M$ is reduced, whereas the relative gains of all other persons are left unchanged, and if, in addition, the relative gain of every person $i \in M$ in x is still greater than the relative gain of person j in x, then y cannot be the solution. The comprehensive closure $\bar{S}$ of S is defined by $\bar{S} = \{x \in \mathbb{R}^n \mid \exists\, s \in S: x \leq s\}$ and $\bar{S}^+ = \{x \in \bar{S} \mid d \leq x\}$.

We now give a formal definition of the condition.

Condition 6. Let f be a bargaining solution, (S,d) a bargaining situation with ideal point $\bar{x}$, and let y be a point in S^+. If there exists a point $x \in \bar{S}^+$ such that $\exists\, j \in N$ and $\exists\, M \subset N$ with $j \notin M$ and

$$\frac{y_i - d_i}{\bar{x}_i - d_i} > \frac{x_i - d_i}{\bar{x}_i - d_i} > \frac{x_j - d_j}{\bar{x}_j - d_j} > \frac{y_j - d_i}{\bar{x}_j - d_j} \qquad \forall\, i \in M$$

and

$$x_k = y_k \qquad \forall\, k \in N \backslash (M \cup \{j\})$$

then

$$y \neq f(S,d)$$

Condition 6 can be interpreted as modeling a particular bargaining step. In view of a proposed point y, person j demands further conces-

[29] M. Klemisch-Ahlert, "Two Axiomatic Characterizations of n-Person Bargaining Solutions," Discussion Paper 8810 (University of Osnabruck: Department of Economics, 1988).

sions from a set M of other persons who would receive greater relative gains in y than person j. Person j claims point x. Following Gauthier, we argue that because the persons in M remain better off in relative gains in comparison to person j, they have to be willing to make the required concessions. Therefore, y will not be a solution. The persons in $N \setminus (M \cup \{j\})$ are not involved in this bargaining step. They do not have to make further concessions when x is claimed.

Condition 6 does not imply that x will be chosen as the solution. The bargaining will continue, some new point in S^+ will be proposed by some person, let us assume a strongly Pareto-efficient one, and some other person will demand concessions until the lexicographic maximin solution in relative gains will be proposed. Then no person has the possibility to enforce a further concession from any other person.

This interpretation captures the intuition of the following theorem.

Theorem 3. For $n \geq 2$ players, there is a unique solution satisfying conditions 1, 2', and 6. It is the lexicographic maximin solution in relative utility gains.

The structure of the comparisons of relative gains between person j and persons in M made in condition 6 is similar to the comparison concerning two individuals made in the formulation of a well-known equity axiom in social-choice theory. But in order to characterize the Gauthier solution in the general case, it is not sufficient to consider bargaining steps in which one person claims concessions from some other person. Klemisch-Ahlert shows that pairwise bargaining leads to the lexicographic maximim solution in relative gains only for a proper subset of all n-person bargaining problems.

It is interesting to note that Gauthier introduced maximin considerations into bargaining procedures. One is, at least to some extent, reminded of Rawls' difference principle, though, clearly, there are major differences between the two proposals. As mentioned before, Gauthier's solution works without assuming any degree of interpersonal comparability of utilities. Rawls' theory, on the other hand, presupposes the possibility of interpersonal comparisons of utility levels, though this is being done in terms of primary goods. Furthermore, in the first section, we presented a quotation from Rawls' book in which the author vehemently argued against considering the disagreement point when problems of distributive justice are to be tackled. Gauthier, on the other hand, points out that he wishes to distinguish between the share of social values each individual would get without cooperation (disagreement point) and the share individuals are able to gain by cooperation. In Gauthier's theory, "the disagreement point for a bargain yielding principles of justice must be a state of nature – a condition characterized by the absence of social cooperation – and not a particular, historically given state of society."[30] For Gauthier, his own proposal is the only procedure a society of rational individuals would agree to from behind a veil of ignorance ("a conception of maximizing rationality"), when deciding on distributive issues. "The person who receives the least extensive share of social benefit, measured in relation to what he might have received," is left "with the knowledge that any alternative social arrangements would have afforded someone a yet smaller share."[31]

Concluding remarks

Yaari and Bar-Hillel[32] have run an experiment on the distribution of commodities between two individuals. The alternative solutions from which the respondents were asked to choose were derived from classical solution concepts such as Nash's, Kalai–Smorodinski's, and others. The results show that for two different distribution problems having the same utility-possibility set, the solution chosen by persons is not always the same point in utility space. Therefore, it seems that the information on a distribution problem that is still available after representation in utility space is not sufficient to decide upon a resolution of the problem.

There are some axiomatic approaches developed from bargaining models that characterize distribution mechanisms on commodity spaces. Binmore[33] models a special distribution problem, where two agents trade in two commodities. His axiomatic characterization is very close to Nash's set on axioms. However, Binmore's setup is such that the solution does not only depend on the utility values, but also on other information given by the preference structure of the agents.

Roemer has criticized the informational simplicity enforced by welfarism. Roemer argues that in bargaining theory, important issues in distributive justice like rights or needs and even preferences are not modeled in a sufficiently broad way because the whole information on a distribution problem is represented by a set of utility vectors. In a bargaining situation, (S,d) rights and needs can only be taken into account when the status quo d is specified. Furthermore, for Roemer, the utility possibility set S, the image of the set of alternatives, is too simple in comparison to the preferences of the individuals over multidimensional alternatives.

Therefore, in cases where the alternatives can be considered as allocations of various commodities to the individuals, Roemer suggests eco-

---

[30] Gauthier, "Bargaining and Justice," p. 46.
[31] Ibid., p. 47.
[32] M. E. Yaari and M. Bar-Hillel, "On Dividing Justly," Social Choice and Welfare 1 (1984): 1–24.
[33] K. Binmore, "Nash's Bargaining Theory III," in The Economics of Bargaining, edited by K. Binmore and P. Dasgupta (Oxford: Basil Blackwell, 1987), pp. 239–56.

nomic environments as objects of distributive mechanisms. An economic environment is defined by an n-dimensional space of commodity bundles to be divided between two persons and the utility functions of the persons on the space of bundles of these commodities. He investigates how classical bargaining axioms work when they are reformulated as axioms on economic environments. Moreover, Roemer[34] presents some axiomatic characterizations of distribution mechanisms using economic information. Roemer's contribution clarifies under which conditions the investigated mechanisms correspond to some of the classical bargaining solutions. One should mention that in his models, Roemer is assuming interpersonally comparable utilities, whereas the models discussed in this essay do without any degree of interpersonal comparability.

Roemer draws the conclusion that only if the dimension of the commodity space is unbounded, the classical bargaining solutions (with interpersonally comparable utilities) can uniquely be characterized by axioms using economic environments, and he does not consider this condition as appropriate for economic bargaining problems.

[34] J. E. Roemer, "Axiomatic Bargaining Theory on Economic Environments," *Journal of Economic Theory* 45 (1988): 1–31.

Part III

The rationality of keeping agreements

Overview of the essays

In his essay Geoffrey Sayre-McCord argues that Gauthier fails to establish that rationality always, or even almost always, requires human agents to dispose themselves to comply with the requirements of morality. For in the real world, people's dispositions are opaque enough that it is often possible to deceive others into thinking that one is trustworthy. Given this possibility of deception, rationality dictates, at least for some real-world agents, that they adopt the policy of pretending to be trustworthy, but breaking agreements whenever it is to their advantage.

David Copp reaches this same conclusion. He also questions Gauthier's unconventional view that a choice is rational if and only if it conforms to a disposition, the having of which would give the agent at least as much utility as any alternative disposition. The more usual view is that a choice is rational if and only if *it* would give at least as much utility as any of *its* alternatives. Copp acknowledges that even if the claimed connection between rational dispositions and rational choice is rejected, Gauthier's argument that it is rational to choose to be disposed to comply with rational agreements is still important. For, if successful, it shows that rationality requires people to become disposed to keep their agreements, and that is still a fairly strong result. Copp challenges, however, Gauthier's claim to have thereby established that rationality dictates that one comply with *morality*. Gauthier's argument for this claim rests on his equation of morality with rational and impartial constraints on the pursuit of self-interest. Copp argues that this equation is mistaken – at least for the sense of impartiality that Gauthier invokes. Copp concludes that Gauthier has not established that rationality dictates that we be disposed to be *moral*. He argues further that if even Gauthier's argument were successful, it would not be an adequate answer to the moral skeptic. At best, Copp claims, it would show that behaving morally is sometimes rationally justified – not that morality itself is.

Holly Smith also criticizes Gauthier's argument for the rationality of keeping agreements. She argues that the advantages of constrained maximization over straightforward maximization are not as clear as Gauthier claims. Gauthier's argument rests on an illegitimate restriction of the policies open to both the agent and his/her potential partners. Moreover, even if all agents are constrained maximizers, and they are transparently so, it does not follow that they will always cooperate. Smith further challenges Gauthier's claim that if it is rational to adopt a given policy (e.g., that of keeping rational agreements), then on each occasion, it is rational to choose on the basis of that policy (e.g., keeping a given agreement). The rationality of adopting a policy, Smith argues, does not guarantee the rationality of a choice that conforms to the policy. Finally, Smith argues that in any case, Gauthier's argument does not succeed in deriving morality from a morally neutral foundation. Close scrutiny reveals that either his derived principles are not genuine moral principles or that his principles of rationality are not morally neutral.

Jody Kraus and Jules Coleman criticize Gauthier's argument that it is uniquely rational to be *narrowly* compliant with agreements (i.e., to be disposed to comply with the terms of *fair* bargains – but not necessarily disposed to comply with the terms of *unfair* bargains). Their main point is that under appropriate circumstances, it can be rational to be *broadly* compliant (i.e., disposed to comply with any mutually advantageous bargain – fair or not). Given that morality (at least on Gauthier's view) is both rational and fair (impartial), they conclude that Gauthier has failed to show that rationality requires that we be moral.

Like these authors, Peter Danielson holds that Gauthier's argument for the rationality of constrained maximization fails. Unlike these authors, however, he holds that it is only the details of Gauthier's argument – not the basic approach – that fail. He argues that there is a policy the adoption of which yields more utility than straightforward maximization, Gauthier's constrained maximization, or any other policy. This is the policy of reciprocal cooperation, which – simplifying somewhat – directs agents to cooperate with others when and only when this cooperation is necessary and sufficient for the cooperation of those others. Unlike Gauthier's constrained maximization policy, reciprocal cooperation directs the agent *not* to cooperate when interacting with others who will cooperate unconditionally (even if they know that the other agents will not cooperate). Thus, reciprocal cooperation yields all the benefits of cooperation that constrained maximization yields, and it yields some benefits from exploiting unconditional cooperators that the policy of constrained maximization does not yield. Where there are just two agents, reciprocal cooperation, not constrained maximization, Danielson argues, is the rational policy to adopt. In the many-person case, however, things are more complicated, since the rationality of cooperation will depend on *how many* agents are willing to cooperate. Here Danielson argues that a policy called "counteradaptive cooperation" is appropriately sensitive to this feature, and is therefore the rational policy to adopt in the many-agent situation. Like Gauthier, then, Danielson holds that it is rational to adopt a policy of cooperation under certain conditions. He disagrees with Gauthier, however, concerning the nature of the conditions under which cooperation is rational.

A caveat: Gauthier holds that under a broad range of circumstances, rationality requires that we conform to the terms of agreements it would be rational to make. He also holds that an action is morally permissible just in case it conforms to rules that it would be rational for the members of society to which to agree. Consequently, he holds that under a broad range of cases, rationality requires that we behave morally. Here there are two distinct issues: (1) Does rationality require us to keep our agreements? (2) Does rationality require us to be moral? Given Gauthier's contractarian theory, the two issues are coextensive, but conceptually they are distinct. Since authors do not always clearly distinguish these two issues, readers should be careful to determine exactly which claim is being assessed.

12. Deception and reasons to be moral*

Geoffrey Sayre-McCord

> There is no vice so simple but assumes
> Some mark of virtue on its outward parts.
> — *Merchant of Venice,* Act III, Sc. 2, L. 81

> The key thing about acting is honesty, when you can
> fake that, you're in.   — *Sam Goldwyn*

> Once you give up integrity, the rest is a piece of cake.
> — *J. R. Ewing*

Why should I be moral? Traditionally two sorts of people have been interested in this question: moral theorists and moral miscreants. One recurrent answer has haunted the moralists and bolstered the miscreants: "There is no (good) reason to be moral."

Glaucon presents the classic version of the problem in the *Republic.* Suppose, he suggests, one were to possess the ring of Gyges – a ring that makes the wearer invisible and guarantees impunity. Would one have any reason to honor commitments or to respect others' belongings? Most people would say, Glaucon reports, that when there is no danger of reprisal, there is no reason to be moral.[1]

Within the framework set by Glaucon's challenge, two standard assumptions conspire to make a rational defense of morality exceptionally

---

*Reprinted by permission of *American Philosophical Quarterly* from "Deceptions and Reasons to be Moral," by Geoffrey Sayre-McCord, in *American Philosophical Quarterly* 26 (1989): 113–22. Copyright © 1989 by *American Philosophical Quarterly.*
[1] *Plato's Republic,* 358e–62c, trans. by G. M. A. Grube (Indianapolis, IN: Hackett, 1974), pp. 31–4.

difficult. The first is that rationality consists solely in the maximization of expected utility, where utility is a relative and subjective measure of an individual's preference satisfaction. The second is that an adequate defense of the rationality of morality must not rely on our all too contingent feelings of sympathy or benevolence. Behind this second assumption is the Kantian conviction that a *rational* morality must apply to us just in virtue of our rational nature and not in virtue of our affective proclivities. And, in any case, relying on affective bonds when defending morality would subvert all attempts to convince the moral miscreants (who have no concern for others). Although I believe both assumptions are mistaken, in the discussion that follows I leave them largely unchallenged (except to the extent that the conclusions of this paper constitute part of the evidence to be marshalled against the conception of rationality contained in the first assumption).

Plato responds to Glaucon by emphasizing the incredible value of a well-ordered soul, and the disruptive effects immoral acts have on that order. According to Plato, no matter what benefits one can expect from acting immorally, they will never compensate for the loss of harmony within the soul.[2] The costs of being immoral, he argues, will always overburden the advantages, even when one's transgressions go undetected by others. As a result, Plato insists, it is always in each person's interest to be moral.

Resisting the substantial and evidently implausible assumptions that Plato needs to support his argument, one might maintain that Glaucon's challenge simply demands too much. All we really need is good reason for us – real people without magic rings – to be moral. This, anyway, would be sufficient for practical purposes, because it would give us an answer to those miscreants we might actually run across. To meet the practical demand, all we need to show is that people, as they really are, stand to gain from being moral. This aim is less ambitious than Plato's, in that it does not involve showing that being immoral is, in principle, irrational. Yet it is ambitious enough. For even if we limit ourselves to real people with no extraordinary means, it seems self-interest will never support anything other than a more careful deployment of self-interested reasoning. It seems egoism begets enlightened egoism, and nothing more.

Importantly, as Aristotle emphasized, a person is moral only if her actions are manifestations of some more or less settled – recognizably moral – character trait.[3] And having a moral character in the relevant sense is more than just having the disposition to behave in those ways that happen to be demanded by morality. People may have dispositions

---

[2] *Plato's Republic*, 444b–5b and 589e–90a, pp. 108 and 236.
[3] See Aristotle's *Nichomachean Ethics*, 1105a30, trans. by Terence Irwin (Indianapolis, IN: Hackett, 1985), p. 40.

that give rise to moral behavior without being moral people. They might, for instance, be so carefully watched that temptation always gave way to fear of detection and punishment. We could certainly expect such people to behave morally; but they would be behaving morally by default, and not because they are moral.[4] What sets the moral apart from enlightened egoists is (at least in part) their willingness to act on considerations other than those of self-interest; unlike enlightened egoists, those who are moral constrain their pursuit of personal benefits on moral grounds.

For this reason, one has not justified *being* moral simply by showing (if one could) that we have self-interested reasons for behaving in each instance as morality demands. To justify morality, it won't do to show just that behaving morally usually, or even always, pays. Instead, we need to show that having the *disposition* to constrain one's pursuit of self-interest in the name of morality pays.[5] That is, we must show that it pays to be a person who acts for moral, and not just self-interested, reasons. Only by concentrating on dispositions, rather than on behavior, are we able to capture the Aristotelian insight (embraced by Kant) that there is a difference between merely doing what one should and doing it the way one should – for its own sake and not for the advantages it may bring.

Moreover, by attending to dispositions, rather than mere behavior or particular actions, we can hope to explain why it is rational to be the sort of person who performs those actions demanded by morality that do not themselves pay. And we *might* even be able to do more; we might be able to show that these nonmaximizing actions are themselves rational to perform. Specifically, we might argue that these actions are rational because they result from a disposition that it is rational to possess. Relying on (what might be called) the "transitivity of rationality," we might hold that the rationality of the disposition carries over to the manifestations of the disposition.

Making this stronger argument has obvious advantages. Most signif-

---

[4] In place of surveillance, people might just be conditioned in such a way that the mere contemplation of immoral actions brings them extreme pain. As long as the conditioning is successful, as long as even immoral thoughts are dreadfully painful, we might reasonably expect them to behave morally. Yet their upright behavior would still not reflect well on their character. See Anthony Burgess, *A Clockwork Orange* (New York: W. W. Norton, 1963), p. 126.

[5] This general approach is advocated by David Gauthier, *Morals by Agreement* (Oxford: Oxford University Press, 1986); by J. L. Mackie, *Ethics: Inventing Right and Wrong* (New York: Penguin Books, 1977), see esp. pp. 115–20; by Edward McClennen, "Prisoner's Dilemma and Resolute Choice," in *Paradoxes of Rationality and Cooperation*, edited by Richmond Campbell and Lanning Sowden (Vancouver: University of British Columbia Press, 1985), pp. 94–104; and by Gregory Kavka, "The Reconciliation Project," in *Morality, Reason and Truth*, edited by David Copp and David Zimmerman (Totowa, NJ: Rowman & Allanheld, 1985), pp. 297–319.

icantly, without it, the rational justification of being moral (even if we can provide one) would not explain the *rationality* of the nonmaximizing actions a moral person would perform. But making the argument requires modifying the maximizing conception of rationality. For the argument involves allowing the possibility that some nonmaximizing actions (if they result from a disposition it is rational to have) are rational. There is an obvious parallel here with rule utilitarianism. In the first place, the *structure* of the positions is analogous. Just as a rule utilitarian justifies particular actions by appeal to rules and then justifies the rules by appeal to their contribution to overall utility, so the stronger argument would have us justify particular actions by appeal to dispositions and then justify the dispositions by appeal to their contribution to the agent's expected utility. In the second place, the *problems* the two positions face are analogous. Just as rule utilitarianism must explain why we should not justify the morality of actions by appealing directly to overall utility, the stronger argument must explain why we should not justify the rationality of actions by appealing directly to the agent's expected utility.[6]

Regardless of whether the rationality of dispositions carries over in the appropriate way to the rationality of particular actions, an emphasis on dispositions gives hope. It suggests there may yet be a rational defense for being the sort of person who does as she should, because she should, even when doing so involves sacrifice. No longer need we think that, in principle, self-interest can justify nothing other than enlightened self-interest – self-interest might actually justify adopting a moral character.

Once the shift to dispositions is made, the question becomes: What grounds might one have for thinking self-interest itself recommends the disposition to reason morally?[7] And the problem of justifying morality becomes one of providing a self-interested rationale not directly for be-

[6] There are serious difficulties lurking behind this assumption of the transitivity of rationality. Most significantly, the transitivity cannot plausibly hold in all cases, since at least in some situations it seems one might actually be rational in making oneself irrational (a possibility that is ruled out by the transitivity assumption). So something has to be said about when the rationality of choosing a disposition carries over to the actions the disposition leads to and when it doesn't. For a discussion of the assumption, see David Gauthier, "Deterrence, Maximization, and Rationality," in *The Security Gamble*, edited by Douglas MacLean (Totowa, NJ: Rowman & Allanheld, 1984), pp. 100–22; his "Responses to the Paradox of Deterrence," in *The Security Gamble*, pp. 159–61; and David Lewis, "Devil's Bargains and the Real World," in *The Security Gamble*, pp. 141–54. See also Derek Parfit, *Reasons and Persons* (Oxford: Oxford University Press, 1984), pp. 18–23.

[7] Unless there are some such grounds, the best we could do is offer a rational justification of enlightened egoism; and this would not be a justification of being moral. As Hume recognized, moreover, a preference for the well-being of others will not of itself provide grounds for choosing to be moral in each particular case. Even the beneficient person, he pointed out, will find herself wishing "that with regard to [a] single act, the laws of justice were for a moment suspended in the universe." *A Treatise of Human Nature*, edited by L. A. Selby-Bigge (Oxford: Oxford University Press, 1978), p. 497.

having morally but for being moral, for having the disposition to reason morally.

Obviously, people may possess any of a variety of immoral dispositions, and even those disposed to reason and act morally may possess such a disposition to varying degrees. Some may have so strong a disposition that they would never do something they thought immoral, while others may have a lower threshold. People will sometimes give in to greed (reasoning morally but acting selfishly) or lethargy (by not reasoning morally at all); and the shakier their disposition, the more frequent we may expect their transgressions to be. Morality will find its rational defense (given our assumptions of what that entails) only if an argument grounded in self-interest can be given for developing the disposition both to reason and to act, when appropriate, in a moral fashion.

Needless to say, a rational defense of morality that appeals to contrived people in contrived situations will not be much help. Even if we could show that someone ideally situated might have reasons for being moral, we would not be showing that real people have good reasons for being moral. Such defenses of morality do not meet the practical concern. What we need are good reasons for people, as they actually are, to be moral. Providing such reasons is a challenge both more pressing and more difficult than one met by showing only that ideal people, in idealized situations, have reasons to be moral.

With this in mind, imagine that we have the opportunity to choose between being an enlightened egoist and being a person with a settled disposition to be moral.[8] Imagine, that is, that we are in the position to choose what kind of people to be.[9] With one hand, say, we might pull a lever that frees us of moral compunction and clears our minds of morality; with the other, we might pull a lever that gives us the will to do what we believe morality demands. Supposing that, when we make

---

[8] Just exactly what it is to have the disposition to reason morally is of course controversial. Within reasonable limits, which exact account one embraces will not matter to the arguments that follow. A self-interested argument for being moral, though, will be plausible only if being moral is compatible with pursuing self-interest in situations where it is known one's companions are irredeemably immoral. Being moral must allow room for rejecting the Golden Rule in favor of, what Kavka calls, the "Copper Rule" (roughly: do unto others as they do unto you). See Gregory Kavka's "Right Reason and Natural Law in Hobbes's Ethics," *The Monist* 66 (1983), pp. 120–33.

[9] I take this way of framing the problem straight from David Gauthier. See his *Morals by Agreement*, and "Reason and Maximization," *Canadian Journal of Philosophy* 4 (1975): 411–33. Gauthier limits the choice to two options: one must choose between being a "straightforward maximizer" (and enlightened egoist) or being a "constrained maximizer" (who is prepared in certain circumstances "to base her actions on a joint strategy, without considering whether some individual strategy would yield her greater expected utility" (*Morals by Agreement*, p. 167). But there is no good reason to limit the choice to these two dispositions; in fact, no disposition will find vindication except by winning out against all realistically possible dispositions one might adopt. This, of course, introduces a whole slew of complications. I won't go into them here.

this choice, all we are interested in is maximizing our own welfare, which lever should we choose?

Initially, it may appear obvious that, from the point of view of self-interest, we should choose to be egoists – enlightened egoists, of course, who enjoy far-sightedness and self-control, but egoists nonetheless. As Hume's sensible knave argues, *"honesty is the best policy,* may be a good general rule, but is liable to many exceptions; and he . . . conducts himself with most wisdom, who observes the general rule, and takes advantage of all the exceptions."[10] To choose otherwise would be to prevent ourselves from taking advantage of opportunities as they arise. Our scruples might get in the way. And this is a worry since it is quite clear that sometimes behaving morally proves a heavy burden. Indeed, it is this fact that makes the rational justification of morality so difficult. Seemingly, an enlightened egoist can expect to come out usually ahead of and never behind a moral person. Given the same opportunities, the two will behave identically except when ignoring moral constraints can be expected to pay. When the chance for profitable exploitation does arise, an enlightened egoist will exploit and reasonably expect to benefit; a moral person will not. Thus, facing equal opportunities, an enlightened egoist may expect to prosper.

Enlightened egoists, however, cannot expect equal opportunities. With changing fortunes and new-found opportunities, they reexamine their options always with an eye toward advancing their own interests. As a result, when opportunities arise, enlightened egoists will break their commitments, and prove themselves unreliable companions. Realizing this, those who are moral will frequently exclude the egoists from their community. "He . . . that breaketh his Covenant, and consequently declareth that he thinks he may with reason do so," Hobbes argued, "cannot be received into any Society, that unite themselves for Peace and Defence, but by the errour of them that receive him; nor when he is received, be retayned in it, without seeing the danger of their errour; which errours a man cannot reasonably reckon upon. . . . "[11] Enlightened

---

[10] *Enquiry Concerning the Principles of Morals,* edited by L. A. Selby-Bigge (Oxford: Oxford University Press, 1975), pp. 282–3.

[11] *Leviathan* (Harmondsworth: Penguin, 1968), chap. 15, p. 205. Hume offers a similar argument, noting that knaves, despite "all their pretended cunning and abilities," will be so wrapped in lies that "they can never extricate themselves, without a total loss of reputation, and the forfeiture of all future trust and confidence with mankind." See *Enquiry Concerning the Principles of Morals,* p. 283. And, as Philippa Foot argues, for an enlightened egoist, "even those who combine with him will know that on a change of fortune, or a shift of affection, he may turn to plunder them, and he must be as wary of their treachery as they are of his." "Moral Beliefs," in *Theories of Ethics,* edited by Philippa Foot (Oxford: Oxford University Press, 1967), p. 100. Whether these observations tell against egoism, or only recommend its careful deployment, depends on how one's character figures in others' willingness to cooperate. Hobbes seems sometimes to think egoists will inevitably suffer reduced opportunities and other times to

egoists, it seems, may well be forced to forego many of the benefits of society because of their character. And, sacrificing the option of cooperation within society, they will find themselves opportunity poor. Egoism's attraction apparently rests on ignoring the impact one's character has on one's opportunities.

This suggests a simple argument for choosing to be moral. A person who is moral can expect to enjoy the benefits of cooperation when they arise. She will be able to cooperate with others who observe moral constraints to take advantage of opportunities that are unavailable to egoists no matter how enlightened. These benefits (so the argument goes) may surely be expected to more than outweigh the burden of moral constraints. To quote from *Ecclesiastes* (4,9), "Two are better than one. . . . For if they fall, the one will lift up his fellow; but woe to him that is alone when he falleth; for he hath not another to help him up." Once the benefits of cooperation are taken into account, it seems that, in choosing one's character, self-interest itself recommends abandoning self-interested reasoning in favor of moral reasoning.[12]

This simple argument depends, unhappily, on the assumption that one's character will reliably affect one's opportunities for cooperation. Yet egoists will be excluded from cooperative ventures only if others are aware of their character. Anyone, including an enlightened egoist, may enjoy the fruits of cooperation as long as others *believe* they are interacting with someone who is moral. Egoists who are mistaken for being moral may take advantage both of cooperation *and* of promising exploitation strategies. We are back again, then, to self-interest recommending that one stick with enlightened egoism as long as one maintains the appearance of constraint.

There is one easy way of avoiding this conclusion. A defense of being moral will be forthcoming if the argument is supplemented by the assumption that people have full knowledge of their cohorts' characters.[13] Assuming the transparency of one's character to one's peers would guarantee that one's character affects which options are available. The transparency assumption would rule out, by fiat, the possibility of deception. Given this assumption, being moral would be reinstated as a real contender. As long as one is a transparent member of a society of transparent people, it would be a sure winner. Otherwise, if one is the lone transparent person (or one of a few) in a society of others not so transparent, the choice between being an egoist and being moral will

---

think that enlightened egoists will recognize the costs of breaking covenants and so will refrain from breaking them.

[12] This argument is advanced by Gauthier in "Reason and Maximization," and in *Morals by Agreement*.

[13] The need for some such assumption is pointed out by Stephen Darwall in *Impartial Reason* (Ithaca, NY: Cornell University Press, 1983), p. 197; and by Derek Parfit, in *Reasons and Persons*, p. 18.

turn on whether the benefits one can expect from cooperation outweigh the risks one takes of being played for a sucker. Either way, the transparency assumption brings the choice of being moral back into the game.

Transparency, however, is not an innocuous idealizing assumption. If *we* are to have a reason to choose to be moral, the calculation of expected utility must be based on *our* expectations. This part of the argument depends crucially on accurate rather than idealized data. Unlike assumptions of full rationality and indifference to others' welfare, which might reasonably be introduced to ensure that the claims of morality depend neither on one's own irrationality nor on one's compassion for others, the idealization of transparency simply renders the argument applicable to almost no one.[14]

Introducing the transparency assumption may generate a defense of being moral, then, but at the expense of robbing the argument of application. We are led, therefore, to ask for some assumption weaker than transparency – one that could allow us to show that *we* (and the miscreants with whom we deal) have self-interested grounds for choosing to be moral.

To this end, we might (following David Gauthier) draw a distinction between those who are transparent and those who are either translucent or opaque, where the distinction is drawn in terms of a person's chances of having her character correctly identified by others.[15] A person is *transparent* if and only if others can always determine her character. She is *opaque* if and only if others have merely an equal chance of correctly identifying her character. And she is *translucent* if and only if others have better than an equal chance of correctly identifying her character but cannot do so unfailingly. So defined, one's relative transparency, while a reflection of one's self, is a reflection in the eyes of others; whether one's character is correctly identified and how often depends largely on the skill of the identifier.

Unlike transparency, translucency appears to be a realistic assumption concerning the extent to which real people are able to identify each other's character; for the most part, we can fairly reliably determine the character of those with whom we interact. Moreover, if we make some reasonable assumptions concerning the relative benefits from being moral and from being self-interested, translucency provides a connection between character and available opportunities that is sufficient to justify the choice of being moral.

The structure of the choice we're imagining shows up if we consider

---

[14] Whether these assumptions really accomplish all they are meant to is questionable; see Christopher Morris, "The Relation Between Self-Interest and Justice in Contractarian Ethics," *Social Philosophy and Policy* 5 (1988): 119–53.
[15] *Morals by Agreement*, p. 174.

a two-person interaction.[16] Suppose that the two will act strictly in accordance with their own self-interest *except*

(i) if both are disposed to be moral and recognize each other as such, in which case they will work together to yield cooperative outcomes (when appropriate); or

(ii) if one is a person who is disposed to reason morally and mistakes the other (an enlightened egoist who recognizes the first for what he is) as a moral person, in which case the first respects moral constraints and the second feigns to but takes advantage of promising exploitation strategies.

The difference between reasoning morally and reasoning with an eye solely to self-interest becomes practically important only when facing opportunities for interaction that proffer the following expected payoffs:

successful exploitation: 1
moral cooperation: u'' (less than 1)
noncooperation: u' (less than u'')
unsuccessful moral cooperation: 0 (less than u')

Three probabilities are relevant to the calculation of one's expected utility under these conditions:

p = probability of correctly identifying another's character
q = probability another will correctly identify one's character
r = probability that one will be interacting with a person disposed to be moral[17]

As one disposed to be moral, one's average expected utility will be equal to one's expected benefits from noncooperative interactions, plus the expected benefits from successful cooperation, minus the expected losses of being played successfully for a sucker. Thus, a moral person's average expected utility equals

$$(A)\ u' + [rpq(u'' - u')] - \{[(1 - r)\ (1 - p)q]u'\}$$

As an enlightened egoist, one's average expected utility is equal to one's expected benefits from noncooperative interactions, plus one's expected benefits from successful exploitation. Thus, an enlightened egoist's average expected utility equals

[16] The argument offered here can be found in *Morals by Agreement*, pp. 175–7.

[17] To avoid confusion, I should note that Gauthier defines the variables differently; he uses p to stand for the probability that constrained maximizers (those who reason morally) will recognize each other and cooperate successfully; and he uses q to stand for the probability that constrained maximizers will fail to identify, yet be identified by, straightforward maximizers who exploit them. For our purposes, the differences do not matter.

(B) $u' + \{[rp(1 - q)](1 - u')\}$

(since $[rp(1 - q)]$ is the probability that one is interacting with a moral person one can correctly identify even while being misidentified oneself; and $(1 - u')$ is the benefit one may expect from successful exploitation).

Choosing to be a moral person may be expected to pay if and only if (A) is greater than (B).

In order to give some flesh to the argument, suppose that, when making the choice of one's character, one can expect the average payoffs from (i) successful immoral strategies (that rely on duplicity and exploitation), (ii) successful attempts at moral cooperation (that respect moral constraints), (iii) noncooperation (that forsakes the benefits and risks of cooperation), and (iv) unsuccessful moral cooperation (where one attempts moral cooperation but suffers from being exploited), to fall along the following lines:

> successful exploitation: 1
> successful moral cooperation: 0.66
> noncooperation: 0.33
> unsuccessful moral cooperation: 0

The following table represents a sampling of the probability distributions that, taken row by row, give the choice of being moral an average expected utility equal to that of enlightened egoism:

p	q	r
0.7	0.7	0.75
0.7	0.75	0.56
0.7	0.8	0.46
0.75	0.7	0.70
0.75	0.75	0.50
0.75	0.8	0.40
0.8	0.8	0.33

Given these average expected payoffs, for instance, a translucent person who has a probability of being correctly identified at least equal 0.7, and who finds herself in a community of (apparently) equally translucent people, should choose to be moral – as long as more than 75% of her companions appear to her to be moral as well. Taking the assumed payoffs, and a populationwide average probability of being correctly identified of 0.7, the 75% figure marks the break-even point for choosing to be moral: with these expected payoffs and probability estimates, being moral will have the same average expected utility as being an enlightened egoist.[18] Of course, the assumptions concerning expected payoffs and probabilities will be sufficient for a rational (i.e., self-interested) choice, even here, only if the probabilities are *unrealistically* taken to be fixed.

[18] Throughout the probabilities are the subjective probabilities of the agent in question.

If they are not fixed, calculations of self-interest will require information concerning the expected utility of attempting to alter the values for p, q, and r, and they will have to take account of the expected utility of deception, deception detection, and moral education.

If the relevant thresholds are met, though, the choice of being moral will find support from calculated self-interest. When the threshold values are not met, of course, self-interest will still recommend enlightened egoism, either because one's character will be so frequently misidentified, or because one is too likely to misidentify a companion, or because one is so likely to run across others who will willingly violate the constraints morality places on self-interest. Simply being a translucent person is not enough to justify the choice of a moral character. If others in one's community are relatively opaque, or if a sufficient number are unvarnished egoists, then being moral would simply set one up as a sitting duck. The choice of a moral character is rational, then, only if one has reason to think one is a (sufficiently) translucent member of a community of (sufficiently) translucent moral people.

So the question arises: Is the translucency assumption really weak enough to apply to almost everyone – even the moral miscreants we want so much to convert? Two attractive arguments, when taken together, suggest it is. First, resorting to random guessing will provide one with an even chance of correctly identifying the characters of one's companions. So, one might argue, we are justified in assuming that everyone has at least an even chance of being correctly identified. Second, since opacity renders one a bad risk, those who are opaque will often be excluded from cooperative ventures regardless of their true character. Thus, each person who is opaque will have reason to increase her translucency so as to be able to take advantage of opportunities closed to those who are opaque.

These arguments work together because the first claims that when it comes to the probability of being correctly identified everyone will fall within the range limited at one end by opacity and at the other by transparency, while the second suggests that anyone who falls near the bottom of that range will have reason to move up the scale toward transparency. Together these arguments appear to support the view that everyone either will be, or will have reason to be, translucent. If the arguments succeed, then they will advance the defense of being moral without sacrificing its applicability to real people.

The two arguments, however, ignore both the availability and the impact of deception. They leave out of account the all-too-large gap that may separate what people are from what they seem to be. The first argument correctly points out that random guessing would result in an even chance of correctly identifying each of one's companions. But there is no good reason to think people will always do as well as they would if they were to guess randomly. After all, people will resort to random guessing only when they lack what they consider to be reliable evidence concerning a person's character. Yet deceptive people will be careful to provide the requisite (though misleading) evidence for those with whom they interact. They will develop winning smiles, travel with a glowing reputation, and cultivate an honest manner. Sadly, this sort of magic is worked (without a ring of Gyges) all too frequently.[19] Such people *seem* both translucent and trustworthy. When the deceptive have worked their magic, their companions will quite reasonably, given their information, misjudge character with regularity. The deceptive may very well become transopaque; successful deception may actually reduce the probability of correct identification to far below what random guessing would allow. There might even be people, the megaopaque (I will call them), who are so successful in their deceptions that their probability of being correctly identified approaches zero. So much for the first argument.

The second argument turns on the claim that opacity will prove to be a burden. There are some people who offer no clues as to their character. They are opaque to others because they have poker faces. And, as the argument emphasizes, having a poker face may well prove a real burden, since some people will hesitate to interact with those they think they cannot predict. So being opaque *may* severely limit one's prospects for cooperation. If it does, then the opaque will have reason to change. But opacity need not be an easily detectable characteristic. One may be opaque (or even trans- or megaopaque) while being the sort of person who inspires confidence. Such people will not be shunned by others. In fact, and unfortunately, those enlightened egoists who can increase their transopacity stand to gain significantly from doing so. The greater their transopacity, the more frequently they will be mistakenly embraced by their fellows as moral. Transopaque egoists can expect to gain all the benefits of being constrained by morality without suffering its cumbersome constraints. Moreover, they will so benefit even within a community of perfectly rational companions.

Certainly, for those who are already confirmed in their disposition to reason morally, as transparency decreases – as long as others are aware of the decreases – opportunities for cooperation will diminish. And, for the same people, increases in their own translucency will be occasioned

---

[19] Think of used car salesmen. They suffer a horrendous general reputation but still manage to convince almost every customer that, this time, the customer is getting honest treatment and a fair deal on that rare used car too good to pass up. Or, to use a fictional but amusingly plausible example, think of Harry Flashman, the cheat, bully, scoundrel, and coward, with the reputation of a hero. See George MacDonald Fraser, *Flashman* (New York: New American Library, 1984). Just how often people carry out successful deceptions is, of course, impossible to tell. That people do, though, is beyond question. For some disturbing research, see R. Christie and F. Geis, *Studies in Machiavellianism* (New York: Academic Press, 1970) and A. Harrington, *Psychopaths* (New York: Simon and Schuster, 1972).

by more opportunities for cooperation, as well as greater risks of being played the fool. For people who are already moral, then, there may be reason to increase translucency (as long as they are in a community of others who are moral).

Yet not everyone benefits from becoming more translucent. Those who may choose both their character and their appearance ought, on self-interested grounds, choose to be transopaque enlightened egoists. They will enjoy many of the benefits and none of the burdens of being constrained by morality (assuming it is cheaper to maintain transopacity than it is to forego exploitation strategies). For some, of course, the burden of keeping up appearances will not be worthwhile.[20] But for others, the costs of the masquerade may well be more than offset by the opportunity to exploit others whenever the dictates of self-interest demand.

Even so, one might object, the plausibility of transopacity itself depends on the assumption that a community will not raise the costs of transopacity so as to protect itself against deception. Since everyone benefits from having translucent and trustworthy compatriots, everyone has reason to increase the proportion of people in the population who are translucent and moral (as long as the benefits are not swallowed up by the corresponding costs of change). Especially in a community of fully rational agents, one might expect, transopacity will disappear as a viable option because the community will work to make the price of successful deception prohibitive. The society might introduce improved socialization procedures and no doubt there would even be a boom in detection-device technology. At some point, it seems, the risks of being a concealed enlightened egoist might outweigh the benefits.

One problem with this argument is that it assumes conditions that do not, and probably never will, hold; it assumes (implausibly) that we live in a community that will raise significantly the risks of deception, and it plays on considerations of what would happen in a community of fully rational agents (a community we surely don't live in now). What it is prudent for us to do, though, does not depend on what would be prudent for us to do in imaginary situations. Other people's limitations and weaknesses, not just their talents and strengths, are clearly relevant

---

[20] Gerald Postema suggests that, according to Hume, the costs of deception include cutting oneself off from others, and to do this "is to cut oneself off *from oneself*, for it is only in the mirror of the souls of others that one finds one's own identity." Yet, as Postema points out, this cost of deception may be avoided by adopting a disposition to be selectively just (say, to one's family or social class). Then one could avoid having to deceive everyone and would thus avoid cutting oneself off from all others and so from oneself. Selective justice allows all the benefits of community without the burdens of uncircumscribed justice. See "Hume's Reply to the Sensible Knave," *History of Philosophy Quarterly* 5 (1988): 23–40. History provides ample testimony to both the possibility and the benefits of such a selective disposition to be just. See Bernard Boxill, "How Injustice Pays," *Philosophy and Public Affairs* 9 (1980): 359–71.

to our own calculations of prudence. Since people are, in fact, both ignorant and irrational, an argument that must assume otherwise is not of practical interest (if one's interest is guided by self-interest). Indeed, given that people are all too susceptible to irrationality, there may even be good self-interested reason for the rational to encourage irrationality in others (at least within certain limits and concerning certain things).[21]

Suppose for the sake of the argument, however, that (when pursuing prudence) we should concern ourselves with what would be prudent for us were we to live in a society of fully rational agents. Why should we think that, in such a society, deceit will be irrational? It may be, of course, that the chances of detection would become so great as to outweigh all benefits of deception. But this need not happen – even in a community of fully rational agents. At some point, detecting the immoral will likely end up costing more than the damage they cause. There is no reason to think that a point of diminishing returns will not be reached before deceit has been completely eradicated. If such a point is reached, the immoral who can remain undetected will have no reason to become moral. Even in a society of perfectly rational agents, then, it may pay to be immoral. Of course, whether it will pay for a particular person cannot be decided in the abstract. The rationality of being immoral depends, in idealized as well as in actual circumstances, on one's ability to deceive others.

In any case when we are talking about real people, in actual situations, it is clear that sometimes the costs of deception may, for individuals, be more than balanced by expected benefits. Those who are able to conceal their character successfully (as many are) will often be better off from the self-interested point of view if they become (or remain) immoral. Perhaps when we consider a community composed of perfectly rational people, the liabilities of being immoral become more substantial. But even for the perfectly rational living amongst their peers, being immoral will be rational if deception is a viable option. So one cannot generate a wholesale condemnation of immorality on grounds of irrationality (as long as one accepts the view that rationality is a matter of maximizing expected satisfaction of one's own preferences whatever they happen to be).

Hobbes and Hume both maintained that being moral may sometimes be irrational. At least, they pointed out, a just person who falls in among rogues ought to act as a rogue (morality be damned, lest one live in hell). Justice, they said, must give way to self-preservation. As Hume argued, if "it should be a virtuous man's fate to fall into the society of ruffians," then

---

[21] As Mary Gibson argues, "in a competitive society, it is, in general, in the interests of each person to be as rational as possible but to have his or her competitors to be as irrational as possible (within certain limits, of course)." "Rationality," *Philosophy and Public Affairs* 6 (1977): 193–225; see p. 218.

" . . . he must consult the dictates of self-preservation alone, without concern for those who no longer merit his care and attention."[22]

Glaucon's challenge, however, concerns not the just person who is among rogues, but the rogue favored with the company of the just. Under such circumstances does the rogue have any self-interested reason to become moral? Our answer must be "no" as long as the rogue can (at reasonable cost) successfully deceive her companions. And this means that the answer that haunts the moralists and bolsters the miscreants may be correct: there may be no self-interested reason, for some, to be moral.

Yet if this answer haunts moralists, a second threatens permanent nightmares. Many have suggested that morality is positively irrational. The moral, they have argued, are victims of an exploitative and onerous myth; paraphrasing Marx, they declare morality an opiate of the masses. Morality, they say, is but a tool in the hands of the powerful used to control the submissive. Better by far to shake off the chains of morality and live a life of enlightened egoism.[23]

This is a nightmare from which we should not suffer. It is not true, unfortunately, that all rational agents, however constituted, have a self-interested reason to become moral. Nonetheless, rationality – *even when very narrowly construed* – permits and sometimes demands that we be, and not merely seem, moral. Many people, in fact, have sound self-interested grounds for abandoning egoism in favor of morality. Specifically, at least three sorts of people may have reason (self-interested reason) to choose to be really moral: (1) those who are permanently translucent (if they are in a community of moral people); (2) those for whom deception comes at significant personal cost (say, to their sense of integrity or pride); and, most importantly, (3) those who have the capacity to participate in a moral community, and so have the ability to embrace as valuable goals other than those fixed by self-interest. This last group is especially important, I think, because almost all human beings belong to it.[24]

---

[22] *Enquiry Concerning the Principles of Morals,* p. 187. See also *A Treatise of Human Nature,* where Hume notes that I am likely to "be the cully of my integrity, if I alone shou'd impose on myself a severe restraint amidst the licentiousness of others," p. 535.

[23] "Any one man," Gauthier once argued, "will always do better if he is prudent." "Morality and Advantage," *The Philosophical Review* (1967): 460–75; see p. 469.

[24] Thanks are due to David Gauthier for the many conversations that prompted this paper, and to Neera Badhwar, David Braybrooke, Douglas Butler, Thomas Hill, Jr., Brad Hooker, Gerald Postema, Nicholas Rescher, Michael Resnik, Daniel Shapiro, Robert Shaver, Laurence Thomas and Gregory Trianosky, for commenting on an earlier incarnation of the arguments. I would also like to thank audiences at the Pacific Division Meetings of the American Philosophical Association, Wake Forest University, Dartmouth College, the University of Oklahoma, Wesleyan University, the University of North Carolina/Chapel Hill, Occidental College, The Ohio State University, the University of Colorado/Colorado Springs, and the Research Triangle Ethics Circle for helpful feedback.

13. Contractarianism and moral skepticism*

David Copp

Contractarian arguments have been offered in several different roles in recent moral theory. I shall focus exclusively on theories offered as a response to a skepticism about the rational credentials of morality.[1] Contractarian theories of this kind are characterized by two central ideas: a conception of the theoretically important skeptical challenge to morality and a conception of how that challenge can be met, by means of a series of results about rational bargaining and choice.

A contractarian sees the main skeptical challenge as consisting in a view of moralities as imposed ideologies that often call on people to act irrationally against their self-interest. The skeptic holds that people are neither rational to comply with morality nor to dispose themselves to comply. To be sure, many of us have preferences that can make it rational to comply with certain moral requirements. We have been socialized to

*This essay was prepared for presentation to the University of Western Ontario Colloquium on Contemporary Contractarian Theory, April 26, 1987. It is grounded in material from my manuscript, *Morality, Skepticism, and Society*, which is in progress. I would like to thank Peter Danielson and Geoffrey Sayre-McCord for helpful comments. I am grateful to the following institutions for their support of my work: the Social Sciences and Humanities Research Council of Canada, for a Research Grant and Research Time Stipend (410–82–0640), which I held during 1983 and 1984; the Campus Research Board of the University of Illinois at Chicago, for granting me a Short Research Leave during 1985; Simon Fraser University for allowing me to take leaves of absence; and, finally, the Research Triangle Foundation and the National Humanities Center, North Carolina, for granting me a fellowship that enabled me to complete my work on this paper.
[1] This idea has a distinguished pedigree that can be traced back through Hobbes to classical philosophy. Plato discussed a simple contractarian account of the origin of justice in the *Republic* (358b–9b), but he regarded it as inadequate, on the ground that it treated justice as merely instrumentally valuable rather than as inherently valuable. It seemed to imply that the man who has "the power to do wrong" would be mad to commit himself not to do wrong. Any contractarian theory in this tradition treats morality as instrumentally valuable.

comply with the going moral code, and we have emotions and feelings and attachments to other people that can make it rational to comply with the going moral code. In addition, certain of the going moral requirements are supported by sanctions in a way that can make it prudent to comply. But the skeptical position is that these are reasons for compliance that obtain only adventitiously or because the going requirements have been imposed on us through socialization or threats of sanctions. A person would not rationally choose to have the preferences, or the emotions, feelings and attachments, or to be subject to the sanctions, that can make it rational to be moral.

The contractarian strategy for defeating this challenge is to argue that there is a set of moral requirements such that, at least under certain conditions, a population of fully rational people would agree to comply with them, dispose themselves to comply with them, and in fact comply with them, given the reasonable expectation of mutual benefit. People would be rational so to agree, and rational to comply, even if, hypothetically, they had no antecedent moral preferences and no attachments to other people, and even if they were bargaining outside of society, where they were not subject to the sanctions of an antecedently accepted societal moral code. The contractarian claims that the moral requirements that are adequately and appropriately justified are those, and only those, if any, that are defensible in this manner, as objects of hypothetical rational agreement and rational compliance.

David Gauthier has developed these ideas in a strikingly sophisticated and interesting way, so I shall discuss his theory in some detail.[2] My aim is to expose the main shortcomings of his approach with a view to drawing some general conclusions about the likelihood of a successful contractarian theory of morality.

I shall not take issue with the contractarian thesis that the skeptical position outlined constitutes a major theoretically important challenge to ethics. I agree that a defender of morality must be prepared to argue that morality is not merely an imposed ideology with no rational justification. However, I suggest that insofar as this challenge is reasonable, it can be defeated without showing, as contractarians think they must show, that commitment to a justified morality is rational for every person in its scope and actual compliance is also rational for everyone. Progress was made in dealing with skepticism about the "external world" when we realized that there is no need to establish certainty, but only knowledge. Similarly, part of the problem with contractarianism is a mistaken conception of what can sensibly be asked of a nonskeptical theory of morality.

---

[2] I refer mainly to David Gauthier, *Morals by Agreement* (Oxford: Oxford University Press, 1986). Unless otherwise noted, references found in parentheses in the text are to this book. When clarity requires, I will cite the book as "Gauthier, 1986."

This criticism would be of little interest if Gauthier's defense of morality were successful. However, I shall argue that it is not successful, and I shall ultimately argue that the contractarian view of the nature of the skeptical challenge, and the constraints that are entailed by a contractarian approach to meeting it, ensure that the challenge cannot be met by a contractarian theory.

After discussing in more detail Gauthier's view of the skeptical problem and his strategy for solving it, I turn to a series of objections. Gauthier believes he can establish that rational agents would dispose themselves to comply conditionally with a set of requirements that would be agreed to in rational bargaining. But, first, even if he is correct about this, he cannot show that people would be rational *actually* to comply with these requirements under the relevant conditions. Second, he cannot show that they are *moral* requirements. Skeptics deny the rational credentials of moral requirements, not of every kind of requirement, and so contractarians must show the relevance of their theory to the concerns of a skeptic. I shall argue that the person-centered nature of contractarian theory ensures that it cannot do justice to the societal nature of morality. Gauthier can perhaps show that a specific conditional disposition to cooperate, by complying with the results of rational bargaining, would be rational for certain people in certain circumstances. Yet, third, a skeptic should concede this, while pointing out it does not follow that this disposition would be rational for other people under other circumstances. In fact, fourth, Gauthier cannot show that this disposition would be rational for people with ordinary preferences and ordinary moral motivations under ordinary conditions. This means he cannot show that ordinary people have any reason to interest themselves in the requirements he claims to be the only rationally justified moral requirements. These are objections that accept the contractarian view of what is required in order to defeat skepticism. Underlying all of them is the fact that the contractarian strategy is grounded in a subjective instrumental and relativistic conception of rational choice. Because of this, the most it can produce is a justification addressed to each individual and relativized to that individual's preferences and circumstances. It cannot yield a justification of any moral code as such. I believe this is the fundamental difficulty with the contractarian approach.

The skeptical problem: First account

David Gauthier opens *Morals by Agreement* with these remarks.[3]

What theory of morals can ever serve any useful purpose unless it can show that all the duties it recommends are also the true interest of each individual?

[3] The quotation is from p. 1. In the original, there is a footnote at the end of the first

David Hume, who asked this question, seems mistaken; such a theory would be too useful. Were duty no more than interest, morals would be superfluous. . . .

But if the language of morals is not that of interest, it is surely that of reason. What theory of morals, we might better ask, can ever serve any useful purpose, unless it can show that all the duties it recommends are also truly endorsed in each individual's reason?

Gauthier goes on to say that he will defend the "traditional conception of morality" by showing that "principles of action that prescribe duties overriding advantage," or principles that constrain the pursuit of individual interest, "may be rationally justified" (p. 2). As he says, "our concern is to *validate* the conception of morality as a set of *rational, impartial constraints on the pursuit of individual interest*" (p. 6, my emphasis). And he claims that if his defense of morality fails, then "a rational morality is a chimera, so that there is no rational and impartial constraint on the pursuit of individual utility" (p. 158).

Philosophers differ in their conceptions of what is required for a "rational justification" of moral principles. Those with an epistemic conception of this would conceive of the central challenge to morality as one that could only be defeated by a showing that we can have moral knowledge. But a contractarian's view of the required mode of justification is quite different in being *practical* and *person-centered*. As Gauthier says, it must be shown that moral principles are "a subset of rational principles for choice," so that "To choose rationally, one must choose morally" (p. 4). The reference is plainly to practical reason, or the theory of rational choice.[4] Hence, Gauthier says, a contractarian theory of morals, "developed as part of the theory of rational choice," establishes the "rationality of *actual compliance*" with moral principles by showing that they are rational constraints "on choice and action" (p. 17, my emphasis).[5]

---

sentence that cites David Hume, *An Enquiry Concerning the Principles of Morals*, sec. ix, pt. ii.

[4] I characterize Gauthier's strategy as involving a practical and person-centered conception of the justification of moral principles, as opposed to an epistemic conception. This does not mean that I disagree with Holly Smith's characterization of Gauthier's strategy, in para. 3 of the sixth section of her "Deriving Morality from Rationality," in Chapter 14 in this volume. My idea is that Gauthier aims to show that certain moral principles are justified by means of an argument that essentially involves premises in the theory of individual rational choice. This is also Smith's idea.

[5] In a reply to three critics, Gauthier insists that a moral theory must show that there is some moral code that each person would be rational to dispose himself to comply with, and actually to comply with, provided enough others do so as well. Only in this way, can the theory show that the considerations the code treats as reasons are genuine reasons with "a hold on the reflectively rational agent," and that the code is not "a system of domination." See David Gauthier, "Moral Artifice," *Canadian Journal of Philosophy* 18 (1988): 385–418. Hereafter references to this article will be placed in the text, and it will be cited as "Gauthier, 1988."

A contractarian theory must begin with a conception of practical reason, for it must give some content to the notion of rational choice. And to avoid begging the question, this conception must be one a moral skeptic could accept. It must be morally neutral at least in not directly entailing that it is rational to be moral. Gauthier assumes a "weak and widely accepted" conception of rational choice, according to which a person chooses rationally if and only if she maximizes her expected utility (p. 182). And, her utility is defined as a measure of her "considered" preferences, where considered preferences are "those that would pass the tests of reflection and experience" (pp. 31, 21–46). Rational choice for a person is a function of the person's preferences.

It seems obviously to follow from the utility-maximizing conception that no one could *rationally* comply with any *constraint* on his pursuit of maximum expected utility. So, if morality is a set of such constraints, then it seems to follow that compliance with morality cannot avoid being contrary to reason, except on those occasions when compliance coincidentally will maximize one's expected utility. Yet Gauthier's approach commits him to showing that compliance with a justified moral code would be mandated by reason. He assumes that an adequate nonskeptical account of morality must show that moral principles are "a subset of rational principles for choice," even while assuming both that moral principles are *constraints* on one's pursuit of maximin expected utility and that rationality requires one to *maximize* one's expected utility. This is an extraordinarily heavy burden of justification, one that looks impossible to discharge.

The contractarian solution

Gauthier's ingenious solution involves moving from the appraisal of one's choices to the appraisal of one's dispositions to choose. This reorientation of rational assessment, coordinated with a key amendment to the theory that rational choice consists in straightforward expected utility maximization, is meant to yield the desired result. He argues that one can maximize one's expected utility in choosing to form a specific conditional disposition to conform with certain constraints on maximizing activity, viz., constrained maximization. Because this is so, constrained maximization is a rational disposition, and, Gauthier claims, any action that "expresses" this disposition *also* counts as rational, even if it involves, as any such action might, the failure to maximize one's expected utility.[6]

---

[6] "Expresses" is the word Gauthier uses in this context. See p. 183. I assume the idea is that an agent's action expresses a disposition to do *A* in circumstances *C* if and only if the agent is disposed to do *A* in circumstances *C*, and the action is a case of doing *A* in circumstances *C*, and the agent's disposition explains his action.

Suppose there is a scheme of cooperation that is mutually beneficial, in the sense that everyone's compliance with it would yield each an expected utility that exceeds the utility he would expect if everyone directly maximized his expected utility. It occasionally might require someone to act in a way that is not to his maximum benefit. Nevertheless, it could be that each of us would maximize his expectation of benefit by being conditionally disposed to comply with this scheme's requirements, as a constrained maximizer. On these assumptions, Gauthier claims, each of us would be rational to comply with the scheme, when compliance expresses his disposition, even on occasions where, in complying, he fails to maximize his expectation of benefit (pp. 169–70).[7]

If the contractarian strategy for defeating moral skepticism is to succeed, two major problems must be solved. Gauthier does not require that a justified moral requirement or code *actually* result from bargaining, nor does he require that it be "the unique joint strategy that *would* be prescribed by a rational bargain" (p. 168, my emphasis). It is enough that a code approximate the result of a hypothetical rational bargain, by affording each agent "a utility approaching what she would expect from fully rational co-operation" (p. 168). Moreover, in Gauthier's view, rational bargaining must take place in the framework of rational moral constraints that are the precondition for rational bargaining (pp. 146, 150, 193, 213–14, 85). So the first problem, that of rational bargaining, is to specify the prescriptions that a group of agents would agree to comply with in a rational bargain, or, at least, to specify criteria such prescriptions must satisfy, and to specify the conditions and constraints that rational bargainers would observe in their bargaining, given a reasonable prospect of striking a bargain. In this connection, Gauthier proposes his proviso and principle of minimax relative concession. The second problem, that of rational subscription, is to show that any agent in the scope of prescriptions that meet these criteria and conditions would be rational to subscribe to them on the condition that enough others do so as well. In this connection, Gauthier argues for the rationality of constrained maximization, as a disposition to comply. To these two problems, Gauthier adds the problem of rational compliance, which grows out of his understanding of the skeptical challenge. The skeptic denies the rationality of complying with any moral code when doing so would fail to maximize one's expected utility. Hence, Gauthier aims to show that each agent in the scope of a contractually based moral code

---

[7] This apparently paradoxical position is analogous to a position one might adopt in a utilitarian moral theory. Truth telling might fail to maximize social welfare on certain occasions, even if the *disposition* to tell the truth is recommended as welfare maximizing. In general, certain *actions* that *fail* to maximize expected social welfare might be prompted by a *disposition* that, arguably, it maximizes expected social welfare for people to have. When this is so, an indirect utilitarian theorist might claim, for example, that truth telling is morally required.

would be rational actually to comply with the code, on every occasion when so doing expresses the conditional disposition of constrained maximization.[8]

The bargainers are idealized, as they must be because of the nature of the skeptical challenge. The skeptic recognizes that people have attachments to other people, and moralized feelings and emotions that have resulted from their socialization, and she recognizes that the requirements of the going morality are often supported by the threat of sanctions of one form or another. Therefore, she does not deny that many people are in fact rational to dispose themselves to comply, and actually to comply, with the going moral code. But she claims that compliance, and the disposition to comply, would not otherwise be rational. Consequently, to meet the skeptical challenge, the contractarian proposes to argue that compliance and the disposition to comply would be rational *even* for people who lacked moral attitudes, attachments to other people, and so on. It would be rational *even* for people who had full information, who were fully rational, and who had the opportunity fully to consider the costs and benefits of proposed bargains. Accordingly, Gauthier idealizes the bargainers. They are imaginary ideal parties bargaining in an hypothetical situation where their bargaining is cost-free.[9] They are equally and fully rational, in that each aims to maximize his expected utility. They lack moral motivations, but they are fully informed. They do not try to influence the bargaining by making threats (p. 156). And they have no (basic) preferences regarding the preference satisfaction of the others with whom they are interacting. In Gauthier's words, they have no basic "non-tuistic preferences" (p. 87).[10]

Gauthier argues that ideal agents of this sort would recognize certain principles as constraining their bargaining. The first of these is the proviso, which "prohibits bettering one's situation through interaction that worsens the situation of another" (p. 205), and which is supposed to set the baseline for bargaining. The second is the principle of minimax

---

[8] It is not the case that a constrained maximizer would always act as he is morally required to act. Compare Gauthier's qualifications on p. 232 with his remarks on pp. 1–2.

[9] Jody S. Kraus and Jules Coleman argue that Gauthier's assumption that the bargaining is cost-free implies that it is irrational. However, they interpret the assumption to mean that the parties have nothing to gain by bargaining, and I think this interpretation is wrong. I believe Gauthier intends us to imagine that the bargaining itself is cost-free, as if time were suspended while it took place. He does not intend us to imagine that nothing is to be gained by agreement. See Kraus and Coleman, "Morality and the Theory of Rational Choice," Chapter 15 in this volume.

[10] A tuistic desire is a desire of a person regarding the desire of some other person. The nontuist has no such desires regarding the desires of those with whom she interacts, unless satisfying or frustrating the desire of another person would be a means to satisfying a nontuistic desire of her own. She neither desires that the preferences of some others be satisfied, nor that they not be satisfied, except where the satisfaction of such desires would be instrumental to the satisfaction of more basic nontuistic desires. She has no "basic" tuistic desires. See p. 311.

relative concession, which, Gauthier argues, governs the bargaining of ideally rational parties.[11] He contends that these principles can be used to specify criteria that a moral scheme must meet in order that compliance with it would be rational.

Constrained maximization may lead a person to restrict her maximizing activity. A straightforward maximizer will cooperate if and only if cooperating would maximize his expected utility. A constrained maximizer is more willing to cooperate. She would be disposed to comply with a scheme of cooperation that restricts her maximizing activity on condition that, among other things, the scheme does not afford her significantly less utility than she would receive from a scheme that ideally rational agents would agree to, bargaining in accord with the principle of minimax relative concession in a situation where the proviso had not been violated (pp. 222–3, 225–7, also 146, 150, 193, 213–14, 85). Notice that the definition of constrained maximization links the bargaining problem to the problems of subscription and compliance. In general, a constrained maximizer will cooperate with a person provided the probability of that person's cooperating, and the payoff from mutual cooperation by comparison with mutual noncooperation are both sufficiently high.[12] Gauthier argues that constrained maximizers have opportunities to benefit from cooperation that are not available to straightforward maximizers. Under certain psychological assumptions, the expected utility of a constrained maximizer exceeds that of a straightforward maximizer (pp. 172–8), and so constrained maximization is a rational disposition.

Hence, Gauthier's response to a skeptic is that constrained maximization is a rational disposition, and the proviso and minimax relative concession are rationally defensible. The skeptic is wrong to think that *no* moral code could be rationally complied with, and be the object of a rational agreement, among agents who have not been coerced or ma-

---

[11] Gauthier contends that ideal parties would agree to minimize the maximum concession made by any party to an agreement; not the maximum in absolute magnitude, measured in utility or in any other way, but the maximum relative concession, where one's relative concession is measured by the proportion between the utility that one concedes and the utility that one would have gained had one been permitted all of the incremental benefits of agreement (p. 136).

[12] More exactly, a constrained maximizer is disposed to do his part in a scheme assigning roles to the members of a group provided that three conditions are satisfied. (1) Everyone's acting on this scheme would yield him at least as much utility as everyone's maximizing his own utility, and (2) it would yield him nearly the utility he would expect from a scheme "determined by minimax relative concession." And (3), his expected utility in acting on this strategy is greater than it would be if everyone maximized his own utility. In evaluating the latter, he takes into account the probability that some members of the group will not comply with the scheme. Gauthier's formulation is slightly different. See p. 167. Notice that a scheme may satisfy these conditions even if there are occasions in which a person's expected utility in acting on the scheme is less than it would be if she straightforwardly maximized her own utility.

nipulated or socialized or otherwise predisposed to prefer to comply with it. Yet Gauthier is inclined to agree with the skeptic that moral codes that a constrained maximizer would not comply with are unjustified and could only gain currency in a society through some form of coercion.[13] For example, he says, a good samaritan morality, or a Rawlsian principle of justice, would require "some to give free rides to others, or to be hosts for their parasitism" (p. 219). If he is correct, then rational agents bargaining in accord with minimax relative concession in a situation where the proviso has not been violated would not agree to comply with principles of this sort. Compliance with such principles would not express a rational disposition, and would not be rational, except among agents who have been coerced or manipulated or socialized or otherwise predisposed to prefer to comply with them.

Rational compliance and skepticism

In the remaining sections, I explore the series of objections to contractarianism that I sketched earlier, beginning with the problem of rational compliance. It is here that Gauthier's amendment to the standard maximizing account of rational choice is critical. He has set himself the requirement to show the rationality of actual compliance with rationally justified moral schemes, but there is a gap between the rationality of disposing yourself to comply and the rationality of actually complying. For the rationality of conditionally disposing yourself to comply with certain constraints does not entail the rationality of *actually* complying with them in circumstances where they require you to act otherwise than would maximize your expected utility.

"The received interpretation," Gauthier says, "identifies rationality with utility-maximization at the level of particular choices" (p. 182). Instead, Gauthier asserts, one chooses rationally if and only if one's choice expresses a rational *disposition* to choose.[14] Here a disposition is

---

[13] See Gauthier's introductory discussion in Gauthier, 1988.

[14] There are two interpretations of Gauthier's position. On one interpretation, which is suggested by Gauthier's words on p. 183, an action is rational if and only if it *does* express a rational disposition. On this reading, an action that would in fact express an irrational disposition would not count as rational, no matter what could be said in its favor. And a morally required action would not count as rational unless it actually expressed a rational disposition to act morally. Hence, on this reading, if Gauthier is correct, only a constrained maximizer would be rational to act morally. I believe that Gauthier wants a stronger result. On the second interpretation, an action is rational if and only if it *could* express a rational disposition, in the following sense: the action is a case of doing A in C, and the disposition of doing A in C is a rational disposition that it is possible for the agent to have. On this reading, if Gauthier is correct, a morally required action would be rationally required even if the agent in question is not in fact a constrained maximizer. I believe that this is the result that Gauthier desires. However, this interpretation severs the evaluation of actions from the evaluation of their actual circumstances. It seems to mean that the rationality of the disposition I *would* have had,

rational for a person if and only if her expected utility from the choices she would make if she had that disposition is no less than it would be if she had any alternative disposition (pp. 182–3).[15] In "parametric" contexts, where one's choices do not affect others' choices, the disposition to maximize one's utility is utility maximizing; hence, we are rational *to be disposed to* utility maximize in parametric contexts, and it is rational *to utility maximize* in those contexts. However, this is not a rational disposition in "strategic" contexts, where interacting agents each choose their action partly on the basis of their expectations of the others' choices. "Constrained maximization" would lead agents to utility maximize in parametric contexts, but in strategic contexts, it would lead them to cooperate and thereby achieve higher utilities than would be achieved if they were straightforward utility maximizers. Constrained maximization is rational both in parametric and strategic contexts, and so we are rational in all contexts to act in ways which express *that* disposition.[16]

Unfortunately, Gauthier does not provide any argument in favor of this amendment, crucial though it is.[17] He does consider objections, and

if I had sincerely promised to meet my friend at his favorite restaurant, implies that I would be rational to meet my friend at the restaurant, even if I did not promise and I know he will not be there. I discuss these two interpretations of Gauthier's position in my "Irrational Deterrence of Rational Retaliation: Coherence and Priority Relations Between Rational Dispositions and Actions" (unpublished).

[15] Gauthier says, "A disposition is rational if and only if *an actor* holding it can expect his choices to yield no less utility than the choices he would make were he to hold any alternative disposition" (pp. 182–3, my emphasis). Does Gauthier mean to say that a disposition is rational just in case *any* actor could expect it to be utility maximizing? Or does he mean to say that a disposition is rational for an agent just in case *that agent* can expect it to be utility maximizing? His wording suggests the former, and if he is right that constrained maximization is a rational disposition for any agent, then the difference between the two wordings is unimportant. However, strictly speaking, he must be taken to mean the latter, for just as, on the received interpretation, choices are rational or irrational only in the context of a given agent's preferences, so dispositions can count as rational or irrational only in the context of a given agent's preferences. If I am correct that different dispositions can be utility maximizing for different agents, given differences among their preferences, then it follows that different dispositions can be rational for different agents.

[16] See pp. 182–3, 169. Gauthier explains that parametric contexts are those in which "the actor takes his action to be the sole variable in a fixed environment." Strategic contexts are those in which "the actor takes his behaviour to be but one variable among others, so that his choice must be responsive to his expectations of others' choices, while their choices are similarly responsive to their expectations" (p. 21). On these definitions, the character of a situation depends on the views of those in the situation. This seems a mistake. For example, sufficiently unimaginative or misguided agents may regard their behavior as the only variable in contexts that in fact involve interaction among agents. Surely the facts determine whether a context is strategic or parametric, not how the agents interpret the facts. The arms race between the Soviet Union and the United States is a strategic context, even if the President thinks that his actions are the only variable in an otherwise fixed environment.

[17] I mean there are no arguments in Gauthier, 1986. Gauthier does provide arguments in essays on the topic of nuclear deterrence, but I do not have the space to discuss them

he claims that his position is not defeated by them (pp. 184–7). But, even if he is right to claim this, as I think he is, it does not follow that his position is correct, and certain examples suggest that it is not correct.[18] I shall briefly consider deterrent threats, since Gauthier concedes that the example of failed threats is a suitable test case for our intuitions about the rationality of actions that express rational dispositions (p. 186). Suppose the effect of enforcing a particular threat against an aggressor, if it failed to deter him from attacking us, would be massive retaliation by him that would cause additional unacceptable losses of things of supreme value, such as would result from a large-scale nuclear exchange between the superpowers. Even on this supposition, it may be rational to make the threat and to *dispose ourselves to carry it out*, if there is a reasonable expectation that this strategy will maximize our safety from aggression, and especially if there is no other way to protect matters of great value. On Gauthier's position, it follows that it would be rational to carry out the threat. Yet I deny that it would be rational to carry it out if it failed to deter, given the known consequences of carrying it out. The example does not sway Gauthier, but it will persuade many other people that his position is mistaken.

Further, one of the skeptic's doctrines is that a rational person would fail to comply with moral standards whenever necessary to maximize her expected utility. Even if Gauthier can show that a rational person would be conditionally disposed to comply with morality, he has no argument against this skeptical thesis unless he can establish his conception of rationality. It begs the question simply to assert that it is rational to comply with a moral constraint when doing so expresses a rational disposition. Of course, there is no argument for the received view of rationality any more than for Gauthier's alternative, but if the goal is to defeat skepticism, it will not suffice to point this out. Gauthier himself thinks that a rational morality is a chimera unless he can make good his case.

It may be thought, however, that skepticism is not a very interesting position if all that remains of it is the gap between the rationality of conditionally disposing oneself to comply with moral constraint and the rationality of actually complying. If the rationality of constrained maximization is given, then a rational and informed skeptic will seek to acquire this disposition. If she succeeds, then her preferences will have shifted in tandem, to correspond with her tendency

here. I do discuss them in my "Irrational Deterrence or Rational Retaliation." There are at least two relevant papers by Gauthier: (1) "Deterrence, Maximization, and Rationality," *Ethics* 94 (1984): 474–95, also published in *The Security Gamble*, edited by Douglas MacLean (Totowa, NJ: Rowman and Allanheld, 1984); pp. 100–22. (2) "Afterthoughts," in the MacLean volume, pp. 159–61.

[18] Holly Smith discusses certain counterexamples in the fifth section of her "Deriving Morality from Rationality," Chapter 14 in this volume.

to comply with moral constraints (under the relevant conditions). As a result, compliance with moral constraint will ordinarily maximize her expected utility, even if it would not otherwise have done so.[19] So even if the gap is not closed by the logic of a nonquestion begging conception of practical reason, it may be enough if it is closed, for the most part, by the psychology of constrained maximization. Indeed, it may be better.[20]

If this is our view, then we have abandoned Gauthier's notion both of what can be shown and of what must be shown in order to defeat skepticism. We are no longer seeing the problem of rational compliance as one that must or can be solved by an adequate nonskeptical moral theory. Yet we have not conceded anything of substance to the skeptic, or achieved anything of substance against him, for whether we accept the received conception of rationality as straightforward expected utility maximization, or Gauthier's rival conception, Gauthier and the skeptic are agreed that compliance with morality may fail to maximize one's expected utility. It is surely beyond question that this is true. Our uncertainty and their disagreement are over the use of the term "rational." From the skeptic's point of view, under Gauthier's usage, "rational choice" would be a term of classification rather than of commendation, for the skeptic would insist that our underlying interest is with the maximization of expected utility. Nothing of substance is to be gained in the context of this debate by denying the label "rational" to the maximization of expected utility.

With this result, whereby we will not require showing the rationality of actual compliance, we can now return to the problems of rational bargaining and subscription. I shall argue that there are insurmountable difficulties in the way of solving these problems. It is not possible to generate an adequate contractarian response to moral skepticism. I begin with an objection about relevance and then continue with internal and external objections to the contractarian account of the justification of morality.

[19] The definition of constrained maximization requires careful interpretation, if I am correct that a constrained maximizer will ipso facto have different preferences than she would otherwise have had. References to the utility of the agent, in the definition of constrained maximization, must be interpreted as references to what the agent's utility would be if she lacked the preferences that she has simply as a result of being a constrained maximizer. When the three conditions identified before in footnote 12 are satisfied by a cooperative scheme, then a constrained maximizer is disposed to do her part in the scheme. This must mean she prefers to do her part, and so, just in virtue of that fact, she gains additional utility from doing her part. This may sometimes be enough to ensure that doing her part maximizes her utility even in cases where, apart from that additional utility, doing her part would not have maximized her utility.

[20] Kraus and Coleman seem to disagree, for they say, "There is no sense in pursuing agreement on a cooperative joint strategy, if rationality precludes compliance." See their "Morality and the Theory of Rational Choice," Chapter 15 in this volume.

The relevance objection: Substantive impartiality

A contractarian aims to justify morality as a set of rationally defensible standards of behavior. Gauthier does not aim to justify the ordinary morality we are familiar with (p. 269), but since he aims to respond to the skeptic, some moral code must emerge as deserving rational support. I argue that Gauthier cannot give the skeptic any reason to believe that what emerges is a *moral* code. The issue here is not a verbal one, nor is it purely technical. It is whether the contractarian has anything to say to the skeptic about the rational credentials of morality; it is whether the topic is still morality. Perhaps Gauthier's argument succeeds in justifying certain requirements of rational choice, such as that rational persons would become constrained maximizers so as to maximize their opportunities for making advantageous agreements. Yet he still needs to show that these are moral requirements. This is the relevance objection.

A symptom of the problem emerges from Gauthier's discussions of the masters and the slaves (pp. 227–32) and of the severely handicapped (pp. 17–18). Gauthier says that, for example, the severely handicapped members of our society would be excluded from rational bargaining by the rest of us, and so would be excluded from the scope of contractarian requirements (p. 18). A rational person would constrain his maximizing behavior only in dealing with those of sufficient power and productivity that agreement with them promises to be advantageous (p. 17). Rational agents cooperate in order to benefit, and they are not disposed to enter schemes from which they do not expect to benefit. I shall soon discuss these issues in more detail. For now, I simply wish to point out that even if it is agreed that Gauthier's argument justifies a set of sophisticated extensions to the theory of rational choice, it can easily seem to show nothing about morality, especially if one has moral intuitions that the argument implies cannot be rationally justified. A person who begins with the belief that morality and reason do not coincide will not be surprised that her moral intuitions do not coincide even with reason as subtly extended by Gauthier. In short, since he aims to defeat skepticism about morality, Gauthier must provide some argument to show that the requirements that allegedly emerge from the contract argument are not simply maxims of rational choice, but are also justified *moral* requirements. And given his other claims, he must also show that there are no other justified moral requirements.

In order to answer the relevance objection, one would need a theory as to the nature of moral codes. Gauthier does not have such a theory, but he does have a criterion that he uses in addressing the problem of relevance. He says, "our concern is to validate the conception of morality as a set of *rational, impartial* constraints on the pursuit of individual interest" (p. 6, my emphasis). That is, in his view, there are two conditions that are jointly necessary and sufficient for a set of constraints on the pursuit of interest to count as justified moral constraints, viz., the rationality condition and the impartiality condition. The contractarian rationality of a set of constraints shows them to be rationally justified. If they are also "impartial," then they are moral constraints.[21] And, in order not to beg the question against the relevance objection, Gauthier recognizes that he must be able to show the impartiality of a constraint on grounds independent of the considerations invoked in the contractarian argument about its rationality (pp. 95, 234).

In fact, there are several criteria of impartiality operating in Gauthier's discussion. Some are substantive, and concern the alleged impartiality of the requirements imposed on people by a constraint, and some are formal, and pertain to the way a principle can be justified. Unfortunately, I argue, neither kind of criterion is adequate in the context of Gauthier's theory. Neither would suffice, even together with contractarian rationality, to ensure that a constraint on the pursuit of self-interest is a moral constraint.

Gauthier sometimes invokes substantive conceptions of impartiality in his argument, claiming that impartiality requires "equivalent shares," and that it would be a failure of impartiality to permit "free rides" or "parasitism." For instance, he says that minimax relative concession counts as impartial because it guarantees equal or equivalent shares to everyone involved (p. 156). And he defends the impartiality of the proviso partly by arguing that a principle requiring some to give "free rides" to others would be "unfair and partial" (p. 219). I shall therefore begin by interpreting the impartiality test as a test of substantive impartiality. Gauthier's position then would be that a justified moral principle must be both rational and impartial in what it requires.

However, a test of substantive impartiality would beg important questions in the context of Gauthier's argument. Impartiality is not simply a matter of treating people "equally" or of giving them "equal consideration." It is a matter of equal treatment or consideration as appropriate in the context. Substantive moral claims about appropriate treatment are presupposed in such judgments of impartiality.

---

[21] A moral conception typically includes things that are not constraints on self-interest, such as permissions and rights to pursue self-interest, and notions of the virtuous. Further, given that self-interest is to be understood in Gauthier's account as a function of the satisfaction of one's considered preferences, conformity with one's moral code may in fact maximize one's "self-interest," if one's preferences are sufficiently well aligned with the requirements of the code. Therefore, it is too simple to define moralities as constraints on the pursuit of self-interest, even impartial ones. I do not believe this is a major problem because, from the point of view of a contractarian, the key problem is to justify constraints on the pursuit of self-interest. So the important question is whether the constraints Gauthier claims to justify can be counted as moral constraints.

For example, impartiality in the treatment of one's children must be appraised in light of substantive views about how children ought to be treated. If one believes in equal allocation of resources to one's children, it will seem that impartiality requires spending equal amounts on the education of each child, or otherwise allocating equal amounts to each, even if one of them has special needs, but if one believes in an equality of opportunity, one may think that impartiality requires being prepared to spend more on a child with special learning disabilities. Then again, one may think that impartiality is compatible with spending more on a more gifted child than on a less gifted child. The principle of favoring more gifted children would not be described as impartial by those of us who reject it, but those who accept it might insist it is impartial on the ground that it requires equal talent to get equal treatment. In general, we will judge these policies as impartial or not depending on our views about the proper treatment of children. In this way, judgments of substantive impartiality presuppose moral judgments about appropriate treatment.

Because of this, there can be disputes about the impartiality of the proviso and the principle of minimax relative concession, and these will amount to moral disputes about their fairness. For example, Jean Hampton objects that the principle of minimax relative concession (MRC) is not impartial because, pace Gauthier, it permits free rides. She attempts to show that "the divisions effected by the MRC principle are not in accordance with what we (and Gauthier) intuitively think of as 'impartial' or 'fair.' "[22] And many would object to Gauthier's claim that the proviso is fair, arguing that if, as Gauthier suggests, the proviso would permit a rich man to keep his goods, while an unlucky woman starves on his doorstep, it is less fair and impartial than a good samaritan principle (see Gauthier, 1986, p. 218; also his 1988). Fortunately, the main line of my argument does not require an investigation of the substance of these disputes over impartiality, for the central point is simply that the dispute is a moral dispute.

There are two major reasons why Gauthier cannot coherently treat the impartiality test as a test of the substantive moral fairness of the proviso and minimax relative concession. First, since he does not claim to defend our ordinary moral views (p. 269), he must regard our intuitions of fairness and impartiality as requiring justification by the contractarian tests of "rationality" and "impartiality." In the absence of such justification, he cannot permit them to be used in evaluating the output of the contractarian argument. Second, he holds that the status of any

---

[22] Jean Hampton, "Can We Agree on Morals?" *Canadian Journal of Philosophy* 18 (1988): 331–55 (reprinted in part in this volume, Chapter 3).

principle as a justified moral principle depends on its being "rational" and "impartial," so it would be circular for him to invoke a moral conception of fairness in arguing that the proviso and minimax relative concession are impartial. He would first have to show that that conception of fairness is "rational" and "impartial," and he plainly could not employ that very conception in attempting to show that it is itself impartial. In short, on the one hand, he cannot regard the test of "impartiality" as involving recourse to *undefended* moral intuitions of fairness, and, on the other hand, in order to defend a principle of fairness, he would need an independent test of "impartiality" that he could use to show that the principle is a principle of moral fairness. Therefore, the impartiality test cannot be understood as a test of moral impartiality or fairness.[23]

There is a further problem. The impartiality test, together with the test of contractarian rationality, is supposed to constitute a necessary and sufficient condition for a constraint on the pursuit of self-interest to be counted as a justified moral constraint. Yet we do not believe that morality always requires impartiality. For example, we do not think that parents should be impartial as between their children and strangers when it comes to deciding whom to feed and clothe, yet we count the requirement that parents be partial to their children as a moral requirement. Gauthier's position cannot accommodate this belief if the impartiality test is a test of substantive impartiality. For if a justified moral principle must be both rational and impartial in its requirements, then it follows straightforwardly that this requirement that parents be partial to their children, and similar requirements, such as requirements of partiality to our friends, lovers, and parents, are not justified *moral* requirements. Perhaps we will ultimately decide that they cannot be *jus-*

---

[23] Kraus and Coleman see Gauthier as arguing "that rational bargains struck from fair initial conditions produce constraints that are fair and impartial in the sense necessary for them to constitute morality." They point out that this strategy may seem to derive "morality from rationality *cum* fairness," rather than "from rationality *simpliciter*." They think that Gauthier can escape this objection only if he can show "that rational persons will bargain only from fair initial bargaining positions, engage only in bargains whose procedures are fair, and dispose themselves to comply only with constraining principles that result from a fair bargain originating from a fair initial bargaining position." However, to accomplish this, Gauthier would have to show both the rationality and, on independent grounds, the fairness of the proviso and minimax relative concession. If Kraus and Coleman have in mind substantive fairness, then this means Gauthier would need to defend a principle of fairness, for he could not use undefended intuitions about fairness. To defend a principle of fairness, he would need to show its "rationality" and "impartiality." As I argue in the text, this means he would need some other criterion of impartiality that he could use to argue that the principle is a principle of *moral* fairness. The impartiality test cannot be understood as a test of substantive impartiality. See Kraus and Coleman, "Morality and the Theory of Rational Choice," Chapter 15 in this volume.

tified, but it would be a mistake to adopt an account that ruled them out without further argument on the alleged basis that they are not moral requirements.

The relevance objection: Archimedean impartiality

I must now canvass the plausibility of a test of formal impartiality, which would judge the impartiality of a principle, not on the basis of what it requires, but on the basis of how it could be justified. The idea is vague, but, roughly, it is that a justified moral principle must be rationally justified in an "impartial manner" with respect to everyone.

A formal notion seems to be involved in Gauthier's remarks that treat the impartiality of a constraint as a matter of its being "acceptable from every standpoint," or "by every person involved" (p. 151).[24] However, the acceptability of a constraint "from every standpoint," or from the perspective of "every person involved," cannot simply be a matter of its rational acceptability to all of the ideal parties to rational bargaining, as some of Gauthier's remarks might suggest (e.g., p. 234). For we need a criterion of impartiality that is independent of the considerations invoked in the argument about rational bargaining. Otherwise there would be no content to the claim that the principles that emerge from the bargaining are also impartial. But acceptability from "every standpoint" also cannot be interpreted as including the actual standpoints of literally every person involved, for it is unlikely that any principle would qualify by this criterion. Neither the ban on "free rides" generated by the proviso, nor a good samaritan rule, would likely be acceptable to everyone concerned: The unlucky poor woman, starving at the gate of a rich man who is meanwhile feasting on caviar and champagne, would be unlikely to accept a principle, such as the proviso, that would permit him to let her starve, and the fortunate rich man might not accept a good samaritan principle that would require him to take a cut in his standard of living in order to help the poor.[25]

Gauthier requires a theoretically powerful, systematic, morally neutral criterion of impartiality, and he finds it in the Rawlsian notion of an

---

[24] The notion that impartiality requires "equal concern" (p. 236) bridges the substantive and the formal notions, for equal concern could be shown either in giving everyone a veto over the distribution of a benefit or burden, or in giving everyone an equivalent share.

[25] The example is Gauthier's. He concedes that, if we ignore how the situation came about, the proviso would permit the rich man to feast while the poor woman starves, and even forbid her from taking the crumbs from his table "if that would deprive him of his pleasure in feeding them to his birds." But he points out that this situation may have arisen in a way that involved violations of the proviso or the principle of minimax relative concession (p. 218). To this, I reply that it need not have arisen in this way.

"Archimedean Point" behind a "veil of ignorance" (p. 235).[26] He says, "The moral status of . . . rationally agreed constraints derives from their impartiality." And, "The role of Archimedean choice is . . . to reveal the moral impartiality implicit in rational agreement" (Gauthier, 1988, sec. 6). Impartiality is ensured because Archimedean choice is from behind a "veil of ignorance." The agent's concern to maximize his own utility, when he is unable to identify who he is in society, ensures that he chooses impartially, with equal concern for all (Gauthier, 1986, pp. 235–6). Rational choice from the Archimedean Point is choice in an impartial manner, and Gauthier argues that the Archimedean Chooser would select exactly what would emerge in rational bargaining among ideal agents – "individual expected utility-maximization, constrained by the proviso and minimax relative concession" (p. 235). If he is correct, then he is in a position to claim that the proviso and minimax relative conces- sion are rational constraints with an impartial justification that accords them a status as moral constraints.

However, I think Gauthier is oversimplifying. Perhaps people choos- ing from the Archimedean standpoint would select the contractarian requirements, *provided* these people were roughly equal in power and productivity so that none of them would rationally be excluded by the others from the scope of rational bargaining. At any rate, I shall not question this conditional claim. Instead, I shall argue that if rough equal- ity does not obtain, then matters are much less straightforward, and Archimedean impartiality cannot be guaranteed. Gauthier discusses two cases that show this.

The first is the case of the severely handicapped members of our society. If Gauthier is correct, they would be excluded from rational bargaining by the rest of us, and "are not party to the moral relationships grounded by a contractarian theory" (p. 18). They do not have sufficient power and productivity for it to be rational for us to constrain our in- teraction with them by the proviso or minimax relative concession. He says that

Only beings whose physical and mental capacities are either roughly equal or mutually complementary can expect to find cooperation beneficial to all. . . . Among unequals, one party may benefit most by coercing the other, and on our theory would have no reason to refrain. We may condemn all coercive relationships, but only within the context of mutual benefit can our condem- nation appeal to a rationally grounded morality. (p. 17)

If *all* the members of society are parties to its Archimedean evaluation, as Gauthier suggests, following Rawls (Gauthier, 1986, pp. 260–1), then the severely handicapped are included in the group of Archimedean

[26] John Rawls, *A Theory of Justice* (Cambridge, MA: Harvard University Press, 1971). See, e.g., pp. 17–22.

Choosers evaluating the arrangements of our society. Moreover, each of the Choosers knows that he may be handicapped, for although he does not know his actual position in society, he knows the basic facts about his society, such as that there are handicapped people in it, and, for all he knows, he could be in the position of any person in the society (pp. 235–6). Hence, it is unlikely that the Choosers would be willing to accept a moral culture that would exclude the handicapped from the protection of constraints on others' maximizing behavior. They would not accept the proviso, unless it is understood to constrain interaction even with the handicapped.

Gauthier seems to agree, for he says the proviso would be chosen from the Archimedean standpoint "as constraining interactions among all of humankind" (p. 261). Yet to rational bargainers outside of the Archimedean standpoint, rational interactions with the severely handicapped are not constrained by the proviso any more than interactions with horses and honeybees (pp. 17, 260).[27] Therefore, it seems that impartial Archimedean choice accords greater scope to the proviso than does rationality. If the scope of the proviso extends to interactions among all of humankind, then Gauthier's argument says it passes the test of Archimedean impartiality, but it fails the test of contractarian rationality. However, if its scope is limited to interactions among people who are roughly equal, among whom there is a prospect of mutually beneficial agreement, then Gauthier's argument says it is rationally justified, but it does not pass the test of Archimedean impartiality, except on the condition that rough equality obtains among all of the people in the relevant society.[28]

---

[27] Gauthier says, if they decrease "the average level of well-being" of our society, the severely handicapped "are not party to the moral relationships grounded by a contractarian theory" (p. 18). Similarly, Gauthier says, people have no reason to constrain their pursuit of self-interest in dealing with horses (p. 17).

[28] Gauthier does not pay attention to quantifiers in stating the proviso. In one of his statements of it, it prohibits "bettering one's situation through interaction that worsens the situation of another" (p. 205). With unrestricted scope, the proviso applies to all of humankind. It says that, for any member of humankind, one is prohibited from "bettering one's situation through interaction that worsens the situation of [that person]." This version is not rationally justified from the standpoint of strategic interaction, but it passes the Archimedean test. The version with scope restricted to people who are roughly equal with oneself, with whom there is a prospect of mutually beneficial agreement, passes the rationality test, but it fails the impartiality test, unless the test is relativized to groups of roughly equal persons. It says that, for any person with whom there is a reasonable probability of mutually beneficial cooperation, one is prohibited from "bettering one's situation through interaction that worsens the situation of [that person]" (see pp. 17–18, 230). Gauthier may recognize that the version that passes the unqualified Archimedean test does not pass the test of rationality from the standpoint of strategic interaction, for he says it is possible that the principles that would be chosen from the Archimedean standpoint would not rationally be complied with by real individuals involved in interaction (p. 266). I claim, in addition, that the proviso would not be a rational basis for bargaining, except perhaps in the restricted version that does not enjoy Archimedean impartiality.

Perhaps Gauthier would reply that the severely handicapped do not count as members of the society. If they do not, then they are not among the Archimedean Choosers, and the Choosers do not consider the position of the severely handicapped as one that they have a chance of occupying. There is some reason for him to take this position, for the severely handicapped are not party to the contractarian requirements and are not included in rational bargaining by the rest of us. If they were excluded from the original position, then perhaps the remaining Choosers would accept constraints that do not protect the handicapped, such as the proviso with narrow scope. But this would not show these constraints to be impartial without qualification. At best, it would show them to be impartial only *relative* to those who are parties to their Archimedean evaluation.

It may seem, in general, that all rational arrangements would pass at least a relativized version of the Archimedean test, if the parties to the evaluation of a given arrangement or principle were exactly those who would be rationally bound by it. But the second case, that of the masters and the slaves, shows that this is not so.

Imagine that the masters want a bargain to eliminate their need to coerce the slaves, and the slaves also want to eliminate coercion from their lives. Yet the masters have acquired their position by actions that violated the proviso. So it may be that, if they were to agree to give up the benefits they acquired in violation of the proviso, they would be made worse off than if they reached no agreement with the slaves. Despite this, if the bargaining could proceed from the status quo, ignoring past violations of the proviso, then a mutually beneficial agreement might be reached, and all of the parties might be rational to dispose themselves to comply with it, or, at least, in the case of the slaves, to dispose themselves to "acquiesce" in it. If so, the scheme that emerged would be the result of rational bargaining, and the parties would be rational to be disposed to comply with it or acquiesce in it.[29] So it would appear to be rationally justified on the same basis that Gauthier's account ultimately relies on in explaining moral justification (pp. 227–32).

Yet it would not be counted as a moral scheme because it is not

---

[29] On the rationality of the slaves' disposing themselves to comply with such a scheme, or to acquiesce in it, see Kraus and Coleman on broad and narrow compliance, in their "Morality and the Theory of Rational Choice," Chapter 15 in this volume. The "unique rationality" of "narrow compliance" would imply that the slaves would not be rational to dispose themselves to comply with the scheme. Yet they might still be rational to dispose themselves to "acquiesce" in it, as Gauthier says (Gauthier, 1986, p. 230). It is not clear how Gauthier could show that schemes an agent would be rational to dispose himself to "comply" with are rationally justified, in a way that defeats skepticism about their rational warrant, but schemes an agent would merely be rational to dispose himself to "acquiesce" in are not rationally justified. Related to this issue is the problem of making sense of a disposition to "acquiesce" except by interpreting it as a disposition to comply.

impartial (pp. 229–31, see pp. 312–13). Perhaps the *masters* would accept it from the Archimedean standpoint *if* they knew they were the masters when they made their choice, but such knowledge of one's position in society is excluded in the situation of Archimedean choice, and a person would not accept the scheme benefiting the masters at the expense of the slaves if she knew she might be a slave, at least not if we accept Gauthier's reasoning about Archimedean choice. The example shows that there are schemes that could be reached in rational bargaining, and that could be the object of a rational disposition to conform, yet which do not enjoy Archimedean impartiality.[30] The masters may be sufficiently powerful and successful that they would not be rational to agree to a scheme, in bargaining between themselves and the slaves, unless it favored themselves in a way that ensured the scheme would not emerge from an Archimedean choice situation that included both masters and slaves. As Gauthier says, "the link between co-operation and mutual benefit must take precedence over the link between co-operation and impartiality or fairness" (p. 229).

These two cases suggest a number of things about Gauthier's notion of Archimedean impartiality. Most importantly, unless everyone in society is roughly equal in power and productivity, schemes or arrangements that would pass the test of contractarian rationality might not pass the test of impartiality, at least not without qualification, and schemes that pass an unqualified impartiality test might not pass the rationality test. The case of the severely handicapped shows that a version of the proviso that would pass an unrelativized and unqualified test of Archimedean impartiality would fail the test of contractarian rationality. For, if Gauthier is correct, ideal agents would not rationally agree to be bound by it, or dispose themselves to comply with it, in interacting with severely handicapped people. And a version of the proviso with restricted scope, which, if Gauthier is correct, ideal bargainers would rationally agree to comply with and dispose themselves to comply with, would not pass the impartiality test, unless the test were relativized so that it would show, at best, impartiality relative to those who are not handicapped. The case of the masters and slaves shows that a scheme that would be rationally agreed to by the masters and slaves, if Gauthier is to be believed, would not pass the impartiality test unless the test were relativized to the masters. Hence, from the point of view of theory, the version of the proviso with scope restricted so that it would pass the rationality test has the same status as the principle defining the arrangement between the masters and the erstwhile slaves. They are rational principles, but they lack moral status.

---

[30] Perhaps an Archimedean choice procedure could be *designed* that would yield the desired result, but it would be ad hoc, and would not appear impartial.

However, for all that I have argued, it remains that if there were rough equality among everyone in society, then there could be schemes and principles that pass both the test of rational compliance and the test of Archimedean impartiality. Gauthier can still maintain that there would be a rationally justified morality if there were rough equality among everyone in society. Yet the impartiality of a scheme or principle, on the condition that everyone is roughly equal, is not impartiality without qualification. For, if there were *not* the required degree and kind of equality in society, a scheme or principle that is rationally justified by Gauthier's test would *not* be impartial among all the members of society. If such a thing is impartial among all the members of society, it is only because, fortuitously, no one in society is weak or unproductive enough to be an object of profitable coercion. I see no reason to believe that an adventitious Archimedean impartiality of this sort would be sufficient to show a rational principle to be a moral principle.

Different specifications of an Archimedean original position, and of the nature of ideal reasoning, would yield arguments for different principles. Rawls has a different conception than Gauthier does of choice from an original position, even though their basic ideas are the same. These different specifications are not, presumably, equally good models of impartiality, or equally plausible generators of moral principles. In fact, Gauthier claims that *Rawls's* conception of Archimedean choice is not impartial because it violates the integrity of human beings (pp. 245–54, esp. p. 254). So Gauthier recognizes the need to show that a particular conception of Archimedean Choice is impartial, and yields moral principles. Rawls relies in part on the content of his principles, claiming they are in "reflective equilibrium" with our considered judgments about justice, but Gauthier's more revisionary approach means he cannot use this Rawlsian argument.

The contractarian strategy should not convince a person who is tempted by the skeptical belief that morality is not sanctioned by reason. The contractarian claims to have shown that there are principles constraining the pursuit of self-interest that would be accepted by idealized agents as constraining their behavior and their bargaining, and that would also be accepted by them from an Archimedean standpoint behind a veil of ignorance, provided everyone in society is roughly equal in power and productivity. These principles would have to be impartial among the bargainers in order to make agreement possible, given they are roughly equal to one another, but the principles represent a pact that rational agents agree to for their own advantage. A skeptic about morality need not also be a skeptic about pacts such as this.

The contractarian argument also should not convince a person who has moral beliefs that the contractarian would claim to be neither rationally defensible nor impartial, such as the belief in a good samaritan moral code. The contractarian claims to have shown both that idealized rational agents, voided of their sympathy and so on, would not accept this code in a rational bargain, and that Archimedean Choosers, ignorant of their own welfare and aiming to maximize their own utility, would not accept it. Was there ever any very good reason to believe that rational utility maximizers, voided of their sympathy, and knowing their position in society, would agree to a good samaritan code? How would this show that we do not have a duty to act as good samaritans?

Better than the criterion of Archimedean impartiality, as a means of dealing with the relevance problem, would be a criterion identifying a moral constraint by its role in a society. After all, a moral skeptic is primarily concerned to deny the rational credentials of societal moral codes. She would want to deny the rational defensibility of moral duties that include duties to others, where the duties are owed by and to all the members of a society. Gauthier does not purport to establish duties owed by and to all the members of a society, except if there happens to be rough equality among the members of society. He holds that one's rationally justified duties are restricted in scope to groups of individuals from whom one can expect to secure certain kinds of benefits. Not even a constrained maximizer would be disposed to restrain his maximizing behavior in dealing with individuals who could not reciprocate in the required way.[31] Differences in power and productivity can lead to the exclusion of certain individuals, such as the severely handicapped, or to the stratification of schemes of cooperation, so that certain individuals, such as the slaves, are rational to acquiesce in a scheme only because of an existing pattern of coercion.

These results could not be overcome in another development of a similarly motivated contractarian approach, for they are a consequence of the underlying practical person-centered approach to justification, combined with the standard account of practical reason as utility maximization. This approach regards a cooperative scheme as justified only if the disposition to comply with it contributes to maximizing the expected utility of everyone in its scope. Differences in power and productivity will obviously affect the comparative advantage different individuals can expect to gain from different schemes and from including different sets of individuals in the scope of the schemes.

---

[31] A group of individuals would be excluded from the scope of a contractarian cooperative scheme if the expected utility of everyone who remained would be greater, if everyone in the remaining group straightforwardly maximized his utility in dealing with the outsiders, than it would be if the outsiders were included in the scope of the scheme. Constrained maximization is defined as a disposition to comply with a scheme only if one's expected utility if *everyone* complies exceeds one's expected utility if *everyone* straightforwardly maximizes his utility (p. 167). But I take it that "everyone" is meant to refer to everyone in the scope of the scheme. At least, the discussion of masters and slaves and of the handicapped suggests as much.

The relevance objection is that Gauthier has not answered the moral skeptic, for he has not shown that the principles that emerge from his argument are *moral* principles. The criteria of impartiality are inadequate. Moreover, the society-centered criterion I vaguely sketched before is simply not satisfied by the schemes that Gauthier's account treats as justified. If a society has eliminated the excessively weak and disadvantaged members, either by eliminating them or by eliminating their disabilities, then it may pay everyone to enter a cooperative scheme that makes room for everyone, and then it might appear that we are dealing with a morality. However, the issue of relevance would still arise. A skeptic would not want to deny the rationality of cooperative schemes that are genuinely mutually beneficial. She would not be concerned to deny the rationality of quid pro quo. And she would not deny that individuals might find themselves in a position where they are rational to dispose themselves to cooperate among themselves, on the basis of a scheme that is beneficial to each of them, in order to facilitate the exploitation of others. She would not need to deny the rationality, from the point of view of the beneficiaries, of schemes whereby masters exploit slaves, or industrial cabals exploit the rest of society for their benefit, or criminal organizations coerce protection money from weak and desperate citizens. And if not, then she need not deny the rationality of a mutually beneficial scheme in a circumstance where, by chance, there is no one to exploit, and everyone affected by it is benefited by it.[32]

Justification: Internal objections

Let us set aside the relevance objection, and suppose it solved. I shall turn to further grounds for doubting that the contractarian argument can answer skepticism.

Ignoring for now the problem we have already discussed regarding the rationality of actually complying with cooperative schemes, the skeptic will query the rationality of conditionally *disposing* oneself to comply with constraints on the pursuit of self-interest, even if they would be suitably related to a bargain among ideal rational agents in appropriate circumstances. Gauthier's claim is that constrained maximization is rational for ideally rational agents who are *transparent*, or at least sufficiently *translucent* that their expected utility as constrained maximizers exceeds their expected utility as straightforward maximizers.[33] Constrained maximizers who recognize one another can successfully co-

---

[32] As Geoffrey Sayre-McCord says, "It seems egoism begets enlightened egoism, and nothing more." See his "Deception and Reasons to Be Moral," Chapter 12 in this volume.

[33] Translucency implies that one's disposition to cooperate or not can be detected by others with some chance of success greater than guesswork but less than certainty (p. 174).

operate, but straightforward maximizers may be able to exploit constrained maximizers if they can recognize them without being recognized by them. Constrained maximizers risk exploitation, and they face some chance that they will fail to recognize one another and fail to cooperate as a result; but straightforward maximizers cannot secure the benefits of cooperation, nor can they secure the benefits of exploitation, except by being sufficiently opaque that constrained maximizers fail to recognize them for what they are. Therefore, a constrained maximizer does better than he would if he were a straightforward maximizer, provided that the probability of interacting with a straightforward maximizer is sufficiently small, provided that people are transparent or sufficiently translucent, and provided that the gains to be expected from the various strategic interactions are in his favor.[34]

The assumption of transparency is quite unrealistic, as Gauthier concedes (p. 174). The assumption of translucency is more realistic, but people vary both in their degree of translucency and in their ability to see through others. Yet Gauthier conducts his argument as if everyone must decide between constrained and straightforward maximization on the basis of the *average* expected utility of each. He discusses *the* gain from defection and *the* gain from cooperation, and he discusses *the* probability that constrained maximizers will successfully cooperate with each other, and *the* probability that they will be exploited by straightforward maximizers, ignoring that both the probabilities and the utilities can be different for different people, depending on their personal characteristics. The conclusions he draws are generalizations, such as that constrained maximizers may expect to do better if people are sufficiently transparent (p. 177).

The skeptic should not be shaken. She can concede that constrained maximization may be utility maximizing for certain nontuistic and amoral people in certain environments, and this can seem a minor concession. For constrained maximization is not a rational disposition without qualification. It is quite possible that some nontuistic and amoral people would do better to be straightforward maximizers, provided that they could successfully appear to be moral while in fact being utility maximizers. If they are less transparent than average, they may be quite rational to dissemble, giving the appearance of constrained maximization while straightforwardly maximizing their own utility. This strategy may be utility maximizing for some people, especially for those who enjoy manipulating and deceiving people, and who are shrewd, clever, and not inclined to experience feelings of guilt. Since the skeptic had no

---

[34] His expected gains from successful cooperation must exceed his expected losses from occasional exploitation by a greater margin than, were he a straightforward maximizer, his expected gains from successful exploitation would exceed his expected losses from missed opportunities to cooperate (pp. 172–8).

reason to deny that moral constraint may maximize the utility of some people in some circumstances, and since she is able to claim that a strategy of dissembling will maximize the expected utility of some non-tuistic and amoral people in some circumstances, she can be content to concede that constrained maximization may maximize the expected utility of some nontuistic and amoral people in some circumstances.

Matters are worse, for in order to show that constrained maximization is a rational disposition, Gauthier would have to show that it is at least as productive of utility as *any* alternative disposition (pp. 182–3). Yet there are more dispositions to consider than just straightforward maximization and constrained maximization. For example, there is a disposition of "reserved maximization." A reserved maximizer has exactly the disposition of a constrained maximizer, except that he will violate a requirement of a cooperative scheme whenever he has the opportunity to win a jackpot. He will take opportunities to make very great gains in utility, when the probability of detection is very low.[35] For example, unlike a constrained maximizer, he may steal the money from a lost wallet, provided enough money is involved and provided he is quite sure he was not observed finding the wallet. A person might do better as a reserved maximizer than as a constrained maximizer.[36]

A further complication is that people have moral motivations, as well as tuistic motivations. People are not mutually disinterested and amoral.[37] Almost everyone likes or dislikes some other person with whom he interacts sufficiently that he has some noninstrumental desires regarding that person's interests. Yet Gauthier attempts to justify morality on the basis of what agents would rationally choose *if they were nontuistic and amoral* (pp. 5, 11).[38] He says, "the contractarian insists" that a per-

---

[35] This suggestion emerged from a discussion of Gauthier's argument among Charles Chastain, Kathleen Cook, John Deigh, Gerald Dworkin, Richard Kraut, and myself.

[36] It is by now common to point out that there are alternatives to constrained and straightforward maximization. Peter Danielson argues, in section 2 of "The Visible Hand of Morality," that the metastrategy of "reciprocal cooperation, not Gauthier's proposed constrained maximization, is the form moral constraint should take for a rational agent." See *Canadian Journal of Philosophy* 18 (1988): 357–84 (reprinted in part in this volume, Chapter 7). See also his "Closing the Compliance Dilemma," Chapter 16 in this volume. And Holly Smith discusses a disposition she calls KM*, in the fourth section of her paper, "Deriving Morality from Rationality," Chapter 14 in this volume. Gauthier expresses sympathy for Danielson's argument in his 1988, section 3.

[37] It should be emphasized that Gauthier does not assume otherwise; he says, "Our theory of morality, although it makes use of the idea of economic man, is not committed to that idea as a full and adequate account of human nature." It is a useful caricature "for both explanatory and normative purposes" (p. 317).

[38] Some moral preferences are not tuistic. For example, I may prefer on moral grounds that animals not be treated cruelly, or that there be no abortions, but these are not tuistic desires. (Of course, preferring that animals not be treated cruelly, I will desire that your sadistic preferences be frustrated. This does not mean that my preference about the treatment of animals is tuistic. It simply indicates that when satisfying or frustrating a desire of another person is a means to satisfying a nontuistic desire, the

son's commitment to a moral scheme is not justified in the relevant sense "if, without appealing to her feelings for others, it afforded her no expectation of net benefit" (p. 11).

The exclusion of moral and tuistic motivations is a deep feature of the contractarian strategy for defeating moral skepticism. It would obviously beg the question to take into account moral preferences in the argument. The rationale for the assumption of nontuism is perhaps less obvious. In part, it expresses the Kantian thesis "that morality makes demands on us that are and must be quite independent of any fellow-feelings we may have" (p. 238). But it is also related to the problem of answering skepticism. An adequate reply to the skeptic must justify morality without relying on special contingencies. A skeptic would not deny that we would be rational to comply with a given moral code if we had an appropriately programmed explosive device in our brains. Nor would he deny that if we have a certain set of tuistic desires, we are rational to comply with the corresponding moral code. Skepticism cannot be defeated by invoking idiosyncratic facts about one's psychology. A different point that leads to the same conclusion is that we should not permit a theory about the rational constraints on how we are to relate to one another to be affected by our antecedent preferences about how we relate to one another.

Hence, the contractarian strategy is to argue that there is a set of moral principles that rational people would agree to and dispose themselves conditionally to comply with *even if* they had no moral preferences and no attachments to other people. Gauthier aims to defeat skepticism, not by invoking actual desires people happen to have, but by invoking facts about "the logic of interaction" among people with conflicting interests, combined with a subjective instrumental relativistic theory of practical reason. He represents his argument as showing that "the need for restraining each person's pursuit of her own utility" emerges from an understanding of "the very structure of interaction" (p. 2). The assumption of nontuism, like the assumption that the contractors have no moral motivations, is basic to the contractarian approach.[39]

Yet these motivational assumptions, together with the standard utility-maximizing conception of practical reason, which also is at the foun-

---

latter may lead one to have a tuistic desire.) On the other hand, some tuistic desires are explained by feelings, such as a love or a caring or a dislike, rather than by moral convictions. My desire that my enemy should eat poison is not a desire explained by moral convictions I have. Hence, the class of moral preferences is not identical to the class of tuistic preferences.

[39] In conversation with me at the University of Western Ontario Conference on Contemporary Contractarian Theory, held in April, 1987, Gauthier said that he now would want to develop his theory without the assumption of nontuism. I do not believe he could do so without radically altering his conception of skepticism or his strategy for meeting it.

dation of Gauthier's argument, lead to a dilemma. For Gauthier does not simply want to show that nontuistic and nonmoral agents would become constrained maximizers. He also wants to show that there is a unique rationally justified moral code, consisting of the proviso and the principle of minimax relative concession, supplemented by the results of agreements that would be reached by rational nontuistic and amoral agents bargaining in accord with minimax relative concession in a situation where the proviso had not been violated. Rational agents would become constrained maximizers, and thereby dispose themselves conditionally to comply with a moral code if and only if it would yield them approximately the expected utility of a code that could be the object of such an agreement.[40]

But according to the standard account of rational choice, our actual preferences are decisive of the rationality of our actual choices. Since we actually do have both tuistic and moral preferences, an argument that takes into account only our nontuistic and nonmoral preferences can be expected to give misleading conclusions about what would be rational for us. The contractarian faces a dilemma: In order to defeat the moral skeptic, he develops an argument that engenders skepticism about the rationality of the contractarian moral scheme for actual people. In order to avoid begging the question against the skeptic, and to avoid having his reply turn on special contingencies, he bases his reply to skepticism on an argument about the choices of hypothetical ideally rational agents who lack moral and tuistic preferences. But this means that the argument cannot show anything about what *we* would choose if we were fully rational, for we have both moral and tuistic preferences. Even if nontuistic and nonmoral agents would be rational to dispose themselves conditionally to comply with the proviso and minimax relative concession, it does not follow that *actual* people, given their *actual* moral and tuistic preferences, would be rational to dispose themselves to comply with these principles. The contractarian response to skepticism requires the exclusion of preferences that the standard theory of practical reason, which is basic to the contractarian strategy, treats as relevant to evaluating the rationality of our actual choices.

Consider people who have moral preferences with overriding importance for them, and suppose that their preferences are widely shared in society. Let us say that these people accept a good samaritan moral code and believe that they are morally required to help those less fortunate than themselves. If they actually prefer compliance with this scheme, and if their preference for it is of sufficiently great importance to them, then, if rational, they would simply dispose themselves to comply with

[40] That is, if and only if the scheme affords them a utility that exceeds their expected utility in the noncooperative outcome and that approaches what they would expect from an outcome determined by minimax relative concession (p. 167).

it. This disposition would maximize their expected utility, given their actual preferences. There is no reason to think they would do as well or better, in relation to their actual preferences, if they became constrained maximizers.[41] If Gauthier is correct, then these people *would* not have been rational to agree to comply with their good samaritan moral code, or to choose to become good samaritans, if they *had* not had any tuistic or moral motivations. Yet this does not undermine their rationality, or the rationality of their acting on their preferences, given that they are in fact good samaritans. *Many* of our preferences are such that we would have no reason to choose to acquire them, if we did not already have them or relatives of them. This is no reason to attempt to get rid of them. Even if my preference of you as a friend is not something I would have rationally chosen, if I had not had any tuistic preferences, this is no reason for me to regret our friendship.

Gauthier remarks at one point that some argument must be given to the Foole, who claims that it may be rational to make an agreement even if it is not rational to comply with it, or to dispose oneself to comply (p. 165). In addition, some argument must be given to the "fool" who claims that it may not be rational to comply, or even to dispose oneself to comply, with a notional agreement that an ideal counterpart to oneself could have reached. This fool claims that the contractarian morality would have to be imposed on ordinary people.[42]

Justification: External objections

The fundamental reason why the contractarian account cannot succeed is not hard to find. To answer the skeptic, a moral code must be justified on a basis that is not idiosyncratic or otherwise dependent on special contingencies. Yet the contractarian strategy employs a theory of practical reason that makes rational choice a function of the subjective states of a person, including those that are merely idiosyncratic and special to

---

[41] I believe that a good samaritan code would not be agreed to by ideally rational nonmoral and nontuistic people, if they reasoned in accord with minimax relative concession in a situation where the proviso had not been violated. The example is relevant to the exclusion of tuistic preferences as well as to the exclusion of moral preferences, for we need not imagine the preference to help those less fortunate than oneself to be grounded in moral beliefs.

[42] Gauthier speaks to this objection in section 6 of his 1988. He says that a person may realize that the moral arrangements of her society are ultimately unjustified "without denying that, given the person she actually is, they afford her a fair share of the benefits of social cooperation. For the person she is may not be the person [she would be] in an essentially just society." So a person's actual preferences and situation may be such that she rationally disposes herself to comply with a moral arrangement that does not even approximate what rational nonmoral and nontuistic agents could agree to. Yet this means that we may exhibit neither a rational nor a moral fault in being disposed to comply with the going moral code, and that we may have no reason at all to interest ourselves in the contractarian moral code recommended by Gauthier.

the person's particular circumstances. And the account relativizes rational choice to the individual making the choice, so that it cannot justify a moral code as such, but, at best, can justify a person in accepting it. The requirement of unanimous agreement imposed by the contractarian is intended to counteract the relative and subjective nature of the justification that can be expected from a person-centered theory based in such a theory of practical reason. However, to achieve unanimity, idealizing assumptions must be made about the imaginary bargainers, and unanimity among ideal rational agents does not guarantee unanimity of rational choice among actual agents, given their actual idiosyncrasies and special circumstances. There is an irreconcilable tension between the need to answer the skeptic with a nonidiosyncratic justification of a moral scheme as such, and the strategy of addressing the answer to each individual's reason, and basing it in a subjective instrumental and relativistic theory of practical reason.

In general, a contractarian aims to justify a code appropriately based in hypothetical rational bargaining, and to show that rational agents would subscribe to a code reached in a rational bargain. Gauthier aims to show that constrained maximization is a rational disposition. But the most that is shown in this way is the rationality of a conditional disposition to comply with a putative moral code. The code itself is not justified in this manner. It is not shown that what the code says is wrong is actually wrong.

The contractarian attempt to show that agreement can be both rational and unanimous does tend to make the argument appear less subjective and idiosyncratic. However, to secure a unanimous result, the contractarian must idealize the agents, as we saw, and ignore the differences among their actual preferences, desires, and values, or else exclude certain individuals from the scope of morality. Gauthier adopts both strategies. Those with little to contribute to our good are excluded entirely. And the remaining bargainers are idealized both to secure rational agreement and to secure the universal rationality of the disposition to comply, among those who would agree. So while unanimity would secure at least intersubjectivity, it is bought at the price of realism and comprehensiveness. And the skeptic can still point to those whose preferences or other psychological characteristics do not in fact line up nicely with the idealizing assumptions. These individuals may still rationally fail to comply, or even to dispose themselves to comply, with the contractarian moral code.

The skeptical problem: Revised account

There is a tension in the contractarian approach between the conception of the skeptical challenge and the conception of rational justification, and this tension ultimately defeats the contractarian strategy. Gauthier's development of contractarianism is ingenious and clear, and so I think it is fair to take its failures as indicative of deep problems with the strategy. From within his theory, the difficulties appear as a lack of fit between various significant perspectives of and on rational choice.

First is a tension between two standpoints that can be taken by an ideally rational nontuistic and nonmoral utility maximizer. In one, the standpoint of ideal bargaining, she aims to solve the structural problem of strategic interaction with relevantly similar rational agents by seeking mutually advantageous and rationally acceptable agreements with them. In the second, she is a constrained maximizer who has disposed herself conditionally to comply with mutually advantageous cooperative arrangements, and now must either comply or fail to comply. The theory of rationality as expected utility maximization implies that even if she is a constrained maximizer, she may not be rational actually to comply, so there is room for the skeptic to insist that rationality does not require compliance with morality, not even on the part of an agent who would be rational both to enter an agreement to comply with it and to dispose herself to comply.

Second is a tension between the standpoint of the rational nontuistic and nonmoral ideal bargainer, aiming to reach mutually advantageous agreements with other rational agents, and the standpoint of the Archimedean Chooser who does not know who he is in society, yet aims to select a system of principles for his society that, if complied with, will maximize his expected utility. From the perspective of the Archimedean Chooser, unless rough equality obtains in society, the agreements that would be made by the ideal bargainer appear ineligible for choice, because the Chooser knows he may have insufficient power or productive capacity to have his interests protected by the bargain. And from the perspective of the ideal bargainer, the arrangements that would be chosen by the Archimedean Chooser appear rationally ineligible because they would require her to limit her utility maximization even in dealing with those with whom an advantageous bargain is not possible. There is room for the skeptic to complain that the constraints that would be agreed to by the ideal bargainers are not moral constraints, but are simply applications of rational choice to subtle problems of strategic interaction. Even if an ideal bargainer would be rational to dispose herself conditionally to constrain her utility maximization, this does not seem to pose a problem for the skeptic.

Third, there is a tension between two views of ideal, rational, nontuistic and nonmoral bargainers. One, mandated by the attempt to answer skepticism, abstracts from any remaining psychological differences among people, but the other, mandated by the account of rational choice as expected utility maximization, emphasizes the fact that the psychological characteristics of a chooser are decisive of what he would be rational to choose, and that ideal rational choosers would not make the same choices unless they had exactly the same preferences, abilities, and so on. The skeptic can insist that different ideally rational nontuistic and nonmoral bargainers would be rational to dispose themselves in different ways with respect to cooperative arrangements. He can insist that it is compatible with the essentials of his view that there are certain circumstances in which a conditional disposition to cooperate would be rational for certain agents.

Finally, there is a tension between the perspective of the ideal nontuistic and nonmoral rational bargainers, regarding cooperative arrangements that are mutually beneficial for them, and the perspective of ordinary tuistic and morally motivated people regarding these arrangements. It is entirely possible that even if ideal bargainers would be rational to become constrained maximizers, ordinary people would not be rational to do so. The ordinary motivations of ordinary people may make it rational for them to comply with ordinary moral standards even if these standards would not be rationally agreed to by ideal bargainers and would not be complied with by constrained maximizers. And it may fail to be rational for them to comply, or to dispose themselves to comply, with cooperative arrangements that ideal bargainers would rationally dispose themselves to comply with, given how different they are from the ideal bargainers.

These problems are deeply rooted in the contractarian conception of the skeptical challenge that moral theory must defeat and the contractarian strategy for meeting that challenge. They are not peculiar to Gauthier's approach. The contractarian conceives the challenge as requiring him to show the rationality of compliance with morality even by agents who lack tuistic and antecedent moral motivations. And he conceives the solution as involving an argument, grounded in the conception of rational choice as individual expected utility maximization, which shows that the structure of strategic interaction makes it rational, even for nontuistic and nonmoral agents, to dispose themselves to conditional cooperation.

Gauthier has shown, I believe, that a conditional disposition to cooperation can be rational, under certain conditions, for certain populations of ideal nontuistic and nonmoral agents. Furthermore, this rational conditional disposition to cooperate would lead to cooperation under schemes that would appear impartial, in that they would be approved from the Archimedean standpoint on the condition that everyone in society is and will continue to be roughly equal in the relevant respects. This showing *does* require an amendment to the form of skepticism with which we began, for it shows that a disposition to comply with impartial cooperative arrangements can be rational in the absence of previously existing moral motivations and psychological ties to other people, and in the absence of coercion and manipulation. The skeptic can still deny that these arrangements are impartial without qualification, since their appearance of impartiality depends on the existence of rough equality among people, and so she can deny that the arrangements count as *moral* arrangements. Yet her position seems to need qualification. The structure of interaction can make cooperative dispositions rational.

Yet I believe that Gauthier's showing can hardly be an adequate justification of any set of moral principles. Nor does the contractarian conception of the skeptical challenge seem one that can or need be answered. We know there are conflicts between morality and individual expected utility maximization, and this by itself is not sufficient to defeat morality. Nevertheless, it is appropriate to seek an understanding of how a moral code could be justified. We need to reconsider what a justification of morality could consist in, and to reconceptualize the skeptical challenge to morality.

Skepticism should be understood to demand a showing that some moral code as such can be justified. The skeptic arguably would be in difficulty if complying with a moral code, or disposing oneself to comply, were rationally justified under every possible circumstance for every agent, but she is not in difficulty if complying, or disposing oneself to comply, is merely justified for certain people under certain circumstances. The explosive device in the brain makes the point. A putative justification cannot be successful if it is grounded in idiosyncracies or special contingencies. This is a reason why justification by the explosive device is uninteresting. It is also a reason why justification cannot succeed on the basis of restrictive assumptions about preferences, such as nontuism, or restrictive assumptions about psychological characteristics, such as transparency. Contractarianism is a practical person-centered account of justification, and I claim that accounts of this kind, if grounded in the standard utility-maximizing theory of practical reason, or any subjective instrumental relativistic theory, *cannot* answer skepticism. For accounts of this kind are ultimately grounded in people's psychological states, such as preferences, which vary idiosyncratically from person to person. And accounts of this kind evaluate people's choices or dispositions, not a moral code as such.

It is hard to see how a nonidiosyncratic justification of some moral code as such could be achieved. If it is impossible within a practical person-centered theory, as I believe, then we need a new model of moral justification. It is unclear what this model could be like, unless we return to an epistemic conception. Our difficulty in knowing where to go from here reflects the unsatisfactory state of our understanding of the nature and justification of morality.

14. Deriving morality from rationality

Holly Smith

Introduction

From its earliest beginnings, western philosophy has attempted to forge a strong link between rationality and morality. Contemporary social contractarian theories derive a good deal of their attractiveness from their claim to have achieved this goal. Such theories argue that the principles of justice, or the principles of morality, issue from a contract that rational individuals would agree to initially, and would comply with once implemented. These theories present moral norms as issuing from rational choice, and so claim to establish the desired connection between morality and rationality.

David Gauthier is the most recent advocate of this approach in his attempt to provide a contractarian justification for moral behavior. In defending his enterprise, Gauthier explicitly invokes the desirability of establishing what he calls "the deep connection" between reason and morality.[1] He asserts that "The main task of our moral theory [is] – the generation of moral constraints as rational...,"[2] and develops this thought in the following passage:

> ... [T]he language of morals is ... surely that of reason. What theory of morals, we might ... ask, can ever serve any useful purpose, unless it can show that all the duties it recommends are also truly endorsed by each individual's reason? ... But are moral duties rationally grounded? This we shall seek to prove, showing that reason has a practical role related to but transcending individual interest, so that principles of action that prescribe duties overriding advantage may be rationally justified. We shall defend the traditional conception of morality as a

---

[1] David Gauthier, *Morals by Agreement* (Oxford: Oxford University Press, 1986). p. 4.
[2] Ibid., p. 7.

rational constraint on the pursuit of individual interest. . . . Our enquiry will lead us to the rational basis for a morality.[3]

Thus, it is essential to the success of Gauthier's project in his own eyes that he can indeed establish the link between rationality and morality. And in taking this stance, he joins a venerable western tradition advocating the importance of this link.

I shall argue, however, that Gauthier fails to show that morality is based on rationality. To see how his argument falls short, let me very briefly describe his main line of thought. Gauthier begins with Hobbes's and Rawls' idea that society is a "cooperative endeavor for mutual advantage." Human beings, living in isolation from each other, can only expect to do poorly in their struggle to survive and flourish. Social cooperation would enable each person to fare better than he or she could do in isolation. Unfortunately, the more common types of potentially profitable cooperation are ones in which individuals' direct pursuit of self-interest paradoxically produces an outcome in which each person is worse off than he would have been if everyone had acted less selfishly. Consider a case in which you and I are two fishermen inhabiting adjoining properties along a dangerous coastline. Hidden sandbars often cause our boats to run aground and our catch to be lost. Each of us can expect two such accidents in the coming year, one on our own sandbar, and one on our neighbor's sandbar. If either of us erected a lighthouse, it would prevent any accidents on the adjacent sandbar. The cost to each of us of a single accident is $500, whereas the cost per year of erecting and maintaining a lighthouse is $600. In these circumstances, if each of us considers only our own welfare, neither will build a lighthouse, since the annual cost exceeds the benefit by $100. But each of us fares worse under this arrangement (where we each suffer an annual loss of $1,000 from accidents) than under an arrangement in which both of us build a lighthouse, for each lighthouse benefits *both* its builder and her neighbor (if both build, each suffers a yearly cost of only $600).

The dilemma posed by this situation can be represented in the following standard diagram:

		I	
		Build	Not build
		−600	−500
You	Build	−600	−1,100
		−1,100	−1,000
	Not build	−500	−1,000

In classic Prisoner's Dilemmas such as this one, an optimal outcome cannot be reached by each agent pursuing his or her own interest. It

³ Ibid., pp. 1, 2.

could be reached, however, if behavior were constrained by principles prohibiting purely selfish behavior: for example, a principle requiring each fisherman to build a lighthouse. According to Gauthier, such principles, if they impartially constrain the pursuit of direct self-interest, qualify as *moral* principles. But Gauthier also argues that it is *rational* for each individual to adopt and comply with such principles – rational in the standard sense of maximizing one's own self-interest. The core of Gauthier's project is to argue for this thesis, which if true would establish morality as part of the theory of rational choice.

When mutually beneficial outcomes are available through cooperation, but purely selfish behavior would disadvantage everyone, individuals have reason to work together to secure mutual benefits. However, many different cooperative arrangements are often available in a given case. For example, one cooperative arrangement just described in the fishermen's case has each of us building her own lighthouse; but a second arrangement, also to the advantage of each, would have each of us building her own lighthouse, but you paying me $50 to defray my expenses; a third would involve my instead paying you $50 to defray your expenses; and so forth. Individuals who might benefit greatly under one arrangement would do far less well under an alternative arrangement that favored others. In these circumstances, members of the group must bargain with each other to determine which particular arrangement they will adopt. Gauthier argues that rational, fully informed people will bargain according to what he labels the "Principle of Maximin Relative Benefit." Bargains reached in accord with this principle mandate cooperative arrangements in which the benefits created by cooperation are distributed so that the return to each individual is proportionate to the contribution (under some interpretation) that he or she brings to the cooperative enterprise. Individuals will bargain with each other to establish the basic terms of their future social interaction – the principles of morality and justice that will govern them – and will agree to norms that require distributing the benefits of interaction proportionally to the contributions of each interactor. Thus, Gauthier argues that they would agree to norms requiring promise keeping, truth telling, and fair dealing, because adherence to such norms permits people to cooperate in ways that may be expected to render the benefits of concrete interactions proportionate to the contribution provided by each party.

People in the state of nature, bargaining with each other to establish mutually beneficial constraints on purely selfish behavior, must look to the future in arriving at their agreement, in the sense that they recognize it is pointless to agree on constraints with which no one will later comply. Thus, Gauthier must show that people would indeed comply with the constraints – that is, the moral principles – agreed to in the original bargain, for otherwise no bargain will be struck.

Hobbes was driven to solve this compliance problem by invoking an all-powerful sovereign to enforce terms of the bargain by threats of harm to disobedient citizens. Many contract theorists have agreed with Hobbes that compliance cannot be secured without coercive measures of some kind. Perhaps Gauthier's most distinctive contribution to contractarian theory is his argument that coercion is unnecessary to secure compliance. He argues that it is rational for a would-be bargainer to "dispose himself" to comply with the terms of the initial bargain as long as he expects similar compliance from others. Agents so disposed may occasionally be exploited by others who take advantage of their willingness to comply with agreements made. But, Gauthier argues, given plausible assumptions about human abilities to ascertain each others' dispositions – assumptions that human beings are "translucent," although not completely "transparent," to each other – a person who disposes herself to comply with fair bargains will enjoy opportunities for beneficial cooperation that will be denied to persons lacking this disposition. Because of these opportunities, she maximizes her self-interest by disposing herself to comply. And, Gauthier argues, having disposed herself to comply, it is rational for her actually to comply when the occasion arises, even when she would maximize her utility by violating the agreement. Thus, compliance with socially adopted norms can be secured by largely voluntary means, and each would-be cooperator knows there is point to agreeing to the bargain, since each will have reason to comply with the bargain once made.

Gauthier's core argument for the rationality of compliance

I begin by examining Gauthier's core argument for the rationality of compliance. To understand Gauthier's official statement of it, we must first introduce his definitions of several key terms. First, Gauthier defines a "constrained maximizer" as

(i) someone who is conditionally disposed to base her actions on a joint strategy or practice should the utility she expects were everyone so to base his action be no less than what she would expect were everyone to employ individual strategies, and approach what she would expect from the co-operative outcome determined by minimax relative concession; (ii) someone who actually acts on this conditional disposition should her expected utility be greater than what she would expect were everyone to employ individual strategies.[4]

---

[4] Ibid., p. 167. Gauthier uses the term "disposition" to describe constrained maximization. It is troubling that he never explains what this crucial term means. Since it is difficult to get a grip on the logic of the argument without an explication of "disposition," I have made the most natural assumption, namely, that a disposition is an intention to perform a certain kind of act. This explication preserves an important feature that Gauthier wants, namely, that the later choice to perform the act is genuinely a free act.

My informal formulation of constrained maximization (immediately following in the text) differs slightly from Gauthier's formal definition. Strictly speaking, Gauthier's

In terms of our fisherman example, what this means is that you are a constrained maximizer if (i) you form the intention to build your lighthouse if I build mine, and the intention not to build your lighthouse if I do not build mine (since the utility you would receive if both you and I build our lighthouses exceeds what you would receive if neither of us built one); and moreover (ii) you actually *do* build your lighthouse if, and only if, you expect me to build mine (since your expected utility of building a lighthouse only exceeds what you would get if we both fail to build lighthouses in a case where you expect me to build mine as well). A *straightforward maximizer*, by contrast, is someone "who seeks to maximize his utility given the strategies of those with whom he interacts" – that is, a normal maximizer of expected utility.[5] In Gauthier's initial statement of his argument, he assumes that the agents involved are *transparent* to each other – that is, each is "directly aware . . . whether he is interacting with straightforward or constrained maximizers."[6] For the sake of greater plausibility, this assumption is then weakened to the assumption that the agents are merely *translucent* – that is, ones whose dispositions "to co-operate or not may be ascertained by others, not with certainty, but as more than mere guesswork."[7] Because it is simpler to state the argument using the stronger assumption of transparency, I shall initially stick with it.

Gauthier's own statement of his argument goes as follows:

Suppose I adopt straightforward maximization. Then I must expect the others to employ maximizing individual strategies in interacting with me; so do I, and expect a utility, u.

Suppose I adopt constrained maximization. Then if the others are conditionally disposed to constrained maximization, I may expect them to base their actions on a co-operative joint strategy in interacting with me; so do I, and expect a utility u'. If they are not so disposed, I employ a maximizing strategy and expect

(somewhat unclear) definition only stipulates what a constrained maximizer does if (in our case) she expects her partner to build her lighthouse; it does not stipulate what she does if she expects her partner *not* to build her lighthouse. However, it is clear from Gauthier's discussion that constrained maximization requires the person to form, and carry out, the intention not to build her lighthouse if she expects her partner not to build. It is this aspect of the disposition that protects the constrained maximizer from exploitation by straightforward maximizers.

My informal characterization of constrained maximization assumes the case of transparency, in which the agent knows that her partner will form, and carry out, the intention to build (or the intention not to build, as the case may be). In the case of translucency, in which the agent may assign probabilities less than 1 to each possible action of her partner, constrained maximization could be stated as "forming and carrying out the intention to build if the expected utility to her of doing so exceeds her expected utility if both partners fail to build; and forming and carrying out the intention not to build otherwise."

5 Ibid., p. 167.
6 Ibid., pp. 173–4.
7 Ibid., p. 174.

u as before. If the probability that others are disposed to constrained maximization is p, then my overall expected utility is $[pu' + (1 - p)u]$.

Since u' is greater than u, $[pu' + (1 - p)u]$ is greater than u for any value of p other than 0 (and for $p = 0$, the two are equal). Therefore, to maximize my overall expectation of utility, I should adopt constrained maximization.[8]

Having argued that it will maximize an agent's expected utility to adopt constrained maximization, Gauthier then claims that *since* it is rational to choose to be a constrained maximizer, it is *also* rational to carry out that choice – that is, to cooperate when the time comes.[9]

Let us lay out this argument, somewhat less technically, in terms of our example of the fishermen. We may envision the situation as a symmetrical one, in which each of us is faced with the same choice. The argument may be stated as follows:

1. I can now choose between constrained maximization (CM) or straightforward maximization (SM), and my choice will bring about my actually carrying out the chosen option. The options are:

   CM. Forming the intention to build if you build, or not build if you do not; and then actually building if I expect you to build, or not building if I expect you not to build.
   SM. Forming the intention not to build whatever you do; and then actually not building whatever I expect you to do.

2. Each of us is transparent, so each will be aware of the other's choice, and will know that the other will actually carry out that choice.
3. If I choose CM, then
   (a) If you choose CM, you will build and I will build.
   (b) If instead you choose SM, you will not build, and I will not build either.
4. If I choose SM, then
   (a) If you choose CM, you will not build, and I will not build.
   (b) If instead you choose SM, you will not build, and I will not build either.

---

[8] Ibid., p. 172. This argument contains what appears to be a (recurrent) misstatement, namely, that others are "conditionally disposed" to constrained maximization. There is never any question of people being *conditionally disposed* to constrained maximization; constrained maximization is already itself a disposition to form certain conditional intentions, and to carry one of them out when the specified conditions occur. "A constrained maximizer is conditionally disposed to co-operate in ways that, followed by all, would yield nearly optimal and fair outcomes, and does co-operate in such ways when she may actually expect to benefit" (ibid., p. 177).

Notice also, as David Schmidtz has pointed out to me, that although Gauthier here describes his argument as showing that CM maximizes expected utility, it is more properly described as showing that CM is the dominant strategy (in cases of transparency).

[9] Ibid., p. 186.

5. Hence, if you choose SM, it makes no difference to my utility whether I choose CM or SM; whereas if you choose CM, I maximize my utility by choosing CM and inducing you to build.
6. So it is rational for me to choose CM.
7. If I am rational to choose CM, then it is rational for me to carry it out when the time comes (e.g., to build my lighthouse if you build yours).

Notice a highly significant feature of this argument: if successful, it entails that I should adopt CM and follow it when interacting with you, *even if you and I will only interact on this single occasion, and even if our interaction will have no effect on my future opportunities to cooperate with other individuals.* Gauthier rejects solutions to Prisoner's Dilemmas that rely on iterated occasions for cooperation, and takes himself to have shown that it is rational to cooperate even in the single-interaction case.[10]

Comment on premises 1 and 2

I have deliberately phrased premises 1 and 2 so as to reveal certain aspects of Gauthier's argument that his own language tends to obscure. Let me comment briefly upon these aspects.

First, I have worded premise 1 to bring out Gauthier's assumption that the choice of constrained maximization at t_1 will actually lead me to form the appropriate unconditional intention at t_2 and then perform the chosen act at t_3. For example, if I form the intention at t_2 of building my lighthouse, then I *will* build it at t_3. There is no possibility that I will fail to carry out what CM requires of me. We might call this assumption the *causal efficacy thesis:* the thesis that forming an intention to do A will cause the performance of A. Gauthier's calculation of my expected utility in choosing CM implicitly incorporates this assumption (for, if I could backslide on an intention to build my lighthouse, the expected utility of intending to build would not simply equal the expected utility of both of us building lighthouses). Indeed, given the truth of the transparency assumption, and the fact that, if you have chosen CM, you will only build your lighthouse if you know I will build mine, Gauthier needs the truth of the causal efficacy thesis to establish that my choosing CM will induce you to build and so maximize my utility. He also needs it to rule out the possibility of my adopting a strategy like the following one:

> KM: Forming the intention to build if you build, or not to build if you do not build; and then not building *whatever* you do.[11]

---

[10] Ibid., pp. 169–70.
[11] Some people object to KM on the ground that one could never intentionally adopt it, since that would involve simultaneously committing myself to (a) intending at t_1 to do A, and (b) intending at t_2 *not* to do A. It is claimed that one cannot, at least rationally,

Under conditions of translucency, adopting KM rather than CM might well maximize an agent's utility because it would enable him to mislead other agents about his future actions. However, KM is ruled out by the assumption of causal efficacy. But we should at least note the extreme strength of this assumption. I find it quite implausible to assume that any intention of mine *inevitably* causes my subsequent carrying out of that intention: some do, but some do not. Upgrading the *kind* of mental state I form (to a commitment or resolution) does not change this fact. Of course, we often change our minds when we acquire new information, or when we adopt new values. Gauthier wants to set such cases aside.[12] But even in cases where none of these factors matter, it is implausible to suppose our commitments always compel our future acts – especially in the kind of case in question, where considerations of utility press the agent to change her mind when the time comes. Indeed, if the causal efficacy thesis were true, it is hard to see how Prisoner's Dilemmas could have been the deep historical problem for social cooperation that they have been. However, in order to turn to other aspects of the argument, I will nonetheless provisionally grant Gauthier the truth of the thesis.[13]

commit oneself to this sort of inconsistent intention formation. Even if this is true, at most it would show that KM could not be recommended to agents by a *decision guide*, that is, a prescription to be used in their actual decision making. It would not show that KM fails to be the best disposition to actually have (even if one could not rationally bring it about that one has this disposition). If the causal efficacy thesis were not true, then KM might well be the best disposition for an agent to have in a Prisoner's Dilemma under conditions of translucency.

[12] David Gauthier, "Afterthoughts," in *The Security Gamble: Deterrence Dilemmas in the Nuclear Age*, edited by Douglas MacLean (Totowa, NJ: Rowman and Allanheld, 1984), p. 159.

[13] Would it raise difficulties for Gauthier's argument if my forming an intention to do *A* only caused me to do *A sometimes*, say, 60% of the time? Suppose you and I are both CMs, and I form the intention to build – but in this particular case, I will not carry through. Since I am transparent, you will detect my future failure to build, and so will form the intention not to build, and will not build. But since you are also transparent to me, I will detect your intention not to build, and so, by CM, should form the intention not to build myself. But by hypothesis, I have formed the intention to *build*. It appears as though failure of the causal efficacy thesis would be inconsistent with Gauthier's other assumptions.

As David Schmidtz points out to me, there is a related problem here, which is that Gauthier makes no provision for the possibility that either prospective partner might fail to carry out the intention to cooperate, not because of any change of mind, but rather because circumstances conspire to make cooperation impossible (e.g., I intend to build my lighthouse, but then am unable to purchase the requisite building materials). Part of this problem could be evaded by stating the constrained-maximization intention as a *doubly* conditional intention, namely, an intention to cooperate, if others do, and if the world permits. Such a restatement would mean that potential partners to whom one was transparent would have to know, not just one's intentions and future trustworthiness, but also whether the world would permit cooperation. But epistemic relations between potential partners would remain complex, and perhaps involve the kind of inconsistencies just described, in any case where the world will not permit cooperation.

The second point to notice is that I have stated the transparency assumption (in premise 2) to bring out the fact that it incorporates not merely the assumption that each person will be aware of the other's choice, but also the assumption that each person will know *that the other will actually carry out that choice*. Gauthier himself tends to discuss the transparency assumption in terms that suggest it merely implies that each person is aware of the other person's current mental state, such

It is worth pointing out that Gauthier's adoption of the causal efficacy thesis appears to raise a special problem for him. In his discussion of deterrence cases, he explicitly rules out cases in which the agent is *im*perfectly rational, unable fully to control her behavior in terms of her considered preferences. As an instance of such a case, he describes an agent whose cool preference not to retaliate will be overcome by her feelings of anger, rage, or panic at the moment action is called for. Gauthier stipulates that he only wants cases in which the person can control her behavior at the time when the choice to retaliate or not must be made. Second, Gauthier rules out cases in which the person, in expressing her intention, delegates her power to choose, by arranging that some other person or some preprogrammed device, capable of ignoring her preferences, will ensue that if the threatener strikes, retaliation will ensue. (Gauthier, "Deterrence, Maximization, and Rationality," in *The Security Gamble*, edited by Douglas MacLean, pp. 100–5.) Thus, we are explicitly confined to cases in which, at the time of action, the agent is rational and in control of what she chooses and does. Clearly, Gauthier wants the same conditions to hold in compliance cases as in deterrence ones.

These restrictions may appear to rule out the causal efficacy thesis, because it may appear that if a person is *caused* to do *A*, then she is not exercising rational choice to do *A* at the time of the action. However, my view, and I suspect Gauthier's as well, is that the causal efficacy thesis is *not* ruled out by the requirement that the person choose rationally at the time she decides whether or not to carry out her intention. (Notice a potentially confusing switch in terminology here: "choose rationally" does not mean, as it usually does in Gauthier's and my texts, "perform the best act"; rather, it means something like "make a reasoned choice given one's evidence.") Since I believe causation is compatible with rational choice, all this requirement entails is that the causal chain initiated by her forming the intention to do *A* must operate by causing her *to choose rationally to perform A*. It must cause her, for example, to deliberate rationally in selecting her alternative. Thus, forming the intention to build a lighthouse must cause her to believe that building a lighthouse is best. Since Gauthier is not interested in misinformed or irrational agents, this belief must be true. But we know that it would not be best for her to build a lighthouse unless she has previously formed the intention of doing so (since building a lighthouse, by itself, merely *de*creases her utility). Thus, forming the intention to build must not only cause her to believe retaliation would be best, it must *in addition make* it the case that building *is* best. So far, however, we have not established that forming this intention would make it best to build. Now, to support the final conclusion of his argument, Gauthier invokes a principle that asserts that if it is rational (best) to form an intention, then it is rational (best) to carry it out. (See the discussion in the fifth section.) Thus, if we could establish that it is rational for the agent to form the intention to build, then we could derive the needed conclusion here, namely, that forming the intention to build does indeed make it best to build. However, we cannot at this point in the argument help ourselves to the assumption that it is rational to form the intention to build, since this is precisely what we are trying to prove. We cannot argue that the intention is rational because it would cause the intended act to be performed, and then turn around and argue that the act itself is best because the earlier intention to perform it was rational. Given Gauthier's desired constraints, the intention is only rational if it would cause the intended act to be performed *rationally*, that is, if it would make the intended act best. And we cannot prove this until we have proved the intention is rational. There seems to be an unavoidable circularity in the argument here.

as the other person's current choice or intention. For example, he states that "A person's expectations about how others will interact with him depend strictly on his own choice of disposition only if that *choice* is known by the others."[14] However, it is clear that Gauthier both needs and relies on the much stronger assumption that others not only know the person's current choice, but also predict infallibly whether or not the person will carry out that choice. For example, Gauthier defines "transparency" as a state in which "each is directly aware . . . whether he is interacting with straightforward or constrained maximizers."[15] Since, as we have just seen, a constrained maximizer is one who *will* carry out her intentions, it follows that awareness that you are a constrained maximizer involves the true belief, not only that you are forming certain conditional intentions, but also that you will carry one of them out when the condition is satisfied. If I did not have this infallible ability to predict your future acts, Gauthier could not argue (as he does) that I maximize my expected utility by choosing CM, since I would sometimes be cheated by defecting partners. Correspondingly, Gauthier's translucency assumption is an assumption that agents' abilities to detect each others' intentions *and* to predict future fulfillment of those intentions surpass mere guesswork. My point here is not to reject these assumptions, but rather to indicate clearly how strong they are, and at least to raise doubts about their credibility.

Does constrained maximization maximize expected utility?

Now let us turn to premise 3, which spells out what the consequences will be if I choose CM as opposed to SM. Here the argument runs into trouble.

The first major problem is that Gauthier mistakenly assumes both that (a) my only options are CM and SM, and (b) my partner's only options are CM and SM. He then argues that CM is my best response to the possibility of these choices on the part of my partner. Both these assumptions seem false – there is no reason to suppose that our options are limited in this fashion. Since discussion of what additional options might be rational for me to choose is complicated, I restrict myself here to pointing out that my partner has a variety of alternatives, and that CM is not my best response to many of these.

I may, for example, face a partner who has chosen what we may call "unconditional cooperation (UC)":[16]

UC: Building one's lighthouse whatever one's partner does.

---

[14] Gauthier, *Morals by Agreement*, p. 173, my emphasis.
[15] Ibid., pp. 173–4.
[16] I am grateful to David Schmidtz for pointing out to me the relevance of this alternative option.

Or I may face someone who has chosen "radical cooperation (RC)":

> RC: Building one's lighthouse if and only if one's partner has chosen unconditional cooperation.

How would someone who has chosen CM fare against a partner who has chosen UC? It is obvious that the best choice is SM rather than CM, since the straightforward maximizer will always obtain -500 and the constrained maximizer will only obtain -600. Similarly, against a partner who has chosen RC, one will maximize utility by choosing UC rather than CM, for in this way one will achieve a constant return of -600 rather than $-1,000$. Of course, a partner who chooses UC or RC may not be rational, since this choice will not fare well against all possible configurations of partners and their choices (although it is certainly arguable that someone choosing UC is *moral*). But CM is hardly an attractive option if it only succeeds against perfectly rational partners. Since many people are in fact irrational, an acceptable option must work against all comers, be they rational or not.[17] Hence Gauthier's argument that CM maximizes utility is significantly incomplete, since it does not take account of cases in which the chooser's partner will select some other option (perhaps an irrational one) besides either CM or SM. To establish whether CM is superior, we would have to know how many potential partners have chosen SM, CM, UC, RC, and all the other options that could be defined; how transparent or translucent these individuals are; what the stakes are in possible interactions with them; and so forth. Gauthier has not performed this task for us, and we can have no advance reason to suppose that CM will emerge ever or often as the best policy.

But even if we restrict ourselves to partners who choose either CM or SM, Gauthier's argument is less compelling than he realizes. Let us look at his first claim:

---

[17] The importance of establishing the rationality of a strategy against irrational opponents has been recognized since von Neumann and Morgenstarn concluded that " . . . the rules of rational behavior must provide definitely for the possibility of irrational conduct on the part of others." John von Neumann and Oskar Morgenstern, *Theory of Games and Economic Behavior* (Princeton: Princeton University Press, 1953). p. 32, as quoted in Brian Skyrms, *The Dynamics of Rational Deliberation* (Cambridge, MA: Harvard University Press, in press), chap. 6.

Even Gauthier, who argues that CM rather than SM is rational, implicitly concedes that CM must succeed against irrational dispositions, of which (in his view) SM is one.

In "Contractarianism and Moral Skepticism" (Chapter 13 in this volume), David Copp describes the contractarian strategy as arguing that there is a set of moral requirements such that a population of fully rational people would agree to comply with them. But if this argument assumes that each person may presuppose the rationality of everyone else in agreeing to comply with these requirements, it idealizes our actual situation beyond any usefulness.

If I choose CM, then
    (a) If you choose CM, you will build and I will build.

Why, precisely, is it supposed to be the case that if I choose CM, then if you choose CM as well, you will build and I will build? Each of us is transparent, so each of us knows the other's choice, plus the fact that the other will carry out that choice. But how does each of us make the relevant choice?

There are actually *two* crucial choices that each of us must make here: the choice between CM and SM, and the choice (if CM is selected) of which unconditional intention to form, the intention to build or the intention not to build. Let's simplify matters by assuming that you have already chosen CM, and, of course, I know this. What should I predict you will do if I choose CM? Gauthier seems to assume that I may simply predict that you will form the intention to build your lighthouse, and then build it. But matters are much more complex than this. Given your choice of CM, what I *can* predict is that you will form the intention to build and carry it out if and only if you predict that I will form the unconditional intention to build and then carry out this intention. But how can I assume you can make this prediction about me? Your position vis-à-vis me is perfectly parallel to my position vis-à-vis you. Even if you know that I choose CM, all you can infer from this is that I will form the intention to build and carry it out *if and only if* I predict you will build. You cannot infer that I will intend and build, simpliciter. But if you cannot infer this, then you will not build. And I will not form the intention to build and then carry it out unless I believe you will build. Neither of us, knowing the other has chosen CM, has sufficient information to predict on that basis what the other will do, so neither of us can decide which intention to form and act to carry out.

What we have just seen is that if "transparency" is interpreted as Gauthier officially interprets it, namely, as awareness on the part of another agent whether he is interacting with a constrained or straightforward maximizer, then transparency is not sufficient to allow two transparent constrained maximizers to predict what the other will do, or to choose any intention or action themselves, since that choice depends on their making this prediction. We might try to avoid this by allowing Gauthier a *maximum* notion of transparency, namely, the assumption that each agent just directly knows (or truly believes) what (unconditional) intention the other agent forms, and knows that the other will carry out that intention. But even this will not solve the problem. To see this, all we need to do is notice that it is perfectly consistent with our both being constrained maximizers that we both form the intention *not* to build, and then carry out that intention. (For being a CM *may* involve forming the intention not to build if you predict the other agent will not build, and then not building yourself; if both of us do this, then we both still qualify as choosing and carrying out CM.) Thus, it is *not* possible, contrary to Gauthier's argument, to show that if we both choose CM, and we are both transparent to each other in this maximum sense, then we will both form the intention to build and then carry out those intentions. We might instead both form and act on the intention *not* to build. But if it is false that two constrained maximizers will necessarily cooperate, it is false that my choosing CM when you have chosen CM necessarily produces greater utility for me than my choosing SM: they might produce the very same utility – the utility I receive if neither of us builds a lighthouse.

It might be hoped that a reformulation of constrained maximization could be found according to which it would necessarily be the case that if two transparent partners both choose CM, then they will both build. Unfortunately, such reformulations do not seem to be available. Consider the following simple candidate:

> CM'. Forming the intention to build, and carrying out that intention.

Two agents, both of who adopt CM', will necessarily both build their lighthouses. But adopting CM' leaves each of them vulnerable to straightforward maximizers, since it directs the agent to build regardless of what her partner does. To avoid this, we need to incorporate the kind of clause adopted by Gauthier, which dictates adopting the same intention as one's partner; and to secure joint building, rather than joint nonbuilding, we need an additional clause that provides pressure, so to speak, in the direction of building. The following option might be thought to solve the problem:

> CM". (i) Forming the intention to build if one's partner will build, or forming the intention not to build if one's partner will not build; and
>
> (ii) carrying out whichever intention one forms; and
>
> (iii) forming the intention to build and actually building if one's partner forms the intention to comply with (i) and (ii).

It may appear that CM" secures the result Gauthier wants, since if both you and I adopt CM", then each of us forms the intention to comply with clauses (i) and (ii), and, hence, each of us must comply with clause (iii) – so we both build our lighthouses. However, CM" must be rejected, for it does not prescribe a consistent set of intentions. For suppose you have adopted clauses (i) and (ii) (but not clause (iii)), and you also form the intention not to build (as we have seen, nothing in clauses (i) and (ii) rules this out). Then, by CM", I must *both* form the intention to build (since that is required by clause (iii)), and *also* form the intention not to build (since that is required by clause (i)). But these intentions, and their attendant actions, are inconsistent. In general, every reformulation of CM I have inspected is vulnerable to some problem or another: either it does not guarantee joint compliance, or it leaves the agent vulnerable to exploitation by a partner who does not adopt CM, or it delivers inconsistent prescriptions. Unless a successful version of CM is forthcoming, we must conclude joint adoption of constrained maximization cannot secure joint compliance as Gauthier's argument assumes.[18]

[18] In "Closing the Compliance Dilemma: Why It's Rational to be Moral in a Lamarckian World" (Chapter 16 in this volume), Peter Danielson recognizes this difficulty, and formulates a version of CM that he claims avoids the problem. He introduces the notion of a "metastrategy," that is, "a function that takes each of the other player's choices (or metastrategies) into a choice." He then introduces the metastrategy CC (intended to be roughly similar to Gauthier's CM), which is defined as "CC = UC → C; MAX → D; CC → C," (where UC and MAX are other metastrategies). But *this* definition is clearly illegitimate, since it refers to the very concept being defined (CC itself). Danielson states that CC can be defined "extensionally" in terms of the game matrix, but this cannot be correct, since he explicitly recognizes (his Figures 16-1 and 16-2) that a first-order game (in which the agents' options are ordinary actions) may have the same matrix as a second-order game (in which the agents' options are metastrategies). Thus, game matrices alone cannot define metastrategies, since such matrices do not distinguish them from ordinary actions or choices. Indeed, since a "metastrategy" is *defined* as a strategy from another player's choice or metastrategy to a choice, it is difficult to see how a metastrategy could be individuated (much less implemented, as Danielson himself realizes, p. 298), without some reference to the other player's choice or metastrategy. In other work, Danielson attempts to solve this problem by use of a quotational device that I have not had the opportunity to examine.

In "Gauthier's Theory of Morals by Agreement" (*Philosophical Quarterly* 38 (1988): 343–64), Richmond Campbell suggests the following formulation of CM to get around this problem: "In a choice situation involving strategic interaction a person has the CM disposition iff: (1) she has property R and (2) she will co-operate with other agents interacting with her iff she believes that each of them has property R." Property R is any property that SMs won't have, such as the property of being ready to reciprocate cooperation when making the second move in *sequential* Prisoner's Dilemmas. It is true that SMs won't have the property Campbell describes, so that someone who adopts CM will not be exploited by SMs. However, there will be other defecting agents who *would* reciprocate cooperation in sequential Prisoner's Dilemmas, but who would *not* cooperate in simultaneous Prisoner's Dilemmas; an agent adopting Campbell's version of CM would be vulnerable to exploitation by these agents. SM agents do not exhaust the list of possible noncooperative agents that CM agents must be protected against. We cannot, of course, without problematic circularity, simply define a CM agent as one who cooperates with all and only other CM agents (or ones she believes to be CM agents). There is a deep problem here about whether the kind of relation Gauthier needs between CM partners is incoherent: it may be that his conditions will only be met if the decision of each partner *causes* the decision of the other partner – a type of causal interaction that cannot be countenanced.

In *Utilitarianism and Co-operation* (Oxford: Clarendon Press, 1980), Donald Regan discusses analogous problems of coordination that might face act utilitarians. In Chapters 8–10, he introduces a new version of utilitarianism that, he argues, enables agents who follow it to protect themselves from "exploitation" by others, and yet enables them as a group to secure the greatest utility available to them as a group. The daunting complexity of this new theory leaves me uncertain as to its success; but readers interested in pursuing this problem for Gauthier would be well repaid to study Regan's contribution.

On Gauthier's original presentation of his argument, I never do worse if I choose CM than if I choose SM, and in one case out of four possible types of cases, I will do better. On my construal of the argument (assuming my partner chooses either SM or CM), I never do worse if I choose CM, and in one case (where you also choose CM) out of four, I *may* do better. This is getting to be pretty slim pickings as support for the rationality of choosing CM. It becomes even slimmer when we move from the strong transparency assumption to the more realistic translucency assumption Gauthier himself uses. Under the transparency assumption, CM is a safe choice, since I can never be exploited by straightforward maximizers: I can always recognize them in advance and protect myself. But under the translucency assumption, CM is no longer safe: it exposes me to exploitation by undetected straightforward maximizers. Both I and potential partners can resort to the *pretense* of being a constrained maximizer, and then prey on those who are deceived. The issue then is whether the gain possibly available through adopting CM is outweighed by the risk of exploitation that it creates.

Gauthier argues that under the translucency assumption, it is rational to choose CM only if the ratio between the probability that an interaction involving CMs will result in cooperation and the probability that an interaction involving CMs and SMs will involve exploitation and defection is greater than the ratio between the gain from defection and the gain through cooperation.[19] In arguing that this will often happen, Gauthier assumes that two constrained maximizers who successfully identify each other will always cooperate. What we have seen is that they will *not* always cooperate. Hence, the probability that an interaction involving CMs will result in cooperation is lower than Gauthier assumes (although we cannot say how much lower). Therefore, it takes a correspondingly *lower* ratio between the gain from defection and the gain through cooperation for it to be rational to choose CM. The less people stand to gain from defection, the more likely it is that CM is rational; but the more people stand to gain from defection, the less likely it is that CM is rational. The rationality of choosing CM is not undermined for *every* case by the phenomenon I have described. What I have shown, however, is that the number of cases in which it is rational to choose CM is smaller than Gauthier supposes, and it may be significantly smaller. And, as we saw at the beginning of this section, it may not be rational at all if one's potential partners adopt options such as UC or RC rather than CM or SM. All this may dramatically reduce the number of occasions on which it is rational to dispose oneself to act morally, and so may considerably shrink the scope of the justification for moral action that Gauthier is trying to provide.

---

[19] Gauthier, *Morals by Agreement*, p. 176.

The alleged rationality of carrying out rational intentions

In the preceding section, I argued that Gauthier succeeds in showing the rationality of choosing constrained maximization in fewer cases than he realizes. Let us now turn to the question of whether it is really rational for me to carry out constrained maximization even in the cases where it is rational to choose it in advance. Line 7 of Gauthier's argument asserts that it is: that, for example, if I rationally choose CM and form the intention to build my lighthouse, then it is rational for me to actually build the lighthouse when the time comes.[20]

Why does Gauthier think it is rational for me to carry out my chosen policy? He admits that doing so is not rational in the usual sense of maximizing utility. It appears that what he relies on here is a general principle, which we may label the "rationality of perseverance" principle (RPP):

RPP: If it is rational for an agent to form the intention to do A, then it is rational for the agent to actually do A when the time comes (assuming the agent acquires no new information, and has not altered her values).

Gauthier asserts, for example, "If it is rational for me to adopt an intention to do x in circumstances c, and if c comes about . . . then it is rational for me to carry out x"; and also, "If [a person's] dispositions to choose are rational, then surely her choices are also rational."[21]

Unfortunately, and surprisingly, Gauthier offers no positive argument in favor of the rationality of perseverance principle. The only argument he appears to provide is the concession that if the agent will suffer from some future weakness or imperfection (such as weakness of will), then it will *not* be rational for her to persevere in carrying out an intention.[22]

---

[20] Part of this claim is the assertion that if I rationally choose CM, and, seeing that you will not build your lighthouse, I form the intention not to build *my* lighthouse, then it is rational for me to carry out this intention as well. But no one disputes that carrying out this particular intention is rational.

[21] Gauthier, "Afterthoughts," p. 159, and *Morals by Agreement*, p. 186.

[22] Gauthier, *Morals by Agreement*, pp. 184–6. In discussing what it would be rational to do for agents who are subject to weaknesses or imperfections, Gauthier states that such rationality "constitute[s] a second-best rationality," and denies that any lesson can be drawn from this about the dispositions and choices that are rational for the perfect actor (pp. 185–6). This seems to be a mistake. It is rational, simpliciter, to do the best one can in the face, so to speak, of the materials that have been given to one. An imperfect agent, one afflicted with future weakness of will, does the best she can in the face of *this* material. The material is imperfect, but her rationality in dealing with this material is not imperfect or "second best." Similarly, an agent facing a threatener, or a straightforward maximizer, does the best she can in the fact of this material. The agents she faces are also imperfect (in Gauthier's view), but this does not show that her rationality in dealing with these agents is imperfect. I can see no principled differences between doing the best one can vis-à-vis one's own future imperfections and doing the best one can vis-à-vis other agents' imperfections.

But, of course, this does not provide positive evidence that rationality requires perfect agents to persevere.

Indeed, it is difficult to know how one could argue for the rationality of perseverance. On the face of it, intentions and the intended acts are two distinct events, sometimes having different features and different consequences. Hence, the appropriateness of an intention appears to imply nothing conclusive about the appropriateness of the intended act. I may, for example, have promised to form a certain intention, but not promised to carry it out; in such a case, I am obliged to form the intention, but not obliged to carry it out, especially if my doing so would be undesirable.[23]

The natural move here for a defender of perseverance would be to appeal to intuitions about rationality in various cases. Unfortunately, such appeals do not appear to support the principle. In standard cases, where the consequences of the intention are the same as those of the intended act, where the agent is rational to form an intention at t_1 to perform A rather than B at t_2, and where she receives no new information and does not change her values by t_2, we all agree that she then would be rational at t_2 to carry out her intention by performing A. But we cannot use this fact to support the claim that the existence of her prior intention to do A *makes it* rational to do A, since it would be rational for her to do A whether or not she had ever formed that prior intention. She has all the same reasons to do A at t_2 that she had at t_1; if it was reasonable to choose A over B at the earlier time, of course, it is reasonable to choose it now. Someone attempting to support the rationality of perseverance principle by appeal to this kind of case would have to resort to a different scenario: a scenario involving two possible worlds, identical to each other except that in the first world, the agent forms a rational prior intention to do A, whereas in the second world, the agent forms no prior intention. It would then have to be claimed that at the time of action, the first agent has *more* reason to do A than the second agent. I, myself, have no inclination to think this: the two agents appear to me to have precisely equal reason to do A.

Gauthier needs the strong interpretation of the RPP, according to which the rationality of the earlier intention *makes* the later action rational. Otherwise, in the kinds of cases with which we are specifically concerned, that is, cases where the agent's reasons for forming the

---

[23] Since this essay was written, I have discovered that similar arguments to those in this paragraph (and a case similar to my subsequent telepathic terrorist case) have already been presented by Gregory Kavka in "Responses to the Paradox of Deterrence," in *The Security Gamble: Deterrence Dilemmas in the Nuclear Age*, edited by Douglas MacLean (Totowa, NJ: Rowman & Allanheld, 1984), pp. 155–9.

A second independent and insightful discussion of what I call RPP (keyed to another article of Kavka's) is contained in Michael Bratman, *Intention, Plans, and Practical Reason* (Cambridge, MA: Harvard University Press, 1987), pp. 101–6.

intention to do A are independent of his reasons for actually doing A, the action would have to be judged irrational according to the normal utility-maximizing criterion of rationality. This presumption of irrationality could only be overturned by the strong interpretation of the RPP. But it is precisely in such cases that we feel the greatest conviction that the agent's reasons for forming the intention to do A seem not to carry over *at all* as reasons to do A itself. Consider the case of a government official negotiating with a terrorist. The terrorist, an infallible mind reader, threatens to blow up a planeload of innocent people unless the official forms the mental intention of releasing the terrorist's imprisoned comrades. When, and only when, the official forms this intention (a psychological event the terrorist will detect telepathically), the bomb will be disarmed. Clearly, under these circumstances, it would be rational for the official to form the intention of releasing the terrorist's comrades. Once he has formed the required intention and the terrorist has permanently disarmed his bomb, it seems equally clear that it would be rational for the official to change his mind and *not* release the comrades. Indeed, we would view a terrorist who merely demanded the formation of intentions as extremely stupid. Here, then, is a clear-cut case where it is rational to form an intention, and yet irrational to carry it out, contrary to the implications of the rationality of perseverance principle.[24] Gauthier might argue that his acceptance of the causal efficacy thesis shows that it is causally impossible for the official both to form the intention to release the comrades and then to change his mind. But this does not show that actually releasing the comrades is *rational*, that is, the best act. Gauthier assumes throughout that the agent has genuine alternatives available to him at t_2, that is, that he *could* fail to release the comrades. And if he could fail to release them, it is open to us to assess this act as the best one.

It may fix this conclusion even more firmly in our minds to notice that Gauthier needs an extremely strong perseverance principle: not just the assertion that prior intentions create *some* reason to carry them out, but rather the assertion that prior intentions create *conclusive* reason to carry them out. For if the reason to comply created by one's earlier intention is not conclusive, there will always be the danger that the disutility of compliance will outweigh the reason in favor of compliance created by the earlier intention, and defection will turn out to be rational after all. The complete counterintuitiveness of such a strong perseverance principle can be seen if we merely raise the stakes at issue in a given case. Consider a case in which a telepathic burglar threatens to steal all my household valuables. I know that if I form the intention of blowing up

[24] Gauthier regards deterrence cases and compliance cases as completely parallel, so he would not dismiss such a case as irrelevant to his argument about compliance with morality. (See *Morals by Agreement*, pp. 184–7.)

the house with the burglar and myself inside, it is nearly certain that he will be deterred. I form this intention, but unfortunately he is not deterred. According to the strong perseverance principle, it is now rational for me to blow up the house and kill myself, merely because I previously formed the intention of doing so under these circumstances. But no one, I think, would want to agree to this. Gauthier's guiding hope in his project is to provide a foundation for moral norms on norms of rationality, because the latter's binding status is much more easily accepted. But if it turns out that the norms of rationality include such principles as perseverance, it appears they may demand greater self-sacrifice from us than even morality typically does, and will be even more difficult to accept. If morality requires rationality of perseverance as its foundation, we are probably worse off than we are with a morality that has no foundation in rationality.

It is also worth noting that nothing in Gauthier's argument for the rationality of choosing constrained maximization really turns on the fact that the means by which I effect my subsequent compliance is a choice to form a certain *intention*. We could restate the entire argument, just as effectively, to show that it would maximize my utility to perform *any* present act that would bring about my subsequent choosing to build a lighthouse. For example, suppose that tonight I open a magazine to an article I want to read tomorrow. Tomorrow I read the article; its mentioning lighthouses triggers the idea that I might build one, and that is precisely what I do. Suppose also that I am transparent to you, in the sense that you detect my opening the magazine tonight and accurately predict that it will stimulate me tomorrow to build a lighthouse. You are a (suitably defined) constrained maximizer. If Gauthier's argument were correct, my opening the magazine in these circumstances would induce you to build your lighthouse as well, and we would have evaded the Prisoner's Dilemma. Hence, since it would (in Gauthier's argument) maximize utility for me to open the magazine, rationality requires that I do so. But, when the time came for me to build the lighthouse, Gauthier would be unable to argue that building the lighthouse is also rational for me, since he can invoke no prior intention on my part to establish its rationality. Since there is no difference between the utility I can secure by forming an intention and the utility I can secure by opening the magazine, there is no way for Gauthier to argue that I must form the intention rather than open the magazine. Agents who bring about their own compliance with moral rules by such means as opening magazines cannot be said to be rational when they do comply.[25]

---

[25] It is clear that in opening the magazine, I have no intention to build a lighthouse. We might investigate whether I could *deliberately* secure my building the lighthouse by performing some act today that would bring about my building the lighthouse tomorrow, without at the time of the act intending to build a lighthouse (it might be claimed,

We should note the flip side of Gauthier's reliance on intentions to make subsequent compliance rational. Imagine a case in which one's partner has performed the cooperative act, even though one did not oneself adopt constrained maximization, or form the intention to co-operate. In such a case, Gauthier must say that it is not rational, and hence not moral, for one to cooperate, since no prior intention to co-operate makes it rational now. (And, since belatedly forming such an intention would have no effect on one's partner's action, there is no reason to do so, even if such an intention, if rational, would make one's cooperating rational.) This seems a clear case in which the recommendations generated by Gauthier's system diverge sharply from those of ordinary morality, which would recommend cooperation even if one had not originally intended to cooperate.

I conclude that the rationality of perseverance principle is false.[26] If this is correct, then Gauthier has not shown that it is rational to carry out constrained maximization, even in those cases where it is rational to adopt it. It follows from this that he has not shown that it is rational to abide with moral rules once accepted, even if it is rational to accept them. Moreover, even if the rationality of perseverance principle were true, it would not apply to cases in which an agent induces himself to

---

for example, that doing A with the intention of bringing about my doing B shows that I *do* have the intention of doing B at the time I do A). I am not at all sure this latter claim is correct, but I shall not try to discuss it here. The important point for us here is that my act of opening the magazine is rational, that is, utility maximizing, whether or not I *believe* it will have the desired effect. And if I open the magazine in ignorance of its effect, I can hardly be said to have the intention of bringing about that effect.

Gauthier might try to assert (and there is some textual evidence that he believes) an analogue of the perseverance principle: that if it is best (rational) for me to do act A (partly because it will bring about later act B), then when the time comes, it must be best (rational) for me to do B as well. Clearly, this is incorrect. Suppose a business student has only two choices: to accept a job with firm 1, or to accept a job with firm 2. If she accepts the job with firm 1, she will subsequently cheat a client out of $100, be caught, and sentenced to spend a month in jail. If she accepts the job with firm 2, she will subsequently cheat a client out of $100,000, be caught, and sentenced to spend ten years in jail. Given the prospects, it would be best for her to accept the job with firm 1 – and best partly because this job will result in her stealing (merely) $100. But it hardly follows that it would then be best (or rational) for her to cheat the client out of $100. She may be destined to do this by her earlier choice, but we can still criticize her action. (See above, footnote 20, for a discussion of whether such cases are sufficiently parallel to the ones in which Gauthier is interested.) In cases such as this, one might question whether act B (stealing $100) is part of what makes act A (accepting the job with firm 1) best – it would be more intuitive to say that act A is best *despite* its leading to act B. But the analogue to the perseverance principle just articulated is only significant if it applies to subsequent acts (such as stealing the $100) that are not rational or best taken in themselves.

[26] In "Contractarianism and Moral Skepticism" (Chapter 13 in this volume), David Copp also argues (in the third section) that actual compliance is irrational even if the CM disposition is rational (except in the sense that the CMs preferences have changed, in virtue of her adoption of CM, so that compliance necessarily becomes the utility-maximizing act).

comply with moral precepts by some means (such as opening a magazine) that do not involve forming an intention to perform the act of compliance. Any agent who maximizes his utility by such means cannot be said to be rational when he then complies. Whether his act of compliance is brought about by a utility-maximizing intention or a utility-maximizing act of another sort, the compliance itself is not rational.

The derivation of morality from rationality

I have argued that Gauthier has not shown that it maximizes expected utility in a significant number of cases for a person to adopt constrained maximization. I have further argued that he has not shown, because it is false, that it is rational for a person to act according to constrained maximization even in the cases where it was rational to adopt it. Now I want to take up a harder and more important question. Suppose my previous arguments were wrong, and Gauthier had indeed shown that it is rational both to adopt constrained maximization in many cases and then to carry it out. Would the success of this argument show, as Gauthier believes it does, that morality is founded on rationality, and hence that rationality provides a "justificatory framework for moral behavior and principles"?[27] If the success of Gauthier's argument *would* provide a rational justification for morality, then we would be well repaid to tinker with the details of his argument in an attempt to salvage it from my previous criticisms. But if success would not provide such a justification, then such tinkering has little or no point.

I shall assume that the point of providing morality with a justificatory framework is to defend it against the moral skeptic, who believes all moral statements are false, or meaningless, or at any rate without epistemological justification. We may characterize what Gauthier has done as arguing that individual rationality, or self-interest, requires a person to dispose herself to perform certain cooperative acts, and then actually to perform those acts when the time comes. Suppose we assume that the acts in question are precisely the same ones that morality requires. Still, the success of this argument would not show that *morality* has been provided with a justification. It would show that we have self-interested reasons to do what morality, *if it were true* (or correct), would demand – but it would not show that morality *is* true (or correct). Such an argument would merely show an interesting coincidence between the purported claims of morality and the real claims of self-interest.[28] In

[27] Gauthier, *Morals by Agreement,* p. 2.

[28] I take this to be one of the points of David Coop's discussion in "Contractarianism and Moral Skepticism" (Chapter 13 in this volume). Copp and I initiated our lines of inquiry into the force of Gauthier's argument independently; reading earlier versions of his stimulating discussion forced me to clarify for myself what I thought Gauthier was really trying to do in connecting rationality and morality.

order for Gauthier to answer the moral skeptic, he must do something more. But precisely what?

One promising strategy for answering the moral skeptic would be to find premises that the skeptic must accept, and then to show that certain moral statements follow from those premises. I believe that Gauthier can be interpreted as trying to follow precisely this strategy. He puts forward certain premises that he believes everyone must accept and then argues that moral statements can be derived from them. In his case, the premises are not factual statements, or definitions of moral terms, but rather normative principles of individual rationality. If these principles cannot be rejected, or at any rate are more readily acceptable than morality itself, then if moral principles can be shown to follow from them, morality will have been provided with a suitable foundation. We need not follow the cognitivist in granting that the principles of individual rationality are *true*, but whatever variety of acceptability they do have will be fully inherited by the moral principles that can be shown to follow from them.[29] The moral skeptic will be hard put to reject such principles.

How precisely is the argument supposed to go? Gauthier posits the following two axioms of individual rationality (where RPP is our old friend, the rationality of perseverance, and RMX is a *qualified* version of he rationality of maximizing expected utility). He characterizes these as comprising a "weak and widely accepted conception of practical rationality."[30]

RPP . If it is rational for an agent to form the intention of doing A, then it is rational for the agent to actually do A when the time comes (assuming the agent acquires no new information, and has not altered her values).

RMX. It is rational for an agent to act so as to maximize her expected utility, unless doing so requires her to violate RPP.[31]

He then argues that these axioms entail the following principles:

1. Under circumstances C, it is rational for an agent to adopt constrained maximization and form the intention to cooperate.

---

[29] Some authors have tried to follow this strategy by deriving moral statements from definitions of moral terms. For example, if we agree what "is morally obligatory" just means "would maximize the general happiness," then we can hardly reject the truth of the statement "It is morally obligatory to maximize the general happiness." The weakness of this version of the strategy is that a skeptic can respond, "Why should anyone care about acts that maximize the general happiness?" Gauthier's version avoids this problem, because it *already starts* with normative principles that have motivational force.

[30] Gauthier, *Morals by Agreement*, p. 17.

[31] Ibid., pp. 43–4 and 182–7.

2. If the agent rationally forms the intention to cooperate, then it is rational for her to carry out this intention (assuming she has acquired no new information and has not altered her values).

The phrase "circumstances C" refers to any combination of empirical factors, involving the intentions of other agents, their degree of translucency, the possible gains and losses associated with cooperation and defection, etc., that makes it true in a given case that the agent would maximize her expected utility by adopting constrained maximization. Principle 1 follows straightforwardly from axiom RMX, if we allow this form of rationality to be applied to the formation of intentions (i.e., adoption of constrained maximization) as well as to external conduct. Principle 2 is a straightforward special case of axiom RPP.

Gauthier claims that the traditional conception of morality identifies any impartial constraint on self-interested behavior as moral.[32] On this account, Principle 1 is not a moral principle, since it in no way constrains self-interested behavior. To the contrary, it recommends adoption of constrained maximization precisely because it will maximize the agent's self-interest. Hence, if this argument provides a justification for morality, the whole weight falls on Principle 2. Principle 2 clearly does constrain self-interested behavior, since it requires the agent to cooperate even when doing so would fail to maximize her utility. Let us grant, for the sake of argument, that Principle 2 is also impartial in some suitable sense.

But does the fact that Principle 2 constitutes an impartial constraint on self-interested behavior show that it is a moral principle? Clearly not. Impartial constraint is *not* sufficient to show a principle is moral. Consider a rule of etiquette requiring thank-you notes to be handwritten rather than typed. Such a rule is certainly an impartial constraint, but it does not thereby qualify as a moral principle.[33] What more is required for morality? This is a difficult question, to which I will not try to supply a general answer. But it appears to me that we can characterize what is lacking in rules of etiquette as something like *appropriate deontic force*. It is by no means easy to say what the deontic force appropriate to morality

---

[32] Ibid., pp. 2, 4.
[33] Another example is the principle of malevolence, which prescribes any action maximizing the general unhappiness. This principle is both impartial and a constraint on self-interest (since it is often highly damaging to an agent's own interests to follow it), yet it hardly seems to be a moral principle. Other examples are supplied by club rules, legal codes, Mafia codes of honor, professional codes, administrative regulations, etc. Of course, some of the prescriptions stemming from these sources will require acts that are morally right, but it does not follow that all such prescriptions coincide with morality, or that any of them *in itself* constitutes a moral prescription. The difficulty with the principle of malevolence is not the one I cite in the text – inappropriate deontic force – but rather inappropriate content.

amounts to. But, borrowing from the traditional literature on the nature of morality, we might suggest the following three features:

I. Moral prescriptions are *overriding*. That is, they outweigh prescriptions from any other source when there is a conflict. In particular, they outweigh the recommendations of self-interest; or perhaps, more accurately, strong moral considerations outweigh weak considerations from any other normative sphere.
II. Moral prescriptions are *categorical*. That is, they hold independently of the agent's actual desires and aversions.
III. Moral prescriptions for action make it appropriate for agents to hold associated distinctive moral attitudes, such as guilt for personal derelictions, blame toward others who violate the prescriptions, a feeling that one is justified when one follows the prescription, etc.

The question before us is whether Principle 2 has the kind of deontic force required of genuine moral principles.[34] Is its recommendation overriding and categorical, and does it support attitudes of guilt and blame, etc.? I am not going to try to answer this question definitively. One can certainly argue that Principle 2 generates prescriptions that are both overriding and categorical. They are overriding because they always outweigh the recommendation of self-interest to maximize one's own utility, and they are categorical for the same reason: they tell the agent what to do regardless of her desires at the moment of action. (On the other hand, there is a sense in which they are neither overriding nor categorical, since these prescriptions only arise because of the agent's prior attempts to satisfy her desires and maximize her self-interest by adopting constrained maximization. This is not the kind of independence from desires that Kant, for example, had in mind.) It is far less clear that one can argue that prescriptions generated by Principle 2 appropriately support attitudes of blame, guilt, and so forth. I myself see no reason why an agent should feel *guilty* (or should *blame* others) for violating Principle 2, which is essentially a demand that one's action and intentions show a certain form of consistency. Inconsistency is not usually the object of blame and guilt.

But this is not the point I want to make here. What I want instead to point out is that whatever deontic force Principle 2 does possess, it inherits this force directly and solely from the axiom of rational persever-

[34] Gauthier's commitment to deriving principles with moral force is shown in the following passage: "A person is conceived as an independent center of activity, endeavoring to direct his capacities and resources to the fulfillment of his interests. He considers what he can do, but initially draws no distinction between what he may and may not do. How then does he come to acknowledge this distinction? How does a person come to recognize a moral dimension to choice . . . ?" (*Morals by Agreement*, p. 9).

ance, since it is simply a special case of that axiom. If that axiom has appropriate deontic force, then Principle 2 will as well, whereas, if that axiom fails to have the appropriate force, then Principle 2 will also fail. What this means is that Principle 2 only qualifies as a moral principle if axiom RPP qualifies as a moral principle. But if axiom RPP qualifies as a moral principle, then Gauthier has not succeeded in deriving morality from some nonmoral source.[35] Instead, he has derived morality from morality itself. This is no help against the moral skeptic. The only possible way in which such an argument could be construed as an effective response to the moral skeptic would be if the RPP, although moral, were somehow less questionable or more readily acceptable than other moral principles. Quite the opposite seems to be the case, as my arguments in the last section aimed at showing.

What we have discovered is that even if Gauthier had succeeded in establishing the truth of Principles 1 and 2, he would not have answered the skeptic by showing how morality can be derived from individual rationality. Either the principles he derives do not qualify as moral principles, because they lack the required deontic force, or if, on the other hand, they possess that force, it is only because a covert moral principle was smuggled into the axioms of individual rationality. No amount of tinkering with the details of Gauthier's argument will circumvent this problem.

This problem is a general one, extending beyond Gauthier's project to other possible attempts to derive morality from individual rationality. It appears to be precisely the powerful deontic force of morality that makes it suspect. It looks as though *any* attempt to derive morality in the manner I have outlined here faces the same dilemma as Gauthier's attempt: either the derived principles will be deontically too weak to qualify as genuinely moral or else the premises will be so strong that they already qualify as moral, and subject to the full blast of the skeptic's suspicion. If morality is to be defended against skepticism by an appeal to rationality, we need some better strategy than the one I have outlined here.

I conclude that the long-sought proof for the rationality of morality still eludes us, despite the hard and illuminating work Gauthier has devoted to the cause of finding it. It may elude us forever.[36]

---

[35] See ibid., pp. 5 and 17, for Gauthier's assertions that he aims to derive morality from a nonmoral source.

[36] I am grateful to Michael Bratman, David Copp, Peter Danielson, Alan Nelson, David Schmidtz, and George Smith for comments on earlier versions of this essay.

15. Morality and the theory
of rational choice*

Jody S. Kraus and
Jules L. Coleman

What is the relationship between morality and rationality? The answer
to this question depends, of course, on how we characterize "rationality"
and "morality." We can begin with the definition of rationality found
in contemporary microeconomics: rationality is utility maximization.[1]
The rational actor seeks to maximize his net, expected, utility. Defining
rationality in this way enables us to give a simple and minimal definition
of morality: morality is constrained utility maximization.[2] The moral actor
sometimes acts so as to constrain his utility-maximizing behavior. Given
these definitions, rationality and morality are incompatible. The purely
rational individual, at least sometimes, must act immorally; the purely
moral individual, at least sometimes, must act irrationally. Recent work
in the theory of rational choice, however, purports to demonstrate not
only that rationality and morality are compatible, but, moreover, that

*Reprinted by permission of the University of Chicago Press from "Morality and the Theory
of Rational Choice," by Jody S. Kraus and Jules L. Coleman, in Ethics 97 (1987): 715–49.
Copyright © 1987 by the University of Chicago. Earlier versions of this essay were pre-
sented at the universities of Arizona and Chicago, at Stanford and Yale universities, and
at the Central Division meeting of the American Philosophical Association in May 1986.
We are grateful for the comments made by participants on those occasions, especially by
David Gauthier. We are indebted as well to Brian Barry, Allen Buchanan, Arthur Fine,
Steve Maser, Ron Milo, Roberta Romano, Chris Shields, Holly Smith, and Oliver
Williamson.
[1] The notion of utility maximization we are employing here is the mathematical notion
  employed by economists whereby the maximization of utility is represented by the
  maximization of a utility function, itself generated from an ordinal preference calculus.
  Talk of utility here does not imply interpersonal comparisons of utility, standard utilitarian moral theory, or any dubious metaphysical commitments. All reference to utility
  maximization can, in fact, be replaced with preference satisfaction.
[2] This definition provides, at best, a necessary condition for a principle to be a moral
  principle. Of course, there may be more to the concept of morality than constraint on
  utility maximization. But we will be concerned here with the property of constraint
  shared by every moral principle, irrespective of what other properties they might share.

moral principles are derivable from rationality, once that concept is correctly analyzed.

It is common to distinguish between the *substantive* and *motivational* aspects of a moral theory. The substantive component specifies the content of the principles of morality; the motivational component explains why a rational person would comply with the principles specified by the substantive theory. If morality is to be derived from rationality, the theory of rationality must generate both the substantive and motivational components of moral theory. In what follows, we hope to show that rationality cannot generate the substantive component of a moral theory. But despite this skeptical goal, we are determined to take seriously the rational-choice framework in which this debate takes place. Understanding this framework is essential in order both to comprehend the argu-ments that follow and to appreciate the relevance of rational-choice theory to moral and political philosophy in general.

The rational-choice framework

One way of framing the question of whether morality is derivable from rationality is in contractarian terms: Under what conditions, if any, would rational agents agree to constrain their utility-maximizing behav-ior? We might begin answering this question by answering another first: namely, can circumstances be specified in which imposing constraints on one's self-interested, utility-maximizing behavior would be irrational? In this light, consider the economist's concept of perfect competition. Under conditions of perfect competition,[3] the individually rational, self-interested behavior of all agents induces a Pareto-efficient outcome.[4] Pareto-efficient states have no states Pareto superior to them. In optimal equilibria, therefore, each actor does as well as he can – that is, his utility is maximized subject to the utility maximization of others. If, by acting purely self-interestedly, each agent does as well as he or she can, then it would be irrational for any agent to impose restrictions on the pursuit of his self-interest. If, given the utility of others, I do the best I can by

---

[3] The conditions of perfect competition can be summarized, roughly, as (1) all individuals in the market behave as price takers (i.e., they choose consumption and production bundles subject to fixed positive prices). (2) All producers sell commodities that are identical with respect to physical characteristics, location, and time of availability. (3) There is no cost involved in exchanging commodities, and there is free entry and exit from the market. (4) Producers and consumers possess perfect information concerning the price, physical characteristics, and availability of each commodity.

[4] Pareto efficiency is usually defined in terms of preferences: A state, S_1, is *Pareto optimal* if and only if there is no feasible alternative state, S_2, such that at least one person prefers S_2 to S_1 and such that no one prefers S_1 to S_2. A state, S_1, is *Pareto superior* to a state, S_2, if and only if at least one person prefers S_1 to S_2 and no one prefers S_2 to S_1. Pareto efficiency can also be defined in terms of utility (roughly) by substituting "is better off in" for "prefers" in the above definitions.

pursuing my self-interest, then I will necessarily do less well by constraining my self-interested behavior. Under conditions of perfect competition, then, the rational actor has no incentive to adopt constraints, moral or other, on his utility-maximizing behavior. Compliance with moral principles would be irrational.

However, when markets fail (which, in the real world, they will do without exception) and conditions of perfect competition do not obtain, the self-interested, utility-maximizing behavior of each individual leads to a Pareto-*inefficient* outcome – that is, one in which at least some individuals could be made better off without worsening the condition of others. The possibility then arises that, by constraining her utility-maximizing behavior, an individual may be made better off than if she continues, unconstrained, to pursue her self-interest. By introducing constraints on the utility-maximizing behavior of individuals, it may be possible to secure Pareto-*efficient* outcomes in which an individual fares better than she would were she to act as an unconstrained utility maximizer. There would then be a rational motivation for compliance with normative principles, possibly even moral principles, which require constraint. Though the perfectly competitive market might well be likened to what David Gauthier calls a "morally free zone" of "moral anarchy," in which moral constraints are irrational, the imperfectly competitive market represents a "normatively constrained zone," in which moral constraints might well be rational.

Morality is a potential solution to the problem of market failure. Because morality is introduced to govern social interactions only under conditions of market failure, it is rendered fundamentally instrumental. The rationality of morality depends on its being a particular kind of solution to the problem of market failure: that is, one that secures a Pareto-efficient outcome by making each individual better off. To be a viable solution to the problem of market failure, morality must be both individually and collectively rational. Moreover, the case for morality generated by the market model is entirely contingent. But the contingency on which it rests is one virtually certain to obtain: markets are never perfectly competitive.

The market model of morality we are developing is not alone in employing the contingent fact of market failure as its theoretical point of departure. In motivating the need for political coercion, Hobbesian political contractarianism also relies upon characterizing the state of nature as, in effect, a failed market. Within the market contractarian framework, morality and politics are alternative solutions to the same problem, that is, the suboptimality of the state of nature. Both morality and politics attempt to "bridge the gap" between the inefficient equilibrium of the state of nature and the potential Pareto-efficient equilibria unavailable if individuals act noncooperatively. Both moral and political contractarians recognize that efficient, mutually beneficial gains are available only when individuals constrain their utility-maximizing behavior. But whereas political contractarianism endorses a political or coercive remedy, moral contractarianism offers a moral one. Where political contractarians claim that state coercion is necessary to prevent individuals from unrestrained pursuit of their self-interest, moral contractarianism claims that individuals rationally and voluntarily will choose to constrain their behavior, thus rendering a political solution otiose.

We have, up to now, cast the rational choice approach to moral and political theory in terms of market failure. However, the textbook illustration of conduct that is both individually rational and collectively irrational is the Prisoner's Dilemma (PD).[5] It is common, moreover, to treat market failure as a PD; Russell Hardin is widely credited with having demonstrated that certain sources of market failure (e.g., the provision of certain collective goods) are themselves extensionally equivalent to n-person PDs.[6] Given the standard conventions, we might discuss the relationship between morality and rationality in terms of the PD.

Recasting the problem of market failure as the problem of escaping the PD emphasizes the relationship between the suboptimality of the state of nature and cooperation. Rational individuals in a PD must choose the noncooperative individual strategy available to them. Were individuals in the PD able to cooperate, they would, in principle, be able to secure the Pareto-efficient outcome. Cooperation in the PD amounts to agreement among all individuals in the dilemma on a *cooperative joint strategy*, which, if complied with by all, will secure a Pareto-efficient outcome. We can characterize the object of agreement, in this context, as a set of collectively self-imposed constraints on individual utility maximization, perhaps even as a set of moral principles. The problem of deriving morality from rationality, then, can be recast as the problem of

5

		B	
		Coop	~Coop
A	Coop	(9, 9)	(0, 10)
	~Coop	(10, 0)	(1, 1)

In the PD, it is rational to agree to the joint cooperative strategy (i.e., where both agree to cooperate), but irrational to comply with such an agreement. According to straightforward utility-maximization considerations, the dominant strategy for both parties in the PD is to agree not to confess and then to defect from this agreement and confess. This means that each party must confess, irrespective of the other party's actions. As a result, the outcome of cooperative interaction in the PD is suboptimal – i.e., in this case, both parties could be made better off.

6 Russell Hardin, "Collective Action as an Agreeable n-Prisoners' Dilemma," *Behavioral Science* 16 (1971): 472–9.

determining the cooperative joint strategy on which all parties in the state of nature would agree and with which all would comply, a strategy the existence of which the political contractarian denies. The rational-choice theory of morality must provide an account of the rationality of agreement and another account of the rationality of compliance. The theory of that agreement will provide the substantive component of morality; the theory of compliance with that agreement will generate the motivational component of morality.

How are we to model in rational-choice terms the process and substance of agreement? We can think of the contract or agreement process as a *rational bargain*. Each actor would agree upon a set of principles only if compliance with them were efficient, that is, only if the principles of moral constraint captured the whole of the available surplus. (This is the collective rationality condition of bargaining theory.) Each actor, as a utility maximizer, however, seeks to maximize his or her share of the gain. (This is the individual rationality condition.) Because the choice problem has both efficiency and division aspects, it is natural to model it as a "mixed bargaining game." Cooperation is necessary to produce the surplus, which is in turn contingent upon agreement on the division of those gains. No agreement upon relative shares, no surplus. Moral principles are the outcome of a rational bargain so conceived.[7]

The theory of compliance must explain why rational agents would comply with the joint strategy to which they bargain. In agreeing on a joint strategy, agents have agreed to abide by normative, perhaps moral, principles. The problem, then, of explaining why rational agents would comply with a joint strategy becomes the problem of determining the motivational component in moral theory – that is, that part of moral theory that explains why it is rational to act in accordance with moral principles.

Compliance and agreement are inexorably linked in the rational-choice framework. There is no sense in pursuing agreement on a cooperative joint strategy, if rationality precludes compliance. And there is no point in demonstrating the rationality of such compliance if rationality precludes securing agreement on a cooperative joint strategy. More importantly, it will not be enough for the rational choice model to demonstrate the rationality of agreement and compliance with any constraining principles. These principles, if they are to be moral principles,

---

[7] There are any number of constraints, various subsets of which would enable individuals to capture the surplus. We might say, then, that various sets of constraints all possess the *efficiency property*, that is, each set will be capable of bridging the gap between the suboptimal equilibrium of the PD and the optimal equilibria of perfect competition. Alternatives differ, however, in the manner in which they *distribute* the gains from cooperation. In pursuing agreement on a set of moral constraints, each actor is exploring alternative ways of distributing the gains from cooperation. Moral maxims, therefore, have an intrinsic distributional component.

must be *fair* and *impartial*. Therefore, we will assume that there is some correct theory of the bargaining process whereby rational agents agree on some principle or other and concentrate instead on the problem of demonstrating that rational agents will agree on fair, and thus moral, principles.

In a bargaining situation, failure to secure agreement returns parties to their prebargain positions. The way in which the parties evaluate their prebargaining position will naturally influence their bargaining behavior in ways that are likely to effect outcomes. If inequity or unfairness exists in the initial position, it is likely to be influential in the bargaining process. Even if it is not influential there, however, it will be transmitted by the bargaining process to the outcomes, thereby raising doubts about the fairness of the resulting principles.[8] The principles chosen in bargaining from unfair initial positions will almost certainly be unfair. On the other hand, the unfairness of the outcome of bargaining does not preclude its rationality. Rational bargains need not be fair ones. So why in the world would someone think that morality could possibly be the outcome of a rational bargain?

One solution to the problem of the status quo ante and its role in bargaining is to emphasize that morality is the outcome of a particular rational bargain, characterized in a particular way. The advocate of the bargaining theory approach need not make the foolish claim that every rational bargain is fair. Only certain rational bargains, struck under certain conditions, need be fair. But which bargains, under what conditions? One argument might be that rational bargains struck from fair initial conditions produce constraints that are fair and impartial in the sense necessary for them to constitute a morality. Why not, in other words, just preclude bargaining from unfair starting points? The point of the enterprise, after all, is to hit upon moral principles, and bargaining from unfair initial positions is unlikely to serve that purpose well.

This simple solution is, alas, too simple. In confining the bargaining problem to "fair" starting points, one cannot end up deriving morality from rationality alone; the best one can do is derive morality from rationality encased within an independently derived moral framework. Our objection is not that it is inappropriate in general to confine the choice problem or to define the environment or circumstances in which actors are viewed as bargaining. After all, every theorist gives a particular characterization of the choice problem including a specification of the environment of choice and a characterization of the decision makers.[9] Our objection is the narrow one that precluding unfair initial bargaining

---

[8] See footnote 17 below.
[9] Recall Rawls' Original Position populated by Kantian rational persons (John Rawls, *A Theory of Justice* [Cambridge, MA: Harvard University Press, 1971]); or Buchanan's contractors bargaining from "anarchistic equilibrium" (James Buchanan, *The Limits of Liberty* [Chicago: The University of Chicago Press, 1975]).

positions a priori simply undermines the enterprise of deriving morality from rationality *simpliciter*. Instead, it derives morality from rationality *cum* fairness. Other constraints on the bargaining problem might be perfectly acceptable. This one is not, unless one can show, rather than assume, that bargaining from unfair initial positions is, believe it or not, irrational.

We shall return to the problem of characterizing the choice problem later. For now it is enough to note that the easy solution will not work. Let us consider a complicated one. The rational-choice theory of morality faces two difficult problems. It must provide a theory of compliance and a theory of the fairness of the bargain. This much we know. Wouldn't it be especially impressive if both could be solved by the same argument? Certainly. Consider the following strategy. To solve the compliance problem, one has to show minimally that it is rational to comply with one's agreements. Presumably these agreements or bargains are them- selves rational. Not every rational agreement is a moral (or fair) one. Suppose, however, one could argue that it is rational to comply with agreements only if they are fair. Then the following argument would be available.

1. Bargaining is rational only if compliance is rational.
2. Compliance is rational only if the bargain outcome is fair.
3. Therefore, bargaining is rational only if it is fair.
4. Therefore, rational bargains must be fair bargains.
5. Therefore, bargaining from whatever unfair advantages one may have ex ante is not rational. (The reason: bargaining from unfair positions yields unfair outcomes with which it is not rational to comply. But if it is not rational to comply, then it is not rational to bargain.)

The upshot of the argument is that a particular solution to the com- pliance problem is sufficient to solve the unfair bargaining problem as well. Once both problems are resolved, the derivation of morality from rationality requires only a particular theory of rational bargaining. More- over, if this argument is sound, the view that bargain-theoretic models of justice necessarily generate the principle "to each according to his threat advantage" turns out to be unfounded.[10] This, then, is the ar- gument one needs to make in order to derive morality from a bargain- theoretic conception of rationality. But is it an argument one can plausibly make? Apparently it is, for it is the central argument in David Gauthier's book, *Morals by Agreement*.[11] Moreover, the fact that Gauthier

[10] This is Rawls' criticism of bargain-theoretic models of justice in "Justice as Fairness," *Philosophical Review* 57 (1958): 164–94.
[11] David Gauthier, *Morals by Agreement* (Oxford: Oxford University Press, 1986).

comes closer to pulling off this "argument of a lifetime" than anyone could legitimately expect makes this book the most important contribution to moral and political theory since Rawls' *A Theory of Justice*.[12]

Fairness and constrained maximization

We noted earlier that any game-theoretic approach to morality requires a solution to the defection or compliance problem. As a general solution to the compliance problem, Gauthier advances the *theory of constrained maximization*. In this essay, we do not take issue with the theory of constrained maximization as such, but several of the arguments that follow require at least a rudimentary understanding of it and of several distinctions upon which it relies.

The question is whether it is rational to comply with bargains into which one has rationally entered. In the course of one's lifetime, one is likely to face this question many times over. In particular, one is likely to be faced repeatedly with PD-structured bargains, that is, bargains embedded within PDs. So one must ask oneself what sort of disposition toward compliance it would be rational to adopt. If one could acquire a disposition that prevented one from abiding by the maxims of straightforward utility maximization (which demand defection) and instead demanded compliance when engaged in a PD-structured bargain, then one could benefit repeatedly from collective action with others similarly disposed.[13] The question then is not simply whether it is rational sometimes, for strategic reasons, to comply with the bargains one strikes, but whether it is rational so to dispose oneself. Gauthier argues that under certain conditions, it is in fact rational to dispose oneself to compliance. The conditions are, roughly, that a threshold number of compliance-disposed persons exists and that individuals are neither "opaque" nor "transparent," but are instead "translucent" with respect to their dispositions for compliance. In other words, if there is a reasonably good chance that you are negotiating with a compliance-disposed person and the chances are pretty good that you will be identified for what you

---

[12] Rawls, op. cit.

[13] The disposition being considered, it would seem, can be no ordinary one. Rather, it would appear to be more akin to a self-imposed psychological guarantee of compliance, one that *cannot* be resisted. If it could be resisted, then it would appear that straightforward maximizers would resist it in PD-structured bargains in order to maximize utility, and so adoption of it would not result in successful collective action. But because Gauthier does want to claim that rational actors so disposed are still making a *choice* when they cooperate in the PD, he wants the disposition to fall short of psychological compulsion; yet, because he wants it to influence their choice to cooperate, it must be strong enough to override consideration of direct utility maximization. It is difficult to conceptualize what such a disposition could be and even more troublesome to contemplate its psychological plausibility. Nonetheless, for present purposes, we allow Gauthier to help himself to such a disposition.

truly are (a complier or a defector), then it is rational to dispose yourself to compliance. To say it is rational to dispose yourself to compliance is to say that you will maximize your utility over time by doing so. Once you are rationally disposed, it will be rational for you to do what you are disposed to do – that is, to comply – even if you may be taken advantage of from time to time by defectors or even if you might do better on occasion by defecting and, thereby, taking advantage of others. The idea is that the benefits from the collective action such a disposition will make possible will outweigh these costs.

In what follows, we grant that constrained maximization is a correct solution to the compliance problem. The crucial issue, as we shall demonstrate, is whether narrow compliance, that is, (roughly) the disposition to comply only with fair bargains, is uniquely rational. So much for clarification on the matter of rational compliance and the motivational component of morality. Now to the matter of fairness.

Fairness and bargaining

Moral principles are constraints. Not every constraint is, however, a moral one. Moral principles are constraints that are "fair and impartial." The outcome of a bargain is moral only if it is fair; it is fair, according to Gauthier, only if it accords each party a share of the gains proportionate to his contribution, which itself must be a function of holdings fairly acquired in the initial position.[14]

---

[14] We accept the property of fairness as an exogenously given, necessary condition to be satisfied by any principles that purport to be moral principles. It is important to note that the rational-choice theory of morality itself does not presuppose the correctness of any theory of fairness. But like any theory of morality, it must accept some criteria of adequacy or correctness against which its results can be tested. In claiming that normative principles must be fair if they are to be moral principles, the rational-choice theory of morality is neither question begging nor circular. Rather, in accepting, pretheoretically, criteria of correctness for moral principles, it seeks to avoid question begging and hopes to demonstrate the conformity of the principles it generates to pretheoretically determined criteria of correctness for such principles. The employment of pretheoretic criteria of adequacy for moral principles is presumably necessary for any theory of morality. The crucial issue concerns the content of such criteria. The rational-choice theory of morality must be judged according to the conformity of its resulting principles with a pretheoretically determined property of fairness. But what is to count as the property of fairness? Gauthier endorses the view, with respect to distributive fairness, that the distributions are fair if and only if they accord each person gains proportionate to his or her contribution. With respect to initial allocations, he endorses a modified theory of the Lockean Proviso. Both these views of fairness, in distribution and acquisition, are, of course, controversial. The former Gauthier assumes but does not defend. The latter, Gauthier claims, is both favored by pretheoretic intuition and would be adopted by ideally rational agents. We do not take issue with Gauthier's substantive claims concerning fairness. Our intention is to demonstrate the failure of *Morals by Agreement* to generate an adequate moral theory on its own terms, i.e., by its own standards. It might be profitable to inquire as to the extent to which the moral theory accords with *other* conceptions of fairness, but it is too easy to endorse a different

Considerations of fairness enter Gauthier's account at three distinct places. The first is within the theory of rational bargaining in which rational persons, it is argued, agree to a set of fair constraining principles as the result of following a uniquely rational bargaining principle.[15] The second is within the theory of constrained maximization in which, it is argued, rational individuals dispose themselves to comply only with fair constraining principles. Bargaining, however, takes place within the context of prior relative bargaining or starting points. Consequently, Gauthier's defense of the rationality of morality requires a theory of fair initial bargaining positions.[16] For Gauthier, rational persons would enter into bargaining only from fair initial bargaining positions. It follows that there are two ways in which constraining principles might be unfair or biased and, therefore, not moral. First, the *bargaining procedure* itself might be unfair. If it is, the principles specifying the distribution of the cooperative surplus might allow some to gain in greater proportion to their contribution than others. Second, the *initial bargaining position* might be unfair, in which case even a fair bargaining procedure (i.e., one in which each individual gains in proportion to his contribution) will embed and transmit this unfairness to the constraining principles to which persons bargain.

Unfairness in the initial bargaining position may be transmitted to the outcome of bargaining in one of three ways. First, if as a result of an unfair initial position, some parties are able to contribute more to a cooperative venture than others, those advantaged individuals will be accorded greater shares of the cooperative surplus. Then, even if the bargaining process itself is fair in that it accords each a share of the surplus proportionate to his or her contribution, the resulting distribution is unfair because it transmits and amplifies the distortions created by unfairly acquired entitlements. Second, even if advantaged parties in the initial position do not contribute more to the bargain and contribute only that portion of their entitlements that would have been acquired in a fair initial position, the outcome may yet be unfair for either of two reasons. Those unfairly advantaged in the initial bargaining

---

substantive criterion of adequacy for moral theory and then to reject the argument of *Morals by Agreement* because it fails to accord with intuitions it does not endorse. In our view, this comes dangerously close to question begging; moreover, it allows one to reject out of hand a view which, if criticized on its own terms, provides a substantial contribution to moral and political theory.

[15] Gauthier argues that the correct principle of ideal rational bargaining is the principle of *minimax relative concession.* This principle and the important condition under which it is thought to obtain are discussed later in the section "Equal rationality and equal compliance."

[16] Gauthier suggests a positive theory of just entitlement for the initial position. He holds that rational individuals will bargain only with those individuals whose possessions have been acquired in accordance with his version of the Lockean Proviso. For a discussion of the role of theories of fairness in Gauthier, see footnote 14 above.

position retain their unfairly acquired entitlements after the bargain. This is just to say that even a fair bargaining procedure need not rectify unjust prior distributions. Fair bargaining does not embed a principle of corrective or rectificatory justice.[17] And, it is also possible that those individuals whose entitlements were fairly acquired might have had more to bargain with in the initial position had no one else acquired entitlements unfairly.[18] Third, advantaged parties in the initial position might use their advantage to "coerce," "railroad," or "extort" a bargain from the disadvantaged, which fails even to accord the disadvantaged a share of the cooperative surplus proportionate to their contributions. Here the unfair initial bargaining position induces an unfair bargaining procedure. In the first two kinds of cases, the distortions existing in unfair starting points are transmitted to outcomes, thus polluting them either because a fair bargaining procedure is unable to rectify or correct prior unfair advantage or because fair bargaining may actually exacerbate prior distortions. In the third case, prior unfairnesses are employed to distort, by "extortion" or "coercion," the bargaining process itself.

In order to derive morality from rational bargaining, the resulting principles must be fair and impartial. To demonstrate their fairness, Gauthier must argue that rational persons will bargain only from fair initial bargaining positions, engage only in bargains whose procedures are fair, and dispose themselves to comply only with constraining principles that result from a fair bargain originating from a fair initial bargaining position.

One last preliminary: Gauthier's argument is state of nature in character and thus treats morality, instead of political coercion, as the solution to the inefficiency problem in the state of nature. We will have occasion to discuss this aspect of his theory more fully in due course. For now, it is enough to note three things about it. First, state-of-nature theory commits Gauthier to the absence of existing third-party enforcement. Bargaining takes place without the benefit of external means of enforcement adequate to induce compliance. If bargaining is to succeed, it must be because the outcome commands rational compliance on its own merits. Second, Gauthier is nowhere committed to the view that

---

[17] We argue, in connection with Gauthier's argument from predation, for narrow compliance, that even this sort of unfairness must be sufficient for a bargain and its outcome to be unfair. Despite the fact that individuals who have prior, unfairly acquired entitlements may enter into new bargains in which those entitlements do not contribute to new unfair results, these new bargains must still be treated as unfair from the point of view of narrow compliance. That is, narrow compliers will not have the disposition to comply with these bargains in virtue of the unrectified unfair entitlements of some parties to the bargain. Otherwise, narrow compliance cannot induce refraining from predation; see the later section "Broad and narrow compliance" and footnote 35 below.

[18] For example, if all players prior to the bargain were playing a zero-sum game, then those who unfairly acquire more entitlements necessarily diminish the entitlements available to others.

all rational bargains, under any conditions, are fair. He is committed only to the claim that rational bargaining in the state of nature yields fair and impartial outcomes. Finally, he explicitly rejects a Buchananlike characterization of the state of nature in which individuals' initial bargaining positions are defined by a state of anarchistic equilibrium.

These preliminaries strongly suggest the kind of strategy Gauthier pursues. Gauthier wants to argue that the only kind of bargains that can command rational compliance are fair ones; that bargaining from a position of anarchistic equilibrium will yield unstable results because the terms of the bargain will reflect the unfairness of the status quo ante; and that once third-party enforcement exists, the outcomes of rational bargaining need not be self-enforcing and, therefore, need not be fair. In effect, the bulk of Gauthier's arguments, therefore, seeks to solve the compliance and the status quo ante problems simultaneously. The first, which is an argument from defection, claims that unfair bargains will be unstable, and since instability adversely affects the rationality of bargaining, only fair bargaining is rational. This argument contains the essence of what he finds wanting in Buchanan and Nash's bargaining.

Fairness and stability

Gauthier begins his discussion of the initial bargaining position by considering a society of rational slaves and masters. In this society, the masters engage in costly coercion in order to force the slaves to do their bidding, while the slaves suffer the effects of coercion. Gauthier observes that this society is suboptimal; alternative forms of interaction can enhance the well-being of some without making others worse off. In fact, there is a mutually advantageous bargain into which the slaves and masters might well enter. It would be rational, for example, for all to agree to continue their society as is, preserving the advantages and disadvantages of the caste system, while eliminating its coercive component. In such an agreement, masters are committed to eliminating coercion and slaves are bound to serve their masters voluntarily. The bargain is Pareto-improving since masters could then enjoy life free of the costs of coercing, and the slaves would be free of the costs of being coerced. Gauthier notes, however, that once coercion has been banned by agreement, and slaves and masters alike have improved their situation, the slaves will no longer find it rational to comply with their part of the bargain. They will simply walk away from the bargain since, in the absence of coercion, they have no incentive to do the bidding of their masters. The bargain, though Pareto-improving, is fundamentally unstable. By demanding pay for services the slaves merely move the bargain along the Pareto frontier, giving them a greater share of the cooperative gains, whereas were the masters to reintroduce slavery, both sides would return to the prebargain state, which would fall within the frontier and which, therefore, would be inefficient. The slaves' walking away and demanding pay is rational; the masters' threat to reintroduce slavery is not credible, since carrying it out would be inefficient. The slaves and masters end up with a situation in which the former slaves sell their labor to former slave owners. This is the stable outcome.

The conclusions Gauthier wants to draw from this example are (1) that a bargain originating in an unfair initial position is unstable, (2) that it is unstable because it is unfair, (3) that it is unfair because it involves "unproductive transfers," and (4) that the stable outcome coincides with what would have been the outcome had the bargain originated in fair initial positions.

It is evident that the slaves would eventually find it irrational to continue to comply voluntarily with their agreement. The reason, as Gauthier puts it, is that they are being asked to make unproductive transfers: "An unproductive transfer brings no new goods into being and involves no exchange of existing goods; it simply redistributes some existing good from one person to another. Thus, it involves a utility cost for which no benefit is received, a utility gain for which no service should be provided" (p. 197).

The slaves have no incentive in the absence of coercion to continue making unproductive transfers. The masters are unable to reintroduce the former coercive arrangement in which slaves were slaves and masters were masters, since doing so would render everyone, including the masters, worse off than they would be under the implicit terms of the postbargain, postdefection arrangement. The masters are stuck with a freer, more egalitarian society – the one, moreover, that all would have agreed to had the initial bargaining position been fair.

Perhaps Gauthier has isolated an example in which a bargain from an unfair initial position will first result in an unstable outcome and eventually in a stable one identical to that which would have resulted had bargaining originated in a fair initial position. It may also be true that the instability in the initial outcome is due to the irrationality, in the absence of coercion, of making unproductive transfers. Gauthier's argument for the rationality of morality requires, however, that the specific case be generalizable: that, in other words, *all* unfair but rational bargains will prove unstable because they will induce rational defection.

One reason for thinking that unfair bargains will occasion rational defection is that unfair bargains involve unproductive transfers, and making an unproductive transfer voluntarily is irrational. We can put the general argument more rigorously:

1. Unfair bargains always require unproductive transfers.

Therefore:

2. Absent coercion, compliance with unfair bargains will always require voluntary unproductive transfers.
3. An act is rational only if it is directly utility maximizing.
4. An unproductive transfer is directly utility maximizing only if it is coerced.

Therefore:

5. Absent coercion, compliance with unfair bargains must be irrational.

Therefore:

6. Unfair bargains between rational individuals are necessarily unstable.
7. Only stable bargains are rational.

Therefore:

8. Only fair bargains are rational.

Were it sound, this would be a great argument. It is surely an interesting one in any case. The problem is that it is unsound. Consider first the claim, in 1, that unfair bargains always involve unproductive transfers. We earlier considered two ways in which an outcome of a bargain might be unfair. It might be the result of an unfair bargaining procedure or it might be the outcome of a bargain from an unfair initial bargaining position. Recall that a fair bargaining procedure is one that distributes the cooperative surplus in proportion to the contributions of individuals. If we consider only those outcomes of bargains that are unfair because they are the result of unfair bargaining procedures, we might suppose that the first premise in Gauthier's argument is correct. After all, if the outcome of a bargain is unfair because it is the result of an unfair bargaining procedure, then some individuals are not gaining in proportion to their contribution and are instead transferring a portion of their fair share to others.

However, if we consider those outcomes of bargains that are unfair in virtue of the unfair initial positions in which they originate, we see that these unfair outcomes need not involve unproductive transfers. Outcomes that are unfair because of the unfairness of the initial bargaining position can be unfair for several reasons, only one of which requires unproductive transfers. This is the case in which, as a result of an unfair bargaining advantage, one individual or group of individuals is able to use his (its) advantages to negotiate in an unfair bargaining process; in other words, bargains in which unfair initial positions induce an unfair bargaining procedure.

But unfair outcomes can result from unfair starting points for reasons other than the unfairness of the starting point inducing extortion, that is, affecting the bargaining process and ultimately resulting in an outcome that requires unproductive transfers. These include outcomes that are the result of a fair bargaining procedure but, nevertheless, either distribute the cooperative surplus according to contributions themselves made possible only because of unfairly acquired entitlements or fail to rectify the unfairness of the initial position so that, though others have not gained in the bargain as a result of their unfair advantage in the initial position, they still retain their relative advantage in the postbargain state of affairs.[19] Neither one of these unfair outcomes requires individuals to make unproductive transfers. If it is not rational for individuals to comply with these outcomes, it cannot be because it is irrational for individuals to make voluntary unproductive transfers, since no such transfers need to be made. It is not true, then, that unfair bargains always require unproductive transfers; 1 is false. Thus, it does not follow that, absent coercion, compliance with unfair bargains will always require voluntary unproductive transfers. In fact, they need not require any unproductive transfers, much less voluntary ones. Therefore, 2 is false.

Is it true, as is claimed in 4, that an unproductive transfer is directly utility maximizing only if it is coerced? No. Whether an unproductive transfer can be directly utility maximizing in the absence of coercion depends on other available options, that is, on the opportunity costs of failing to make the unproductive transfer. We can, in fact, imagine cases in which unproductive transfers may be directly utility maximizing not because they are coerced, but because the only alternative is a return to the initial bargaining position, an alternative that is mutually disadvantageous and thus irrational.[20] Return to the initial bargaining position

---

[19] These bargains, according to Gauthier's arguments, must be treated as unfair; see footnote 17 above.

[20] For example, suppose that the community of masters and slaves were to strike a somewhat different mutually advantageous bargain. According to it, the masters would no longer coerce the slaves as long as the slaves would fill undesirable jobs in the masters' manufacturing plants. It so happens, in virtue of contingent features of the relevant labor markets, that no manufacturing is possible without the slaves filling these positions at the plants. Once manufacturing begins, there is a huge cooperative surplus that is put to use in a mutually advantageous way. In this arrangement, the slaves are better off because they are no longer being coerced and they are getting paid for their work. The masters are better off because they no longer bear the costs of coercing and they enjoy the benefits of production without having to participate in the undesirable tasks involved in manufacturing. Since the masters handle all financial matters, we might suppose that they retain control over the distribution of the surplus. The masters pay themselves more for their jobs than they pay the slaves for working their jobs. Here the cooperative surplus, ex hypothesi, is not being distributed in proportion to relative

need not be the result of coercion; rather, it may be the result of contingent features of the nature of the joint strategy on which all parties agree. Nevertheless, it is a result rational parties must seek to avoid, even at the cost of making an unproductive transfer.

Gauthier believes that unfair bargains are inherently unstable because they involve unproductive transfers. Making an unproductive transfer is irrational because it is not directly utility maximizing. We have shown so far that bargains can be unfair without involving unproductive transfers. Moreover, we have suggested that unproductive transfers, given the opportunity costs of noncompliance, can be directly utility maximizing and, therefore, can be rational in the absence of coercion.[21] But even if we are mistaken in claiming that unproductive transfers sometimes can be directly utility maximizing, it does not follow that unproductive transfers are irrational on those grounds alone.

An act can be rational even if it is not directly utility maximizing and for the very same reasons that Gauthier thinks that the disposition to comply with certain cooperative strategies, and thus compliance itself, can be rational.[22] Simply recall Gauthier's solution to the compliance problem: the principle of constrained maximization. In the single play or ordinary PD, defection is the dominant strategy. Consequently, rational individuals will not comply with the agreements they make because the agreements themselves have the logical structure of the PD.

---

contribution. Though the slaves might threaten to strike, such threats would be irrational to carry out. A strike would return the entire community to the mutually disadvantageous initial bargaining position. And, as Gauthier recognizes, bringing about mutually disadvantageous states of affairs is paradigmatically irrational. In this revised slave/master bargain, part of the portion of the cooperative surplus to which the slaves directly contribute is "redistributed" to the masters. Gauthier claims that, in the original slave/master example, the voluntary provision of unremunerated services to the masters by the slaves constitutes an "unproductive transfer." In this example, unlike the original slave/master example, the slaves do not directly "transfer" part of their share of the surplus to the masters. Rather, they voluntarily contribute to the creation of the cooperative surplus knowing that they will not be given their fair share of it. In this case, the unfair distribution of the surplus constitutes an unproductive transfer. Thus, it is not true that an unproductive transfer is directly utility maximizing only if it is coerced. Premise 4 is, therefore, false. We then can say of the "slaves" in our example that they voluntarily comply with an arrangement involving unproductive transfers and that their doing so is *rational*. Therefore, contrary to 5, compliance with unfair bargains in the absence of coercion can be rational.

[21] See footnote 20 above.

[22] Gauthier argues that if it is rational to choose the disposition to comply with certain agreements, then the actual compliance with those agreements is itself rational, even if it is not straightforwardly, or directly, utility maximizing. We will grant this point. Gauthier's argument for the claim is too extensive to be reconstructed here. He makes and defends the claim in chap. 6, sec. 3.2, pp. 184–7: "An objector might grant that it may be rational to dispose oneself to constrained maximization, but deny that the choices one is then disposed to make are rational. . . . [But] our argument identifies practical rationality with utility-maximization at the level of dispositions to choose, and carries through the implications of that identification in assessing the rationality of particular choices."

Agreement on a set of constraints will not produce the desired outcome because defection will set in when agreement reaches closure. In order for cooperation to succeed, compliance with rational agreements must itself be rational. But defection, not compliance, is rational; or is it?

To solve the dilemma, Gauthier introduces a distinction between directly and indirectly utility-maximizing conduct. Compliance with PD-structured agreements, he argues, can be rational even when it is not directly maximizing. Why? Because compliance in particular cases is the result of choosing to have a certain disposition on the basis of directly utility-maximizing considerations. The rationality of compliance is completely a function of the rationality of the choice to dispose oneself to comply.[23] Compliance with PD-structured bargains is rational, then, in virtue of the directly utility-maximizing choice to be disposed to compliance in PD-structured bargains. The disposition to comply is utility maximizing even if on occasion compliance is not directly utility maximizing. In Gauthier's view, the rationality of a course of conduct, the choice of a disposition, or anything, for that matter, cannot be determined entirely by inquiring whether or not it is directly utility maximizing.

Similar reasoning can be used to defend the rationality of other non-directly utility-maximizing acts such as unproductive transfers. Even if compliance with certain mutually advantageous joint strategies that require voluntary unproductive transfers is not directly maximizing, it may be rational to make such transfers in virtue of the rationality of the choice to dispose oneself to make such transfers. At the very least, Gauthier's own argument for the rationality of compliance shows that we cannot infer that certain actions or choices are irrational from the fact that they are not directly utility maximizing. If unproductive transfers are irrational, their irrationality does not follow from their not being directly utility maximizing, at least not if Gauthier's argument for the rationality of constrained maximization is compelling. So 3 is false.

The argument from the instability of unfair bargains is unsound. Were Gauthier seriously to defend the claim that only directly utility-maximizing behavior can be rational, he would be forced to abandon the argument for rational compliance. Were Gauthier to give up the argument for rational compliance, his entire enterprise would quickly unravel and for the obvious reason stated earlier. If it is not rational to comply, it cannot be rational to bargain. It would appear that Gauthier would do better to hold onto the possibility that some nondirectly utility-maximizing behavior can be rational and to give up instead the argument from the instability of unfair bargains.

But there is another, more attractive, line of argument for Gauthier

---

[23] See footnote 22 above.

that may allow him to have both constrained maximization and the argument from the instability of unfair bargains. This argument depends on a distinction he draws between two kinds of constrained maximization. In the end, Gauthier does not want to argue that constrained maximization in just any form is rational. Rather, he wants to argue that it is rational to dispose oneself to comply with bargains only if they are fair (p. 178). This is a particular form of constrained maximization, what Gauthier calls "narrow compliance." Because narrow compliance is a form of constrained maximization, its rationality does not depend on its being directly maximizing. So Gauthier's commitment to the rationality of narrow compliance means that he is committed to the principle that nondirectly maximizing behavior can be rational. But, in order to save the argument from the instability of unfair bargains, Gauthier has to give up reliance upon the claim that because unproductive transfers are not directly utility maximizing they are irrational. He can do this by claiming instead that nondirectly utility-maximizing behavior can be rational only when it is required by narrow compliance. Thus, unproductive transfers, which are involved in unfair bargains only, cannot be rational. They are not directly utility maximizing and are never required by narrow compliance. Moreover, given the unique rationality of narrow compliance, unfair bargains necessarily will be unstable because it will be rational for all parties in unfair bargains to defect. They will not have the disposition to comply necessary to secure the success of PD-structured bargains.

However, if narrow compliance is uniquely rational, then Gauthier's argument for the instability of unfair bargains is rendered entirely unnecessary. All of its central premises are abandoned. Because narrow compliance compels compliance only with fair bargains, unfair bargains, whether the result of unproductive transfers or not, are unstable. The entire discussion of the irrationality of unproductive transfers is beside the point. In short, if Gauthier is going to end up arguing for the unique rationality of narrow compliance, as in fact he is, it serves no purpose to show that unfair bargains unravel. The unique rationality of narrow compliance demonstrates a more fundamental flaw in them. Namely, it would not be rational to negotiate an unfair bargain because it is not rational to bargain in the absence of compliance, and narrow compliance precludes abiding by the terms of anything other than fair bargains.

It is clear to us – and, one hopes, to others – that the most important arguments in Gauthier's book are those presented on behalf of the unique rationality of narrow compliance.[24] We, therefore, turn our attention to them.[25]

---

[24] Even if one is persuaded of this point by the instability argument, note that by undermining the arguments for narrow compliance that follow, the instability argument will

Broad and narrow compliance

There is an important distinction between a person "who is disposed to cooperate in ways that, followed by all, merely yield her some benefit in relation to universal non-cooperation" and a person "who is disposed to cooperate in ways that, followed by all, yield nearly optimal and fair outcomes" (p. 178). The former are *broad compliers*, the latter *narrow compliers*. As it stands, the definitions of broad and narrow compliance are seriously and importantly ambiguous.

Cooperation consists in both agreement and compliance. From what Gauthier says, we cannot be certain if narrow compliers have the disposition *to agree to and comply with* fair bargains only, or if their disposition is *to comply* with whatever fair bargains they strike, though they have no particular disposition with respect to the striking of bargains, fair or otherwise. On both accounts, narrow compliers are disposed to comply with any fair bargains they make. The difference is that, on the first account, the disposition they have is compound: it includes not only a disposition to comply with fair bargains but a disposition to accept any and all fair bargains and to reject all unfair ones as well. Thus, for them the question of whether to comply with an unfair bargain into which

be undermined, for without an argument for the unique rationality of narrow compliance, there is no argument for the irrationality of unproductive transfers.

[25] In a recent commentary, Gauthier seems to view his argument in *Morals by Agreement* in a different light. He suggests that the case for fair principles is based on establishing the unique rationality of acting in accordance with his version of the principle of ideal rational bargaining, minimax relative concession: "I claim then that it is rational to dispose oneself to narrow compliance, rather than to either broad or less-than-narrow compliance. The argument requires (i) a defense of the rationality of the principle of minimax relative concession; (ii) a defense of the rationality of the proviso constraining interaction to ensure a no-advantage basepoint; (iii) a defense of the rationality of narrow compliance given (i) and (ii)" (David Gauthier, "Reply to Kraus/Coleman" [paper read at the meeting of the American Philosophical Association central division, St. Louis, MO, May 2, 1986], p. 14). Though this may have been Gauthier's intention in *Morals by Agreement*, the arguments he presents for the rationality of the proviso, in our view, themselves depend on independent arguments he presents in defense of narrow compliance. First, Gauthier claims he will show the proviso to be rational: "It may seem that reason and the proviso part company, and so, since the proviso ensures impartiality, do reason and morals . . . we deny this" (*Morals by Agreement*, p. 224). But the case for the rationality of the proviso rests entirely on the arguments from *displaced costs* (p. 225) and from *equal rationality* (p. 226), both of which are arguments for the unique rationality of narrow compliance. Thus, Gauthier seems to misunderstand the order of his own analysis. The arguments for the rationality of the proviso *presuppose* the soundness of his arguments for narrow compliance, not vice versa. Moreover, the strategy we suggest in the text provides a more powerful case for narrow compliance, which does not rest on the rationality of the proviso or on the correctness of minimax relative concession. Additionally, Gauthier's arguments for minimax relative concession rest on assumptions that do not obtain in the state of nature, where Gauthier holds rational individuals would employ that principle (see the discussion in the text of ideal rational bargaining). Thus, if the only argument for narrow compliance presupposes the successful defense of the rationality of the proviso and of minimax relative concession, the argument would be circular and unsuccessful.

one has entered never arises. Narrowly compliant persons of this sort just do not make unfair bargains. The disposition to be narrowly compliant in the second sense, however, ensures only that, if a fair bargain is struck, a narrowly compliant person will abide by its terms. Narrow compliers, however, would be free to refrain from striking fair bargains and free to make unfair ones.

For the narrowly compliant person of the second sort, the decision whether or not to strike a particular bargain will be made on straightforward utility-maximizing grounds. Among the factors relevant to assessing the rationality of entering negotiations with others is the likelihood of their compliance with its terms. A narrowly compliant person in the second sense will strike either fair or unfair bargains only if she believes the compliance of others is likely. If compliance is likely and the bargain struck a fair one, the narrowly compliant person is compelled to cooperate. If the compliance of others is likely and the bargain struck an unfair one, the narrowly compliant person is not compelled to comply. This does not mean she is compelled to defect. She is compelled in no way at all. She is free either to comply or defect. If the bargain is embedded in a PD, she will defect. But her decision to defect follows from the PD structure of the bargain and the dominant rationality of defection in the absence of a disposition to do otherwise. If the bargain is not a PD, however, she can comply or defect, depending on the counsel of straightforward maximization. If we restrict discussion to a state of nature in which all bargains are embedded in the PD, then she will always defect from unfair bargains she makes – but not because she is disposed to defect and not because she is disposed not to make unfair bargains.

Now consider the narrowly compliant person of the first sort. Because he is compelled to enter into and comply with only fair bargains, no decision he makes requires that he take into account straightforward maximizing considerations. Those factors enter only when he chooses so to dispose himself. From then on, he is compelled to turn his back on bargains that are unfair, even if the compliance of others is likely and the terms offered benefit him in disproportion to the gains accorded others.

In this essay, we adopt the second formulation of narrow compliance and, thus, define broad compliance accordingly.[26]

---

[26] There are two theoretical considerations that are relevant to the choice between the two alternative formulations of narrow compliance. The first consideration is *psychological*. Because it is difficult enough to suppose that individuals can voluntarily choose to adopt a disposition to comply with bargains and that, moreover, this disposition is conditional upon the fairness of the bargain, it would seem theoretically prudent to avoid adopting an even less plausible definition that requires the same voluntarily adopted disposition *in addition to* another disposition for accepting and rejecting bargains on the basis of their fairness. Perhaps the bounds of our imaginations can stretch to accommodate the

Narrow compliers have the disposition to comply with fair bargains, though, as a matter of their disposition, they need not accept them in the first place. Because their disposition is confined only to fair bargains, they are dispositionally free with respect to their compliance decisions regarding unfair bargains.[27]

Broad compliers have the disposition to comply with any mutually advantageous bargains they enter, though they may choose not to enter certain bargains, fair or not.

We have adopted these formulations for three reasons. First, and foremost, the theoretical motivation for constrained maximization is the PD. The adoption of a disposition to comply with bargains is motivated for rational agents as a strategy for avoiding the suboptimality of the PD. Rational agents can avoid the PD by the adoption of a disposition for compliance simpliciter. A more complex disposition that disposes agents both to comply and to accept bargains is unmotivated for rational agents.[28] Second, the relevant disposition for compliance must be psychologically plausible. The disposition to comply only with certain bargains is psychologically more plausible, we believe, than the disposition to enter into and to comply with certain bargains only.[29] Finally, Gauthier's own discussions[30] of narrow and broad compliance in *Morals by*

first account, but they positively explode when contemplating the second. The second theoretical consideration is *epistemic*. Gauthier's argument for constrained maximization depends on individuals' being translucent with respect to their dispositions for compliance. Translucence in turn requires some practical explanation of how individuals might be able to tell whether others are constrained or straightforward maximizers. Yet if both narrow compliers and straightforward maximizers can be observed defecting from agreements, "defection records" would not be reliable indicators of individuals' dispositions. Ideally, only straightforward maximizers would ever defect from their agreements. Once an individual defects from an agreement, then it might be plausible to suppose that society has a good chance of marking him as a straightforward maximizer. Epistemic considerations, therefore, favor the first alternative definition, which precludes, analytically, the possibility of a narrowly compliant person's defecting from his or her agreements. Psychological factors favor the second characterization of narrow compliance; epistemic ones favor the first.

27 This point bears amplification. In the state of nature, a narrowly compliant person will always comply with fair bargains and always defect from unfair ones. The reason is this. The state of nature is a PD in which defection is rational unless one is disposed always to do otherwise and so will never defect. A narrowly compliant person will defect in a PD except when he is disposed to do otherwise; and he is disposed to do otherwise only if the bargain is fair. If an unfair bargain is not a PD, a narrowly compliant person need not defect, though he is not compelled to comply either.

28 In addition, Ockham's razor would mitigate against the more complex disposition. It is theoretically unnecessary.

29 See footnote 26 above.

30 In *Morals by Agreement*, Gauthier clearly holds that narrow compliers will not have the disposition to comply with unfair bargains, irrespective of whether they benefit or suffer from the unfairness: "The narrowly compliant person is always prepared . . . to be co-operative whenever co-operation can be mutually beneficial on terms equally rational and fair to all. In refusing other terms . . . she ensures that those not disposed to fair co-operation do not enjoy the benefits of any co-operation, thus making their unfairness costly to themselves, and so irrational" (pp. 178–9). If a narrow complier has the disposition to comply with certain fair bargains (i.e., ones according her the greater, unfair

Agreement strongly suggest this interpretation.[31] However, as concerns the arguments of *Morals by Agreement*[32] and our criticism of them, the two definitions can be shown to be *extensionally equivalent*,[33] so someone unpersuaded by our characterization of narrow compliance can sub-

share), then she would be defeating herself by trying to ensure "that those not disposed to fair co-operation do not enjoy the benefits of any co-operation." But in a recent commentary, Gauthier changes the definition of narrow compliance: "A narrowly compliant person, as I define her . . . does not refuse to enter, or to comply with, agreements if her share is more than fair; she refuses only if she would get less" (Gauthier, reply to Kraus and Coleman, p. 13). His strategy is to strengthen his argument *against* the rationality of broad compliance (i.e., the disposition to comply with mutually advantageous bargains that accord one the smaller portion of the cooperative surplus). As it stands, even this redefinition does not help Gauthier's case, for the definition of narrow compliance we adopt enables narrow compliers to enter into and comply with unfair bargains *as a matter of disposition* (i.e., their disposition does not prevent them from doing so). But narrow compliers, being utility maximizers, will not comply with unfair, PD-structured bargains, even when the unfairness is in their favor, because they lack the disposition to comply necessary to override the straightforward, utility-maximizing strategy of defection in PD-structured bargains. We might suppose, however, that Gauthier here allows for narrow compliers *to be disposed to comply* with unfair bargains on the condition that the unfairness is in their favor. This redefinition not only makes the envisioned disposition extremely psychologically unrealistic, but it also fails to increase sufficiently the profitability of being a narrow complier. For the set of bargains available to narrow compliers is a proper *subset* of the larger set of bargains available to broad compliers. Thus, broad compliance is more profitable than narrow compliance and hence is the rational disposition to choose. See the discussion of the equal rationality argument below.

[31] Consider two of Gauthier's statements. First, he says "in interacting with you I should dispose myself to comply with a joint strategy only if it offers me, not a fair share, but a lion's share of the cooperative surplus" (*Morals by Agreement*, p. 226). Here Gauthier is clearly isolating a disposition for compliance, and compliance only. No mention is made of a disposition to accept or reject bargains. Second, he says, "A person disposed to broad compliance compares the benefit she would expect from co-operation on whatever terms are offered with what she would expect from non-co-operation, and complies if the former is greater" (p. 225). Though this definition seems to conflate agreement and compliance, he seems clearly to think that the choice to accept a bargain is a straightforward maximization consideration, not a matter of disposition. The question the broad complier faces is whether to accept the bargain knowing that she will comply with it if she does.

[32] Gauthier presents different arguments in his recent commentary, "Reply to Kraus/ Coleman." There Gauthier reformulates the definition of narrow compliance. We respond to this reformulation and the argument that relies upon it in footnote 30 above.

[33] To say that the two alternative definitions of narrow compliance are extensionally equivalent, in this context, is to say that all and only the bargains that narrow compliers can (or will) make in the state of nature given the first definition are bargains that narrow compliers can (or will) make in the state of nature given the second definition. To see that the definitions are extensionally equivalent, consider first the bargains broad and narrow compliers will make if we use the first definition. Broad compliers will be able to make fair and unfair bargains among themselves, and as long as they do not have unfairly acquired entitlements as a result of unfair bargaining, they will be able to make fair bargains with narrow compliers. Narrow compliers will be able to make fair bargains with other narrow compliers and with broad compliers who have legitimately acquired entitlements (if their entitlements were unfairly acquired, then bargains with them would be necessarily unfair (see footnote 35 below). No unfair bargains involving narrow compliers will be possible. Next, consider the bargains made by broad and narrow compliers if we use the second definition. Broad compliers will be able to make fair

stitute the more complex characterization in most arguments, salva veritate.[34]

In order to solve the compliance and status quo ante problems simultaneously, the rational-choice model of morality requires that narrow compliance be uniquely rational. In what follows, we distinguish among four arguments for the irrationality of broad compliance and the rationality of narrow compliance. These are arguments from predation, displaced costs, translucence, and equal rationality. We consider each in turn.

Narrow compliance and predation

Gauthier writes: "Someone disposed to comply with agreements that left untouched the fruits of predation would simply invite others to engage in predatory and coercive activities as a prelude to bargaining. She would permit the successful predators to reap where they had ceased to sow, to continue to profit from the effects of natural predation after entering into agreements freeing them from the need to invest further in predatory effort" (p. 195). It is irrational to dispose oneself to comply with less than fair bargains because it would encourage others "to engage in predatory and coercive activities as a prelude to bargaining" (p. 195). According to the argument from predation, it is rational to exclude from bargaining those individuals who have unfair initial entitlements because doing so would discourage them from stealing as a prelude to

bargains among themselves and with narrow compliers just as above. However, they are, in principle, also able to engage not only in unfair bargains among themselves, as above, but also in unfair bargains with narrow compliers, for narrow compliers now may make any bargains they wish. However, even though narrow compliers presumably might, under certain conditions, like to make advantageous, unfair bargains among themselves and with broad compliers, rationality prevents any such bargains from taking place. Broad compliers will not make any unfair bargains with narrow compliers because narrow compliers are not credible in unfair bargains. Their disposition to comply with bargains, unlike the broad compliers' disposition, is contingent upon the fairness of the bargain. In the state of nature, all bargains have the structure of the PD, and so narrow compliers will defect from unfair bargains because it is the uniquely rational action, in lieu of a disposition to comply. Broad compliers, who will comply with such bargains, know that narrow compliers cannot comply, as a matter of straightforward utility maximization, and so will not enter into unfair bargains with narrow compliers. Likewise, narrow compliers will not make unfair bargains among themselves because each knows the other is bound by rationality to defect. Thus, irrespective of the definitions of narrow and broad compliance we adopt, the same set of bargains are available to narrow and broad compliers: unfair bargains can take place only among broad compliers, and fair bargains can take place among both narrow and broad compliers as long as they have not already profited unfairly in previous bargaining, thus rendering all bargains they enter unfair.

[34] When we later have occasion to discuss the rationality of "less-than-narrow" compliance, the difference between the two formulations we have just considered and the two analogous definitions of less-than-narrow compliance will be important. There we will not be able to treat the two as extensionally equivalent.

bargaining. Narrow compliance, as we have defined it, ensures the exclusion of individuals with unfair entitlements from bargains with narrow compliers.[35]

It is clearly desirable and rational to attempt to discourage individuals from attacking in the state of nature. Suppose there were so many narrow compliers in the state of nature who excluded those with unfair initial entitlements from the benefits of cooperation that the benefits from predation did not exceed the costs of exclusion from cooperation. Then, as Gauthier claims, it would be irrational to engage in predatory behavior, and individuals would be discouraged from doing so. But we cannot simply assume that there are, or always would be, a sufficient number of narrowly compliant individuals in the state of nature to make prebargain predation irrational, and even once a threshold population of narrow compliers has been reached, and prebargain predation becomes irrational, it does not follow that it is rational for any particular individual to be narrowly compliant.

Consider two possible scenarios. In one, the population of narrowly compliant individuals falls below the threshold necessary to induce others to refrain from predation. In the other, the population exceeds that necessary to deter predation. Should the threshold population of narrow compliers in the state of nature not obtain, there is no reason to think that the members of the narrow compliance population will be spared from predation by nonnarrow compliers. Narrow compliance would be costly since it would require someone to forgo certain mutually advantageous, but unfair, bargains; at the same time, the potential benefit of

---

[35] In order for the argument from predation to get off the ground, it must be the case that anyone who acts as a predator in the state of nature will be excluded from bargains with narrow compliers. But the criterion for exclusion from bargains with narrow compliers exclusively concerns the fairness of the bargains they are considering and is connected to prebargain predation only via the effect such predation will have on the fairness of bargains entered into by formerly predatory individuals. Thus, the argument can work only if bargains with formerly predatory individuals will be necessarily unfair. Prebargain predation must "taint" an individual so that all the bargains he enters necessarily will be unfair. These bargains will be ones with which narrow compliers will not comply (they will defect in PDs unless disposed to comply), and thus ones into which narrow compliers will not even enter. It is a consequence of this argument, then, that an individual who has unfairly acquired entitlements is analytically unable to enter into a fair bargain. Even if he bargains according to a fair bargaining principle, and his unfairly acquired entitlements in no other way adversely affect the other parties' bargaining gains (e.g., the prebargain situation is not a zero-sum game where unfairly acquired entitlements for A necessarily mean unfairly less entitlements for B and C), the fact that he retains his unfairly acquired entitlements in the postbargain outcome renders the distributions necessarily unfair. Thus, bargains that fail to rectify prior unjust distributions are necessarily unfair. If this were not the case, then individuals would be free to engage in prebargain predation as long as they did not use the fruits of their predation in future unfair bargains, bargains where their unfair advantage enables them to coerce others into complying with bargains resulting from unfair bargaining principles.

narrow compliance, that is, deterring predation, would not obtain. Thus, narrow compliance would not be rational, let alone uniquely rational.

Now consider the case in which the threshold of narrowly compliant persons in the overall population is met or exceeded. When this condition is satisfied, it is rational to refrain from engaging in predatory behavior. But is it rational to be narrowly compliant? No. Whether or not an individual is narrowly compliant, others will not prey on him. If they do, they will be excluded from advantageous bargains with the narrow compliers. But being a narrow complier is not a necessary condition for cooperative interaction with narrow compliers. The only precondition is that one not engage in predation. Nonnarrow compliers who do not engage in predatory behavior will not be excluded from cooperative bargains with narrow compliers. It is rational not to be excluded. Broadly compliant persons also will be included as long as they are not predatory. Thus, broad compliance is a rational disposition both when the number of narrowly compliant persons in a population falls below or exceeds that necessary to foreclose predation. The only circumstance in which it is uniquely rational to be narrowly compliant occurs when one's decision is decisive in reaching the threshold population in which predation becomes disutile and thus irrational. The probability that any one person's choice of a disposition toward compliance could be decisive is extremely low. And even where one person's choice could affect the expected utility of predation, the probability of any one particular choice being decisive is even lower. So the rationality of narrow compliance is simply not established by the argument from predation.

Displaced costs and rational compliance

The argument from displaced costs is really just Gauthier's earlier argument that, because unfair bargains involve unproductive transfers, narrow compliance is uniquely rational. Gauthier writes:

If interaction is to be fully cooperative, it must proceed from an initial position in which costs are internalized, and so in which no person has the right to impose uncompensated costs on another. For if not, the resulting social arrangements must embody one-sided interactions benefitting some persons at cost to others. Even if each were to receive some portion of the cooperative surplus, yet each could not expect to benefit in the same relation to contribution as his fellows. *Interactions based on displaced costs would be redistributive, and redistribution can not be part of a rational system of cooperation.* (P. 225, emphasis added)

The claim is that unfair bargains always result in displaced costs and that because displaced costs are redistributive, they are irrational. Redistributive outcomes are irrational, according to Gauthier's earlier claim, because they require unproductive transfers. But recall that (in the instability argument) his argument for the irrationality of unproductive transfers, and thus redistribution, depended on the claim that unproductive transfers were not directly utility maximizing. However, as we earlier pointed out, Gauthier cannot claim that any act that is not directly utility maximizing is necessarily irrational, for his central thesis of constrained maximization, if correct, proves the exception: it is rational to dispose oneself ex ante to comply with certain bargains; thus compliance with these bargains, even when not directly utility maximizing, is rational. In order to prove that unproductive transfers are irrational, Gauthier has to argue that only one brand of constrained maximization is rational, namely, narrow compliance. He could then hold that all nondirectly utility-maximizing behavior is irrational unless it is required by narrow compliance. Since unproductive transfers will never be required by narrow compliance, it follows that unproductive transfers cannot be rational. But this strategy cannot work. On pain of circularity, Gauthier cannot, in the displaced costs argument, argue for the unique rationality of narrow compliance on the grounds that the alternative of broad compliance involves unproductive transfers[36] and is thus irrational, when his only argument for the necessary irrationality of unproductive transfers (made earlier in connection with the instability argument) relied upon the claim that narrow compliance is uniquely rational. We had best move on.

Translucence and compliance

The rationality of constrained maximization depends, in part, on the ability of constrained maximizers to recognize straightforward maximizers and other constrained maximizers. The easier it is to recognize what sort of maximizer an individual is, the more probable it will be that (i) constrained maximizers successfully bargain to mutual advantage with other constrained maximizers, (ii) constrained maximizers will not be exploited by straightforward maximizers, and (iii) straightforward maximizers will be excluded from cooperative interaction. As the probability of i–iii increases, the expected utility of being a constrained maximizer increases and the expected utility of being a straightforward maximizer decreases.

A "transparent" individual is one whose disposition is unmistakable. Transparent individuals are always recognized correctly for the kind of maximizers they are. An "opaque" individual is one whose disposition is very difficult to detect. Opaque individuals are often mistakenly identified as constrained maximizers when they are in fact straightforward

---

[36] A claim we earlier undermined; see the previous section, "Fairness and stability."

maximizers and vice versa. Gauthier claims that in fact individuals are "translucent." They admit of various degrees of translucence so that some individuals, who have finely honed skills of recognition, can do very well at recognizing constrained and straightforward maximizers, and most people stand a pretty good chance of recognizing individuals to be the type of maximizers they are.

We can reformulate Gauthier's claim about the relationship between the rationality of constrained maximization and the recognizability of constrained maximization as follows: the higher the degree of translucency, the less the potential benefit of cooperation must be in order for constrained maximization to be rational; or, the lower the degree of translucency, the greater the potential benefit of cooperation must be in order for constrained maximization to be rational.

Gauthier claims that "as practices and activities fall short of fairness, the expected value of cooperation for those with less than fair shares decreases, and so the degree of translucency required to make cooperation rational for them increases" (p. 178). The point is that it can be rational to be a constrained maximizer who accepts unfair bargains only as individuals approach transparency. The expected utility of constrained maximization is a function of the likelihood of interacting with constrained maximizers, the potential gain from such interaction, and the potential loss from interacting with a straightforward maximizer. In turn, the likelihood of interacting with a constrained maximizer, and not interacting with a straightforward maximizer is, in part, a function of translucency. So if it is going to be rational to dispose oneself to comply with unfair bargains, in which the potential gain need not be considerable, the likelihood of success must be very high. Thus, the rationality of disposing oneself to compliance with unfair, though mutually advantageous, bargains will be in part a function of translucency. Individuals will have to be very translucent in order for the expected utility of compliance with unfair bargains to be greater than the expected costs. Thus, a disposition to comply with unfair bargains is unlikely to be rational.

Gauthier's account of the relationship between the rationality of the disposition to comply with unfair bargains and translucency is essentially correct. But the translucency argument fails to take degrees of unfairness into account. Surely not all unfair bargains are equally unfair. And where the stakes are large enough, even unfairly small portions of a surplus may be large enough to make the expected utility of broad compliance high enough to outweigh its expected loss. Our principal objection to the translucency argument is that Gauthier cannot assume that all unfair bargains are ones in which the potential gain, the unfair share of the surplus, will be critically low. It may be sufficiently high if either (i) the bargain is not extremely unfair and/or (ii) the cooperative surplus is very large (even an unfair share of a million dollars may be significantly large). There will surely be some unfair bargains with which no rational person ought to comply. But from this it cannot follow that there are no unfair bargains with which rational persons ought to comply. The latter claim must be true, however, for narrow compliance to be uniquely rational.

Narrow compliance and equal rationality

In some sense, Gauthier's entire enterprise rests on his demonstrating the unique rationality of narrow compliance, that is, the disposition to comply only with fair bargains. It is one thing, though no small or insignificant thing, to establish the rationality of self-restraint; it is another thing to establish that compliance is rational only if the terms of an agreement are fair. Considerations of predation, displaced costs, and the translucence of character do not appear to provide the argument Gauthier needs. The deepest and, in many ways, the most compelling argument for narrow compliance relies upon the concept of *equal rationality*. Basically the argument is this:

1. Equally rational individuals will comply under the same conditions.

Therefore:

2. If some individuals comply under different conditions than others, these individuals cannot be equally rational.

Therefore:

3. If some people are narrowly compliant, and others are broadly compliant, some individuals are not as rational as others.
4. But all individuals are equally rational, ex hypothesi.

Therefore:

5. Either everyone must be broadly compliant or everyone must be narrowly compliant.
6. It is never rational for everyone to be broadly compliant.

Therefore:

7. It is uniquely rational for everyone to be narrowly compliant.

The argument rests on two extremely controversial claims. The first is that it cannot be rational for everyone to be broadly compliant, 6. The second is that, 1, equally rational individuals will comply under the same conditions; thus, broadly and narrowly compliant persons cannot both be equally rational.

The irrationality of broad compliance. Gauthier's argument for the claim that it is not rational for everyone to be broadly compliant is:

1′. "If you will comply for any benefit whatsoever, i.e., if you are broadly compliant, then in interacting with you I should dispose myself to comply with a bargain we strike only if it offers me, not a fair share, but the lion's share of the surplus."

Therefore:

2′. "If some persons are broadly compliant, then others, interacting with them, will find it advantageous not to be broadly compliant, or even so much as narrowly compliant. It is rational for them (those demanding the lion's share) to be less-than-narrowly compliant."

Therefore:

3′. "It is not and cannot be rational for everyone to be . . . broadly compliant" (pp. 226–7).

Consider premise 1′ of the argument. According to Gauthier, constrained maximizers, whether narrowly or broadly compliant, cooperate only with persons they have reason to believe are similarly constrained. They want to make it costly for others to be straightforward maximizers (by excluding them from the benefits of cooperation) and beneficial for others to be constrained maximizers. This will increase the desirability of being a constrained maximizer and thus increase the number of constrained maximizers in the population. And this, in turn, increases the probability of constrained maximization being rational. Now suppose that you have the disposition to comply with any mutually advantageous bargains into which you enter, and I know this.[37] That is, I know you are broadly compliant. Does it follow that I should dispose myself to comply only with agreements that afford me a lion's share of the cooperative surplus (i.e., does it follow that I should be less-than-narrowly compliant)? Surely not.

First, from the fact that you are broadly compliant, it does not follow that you will enter into any mutually advantageous agreement. All that follows is that you will comply with any mutually advantageous agreement into which you enter. And were you to know that I am not even narrowly compliant (which you would be as likely to know as I am likely

---

[37] Note that this supposition presupposes my knowledge of whether you are a broad or narrow complier. But even if constrained maximizers are transparent, it does not follow that broad and narrow compliers can be easily distinguished. This is yet another obstacle facing the view that only narrow compliance is rational: it requires a further epistemic ability to distinguish not only constrained from straightforward maximizers, but narrow from broad compliers as well.

to know that you are broadly compliant), you would know that the only successful cooperative agreements between us would be ones that accorded me the lion's share of the surplus. You would enter into a bargain with me only if your squirrel's share of the surplus were sufficiently great to make such a bargain rational for you. Depending on your other opportunities, you might be disposed not to strike a deal with me at all. In general, broad compliers might well enter into few bargains with less-than-narrow compliers – those affording the broad compliers enough to make the bargain rational. And since less-than-narrow compliers are known not to comply with bargains affording them less than a lion's share of the surplus, broad compliers will find it rational to enter into bargains with them only when the surplus is so large that their small share is still worth pursuing.

Whether it is worth pursuing depends, of course, on the opportunity costs. The range of unfair bargains worth entering into for those destined to receive the unfair, extremely small reward is nowhere near as large, we might reasonably suppose, as the range of unfair and fair bargains into which broad compliers might enter, for example, with one another. Were I a broad complier, the range of bargains in which each of us could count on the other to comply would be maximal, so we would likely strike more bargains and gain more as a result. Broad compliers faced with other broad compliers will know that they can successfully cooperate on a much larger set of joint ventures and so will almost always find some strategy on which to agree. But broad compliers know that less-than-narrow compliers will have the disposition to comply only when they get the lion's share. Thus, it is less likely to be rational for broad compliers to interact with less-than-narrow compliers than it will be for them to interact with other broad compliers. If I am considering demanding the lion's share, then I must realize that one consequence of my doing so is that you might be a broad complier and yet decide not to bargain with me at all. So it may be irrational for me to be less-than-narrowly compliant even if I know you are broadly compliant! Certainly we can draw no inference about what it would be rational for me to demand of you in the absence of my knowledge of your other alternatives.

Second, even if it would be desirable for me to be a less-than-narrow complier when interacting with a broad complier, it does not follow that it is rational for me to *become* less-than-narrowly compliant. The dispositions of narrow and broad compliance are not conditional upon certain bargains *with certain sorts of people*. Individuals are either broad or narrow (or less-than-narrow) compliers, period. They cannot be broad compliers when interacting with some people but narrow compliers when interacting with others. Though I might rationally prefer to be a less-than-narrow complier while I am interacting with you, the rationality of my actually being a less-than-narrow complier will depend on the distribution of dispositions throughout the population with whom I interact. If everyone but you were narrowly compliant, then it would still not be rational for me to be a less-than-narrow complier, even if you are broadly compliant.[38]

The central premise in the argument, that is, 1', is false. It does not follow from the fact that someone is broadly compliant that others ought to be less-than-narrowly compliant. In fact the reverse might be true. Thus, 2' does not follow: if some persons are broadly compliant, then it is not necessarily the case that others interacting with them will find it advantageous not to be broadly compliant, or even so much as narrowly compliant. Premise 3' is also false: it can be rational for everyone to be broad compliers. For being a broad complier may afford everyone the best opportunity to reach agreement and to benefit from cooperative ventures.

Equal rationality and equal compliance. What we have demonstrated so far is that 6 in the equal rationality argument is false: it can be rational for everyone to be a broad complier. Thus, the truth of 7 does not follow

---

[38] This lengthy footnote is for the reader who still remains a fan of the alternative definition of broad and narrow compliance. No doubt you have noticed that our argument against the rationality of less-than-narrow compliance relies upon defining the dispositions in question *not* to include a disposition to accept certain bargains. So for you, we will show that the claim that broad compliance of some leads to less-than-narrow compliance of others is incorrect, even on the alternative definition. Suppose that broad compliers do in fact have the disposition *both* to accept and comply with *any* mutually advantageous bargain, no matter how unfairly small their share of the cooperative surplus. Then, presumably, a less-than-narrow complier would have the disposition to accept, offer, and comply with only those unfair bargains that accorded him a lion's share of the surplus. Now, does it follow that it is rational to be a less-than-narrow complier if someone else is a broad complier? We have already seen that the presence of one broad complier will be unlikely to affect the rationality of being a less-than-narrow complier for anyone else. The rationality of the latter will, at best, be a function of the number of broad compliers in a population. But the number of broad compliers required in order to make less-than-narrow compliance rational is very large. For less-than-narrow compliers will never be able to strike cooperative agreements with each other. There must be so many broad compliers, and so few less-than-narrow compliers, that the costs of being a less-than-narrow complier (i.e., of failing to make agreements with other less-than-narrow compliers) is outweighed by the benefits of exploiting broad compliers. But these benefits are possible only when cooperative efforts consist of agreement between few enough narrow compliers, and enough broad compliers, that the less-than-narrow compliers can still receive their lion's share. The more less-than-narrow compliers involved in a cooperative venture along with the broad compliers, the less the lion's share for each less-than-narrow complier. And so the more less-than-narrow compliers in the world, the less there will be opportunities to engage in cooperative bargains according lion's shares to some and squirrel's shares to others. One wolf among a flock of sheep fares well. Ten wolves among two sheep fare poorly. So even if we define broad and narrow compliance to include a disposition to accept and comply with certain agreements, we see that even in a population of many broad compliers, it does not necessarily follow that it is rational to be a less-than-narrow complier.

from the conjunction of 5 and 6, and the argument for the unique rationality of narrow compliance is now incomplete. But the crux of the argument, premise 1, so far remains intact: equally rational individuals will comply under the same conditions, and thus, everyone must be either broadly or narrowly compliant. Some people cannot be narrowly compliant and others broadly compliant. The "impossibility" is presumably a conceptual one, following from the definition of "equal rationality."

The equal rationality of the parties in the initial position, however, is largely irrelevant in determining the rationality of broad and narrow compliance. One's reasons for being a broad or narrow complier depend on one's bargaining advantage in the state of nature and the preexisting size of the populations of broad and narrow compliers. Given acceptable populations of broad and narrow compliers, if one is advantaged, then one can afford to hold out for unfairly profitable bargains. If one is disadvantaged, one may not be able to hold out for fair bargains. Opportunity costs will often force the disadvantaged to acquiesce to unfair bargains. Though parties in the initial position may be equally rational, they are not necessarily equally advantaged. Thus, they may comply with bargains under very different conditions.

For advantaged individuals, it will never be rational to be narrowly compliant, for the adoption of that disposition would preclude them from ever profiting from their advantage. The only question they must face is whether it is rational to engage in unfair bargains. Because anyone who gains unfairly in a bargain will be excluded from bargaining with a narrow complier even on fair terms,[39] even advantaged individuals must weigh the benefits of using their advantage against the costs of being excluded from whatever population of narrow compliers exists or will exist in the future.

Ultimately, then, the only question that an advantaged individual must confront is whether he ought to engage in unfair bargaining, not whether he ought to be a narrow complier. Under no circumstances will it be rational for an advantaged individual to be a narrow complier, for by becoming narrowly compliant, he forfeits the possibility of profiting from his advantage when the benefits of so doing outweigh the costs (i.e., of exclusion from bargaining with the population of narrow compliers). Individuals who are not advantaged will, of course, desire that

[39] The reason that unfairly acquired prior entitlements render individuals ineligible in otherwise fair bargains in the future is that even bargains with fair bargaining principles must be treated as unfair if they transmit prior unfairnesses. This was an assumption necessary to make sense of the argument from predation (see footnote 35 above). If we drop this assumption, then advantaged individuals could, in principle, profit unfairly in bargains and then bargain on fair terms in the future with narrow compliers. So much the worse for the case against the rationality of exploiting one's advantage: it would be possible to avoid incurring *any* costs for using one's unfair advantage!

there be a large enough population of narrow compliers so that advantaged individuals have incentive only to engage in fair bargaining. But, as we earlier demonstrated,[40] even from this, it does not follow that any one particular disadvantaged individual ought to become narrowly compliant. In fact, unless his decision to become narrowly compliant can break the threshold beyond which the costs of unfair bargaining for advantaged individuals outweigh the benefits, it is irrational for any single disadvantaged individual to be narrowly compliant. Broad compliance allows him to benefit from all bargains with narrow compliers and from those unfair bargains with advantaged individuals in which he gains the lesser, unfair, share.

What, then, can we say about the possibility of a population of equally rational individuals being divided between broad and narrow compliers? Simply this: in the absence of a preexisting large population of narrow compliers, it is not and will never be rational for anyone, advantaged or not, to become a narrow complier. For advantaged individuals, narrow compliance is never rational. For disadvantaged individuals, it is rational only when their choice to become narrowly compliant is decisive. Their choices being decisive requires at least some preexisting population of narrow compliers. But if this is so, then there will never be any population of narrow compliers, for it will never be rational for any one individual to become narrowly compliant in the first place! Alternatively, if we stipulate the existence of a large population of narrow compliers, without explaining how it was ever rational for any of them to become so, then it still would be irrational for any of the remainder of the total population to become narrowly compliant. They might just as well be broad compliers who restrict their bargains to fair ones. In this case, we see that a population of rational individuals could include both broad and narrow compliers, though the evolution of such a population would remain a mystery. In any event, equal rationality, it appears, does not entail equal compliance, and the last argument for the unique rationality of narrow compliance has failed.[41]

The arguments from rational and costless bargaining

We cannot discuss every argument Gauthier advances for the rationality of morality. We are convinced the arguments from narrow compliance

---

[40] See the discussion in the last section, "Narrow compliance and predation."

[41] We have not discussed Gauthier's argument that the correct principle of ideal rational bargaining *entails* that rational individuals will not bargain from anything less than fair initial positions. We discuss his principle of ideal rational bargaining below. It is our claim that the correctness of this principle depends on the implausible, if not incoherent, characterization of the initial choice problem as being costless. Thus, we need not wonder whether his principle, if correct, would entail the fairness of the initial bargaining position. We have yet to see a proof of its correctness that does not depend on an assumption we reject.

are the most powerful available to him, and that is why we have focused on them in such detail. We want to close the body of this essay by considering somewhat more quickly two other arguments available to Gauthier.

Rationality and fair bargaining

Suppose we are right that the argument from narrow compliance is unsound. It can be rational to dispose oneself to comply with the rational bargains one strikes, even if those bargains are not fair. That is, we cannot derive the fairness of bargained outcomes as a consequence of a theory of rational compliance. This does not mean that we cannot derive it from a theory of rational bargaining. Suppose the correct theory of rational bargaining had as its consequence that a rational bargain was a fair one. Then, if moral principles must be fair ones, they might still be determined by the outcome of a rational bargain.

Gauthier advances a theory of rational bargaining, the principle of minimax relative concession. According to this principle, each individual shares in the surplus proportionate to his relative contribution. Since fairness requires proportionate distribution, rational bargaining turns out to be fair bargaining. The outcome of every rational bargain is fair. Therefore, even if it is rational to be broadly compliant, the bargains with which one complies are fair ones.

The problem with this argument is that it ignores the potential unfairness of the initial positions. As we have repeatedly noted, even if the rational bargaining process itself is fair, it may exacerbate and will, in any event, transmit rather than rectify preexisting inequalities. Unless rational bargaining is rectificatory as well as contributorally just, the outcome of a rational bargain can be unfair even if rational bargaining is procedurally fair.

The possibility remains that this sort of unfairness need not concern the rational-choice model of morality. After all, the substantive principles of morality will be fair, they just will not be rectificatory. But why think that correct moral principles ought to address issues of corrective justice? We think that a theory of morality that ignores corrective justice is unacceptable. But even if it were acceptable, a rational-choice theorist of morality would still have to prove that the correct ideal principle of rational bargaining was a fair one. Gauthier claims to have done this, but his proof depends crucially on the characterization of the initial choice problem as taking place within the context of costless bargaining.

Costless bargaining

One of the most common objections leveled against Rawls is that his characterization of the decision problem is not normatively neutral. Because it is not, the two principles of justice do not derive from pure rationality fleshed out as Rawls thinks it should be, namely, as individual rational decision under uncertainty. Instead, the principles are derived from rationality embedded within a Kantian normative framework. One way of understanding the rational-choice model of morality is as an effort to derive morality from "pure rationality." This explains Gauthier's efforts to impose minimal constraints on the decision problem. The one important constraint he imposes, but inadequately discusses, is that bargaining in the state of nature is costless in terms of utility and time.[42] This constraint is motivated by his desire to isolate "pure rationality."

If bargaining is in fact costless in time and utility, it is possible to argue that rational bargaining will invariably lead to fair outcomes. Rational bargaining will give rise to unfair outcomes if initial inequities allow one party to extort shares that exceed his relative contribution, or if the inequities are simply transmitted in toto to the outcomes. If bargaining is costless, however, then those disadvantaged in the state of nature have nothing to lose by refusing to join in a cooperative effort unless the terms of the bargain are fair. At the same time, they cannot expect to receive terms more favorable to them than fair terms, since other cooperators will object and hold out for fair terms at no cost to them. Thus, everyone can expect fair terms, regardless of the initial distribution of holdings. Provided they are equally rational, they will get fair terms. Cooperation assumes that the contribution of others is necessary; the costlessness assumption guarantees that all bargaining will be on terms that are fair to all contributing parties. The costlessness assumption, which is aimed at isolating pure rationality, turns out to have extraordinary normative consequences. It nullifies all advantages and induces all parties to comply under exactly the same terms. It does what the arguments for narrow compliance could not do, that is, solves both the compliance and status quo ante problems. It has to be too good to be true, and it is.

The assumption enables Gauthier to derive morality from rationality but at the cost of robbing the argument of its essential state-of-nature character. The motivation for rational individuals to cooperate in the state of nature, after all, is the existence of costs. These are forgone opportunities in the form of a surplus unattainable given the defection problem. If the state of nature were itself costless in Gauthier's sense, no need for a theory of rational bargaining would arise. Truly costless

---

[42] Gauthier writes that "bargaining is cost-free, both in terms of utility and time, so that no one need come to a decision without full consideration; bargaining is unpressured. Thus, each bargainer can employ only his rationality to appeal to the equal rationality of his fellows. In addition to rationality, there are only each person's preferences and possible actions to consider, and it is about these that everyone bargains" (*Morals by Agreement*, p. 156).

interaction would be efficient, and no need for a mechanism to solve a market failure problem would emerge. In a costless world, no market failures would emerge. The entire state-of-nature enterprise unravels quickly once one introduces the costlessness condition.

A sympathetic reading of Gauthier sees the costlessness assumption as part of his attempt to isolate a concept of "pure rationality." But we are not sure that the concept of "pure rational bargaining," by which is meant "costless bargaining," is coherent. Rational individuals who incur no costs for failing to reach agreement have, a fortiori, nothing to gain in bargaining. For if they did, there would be, necessarily, costs (opportunity costs) of forgoing, or delaying, agreement. Bargaining is rational, therefore, only if it takes place within the context of costs, and costless contexts necessarily render bargaining irrational. The costlessness assumption, far from being an innocent attempt to constrain the decision problem in a normatively neutral way, turns out to be too strong. It may even be incoherent.[43]

Conclusion

There is, we believe, a significant theme that emerges from our discussion: the very problems of collective action that motivate the need for constrained maximization emerge again at the level of choice between the alternative forms of constrained maximization, broad and narrow compliance. The rationality of narrow compliance ultimately depends upon the incentives available for inducing individuals to be narrow compliers. And while we can imagine it sometimes being rational to want a population that is largely, if not exclusively, narrowly compliant, the problems of collective action prevent individuals from forming such a population. Only this time, constrained maximization cannot be enlisted to overcome the problems of collective action. Once again, what is collectively rational is individually irrational. The conundrum of collective action, even when solved at one level, reoccurs at another, in this case foiling an ambitious attempt to ground morality in rationality.

In spite of our objections to it, Gauthier's rational choice, moral con-

---

[43] Note that even if we hold the costlessness assumption to be coherent, and legitimate within the context of deriving a principle of ideal rational bargaining, this will not help Gauthier's case for the fairness of bargaining in the state of nature. For even though we assume individuals to be perfectly rational in the state of nature, it is doubtful that rationality requires that they employ a principle of bargaining the unique rationality of which has been proved only in a costless setting. The principle of minimax relative concession, even if uniquely rational in costless contexts, need not be, indeed is unlikely to be, uniquely rational in costly contexts. And the state of nature is, by definition, costly. Thus, we see that "ideal rational principles" of this sort have no implication even for ideally rational agents when the derivation of such principles depends on artificial conditions considerably different from those in which even ideally rational agents might find themselves (e.g., the state of nature).

tractarianism, remains important. From a moral theorist's point of view, the importance of Gauthier's work is that it attempts to answer the moral skeptic. It does so by grounding moral theory in a particular conception of rationality. For analytic political theorists, like ourselves, Gauthier's work is important for two reasons. First, and in our minds foremost, it demonstrates the importance of a unified theory of the social sciences: the sense in which political theory, economics, and political science are, at some level, the same discipline, namely, rational-choice theory. Second, it is an impressive, extremely imaginative, and thoughtful attempt to resurrect anarchism: an effort that rests on neither the implausible motivational theory of ideal communitarianism nor the questionable mathematics of the iterated Prisoner's Dilemma.[44]

[44] John Carroll, "Indefinite Terminating Point and the Iterated Prisoners' Dilemma," *Theory and Decision* 22 (1987): 247–56.

16. Closing the compliance dilemma: How it's rational to be moral in a Lamarckian world*

Peter Danielson

The compliance problem

The most striking feature of *Morals by Agreement*[1] is David Gauthier's argument that morality can be individually rational. We should welcome this conclusion, which undercuts the rationale for much coercion and also the need for irrational moral motivators. Of course, welcoming a conclusion is generally irrelevant to its truth. However, Gauthier is a pragmatist about rationality, so welcoming something is not irrelevant to its rationality. This suggests an easy argument to the desired conclusion: we all want agents to be impartially constrained, therefore, morality is rational. However, this gets things turned around by confusing Gauthier's conclusion with one of his premises. He assumes that morality aims at what we all want (what is collectively rational); the problem is

*This essay is based on one read at the Conference on Contemporary Contractarian Thought, subtitled: "Why It's Rational to Be Schmoral in a Darwinian World." The new subtitle indicates a stronger argument in three respects: (i) the argument for the rationality of reciprocal cooperation now has a weaker evolutionary premise, (ii) I answer procedural objections by showing how reciprocal and conditional cooperators are coherent, and (iii) I argue for the morality of reciprocal cooperation as well as its rationality. Points (i) and (ii) respond to Holly Smith, whose criticisms of Gauthier are so interesting that I have taken this opportunity to show how my approach can answer some of them. Finally, in the years between the conference and this paper, I have written a book, *Artificial Morality* (London: Routledge, in press), that elaborates much that is briefly sketched in this essay and thanks all those who have helped me to think about these issues. Here I would like to thank Peter Vallentyne for organizing the conference and this volume.

[1] David Gauthier, *Morals by Agreement* (Oxford: Oxford University Press, 1986); all bare page references in the text are to this book. Gauthier has explained, extended and modified his theory in response to critics on two occasions: "Moral Artifice," *Canadian Journal of Philosophy* 18 (1988): 385–418, and "Morality, Rational Choice, and Semantic Representation," *Social Philosophy and Policy* 5 (1988): 173–221. I will refer to these articles as Artifice and Semantic, respectively.

to show that moral constraint is rational for each of us. The gap between morality and individual rationality is a real problem, because, while I benefit from others' impartial constraint, my own constraint is a pure cost to me. What is obviously (although deviously) rational for me is that everyone *else* should be moral. (No wonder rational agents need costly policing or appeals to motivational magic to keep them in line.)

This is the compliance problem. Gauthier formulates this central problem of ethics in a particularly sharp and fruitful manner. Can an agent do better in terms of her amoral preferences by imposing a constraint on herself that benefits agents impartially? Gauthier also proposes a promising solution: the device of conditional moral principles. Nonetheless, like the other contributors to Part III of this volume, I do not find that Gauthier's principle of constrained maximization closes the gap between rationality and morality. Indeed, I shall argue that constrained maximization is rationally and morally criticizable. However, unlike the others, I think that Gauthier's argument is *almost* successful. In this essay, I extend Gauthier's theory to solve the compliance problem by developing a principle, reciprocal cooperation, that is substantively rational, procedurally coherent, and satisfies minimal moral standards.

Fundamental justification

Morality is a rich and varied phenomenon that likely appeals to us humans, with our complex motivations, for many reasons. However, a rudimentary morality of impartial self-constraint should be attractive even to the meanest sort of agents, the rational agents of the theoretical social sciences, because morally constrained agents can solve difficult social problems better than unconstrained agents. This minimalist approach to morality promises to answer a deep source of moral skepticism by providing a fundamental justification of morality that appeals to amoral agents.

Why should agents concerned only to satisfy their own preferences constrain themselves by impartial moral principles? Because they sometimes interact so that each gains less by choosing his preferred option than what his choice costs the other agent(s). Some of these situations have the payoff structure known as the Prisoner's Dilemma (PD); see Fig 16-1.[2]

When we each choose what is best for himself (*d*), we end up with only the third best outcome. Such situations are common and practically

---

[2] This abstract Prisoner's Dilemma uses Gauthier's "typical" outcome values, measured in utility units multiplied by 3 to yield convenient integers. Row chooser gets the lower-left payoffs; column chooser gets those in the upper right. The two-player PD is the most studied, but also one of the simplest, test cases for a rational morality. I take up some harder cases in *Artificial Morality*.

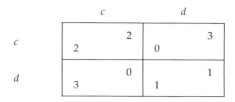

Figure 16-1.   The Prisoner's Dilemma.

important. (For example, in Toronto, each of us does better for himself by driving his car to work, but each of us suffers even more from the traffic congestion caused by others driving.) More relevant to our topic, these situations are *theoretically crucial* to fundamental justification. They provide a chance – indeed, the only chance – for morality to prove itself useful in a world of rational agents. (Roughly, unconstrained rationality suffices for easier problems and harder problems resist even moral solutions.) This theoretical point has two methodological consequences. First, it drives us to abstraction. Any temptation to interpret the Prisoner's Dilemma brings with it the possibility that our moral solution is due to the particular interpretation and, therefore, does not solve the underlying problem. Second, those who seek a fundamental justification are stuck with the Prisoner's Dilemma. We must solve this problem, which, we shall soon see, is very deep.

First, consider the attraction of morality for rational agents in a Prisoner's Dilemma. Self-interested rationality directs us each to choose option d, because the utility of d's payoff is always one better than the payoffs to option c. However, we both do better if we both choose option c than if we both choose option d. If we could choose together, we would agree to choose c. From this impartial moral point of view, the Prisoner's Dilemma is a simple problem. We would constrain ourselves by the following rudimentary moral principle:

Cooperate: Choose what is impartially better for all. This is not intended to trivialize the task of selecting moral principles. The PD is particularly simple. Some of the most intriguing arguments in *Morals by Agreement* address the harder cases, where there are several alternative ways to cooperate that distribute the gains from social cooperation differently. Gauthier proposes an elaborate, innovative, and controversial theory of distributive justice based on bargaining from morally constrained initial holdings.[3] As he acknowledges, without a solution to the compliance problem, his theory of agreement through rational bargaining is in vain:

---

[3] For some criticisms, see Peter Danielson, "The Visible Hand of Morality," *Canadian Journal of Philosophy* 18 (1988), introduction and sec. 1, reprinted in this volume under the title "The Lockean Proviso," Chapter 7.

"The genuinely problematic element in a contractarian theory is not the introduction of the ideal of morality, but the step from hypothetical agreement to actual moral constraint" (p. 9).

Partial compliance

One does better constraining oneself by an ideal moral principle of co-operation as long as everyone does the same. But rationality is a theory of *individual* choice; none of us can choose for all. For moral constraint to be rational, it must pass the test of partial compliance. Morality asks: What if everyone did *X*? Rationality rejoins: What if everybody isn't moral? The power of the abstract Prisoner's Dilemma comes to the fore here; it helps us to answer this second question as it did the first. We need only interpret the *c* option in the Prisoner's Dilemma as disposing oneself to be moral by cooperating and the *d* option as not constraining oneself and not cooperating (defecting). If you cooperate, then I do better by not cooperating, and if you do not cooperate, I also do better by not cooperating. This constructive dilemma in favor of defection is called a *dominance* argument. It shows amoral opportunism is better for each than moral constraint. Not only is it not rational to be moral, but the problem of choosing a moral disposition has the same structure as the original problem morality was supposed to solve. This shows that the compliance problem is a deep problem; I call it the *compliance dilemma*.

Gauthier proposes to solve the compliance problem by introducing a more sophisticated moral principle: constrained maximization. To be rational, moral constraint must be *conditional* upon others' similar constraint. Gauthier uses this conditional disposition to rebut the dominance argument in favor of noncooperation:

> Since persons disposed to co-operation only act co-operatively with those whom they suppose to be similarly disposed, a straightforward maximizer does not have the opportunities to benefit which present themselves to the constrained maximizer. Thus [the dominance] argument . . . fails. (P. 172)

In the Prisoner's Dilemma, a constrained maximizer (CM) refuses to open herself to exploitation by acting cooperatively with an amoral straightforward maximizer (SM). Her conditional disposition is a new option that gives rise to a new set of payoffs in the choice of dispositions for dealing with partial compliance. These new payoffs are shown in Figure 16-2. Gauthier's constrained maximizers do as well or better than straightforward maximizers. They escape the compliance dilemma and show moral constraint to be individually rational.

This claim is obviously significant. Derek Parfit writes about an earlier version of Gauthier's compliance argument:

	CM	SM
CM	2 / 2	2 / 1
SM	1 / 1	1 / 1

Figure 16-2.   Compliance resolved.

If this argument succeeds, it has great importance. It would show that, in many kinds of case, it is rational to act morally, even when we believe that this will be worse for us. Moral reasons would be shown to be stronger than the reasons provided by self-interest. Many writers have tried, unsuccessfully, to justify this conclusion. If this conclusion is justified by the argument that I am discussing, this argument solves what Sidgwick called "the profoundest problem of Ethics."[4]

Moral pluralism

Does Gauthier's argument succeed? Does constrained maximization solve the compliance problem? Unfortunately, not. Gauthier's formulation of Sidgwick's problem of fundamental justification in terms of the theory of rational choice and his appeal to conditional dispositions are both major advances. He moves us from moral monism (that focuses on the ideal situation where all agents follow the same principle) to rational dualism. Setting out the conditions of constrained or moralized rational choice, Gauthier notes that "A just person must however be aware that not all (otherwise) rational persons accept this reading . . . ; 'rational response' remains . . . open to several interpretations" (p. 158). Therefore, partial compliance is a problem. Rational moral principles need to be robust enough to resist amoral predators. However, why stop here? What about dealing with the other sorts of agents – in particular, other moral agents? Gauthier does not consider this complication. I shall argue that when we reintroduce the naive unconditional cooperator, the gap between morality and rationality opens again. A new sort of constrained agent, the reciprocal cooperator, exploits unconditional cooperators, and so does better than Gauthier's constrained maximizer. Since this exploitation is apparently immoral, the compliance

[4] Derek Parfit, *Reasons and Persons* (Oxford: Clarendon Press, 1984), p. 18, referring to *The Methods of Ethics* (London: Macmillan, 1907), p. 386, fn. 4. Parfit's previous footnote links his discussion to Gauthier, "Reason and Maximization," *Canadian Journal of Philosophy* 4 (1975): 411–33. This quotation shows the wide agreement on the importance of a fundamental justification of morality based on rational self-interest, since Parfit is one of the strongest critics of this form of justification. For more on fundamental justification, see C. W. Morris, "The Relation between Self-Interest and Justice in Contractarian Ethics," *Social Philosophy and Policy* 5 (1988): 119–53 and Gauthier's reply, Semantic, sec. VI.

dilemma threatens again. Moreover, the problem of identifying similarly constrained conditional agents is procedurally more complex than Gauthier allows.

Artificial morality

I join other critics in this volume in finding Gauthier's argument for compliance to be incomplete. Unlike them, I believe that Gauthier's approach is sound; his theory can be extended to solve the compliance problem. In this essay, I work on both horns of the compliance dilemma by showing that my alternative principle, reciprocal cooperation, is substantively more rational (the second section) and no less moral (the fourth section) than Gauthier's proposed principle of constrained maximization. In addition, the sophisticated conditional strategies needed to close the compliance dilemma are procedurally coherent (the third section).

Since I aim to extend Gauthier's theory, I should argue from his premises. However our approaches differ in one important respect. Gauthier is concerned with rationality and morality for human beings. In contrast, I prefer a more abstract, functional approach, which I label *artificial morality*. Fundamental justification raises the question whether rational morality is possible. We need to ask how impartial constraint is rational for any sort of agent whatsoever. Notice that the other contributors to Part III fall roughly into two classes. The first group, Copp and Sayre-McCord, stress the *practical* criticism that Gauthier has not shown compliance with moral principles to be rational for "people with ordinary preferences and ordinary moral motivations under ordinary conditions."[5] The second group, Smith and Kraus and Coleman, focus on more *theoretical* problems. They criticize constrained maximization under

---

[5] From the introduction to David Copp, "Contractarianism and Moral Skepticism," Chapter 13 in this volume. In "Deception and Reasons to Be Moral," Chapter 12, Geoffrey Sayre-McCord writes:

> [A] defense of morality that appeals to contrived people in contrived situations will not be much help. . . . Such "defenses" of morality do not meet the practical concern. What we need are good reasons for people, as they actually are, to be moral. Providing such reasons is a challenge both more pressing and more difficult than one met by showing only that ideal people, in idealized situations, have reasons to be moral.

> We agree that a theory that shows morality to be rational for people is practically more pressing and may be more difficult. However, the alternative, artificial morality, need not be so idealized as Sayre-McCord suggests. For example, although my agents are contrived, their situations are not; I introduce a test for substantive rationality designed to eliminate contrived situations. Also, agents who do well against whatever rational self-interest can throw at them are not limited to ideal situations; the problem of partial compliance is central to our argument, as it is to Gauthier's.

quite optimistic assumptions about agents' capacities and the transparency of their situation. I focus on the theoretical criticisms, as these challenge the entire rational-choice project of fundamental justification. In addition, I find the compliance problem sufficiently difficult even under the drastic simplifying assumption that artificial agents are available who can do whatever substantive rationality requires and procedural rationality permits. While it is interesting to speculate why rational morality might not apply to us humans, first, we must establish what – if anything – rational morality requires.[6]

Substantive rationality

Gauthier's argument for constrained maximization depends on showing that this disposition is substantively rational, that it is a better means to an agent's ends. We are led to ask: Better than what and amongst whom? This section answers this question by sketching some alternative constraining principles and developing a test for substantive rationality. I argue that there is a rationality superior alternative to Gauthier's proposed principle.

Conditional cooperation

The compliance dilemma is caused by a failure to discriminate. An unconditional cooperator (UC) is a naive moral agent who indiscriminately cooperates with all agents. Unconditional cooperators fail to protect themselves from exploitation by straightforward maximizers. Unconditional cooperators fail to satisfy what Lyons calls "minimizing conditions"; they do not know how "to make the best of a generally bad situation."[7] To protect himself from straightforward maximizers, a moral agent should differentially cooperate only with other cooperators. Gauthier's principle of constrained maximization (CM) embodies such a conditional disposition; "the just person is disposed to comply . . . in interacting with those of his fellows whom he believes to be similarly disposed" (p. 156). Simplifying somewhat, I identify this component of constrained maximization as the principle (or strategy) of conditional cooperation:

---

[6] Gauthier acknowledges this problem: "Constrained maximization may, for all that I say in *Morals by Agreement*, be incompatible with our psychology" (Artifice, p. 416). I do think that artificial morality has application to organizations; see Danielson, "The Lockean Proviso," fifth section in Chapter 7 of this volume.

[7] David Lyons, *Forms and Limits of Utilitarianism* (Oxford: Clarendon Press, 1965), p. 128. G. Kavka, *Hobbesian Moral and Political Theory* (Princeton: Princeton University Press, 1986), sec. 9–4, extends Lyons' categories from utilitarian rules to self-interested principles.

Conditional Cooperation (CC): Cooperate with and only with those who can be expected to cooperate.[8] The principle of conditional cooperation protects an agent from exploitation, allowing her to escape the compliance dilemma, as we saw in Figure 16-2, which displayed the possible outcomes open to two agents, each of whom can choose between straightforward maximization and conditional cooperation as her strategy for the Prisoner's Dilemma.[9] The availability of conditional cooperation has changed the compliance problem from a Prisoner's Dilemma into a simple coordination game. If I choose CC, I am protected should you choose SM, as I will then defect as well, so CC meets minimizing conditions. Moreover, my choice of CC makes CC your best choice, so choosing CC is the dominant equilibrium choice. Finally, since we both do better choosing CC than choosing anything else, the outcome is optimal. Conditional cooperation is rational *and* moral; CC appears to resolve the compliance dilemma.

So far I have followed Gauthier's line of argument; now we diverge. Gauthier, convinced of the rationality of CC in the simplest case where agents' dispositions are transparent, proceeds to discuss more complex and realistic cases where transparency fails. In contrast, I see two problems with the justification of conditional cooperation as rational even in the most favorable case. First, although CC does better than SM, these are not the only alternatives that need to be considered. For example, CC does not do better than SM when interacting with an unconditional cooperator, so Gauthier's argument for the substantive rationality of constrained maximization is incomplete. Second, conditional cooperators do better than SMs only because CCs cooperate with each other. However, the interaction of *conditional* agents is problematic. For example, Alphonse will cooperate if Gaston will, but Gaston will only if Alphonse will, and so on. This symmetrical situation seems to throw conditional cooperators' decision procedures into a vicious regress; the

---

[8] The connection between constrained maximization and conditional cooperation is complicated by Gauthier's use of the phrases "similarly disposed" and "like-disposed" (p. 169), which leave unclear the level of similarity required. Is a disposition to cooperate sufficient or is a *conditional* disposition required? The canonical specification of constrained maximization on p. 167 indicates that the former suffices. Therefore, constrained maximizers are conditional cooperators, as Gauthier agrees (Artifice, p. 399). Cf. Peter Danielson, "The Visible Hand of Morality," sec. III.

[9] The matrix in Figure 16-2 simplifies matters in two ways. First, I assume that CC will always recognize SM. Otherwise, the payoff structure will likely be that of the Assurance Game; cf. Gauthier, "Reason to Be Moral?" *Synthese* 72 (1987): 21. Second, I assume that SM and CC never cooperate together. Gauthier stresses the need for an additional disposition to refuse to cooperate with straightforward maximizers on p. 180. However, in *sequential* Prisoner's Dilemmas, SM would sometimes cooperate. Cf. Edward F. McClennen, "Constrained Maximization and Resolute Choice," *Social Philosophy and Policy*, 5 (1988): 95–118, and Gauthier's discussion in Semantic, p. 208f. This case raises interesting questions that are related to the choice between broad and narrow compliance. I address this problem in *Artificial Morality*.

	UC	SM	CC	RC
UC	2 / 2	3 / 0	2 / 2	3 / 0
SM	0 / 3	1 / 1	1 / 1	1 / 1
CC	2 / 2	1 / 1	2 / 2	2 / 2
RC	0 / 3	1 / 1	2 / 2	2 / 2

Figure 16-3. Moral pluralism.

compliance dilemma leads to a procedural dilemma. It will simplify discussion to separate these two problems. I begin with the substantive problem in the remainder of this section, introducing and comparing principles without concern whether the corresponding decision procedures are possible. As it turns out, a new strategy that I defend as substantively rational simplifies the problems of procedural rationality that I take up in the third section.

Reciprocal cooperation

Conditional cooperators cooperate when this is sufficient for the other agent's cooperation. They cooperate with fellow CCs but they also co-operate with unconditional cooperators. This extension of moral constraint seems rationally unmotivated. An agent should do better defecting against those who will cooperate in any case. While CC meets minimizing conditions, it does not meet maximizing conditions. It does not make the best of a generally good situation where predatory benefits are freely available. Therefore, I propose, as a rational improvement over conditional cooperation, the principle of reciprocal cooperation.

Reciprocal Cooperation (RC): Cooperate when and only when cooperation is necessary and sufficient for the other's cooperation.[10] RC agents only constrain themselves when cooperation is a *necessary* condition for the other's cooperation. Figure 16-3 shows how reciprocal and conditional cooperation differ. RC cooperates with CC and RC itself and defects with SM and UC.

---

[10] Peter Danielson, "The Visible Hand of Morality," sec. III. The label "reciprocal cooperation" recalls and specifies the sociobiological concept of reciprocal altruism.

Again, I leave until the third section the procedural question of how – indeed, whether it is possible – to compute effectively the RC strategy. Here we focus on the question of substantive rationality: Should an agent choose RC as her strategy for use in the Prisoner's Dilemma? Like CC, RC is an optimal equilibrium strategy. There is no strategy better for both agents, and RC is the best response to the other player's best response to it. Thus, RC is both morally and rationally attractive. More- over, RC (weakly) dominates the other strategies, including CC. That is, no matter which of these principles the other uses, one never does worse and sometimes does better using RC. Therefore, reciprocal co- operation appears to be substantively more rational than Gauthier's prin- ciple of constrained maximization.

However, reciprocal cooperation differs from conditional cooperation only in its poor treatment of unconditional cooperators. This distin- guishing feature is a vulnerable point in my defense of RC as rational and moral. Exploitation of the innocent appears to be morally indefen- sible; I address this problem in the fourth section. On the side of ra- tionality, since UC is irrational, why include it in the test situation in Figure 16-3? I turn to this criticism now.

The arbitrariness of a population containing UC is symptomatic of a more general problem. Like Gauthier's defense of constrained maximi- zation, our argument for reciprocal cooperation is limited to the range of alternatives it considers. Indeed, the argument seems to depend on a *contrived* population; without the presence of UC, RC does no better than CC. Moreover, because UC does so badly, it is evidently irrational. It appears that the only reason to insert this irrational agent into the population is to provide something for RC to exploit. Including UC, therefore, appears to bias the test against CC. Finally, if we can add contrived agents, why not add one who refuses to cooperate with RC, thus making RC do worse and CC do better and undermining my claim for the substantive superiority of the former?

Arbitrariness and parametric choice

Introducing additional agents creates problems for claims about sub- stantive rationality that Gauthier has not considered. Substantive ra- tionality is doubly relative. A strategy is rational compared to some set of alternative strategies, A, depending on their interaction with a pop- ulation of strategies, P. For simplicity, let A and P be the same; how should this population be specified? Very roughly, there are two ways this might be done. As an example of one extreme, when I consider whether to vote or to support the regional noncommercial radio station, I can take the actual population with its distribution of dispositions as given to me as a fact of nature. Because this population consists of agents whose choice is largely independent of mine, my decision problem is a *parametric* one of choosing the best strategy without concern for others' strategic responses. At the other extreme, there are *strategic* situations in which the other agents can be expected to respond in a rational way to one's own choice. How should Gauthier, who claims that moral theory is a part of rational-choice theory, specify the relevant choice situation?

In *Morals by Agreement*, Gauthier stresses that the choice of a disposition is a parametric choice.[11] This leaves him open to objections such as the one Holly Smith presses by introducing two additional principles, unconditional cooperation and a restricted form of conditional cooperation, which cooperates with and only with UC, which I will label CUC. She then asks,

> How would someone who has chosen CM fare against a partner who has chosen [UC]? It is obvious that the best choice is SM rather than CM, since the straightforward maximizer will always obtain [3] and the constrained maximizer will only obtain [2]. Similarly, against a partner who has chosen [CUC], one will maximize utility by choosing [UC] rather than CM, for in this way one will achieve a constant return of [2] rather than [1]. Of course, a partner who chooses [UC] or [CUC] may not be rational, since this choice will not fare well against all possible configurations of partners and their choices (although it is certainly arguable that someone choosing [UC] is *moral*). But CM is hardly an attractive option if it only succeeds against perfectly rational partners. Since many people are in fact irrational, an acceptable option must work against all comers, be they rational or not. Hence Gauthier's argument that CM maximizes utility is significantly incomplete. . . .[12]

I agree that this objection has force against Gauthier; his defense of constrained maximization *is* incomplete. Since Gauthier stresses that his argument is parametric, it is fair to demand, as Smith does, a general account of how CM fares against and among all possible configurations of agents. Gauthier does not and cannot provide such a general defense of constrained maximization. On the one hand, once agents are allowed to react to other's principles (as CUC does), complexity explodes and there are infinitely many agents to consider.[13] On the other hand, even

---

[11] Gauthier writes:

> We have defended the rationality of constrained maximization as a disposition to choose by showing that it would be rationally chosen. Now this argument is not circular; constrained maximization is a disposition for strategic choice that would be parametrically chosen. (P. 183)

[12] Holly Smith, "Deriving Morality from Rationality," the fourth section, Chapter 14 in this volume; abbreviations and payoffs changed to my conventions.

[13] A diagonal argument establishes this result. Begin with the two simple strategies, UC and UD. There are four ways to react to this pair; so now we have four strategies. But each strategy needs to be specified further according to the two possible answers to the questions whether it cooperates with each of these two (this is the diagonal generator)

World

		UC	CUC
	UC	2	2
Agent:	CC	2	1
	SM	3	1

Figure 16–4.   A parametric dilemma.

with very simple sets of agents, there is no one strategy that is rational for all possible social worlds. Smith has, in effect, constructed a world that presents Gauthier with a new parametric dilemma, as shown in Figure 16-4.

For any population mix of UC and CUC, either SM or UC does best; CC never does best in this world. It is a world in which a principle requiring either more or less constraint does better than CC. I shall return to Smith's counterexamples after reconsidering Gauthier's insistence on parametric reasoning, which led to this problem.

Several considerations favor a strategic over a parametric test for substantive rationality. First, a strategic test is better suited to the problem of fundamental justification. As the examples before suggested, applied moralists can often take the distribution of dispositions in the actual population as given. However fundamental justification should not allow these crucial variables to be exogenously determined.[14] Strategic arguments address the problem of arbitrariness by rationalizing the populations. Agents adapt by shifting to rationally preferable strategies. Second, an attractively weak form of Gauthier's assumption of equal rationality favors strategic arguments. As Elster notes,

There is something strange or even contradictory in the notion of parametric rationality. A parametrically rational agent believes himself to be free to adjust optimally (given his end) to a constant environment, and at the same time he can hardly fail to have some awareness of the fact that this environment is made up in part of other agents similar to himself.[15]

Third, we shall shortly see that Gauthier's own arguments are strategic, not parametric. These reasons support a move to a strategic test for substantive rationality.[16]

yielding sixteen strategies, and so on. The source of this complexity cannot be avoided, as the substantively rational RC is similar to CUC in the crucial respect; both are meta-strategies. Cf. the later section entitled "Strategies and metastrategies."

[14] How little natural support can be found for the assumption of a nonarbitrary situation can be seen from Gauthier's recent remarks on the problem of arbitrariness, ending with: "I ... assume ... (probably falsely) that our world is not one in which arbitrary rewards are provided. . . ." Gauthier, "Reason to Be Moral?" p. 22.

[15] Jon Elster, *Ulysses and the Sirens* (Cambridge: Cambridge University Press, 1984), p. 117.

[16] What of the worry about circularity that leads Gauthier to a parametric test? This is a large issue, which I take up in *Artificial Morality*.

An evolutionary test

Several of Gauthier's arguments turn on strategic consideration of how other agents will choose their principles in response to the agent's own choice. In particular, Gauthier's defense of narrow over broad compliance (p. 178 and p. 225ff.) and his response to our defense of reciprocal cooperation have this form. I focus on the latter:

> . . . [R]eciprocal cooperation helps to sustain the conditions in which cooperation flourishes, and so in which fair mutual advantage is realized. Unconditional cooperation is a disposition that is inimical, not only to its own survival, but to that of any form of cooperation. For a world of unconditional cooperators is easily invaded by straightforward maximizers, who exploit their guileless if benevolent fellows at every turn and whose presence, except in conditions of full transparency, increases the risk run by other cooperators by mistaking their fellows' dispositions and consequently being victimized. Conditional cooperators, although defending themselves directly against predators and free-riders, fail to defend themselves indirectly, by sustaining the unconditional cooperators whose presence enables straightforward maximizers to thrive. Reciprocal cooperators defend themselves both directly and indirectly; by exploiting unconditional cooperators, reciprocal cooperators help eliminate the natural victims of straightforward maximizers, placing the latter at a competitive disadvantage. Reciprocal cooperators thus help make the world safe for morality. ("Artifice," pp. 400–1)

Gauthier's talk of invasion and survival should put us in mind of sociobiology and, in particular, the strategic concept of an evolutionary stable strategy (ESS). Indeed, the trajectory of populations of interacting strategies in Maynard Smith and Price's model almost exactly parallels what we should expect to happen to conditional cooperators (although they used a game of Chicken instead of Prisoner's Dilemma).[17]

> In a population of retaliators [CC], no other strategy would invade, since there is no other strategy that does better than retaliator itself. However, dove [UC] does equally well in a population of retaliators. This means that, other things being equal, the numbers of doves could slowly drift upwards. Now if the number of doves [UC] drifted up to any significant extent, prober-retaliators [RC] (and incidentally, hawks and bullies [SM]) would start to have an advantage, since they do better against doves [UC] than retaliators do. Prober-retaliator, unlike hawk and bully, is almost an ESS. . . .[18]

---

[17] J. Maynard Smith and G. R. Price, "The Logic of Animal Conflict," *Nature* 246 (1973): 15–18. The game of Chicken differs from Prisoner's Dilemma in reversing the ordinal ranking of the *S* and *P* outcomes in footnote 41, Figure 16-5. Chicken models a situation where punishing a defector with defection is more costly than acquiescing to exploitation.

[18] R. Dawkins, *The Selfish Gene* (New York: Oxford University Press, 1976), p. 80. In the game of Chicken, hawk, who always defects, is distinct from bully, who is a SM; prober-retaliator is only "almost an ESS" because in Maynard Smith and Price's iterated se-

Evolutionary stability provides the ideas we need to develop a strategic test for substantive rationality. The main problem is to specify a non-arbitrary population appropriate for fundamental justification. In the example just given, UC is a nonarbitrary addition to the population P_1 = $\langle CC \rangle$ because UC does as well as CC in the augmented population P_2 = $\langle CC, UC \rangle$.[19] RC invades CC by doing better than CC in P_3 = $\langle CC, UC, RC \rangle$. I will say that UC is a (weakly) rational addition to P_1. P_2 and P_3 rationally extend $\langle CC \rangle$. Therefore, P_2 and P_3 are nonarbitrary populations in which to test CC. With these rough definitions in hand, I can state an informal account of substantive rationality: A strategy S_1 is substantively more rational than a strategy S_2 if and only if S_1 can invade some rational extension of $\langle S_2 \rangle$, but S_2 cannot invade any rational extension of $\langle S_1 \rangle$.

According to this standard, reciprocal cooperation is substantively more rational than conditional cooperation. Conditional cooperation is unstable; it allows agents to drift to another strategy, UC, which then allows other strategies to do better than CC itself. CC can be indirectly invaded. What would invade the resulting $\langle CC, UC \rangle$ population? Gauthier points to SM; eventually, SM could invade, showing that by my standard, CC is *not* more rational than SM. However, since CC cooperates with RC but not SM, RC can invade immediately, whereas SM would need to wait until the number of UCs so increased that the gains of predation outweighed the penalty CC exacts. Therefore, CC is unstable; it would be invaded indirectly by SM and RC. Conversely, RC cannot be invaded by SM or CC (nor by any other strategy that I know of). RC allows a drift to CC, but the presence of RC blocks the possibility of CC drifting to UC, and CC never does better than RC. We conclude once again that reciprocal, not conditional, cooperation is substantively rational in the following strong sense: RC is rationally superior to CC and SM and CC is not rationally superior to RC or even to SM.

This test is evolutionary rather than ecological because it starts with the agent to be tested and assumes that new agents come into existence to fill niches as they arise. The test is far from completely specified. I have not provided a generator of alternative strategies, nor dealt with the question whether newcomers arrive alone or in clusters.[20] However, this sketch of a test is enough to allow us to deal with Smith's counter-

quential game, where knowledge is acquired by probing (defecting), prober-retaliator pays epistemic costs, which RC does not.
[19] The test is historical, beginning with the strategy to be tested, so I represent populations as *ordered* sets of strategies.
[20] In order to secure the result that CC and RC can invade SM, the evolutionary test must assume that newcomers arrive in clusters; cf. Axelrod, *The Evolution of Cooperation* (New York: Basic Books, 1984), chap. 3. I leave further consideration of clustering and generation to *Artificial Morality*, but take up one aspect of generation, namely, learning by selective imitation, in the later section entitled "Indirection in a Lamarckian world."

examples. I agree with Smith's first counterexample and even strengthen her criticism of CC. By my evolutionary standard, UC is rational in the environment CC creates. Therefore, I can object to CC in that it allows the drift to UC and thereby the invasion of UC's predators without recourse to exogenously determined (human) irrationality.

However, there may be objections to my claim that UC is rational in the sense that it is equally advantageous in a population of CC agents. First, I allow merely equally advantageous strategies to drift into the test population. This may seem undermotivated and therefore designed to admit UC in order to embarrass CC. But there are other reasons to allow drift. Equally advantageous agents are indistinguishable to some learners. Indeed, CC, like Tit For Tat, *teaches* simple learners to become unconditional, not conditional, cooperators.[21] Also, once we admit procedural considerations, UC's simplicity may make it on balance rationally better than CC (at least until predators appear on the scene). A second objection is that UC will be short-lived; its presence in a population makes the entry of SM rational (where it was not in an CM population) and leaves UC as the worse-off strategy. Wouldn't UC agents die out or change to CC at this point? Not necessarily. First, unconditional cooperators need not die out because there is no necessary connection between one's preferences and survival. Rational ethics is not sociobiology; we should not identify the preferences that rationality aims to satisfy with objective fitness values. Ethics – even rational ethics – must admit the survival of the frustrated. Second, UC agents may not be able to change their principles. The assumption that agents can rationally constrain themselves introduces hysteresis.[22] Until we have investigated the procedural mechanisms of rational constraint, it is not obvious that what can be bound can also be unbound. Therefore, I conclude that even in a world of rationally chosen constraint, there may be unconditionally cooperative agents. From this, Smith concludes that SM would be more rational than CC, which is bad news from the point of view of solving the compliance problem. Our conclusion is more hopeful. In a world where UC enters because CC allows it, RC, but not SM, is rationally superior to CC. This is better news, because RC, unlike SM, is a morally constrained principle, which helps to close the compliance dilemma.

Now consider Smith's second counterexample, CUC. This is less directly interesting, since CUC is neither rationally nor morally attractive.

---

[21] Cf. Peter Danielson, "The Moral and Ethical Relevance of TIT FOR TAT," *Dialogue* 25 (1986): 455.

[22] Gauthier makes stronger assumptions, tying preferences to survival: "Now suckers are unlikely to do well in the struggle for survival, so that our maximizer may not expect to find many around." "The Unity of Reason: A Subversive Reinterpretation of Kant," *Ethics* 96 (1985): 85. On "moral hysteresis," cf. Jon Elster, *Ulysses and the Sirens*, p. 147.

CUCs are not rational (as Smith admits). Indeed, CUC is the most easily invaded strategy I know of. Because it does not even succeed in cooperating with its twin, CUC can be directly invaded by UC. (CUC takes symbiotic cooperation to the extreme of self-sacrifice.) Failure to cooperate with its twin also undercuts any moral justification for CUC. If cooperating with UC is morally required, why punish those who so cooperate? The only rationale for CUC seems to be to undermine CC; it is a CC *devil*. This would be a good reason to eliminate it. A derivation of impartial constraint in a world contrived to include only constraint lovers begs the question. Conversely, the failure of a principle, *P*, in a world of otherwise irrational *P* haters should be excluded for methodological reasons. So I am happy to be able to exclude CUC by a general evolutionary test of substantive rationality. Nonetheless, CUC suggests that more might be done to protect unconditional cooperators. In this respect it is morally interesting, as we shall see in the fourth section.

Conclusion

I conclude that reciprocal cooperation is substantively more rational than Gauthier's constrained maximization. Our evolutionary test, which models the type of argument Gauthier generally uses, establishes this result in a nonarbitrary world of varied rational agents. Reciprocal cooperation helps to close the gap between rationality and morality because it is more rational than Gauthier's proposed principle and cannot be invaded, even indirectly, by straightforward maximizers.

Procedural rationality

In the previous section, we found reciprocal cooperation to be substantively more rational than its rival, conditional cooperation, on which Gauthier builds constrained maximization. However, my argument for RC's rational superiority is thin, because it ignores procedural issues entirely. Minimally, it must be possible to implement a strategy. More generally, procedural complexity may incur substantive disadvantage when it causes errors or makes recognition and learning by others difficult. This section begins by showing how reciprocal cooperation is more complex than conditional cooperation. As a result, reciprocal cooperation faces a serious objection. Critics have argued that CC is already prohibitively complex – indeed, incoherent. A fortiori, RC would appear to be procedurally objectionable. This section addresses the incoherence objection. Reciprocal and conditional cooperation are shown to be coherent by indicating how artificial agents that embody RC and CC decision procedures can be constructed. A consequence of the technique I introduce is that RC need be no more difficult to implement than CC.

Strategies and metastrategies

Reciprocal cooperation is more complex than conditional cooperation. This difference between RC and CC is best explained in terms of the distinction between strategies and metastrategies, which also illuminates the question whether Gauthier's constrained maximization is a matter of new *preferences*.[23] The CC principle may be represented as a preference for cooperation in response to cooperation and a preference for defection in response to defection. Sen calls these preferences, "Assurance Game Preferences."[24] In contrast, the RC principle cannot be represented as a set of preferences over pairs of actions. The RC response to someone choosing to cooperate depends on what the other player would do were RC to defect. Therefore, CC is simpler than RC. Conditional cooperation can be represented as a simple preferential strategy, whereas reciprocal cooperation can only be represented as a *metastrategy*: a strategy defined over others' strategies (or metastrategies).[25] This extra complexity may seem daunting. Roughly, whereas CC is a conditional principle that sometimes cooperates with other conditional principles, RC *only* cooperates with other conditional principles. One may suspect that reciprocal cooperation will require such complex decision procedures that it will be procedurally doomed. This brings us to the coherence problem.

The coherence problem

Again we turn to Holly Smith's essay, "Deriving Morality from Rationality" (Chapter 14 in this volume) because she states the coherence objection in its strongest form, by allowing Gauthier maximally transparent agents.

Let's simplify matters by assuming that you have already chosen CM, and, of course, I know this. What should I predict you will do if I choose CM? Gauthier seems to assume that I may simply predict that you will form the intention to [cooperate]. But matters are much more complex than this. Given your choice of CM, what I *can* predict is that you will [cooperate] if and only if you predict

---

[23] On McClennen's theory of resolute choice (see Edward F. McClennen, "Constrained Maximization and Resolute Choice," *Social Philosophy and Policy* 5 [1988]: 95–118), the job of CM is done by contextually defined preferences over actions. Gauthier replies that CM gives reasons, not new preferences (Semantic, sec. V). Cf. D. MacIntosh, "Two Gauthiers?" *Dialogue* 28 (1989): 43–61, on the distinction between preferences and principles.

[24] A. K. Sen, "Choice, Orderings and Morality," in *Practical Reason*, edited by S. Körner (New Haven: Yale University Press, 1974), pp. 54–67.

[25] The device of a metastrategy originates in N. Howard, *Paradoxes of Rationality: Theory of Metagames and Political Behavior* (Cambridge, MA: The MIT Press, 1974). Symmetrical metastrategies are introduced in N. Howard, " 'General' Metagames: An Extension of the Metagame Concept," in *Game theory as a Theory of Conflict Resolution*, edited by A. Rapoport (Dordrecht, Holland: D. Reidel, 1971), pp. 261–83.

that I will [cooperate]. But how can I assume you can make this prediction about me? Your position vis-à-vis me is perfectly parallel to my position vis-à-vis you. Even if you know that I choose CM, all you can infer from this is that I will [cooperate] *if and only if* I predict you will [cooperate]. You cannot infer that I will [cooperate], simpliciter.[26]

This decision problem is certainly complex enough to befuddle human agents, but Smith's objection is stronger, as it applies to ideally competent, transparent artificial agents as well. We encounter a methodological problem: How can we (humans) *tell* if a complex artificial agent is coherent? I suggest that since agents embody decision *functions*, coherence requires returning a choice for all legitimate imputs, that is, decision contexts. An ideal test for procedural soundness would mechanically test logical definitions of agents considered as decision algorithms. The computer language Prolog comes very close to what we need. Examining a pair of conditional cooperators (named Loopy1 and Loopy2) implemented in Prolog makes the procedural problem plain:[27]

    cooperate(loopy1,Other) if cooperate(Other,loopy1).

    cooperate(loopy2,Other) if cooperate(Other,loopy2).

Each of Loopy1 and Loopy2 will cooperate with whatever will cooperate with them. For example, both will cooperate with the following unconditional cooperator:

    cooperate(uc1,Anything).

But the outcome of the two conditional decision procedures is indeterminate in the presence of each other: cooperate(loopy1,loopy2) calls cooperate(loopy2,loopy1), which calls cooperate(loopy1,loopy2) again. These decision procedures fail to terminate because of the way in which they try to predict each other's decision. Call this the *prediction problem*.[28]

There is another way to see why conditional cooperators might lapse into incoherence that is related to Gauthier's conception of constrained maximization as a form of moral impartiality or equality. In our formulation of the CC procedure before, each loopy agent asks for more from the other – that is, cooperation – than the conditional cooperation it is willing to offer itself. (Paradoxically, this means that CC agents

---

[26] Holly Smith, "Deriving Morality from Rationality," the fourth section in Chapter 14 in this volume. I have simplified the argument by substituting "cooperate" for Smith's more complex "form the intention to build and then carry out this intention." The coherence problem is least tractable in games where agents must choose simultaneously. Therefore, I shall answer Smith's objection in that context. However, I note that it would be preferable, were there more space, to develop procedural solutions more gradually by first working through the easier *sequential* Prisoner's Dilemma discussed by Gauthier and McClennen; cf. footnote 23 above.

[27] Prolog is a computer programming language based on predicate calculus. However, contrary to standard syntax, constants are written in lowercase and variables, all of which are free, are indicated with initial capitals.

[28] On the prediction problem, see Richmond Campbell, "Gauthier's Theory of Morals by Agreement," *Philosophical Quarterly* 38 (1988): 343–64.

implemented in this way will *only* succeed in cooperating when interacting with UC. Since this is precisely the case that we criticized in the
second section, CC's procedural success is coincident with its substantive
failure.) Call this the *assurance problem:* CC agents demand more assurance than they offer.

We conclude that Smith's coherence objection is no minor procedural
problem. Gauthier underestimates the procedural complexities that his
conditional principle introduces, even for artificial agents:

> If one thinks of morality, not only as artifice, but as intended for such artifacts
> as corporations and governments, then one need consider only problems of
> institutional design. In principle, a constrained maximizer is no more difficult
> to construct than a straightforward maximizer. (Artifice, p. 417)

This is not so; it appears that constrained maximizers must work in an
entirely different way from straightforward maximizers.

It may seem as if Smith and I exaggerate the coherence problem. After
all, a conditional cooperator's prediction problem is familiar. It is closely
related to the original prediction paradox faced by interacting strategic
agents. That problem was solved by the fundamental result of game
theory: the existence of equilibria over mixed strategies. However, the
accompanying note, which works through this analogy, concludes that
CC agents cannot solve the coherence problem in just the same way
straightforward maximizers solve the original prediction problem.[29] In
any case, RC cannot be represented as a set of preferences, so it cannot
be rescued in this way. Therefore, I turn to the task of reformulating
constrained maximization in order to solve the coherence problem in a

---

[29] This note develops the parallel between the symmetrical decision problem for CC agents
and the strategic problem of SM agents generally. For example, in a pure competitive
game of coin matching, I would like to show heads if I expect you to show tails, but if
I show heads, you would like to show heads as well. As Gauthier explains in chap. III,
game theory resolves this paradox of interdependent expectations with the concepts of
the Nash equilibrium and the mixed strategy. Once we emphasize that the CC strategy
requires cooperation when one *expects* the other to cooperate, can't CC agents base their
expectations on the undominated equilibrium of joint cooperation?

> A unique undominated equilibrium must . . . be preferred by everyone to every
> other equilibrium outcome. It affords a natural focus for the expectations of
> persons who identify rationality with utility maximization. (P. 71)

This solution to the coherence problem is attractively elegant, as it applies the standard
theory of rational choice to achieve what Gauthier sees as its moral extension. However
the application is not so simple for several reasons. First, CC agents *don't* identify
rationality with utility maximization. Second, we could only argue that joint cooperation
is in equilibrium if both agents *prefer c* to *d* in case the other chooses *c*. But the Prisoner's
Dilemma is defined by each agent preferring *d*'s outcome to *c*'s outcome in this case.
It is true that CC agents choose *c* if the other does, but this is not a matter of simple
preference; their choice of *c* is *counterpreferential*. (That's what makes it a matter of moral
constraint.) Third, a complex procedure is required somehow to reveal these new preferences, hypothetically in a simultaneous game and, since the new preferences are
based on the CC procedure itself, the danger of incoherence remains.

general way applicable to both conditional and reciprocal cooperation. Smith issues a skeptical constructive challenge:

> It might be hoped that a reformulation could be found according to which it would necessarily be the case that if two transparent partners both choose CM, then they both would [cooperate]. Unfortunately, such reformulations do not seem to be available.

Elsewhere I have argued that there is a coherent reformulation of CM that does not run afoul of the problem of circularity.[30] That is, one *can* define a CM agent that cooperates with all and only CM agents. Smith is also skeptical about this approach. She continues in a footnote:

> We cannot, of course, without problematic circularity, simply define a CM agent as one who cooperates with all and only other CM agents. . . . There is a deep problem here about whether the kind of relation Gauthier needs between CM partners is incoherent.[31]

We grant Smith that it is not "simple" to do this, but it can be done with modern logical tools. The incoherence problem is caused by agents trying to predict each other's behavior by invoking the other's decision procedure. In the faulty formulation of CC given before Loopy1 invokes or *uses* Loopy2's procedure, which in turn uses Loopy1's, and so on. This suggests a way out of the problem: design agents who forsake prediction by direct simulation for a cruder similarity test based on matching *mentioned* principles. The metalogical device of quotation allows us to design coherent symmetrical metastrategies.

Selfsame cooperation

As we saw in the second section, the substantively rational agent, RC, must be able to pick out not only agents similar to herself, but some dissimilar agents as well (CC in the case of RC). This discrimination task calls on procedures more complex than matching. To simplify the task of constructing a coherent symmetrical metastrategy, I temporarily drop concern with substantive rationality and focus on procedural matters in this subsection. I begin with a procedurally simpler matching principle and work up to more complex varieties. Consider the simplest matching principle:

Selfsame Cooperation (SC): Cooperate with and only with similar agents.

How does a selfsame cooperator solve the coherence problem? First, she addresses the assurance problem by not demanding more constraint

---

[30] Holly Smith, "Deriving Morality from Rationality," fourth section; cf. Peter Danielson, "Visible Hand," sec. III.

[31] Holly Smith, "Deriving Morality from Rationality," footnote 18.

from the other agent than she is willing to offer herself. It will be useful to introduce the class of *assurance modulators* here. A principle can be seen as modulating cooperativeness; given some degree of assurance of cooperation, it will provide some degree of assurance. For example, in the iterated Prisoner's Dilemma, the strategy of tit for tat always co-operates in the first round, before it knows whether the other agent will cooperate. Tit for tat is an assurance amplifier; it gives more assurance than it demands. UC is the limiting case; it asks for no assurance and gives certain cooperation. Conversely, a strategy that demands uncon-ditional cooperation before it will cooperate is an assurance damper; it demands more assurance than it gives. As we saw earlier, CC has this property, since it requires cooperation but provides only conditional cooperation. Finally, a procedure is assurance neutral if it returns just what it gives. Returning to selfsame cooperation, it appears to be neutral because of its appeal to similarity but it is an assurance amplifier. In return for a conditional commitment to cooperation, SC offers cooper-ation, thus solving the assurance problem.

How do selfsame cooperators avoid the prediction problem? A SC agent need not know that the other agent will cooperate, but only that the other is similar, that is, also an SC agent. Notice that the definition of selfsame cooperation guarantees that both will cooperate in case of a match (in contrast to Smith's account of CM, according to which CM allows joint defection). However, this might seem merely to put the procedural problem off one step. How, in a situation of simultaneous choice, with no previous interaction, is one SC agent to test another agent for the requisite similarity? Moreover, similarity is a vague notion; how much similarity is required? I use metalogical matching to answer both questions. Here is one way we might implement selfsame coop-eration. Compare a quotation of the other agent's procedure, O, with a quotation of your own decision procedure, S. Check if O is the result of substituting the other agent's name for one's own in S. If this is the case, cooperate. This is probably too sketchy to allay fears of incoherence. Unfortunately, a more technical discussion may be required. (The next paragraph may be skipped without loss of continuity.)

To assure the reader that SC can be implemented coherently, here are two versions that will pass the test of machine execution under a Prolog interpreter. The SC agent described before looks like this:

```
cooperate(sc1,Other) if

    clause(cooperate(sc1,Other),My _ principle) and

    clause(cooperate(Other,sc1),Others _ principle) and

    substitute(sc1,My _ principle,Other,Others _ principle).
```

"Clause(Head,Body)" is a metalogical predicate that is true of the head and body of a then–if clause. For example, given "p if (q and r)" clause(p,Body) is true of Body = (q and r). If one defines another agent, sc2, similarly, sc1 and sc2 will cooperate with each other without regress or the chance that either can be exploited. However, this self-contained formulation of SC takes a logical liberty. The variable My _ principle gets bound to something that includes My _ principle itself, violating a constraint needed to block the invalid introduction of existentially quantified expressions. We can avoid this problem by making SC a separate predicate exterior to agents' decision procedures, resulting in this elegant implementation of SC:

```
cooperate(sc3,Other) if sc(Other,sc3).

sc(Ego,Alter) if clause(cooperate(Ego,Alter),sc(Alter,Ego)).[32]
```

Notice that the predicate $sc(X,Y)$ does not call $sc(Y,X)$, so coherence is preserved. Finally, note that sc1 will not cooperate with sc3. This creates a coordination problem to which we return in the section entitled "Indirection in a Lamarckian world." (The technical discussion ends here.)

I conclude that conditional metastrategies that cooperate with similar conditional metastrategies can be coherently defined. However, gaining coherence in this way has its price. A metastrategy that cooperates as a function of the other's metastrategy produces the desired results only when it is possible to determine the other agent's metastrategy. Have we merely exchanged one procedural problem for another? Yes, if it is difficult to determine another's metastrategy, SC's tactic will fail, and I grant that there are real problems about trust and transparency in the case of human agents. However, recall the goal of this essay is to show how rational morality is possible. To this end, I have postulated artificial agents able to choose under complex constraints. Now I postulate, in addition, that they may reveal these constraints if they so choose. This amounts to assuming that they can publicize their decision procedures and that dishonesty is impossible.

Second, straightforward maximizers have no interest in others determining their strategy. Therefore, a critic might suggest that the com-

---

[32] I owe this formulation to Andrew Rau-Chaplin. In footnote 16, Holly Smith notes the analogy between this coordination problem and that faced by D. H. Regan's cooperative utilitarians (*Utilitarianism and Co-operation* [Oxford: Clarendon Press, 1980]) with concern about the "daunting complexity" of Regan's solution. To assure readers that that our solution to the coherence problem is workably simple, I defined SC in (nearly) executable Prolog code in the text (which adds to the original version in Danielson, ibid.,) J. V. Howard, "Cooperation in the Prisoner's Dilemma," *Theory and Decision* 24 (1988): 203–13, proposes something similar to sc1 and presents a program that will recognize identical copies of itself. Unfortunately, Howard's self-matching program is written in BASIC, a language ill-suited for mapping programs onto data. Notice that sc1's three-line predicate does more (because it recognizes its own type by matching with substitution and cooperates) than Howard's one-page BASIC program.

pliance dilemma will recur on the question of revealing one's metastrategy versus nonrevelation. However, this will not happen. Recall that SC agents only cooperate when the other player is known to be an SC agent. SC defects on indeterminate agents. This gives adherents of SC a reason to reveal their metastrategies, otherwise fellow SC agents will not cooperate with them. Finally, there is no danger in revealing the SC metastrategy, since it is individually rational and not open to exploitation. Therefore, this revelation game is not another Prisoner's Dilemma, but a benign coordination problem.

I have sketched an answer to the procedural objection to symmetrical conditional metastrategies. It is possible to be committed to cooperate on condition that others are committed conditionally to cooperate. First, it is possible to devise metastrategies that take other metastrategies as their antecedents. Second, the publicity required by this linkage of principles is motivated by the conditional metastrategies themselves. One runs no risk by revealing a key to one's compliance that can only be used by an agent transparently committed to comply with you.

Indirection in a Lamarckian world

The objector might continue: coordination by matching only works if agents happen to have *exactly* the same decision procedure. The SC agents I have constructed cannot determine whether agents with different decision procedures are functionally equivalent to each other. In order to avoid incoherence, my SC agents were forced to give up actually testing (use) the other's decision function in favor of matching (mention). Moreover, as I indicated at the beginning of the section entitled "Self-same cooperation," selfsame cooperation falls short of what substantive rationality requires. For example, SC fails to cooperate with CC, whereas a rational RC agent should cooperate in this case. Our SC solution to the coherence problem appears to be a dead end, as it supplies no hints how to go on to discriminate those dissimilar agents suitable for safe cooperation.

Note that the first objection is not a problem for *Morals by Agreement*, which uses a social contract to resolve coordination problems. Rational contractors presumably would agree to use the same decision procedure to avoid a coordination problem. The second problem remains: How can we generalize coherent but intolerant selfsame cooperation into more tolerate metastrategies, like RC? I will now sketch one solution to this problem. (Only sketch because the decision procedures quickly get quite complex. The details are worked out in *Artificial Morality*.)

Gauthier's argument for constrained maximization is, roughly, a form of indirect self-interested maximization. Self-interested agents can be seen as choosing a principle, or disposition, that they use to select particular actions that a directly self-interested straightforward maximizer would not select. Gauthier emphasizes that that no actual second-order choice is required; it is merely a "heuristic device."[33] For all that I have said so far, it is possible that constrained maximizers come hardwired for rational morality. However, I want to go beyond Gauthier's argument in this respect as well and suggest procedural reasons to make this second-order choice actual and to introduce it into the interaction. Consider an indirect maximizing (IM) agent, who can in *each* interaction choose that principle that will best satisfy her preferences. Should an IM agent meet a SC agent in a Prisoner's Dilemma, she will adopt the SC principle. More precisely, she will adopt *whatever decision procedure* the SC agent reveals, since this is the only way to get the SC agent to cooperate (and there is no way to exploit the SC agent). Therefore, indirect maximizers can solve the coordination problem that arises between different variations on the SC theme. They adapt by learning. They generate trial principles by copying with substitution the principles that SC agents willingly reveal and select by appeal to a maximizing test.

Moreover, IM agents can extend their principles beyond selfsame co-operation. For example, consider an IM agent meeting a conditional cooperator. Now the SC principle does poorly (it leads to joint defection) so the IM agent will adopt CC as her own principle. (I skip over important details such as why she doesn't learn UC and indeed how CC works procedurally.) Finally, an IM agent meeting UC or SM will adopt SM. Thus, an IM agent is a coherent procedural implementation of the RC principle. The resulting IM/RC agent solves the coherence problem and also the second-level coordination problem between principles. Self-interested agents, capable of selectively copying other's public-constraining principles can implement reciprocal cooperation. RC is procedurally possible in what I label a Lamarckian world.[34]

---

[33] Gauthier writes:

> But the idea of a choice among dispositions to choose is a heuristic device to express the underlying requirement, that a rational disposition to choose be utility-maximizing. In parametric contexts, the disposition to make straight-forwardly maximizing choices is uncontroversially utility-maximizing. We may therefore employ the device of a parametric choice among dispositions to choose to show that in strategic contexts, the disposition to make constrained choices, rather than straightforward maximizing choices, is utility-maximizing. We must however emphasize that it is not the choice itself, but the maximizing character of the disposition in virtue of which it is choiceworthy, that is the key to our argument. (P. 183)

[34] Why Lamarck and not Darwin? Because of the emphasis on learning as more appropriate to a rational moral theory than genetic inheritance and random variation. Also Lamarck's pioneering functionalism deserves recognition, cf. Steven Gould, *The Flamingo's Smile* (New York: Norton, 1985), p. 35ff.

Reciprocal versus conditional cooperation

Having shown reciprocal cooperation to be coherent, the question arises whether it is uniquely favored by procedural considerations. In particular, is reciprocal cooperation easier to implement than conditional cooperation? I think not. Conditional cooperation can be implemented in a way similar to reciprocal cooperation.

Indirect maximization shows the reciprocal cooperator to be an opportunist at the second level of choice. An agent who rejected maximization here as well as at the first level would differ from IM/RC; when it met UC, it would choose a cooperative principle. This indirect cooperator implements conditional cooperation. The indirect cooperator is otherwise similar to the indirect maximizer. They share the ability to solve coordination problems between principles, for example. Therefore, it is possible to implement CC in a way parallel to RC. Neither is procedurally impossible; CC is as easy to implement as RC.

Indeed, it may seem that conditional cooperation is procedurally much easier to implement than reciprocal cooperation. This is true in iterated Prisoner's Dilemma, where CC can be implemented by the elegantly simple strategy of tit for tat. (Something similar is true in sequential Prisoner's Dilemmas, mentioned in footnote 26.) But in the standard case of the simultaneous Prisoner's Dilemma, CC is no easier to implement. In particular, it may seem that CC could use its willingness to cooperate with UC to avoid regress, say, by cooperating with and only with those who cooperate with UC. But a moment's reflection will show that this strategy, although procedurally appealing, is both over- and undercooperative. It will cooperate with, and so be exploited by, an agent who cooperates *only* with UC, and it will fail to cooperate with RC, who is willing to cooperate with CC but not UC.

Although it does not cash out into narrow procedural advantage, there remains something appealing about conditional cooperators' willingness to cooperate with unconditional cooperators. I shall turn to the moral aspect of this appeal in the next section. In addition, indirect maximizers acquiesce to threats that indirect cooperators may be able to resist. This difference raises important issues that I take up elsewhere.

Conclusion

To answer the criticism that all forms of constrained maximization must be incoherent, I have shown how to build coherent conditionally constrained agents. Reciprocal cooperators can be implemented as indirect maximizers. They are no more difficult to build than conditional cooperators.

Morality

Although reciprocal cooperation is both substantively and procedurally rational, it may seem surprising that I propose it as a solution to the compliance problem. The compliance dilemma pits rationality against morality. Reciprocal cooperators, whose distinguishing feature is their willingness to exploit innocent unconditional cooperators, are evidently morally defective. By showing that rationality directs one to exploit innocent unconditional cooperators, reciprocal cooperators reopen the gap between rationality and morality. They are part of the compliance problem, not part of its solution. In this new compliance dilemma, rationality points to RC and morality to CC. This section addresses this new dilemma. First, I examine the moral criticism of reciprocal cooperation in order to establish its basis in moral principle. Then I show that Gauthier's principle of constrained maximization also fares badly by this moral standard. Finally, I admit that there are morally more attractive solutions to the problem of innocents, but the most obvious of these may be procedurally unattainable.

A gap between rationality and morality

Since rationality points to RC and morality to CC, there are two strategies that one might pursue to close this new gap. On the one hand, one can try to show conditional cooperation to be more rational; on the other, one can try to show reciprocal cooperation to be less immoral. Gauthier works in both these ways. For example, to make CC rationally more appealing, he speculates about the role of emotion:

What if these dispositions are themselves objects of preferences? Danielson, focusing on artificial morality, can avoid this problem by the appropriate construction of his agents. I cannot. . . . [H]uman beings have . . . emotions that affect their willingness and ability to behave in different ways. The desirability of cultivating feelings supportive of cooperative practices and inimical to predation, exploitation, and free-riding may well support, at this richer level of analysis, conditional cooperation. (Artifice, p. 401f.)

This is not an appeal to ad hoc higher-order preferences that make CC substantively rational. Instead, I take it to be a claim that constraints on human decision making make conditionally cooperative emotions procedurally rational in terms of preexisting preferences. I do not deny that there are situations in which CC is rational. For example, there is strong evidence that in indefinitely iterated play of the Prisoner's Dilemma, tit for tat, which is a version of CC, is rational. Axelrod argues that tit for tat's success is due to the ease with which it is recognized. This reason might carry over to noniterated play in conditions of less than complete transparency. Also, Hobbes argues for a principle closer to CC than RC for humans.[35] But any appeal to emotional rigidities in humans sits uncomfortably in Gauthier's rational-choice framework with its appeal to perfect agents. Is it rational to be emotionally constrained? Does the argument for constraint depend on human cognitive shortcomings? Leaving aside these speculations about complex human rationality and morality, let us turn to the other horn of the dilemma, and look at ways to defend RC morally.

Why is reciprocal cooperation immoral?

Reciprocal cooperators may seem nastier than they are, so I begin by clearing away one possible misperception. Notice that my argument for reciprocal cooperation is not based on the possibility of deception (cf. Sayre-McCord, "Deception and Reasons to Be Moral," Chapter 12 in this volume). As Gauthier points out, "To avoid misunderstanding, note that a reciprocal cooperator is not engaged in a game of 'second-guessing.' He does not seek to fool others, to take advantage of those who are taken in by his cooperative disposition" (Artifice, p. 400). The argument for RC over CC is valid in a strongly transparent artificial world where deception is impossible. Reciprocal cooperators are not deceivers.

Now I address the main question: Is reciprocal cooperation moral according to Gauthier's own standard of impartiality? It may seem obvious that reciprocal cooperation lacks "the impartiality characteristic of morality" (p. 4). However, this is not so clear, due to the character of Gauthier's argument for constrained maximization. Unlike his arguments for the principle of rational bargaining and the proviso constraining the initial bargaining position, Gauthier devotes his entire effort in Chapter VII to showing that constrained maximization is rational, not moral. This is understandable, since, as I noted earlier, he considers no alternative to constrained maximization but straightforward maximization.[36] Since the former aims at fair optimal outcomes, its moral superiority to the latter is evident. However introducing additional alternatives to the conditionally cooperative strategy contained in constrained maximization leads to new questions of comparative moral value, even in terms of impartiality.

It is not clear how the moral standard of impartiality regards retri-

[35] See G. Kavka, *Hobbesian Moral and Political Theory*, sec. 9-4, on the asymmetry of Hobbes' laws of nature with respect to maximizing and minimizing conditions. R. Axelrod, *Evolution of Cooperation*, defends tit for tat as rational in the iterated PD; since tit for tat cooperates with unconditional cooperators, it is analogous to CC.

[36] Gauthier does distinguish two strategies *within* constrained maximization, broad and narrow compliance.

butive defection. It seems appropriate that CC and RC defect against a defecting straightforward maximizer, but some claim that impartiality requires cooperation even in this case.[37] Matters become less clear when we attempt morally to rank CC and RC. CC cooperates with unconditional cooperators and so expresses impartiality at the level of behavior: cooperate with cooperators. RC defects on UC, but may rejoin in her own moral defense that UC is immorally indiscriminate in cooperating with defectors. Thus, reciprocal cooperation can be seen as expressing impartiality at the level of principle: cooperate only with the morally discriminating. However, there is a problem with this defense of reciprocal cooperation as impartial. Since cooperating with amoral defectors makes UC amoral, shouldn't CC's cooperation with amoral UC brand her also as indiscriminating and hence amoral? But RC cooperates with CC.[38]

I conclude that the moral standard of impartiality is not easy to apply to a situation consisting of several different sorts of agents. Nonetheless, RC is not clearly inferior to CC according to this standard. First, like CC, reciprocal cooperation requires genuine self-constraint in the keeping of distributively fair agreements in the Prisoner's Dilemma. Second, RC is impartial to all moral agents, if we are careful to delimit the set of moral agents by their compliance with conditional principles of rational morality rather than by simple cooperation. Third, RC also encourages others to cooperate, because, although it penalizes UC, the lesson communicated is cooperate in a more sophisticated, discriminating manner. As Gauthier writes, "Reciprocal co-operators . . . help make the world safe for morality" (Artifice, p. 401).

Protecting innocents

But Gauthier continues:

This is not an appealing argument. If the farmer, in order to protect his chickens from the foxes, eliminates the local rabbits, thus reducing the foxes' overall food supply and encouraging them to go elsewhere, it does seem rather hard on the innocent rabbits. But of course rabbits cannot help being rabbits, whereas unconditional cooperators can presumably mend their guileless but costly ways. . . . [M]any of us might prefer reeducating unconditional cooperators to exploiting them. (Artifice, p. 401)

---

[37] See Regan, *Utilitarianism and Co-operation*, p. 73, for an argument against punishment where expectations cannot be altered. Applying this argument to the Prisoner's Dilemma requires stronger interpersonal comparisons of utilities than Gauthier's theory requires or supports.

[38] Contrast Maynard Smith's more consistent principle: "I will cooperate; I will join in punishing any defection; I will treat any member who does not join in punishing as a defector." "The Evolution of Animal Intelligence," in C. Hookway, ed., *Minds, Machines, and Evolution* (Cambridge: Cambridge University Press, 1984), pp. 68–9.

I agree that it would be better costlessly to reeducate unconditional cooperators. But this is not an option in the stark situations that Gauthier and I employ to test various principles. Of course, one can teach by example (as we saw in the section entitled "Indirection in a Lamarckian world"), but the only way to *motivate* another rational agent is through the carrot and stick of cooperation and defection. (Does this conclusion make our minimalism objectionable? No. The point of projecting the problems of rationality and morality onto such meager landscapes as the Prisoner's Dilemma is to force hard decisions upon us, to reveal problems starkly and to avoid appeals that would undermine a fundamental justification of morality.) So Gauthier's call to reeducate UC instead of exploiting her is moot. We are left with the alternatives of exploiting UC or maintaining her.

What does morality require here and why? I conjecture that we need to go beyond impartiality to a standard focusing on the treatment of innocents. Impartiality does not adequately address the problems introduced by the presence of naive unconditional cooperators. Although CC is more impartial toward UC, CC can still be criticized for failing to protect UC from RC. Reciprocal cooperators *exploit* unconditional cooperators; that is, RC makes UC worse off than the noncooperative baseline even when this is not necessary to protecting RC from SM. Reciprocal cooperators violate our sense that innocents ought not to be exploited, at least in cases where this is not required for self-defense. (Note that while Gauthier defends RC as protecting itself indirectly from SM, he sees that this rationale does not hold under the conditions of full transparency that I have assumed, where SM can never exploit RC; cf. Artifice, p. 401, quoted in the earlier section entitled "An evolutionary test.") Therefore, I introduce a second moral standard (impartiality is the first): minimize the exploitation of innocents.[39]

As I have already hinted, in terms of this moral standard, conditional cooperators do no better than reciprocal cooperators. Conditional cooperators encourage unconditional cooperators, which the conditional cooperators then fail to protect from exploitation from RC. By cooperating with RC, CC acquiesces in RC's treatment of UC. So, in an evolutionary perspective, RC, by making UC irrational, prevents the exploitation of these innocents. CC, on the other hand, is inconsistent in its treatment of unconditional cooperators. It encourages UC agents, only to let them be exploited. Therefore, we can grant that RC is morally criticizable for preying on UC, but CC is also criticizable. Indeed, since our standard aims to minimize the number

---

[39] This is a teleological standard; a deontological standard that prohibited only the direct exploitation of innocents would favor CC.

of innocents exploited, conditional cooperation may fare worse than reciprocal cooperation.

A moral alternative

The foregoing is unsatisfactory. Must rational morality choose between two evils: CC, which abandons innocents, and RC, who preys upon them? No; it need not. Once again, we should explore additional principles. I introduce a new strategy that protects innocents directly and indirectly by refusing to cooperate with those who refuse to cooperate with UC:

Unconditional Cooperator Protector (UCP): Cooperate with and only with those who (a) Cooperate with Unconditional Cooperators and (b) Cooperate with Unconditional Cooperator Protectors. Like a conditional cooperator, UCP cooperates with an UC; unlike CC, UCP carries through on the defense of UC by refusing to cooperate with anyone who defects with an UC, such as RC. UCP is morally more attractive, than CC. Notice that although inspired by Smith's CUC, UCP is a great improvement, both morally and rationally, since it cooperates with itself. UCP protects the unconditional cooperators that it fosters, making it morally superior both to CC, who lets innocent unconditional cooperators be exploited, and RC, who exploits them.

Recall that this section began with a new compliance dilemma, with rational RC vying with purportedly moral CC. UCP changes this picture. UCP is the alternative that should hold down the moral side of the dilemma. This leads us to examine more closely the rationality of UCP. UCP refuses to cooperate with RC not because RC refuses to cooperate with it, but because of RC's treatment of UC. UCP embodies what Axelrod calls a metanorm supporting cooperation.[40] As a result, UCP cannot invade any population that contains RC; CC will always do better than UCP. This may lead one to think that UCP is irrational. But the population containing RC is not canonical for the evolutionary test of substantive rationality. Indeed, if UCP enters the population first, RC cannot invade, so the situation is almost symmetrical. "Almost symmetrical," because should UCP allow too many

---

[40] Robert Axelrod, "An Evolutionary Approach to Norms," *American Political Science Review* 80 (1986): 1095–111. UCP is not completely free of moral inconsistency. It cooperates with CC, who tolerates RC, who is immoral by UCP's principle. A stronger metanorm excluding CC from cooperation with UCP would be costly on the substantive rationality side.

unconditional cooperators to enter the population, RC can invade.[41] As long as UCP is careful to keep the number of UC below this limit, it can keep RC out. Summing up, neither RC nor UCP is rationally superior according to our substantive standard based on the ability to invade the other.

This suggests a way to close our second compliance dilemma. Rational morality should recommend UCP over RC. Rational moral agents should try to make their world safe for morality *and innocence,* and this is not irrational. However, this conclusion is premature. Although UCP is not substantively irrational in tiny situations, we have not considered whether it is procedurally possible or workable in more complex situations. UCP's need to check for indirect defection against UC and the requirement to maintain a population control on UC suggest formidable procedural difficulties. For example, why should an indirect maximizing RC agent admit to exploiting unconditional cooperators? Therefore, UCP agents will need to restrict their cooperation to indirect cooperators – but UCP is not herself an indirect cooperator. Therefore, a more thorough test of the rationality of UCP versus RC will depend on the robustness of indirect maximization in other situations (for example, where threat resistance is valuable) and the feasibility of implementing UCP. Although I suspect that the balance of procedural and substantive factors will favor RC, I must leave their consideration to another occasion.

Conclusion

I am ambivalent about the conclusions of this section. I set out to argue for several theses that do not run together here. First, my defense of reciprocal cooperation is strengthened by its positive moral showing compared to conditional cooperation, in terms of Gauthier's own standard of impartiality and even on the standard of protecting the innocent. Second, and more importantly, the compliance dilemma appears more tractable when we see that the morally appealing alternative of protecting unconditional cooperators is not substantively irrational. Finally, I am pleased that the method of artificial morality generates new strat-

---

[41] Using the standard notation for payoffs in the PD (see Figure 16-5), the threshold is that point when the product of the number of UC agents times $(T - R)$ equals the product of the number of UCC agents times $(R - P)$.

	c	d
c	R R	R S T
d	S T	P P

Figure 16-5.

egies as interesting as UCP and provides a way to test them, even though they may prove superior to reciprocal cooperation.

Conclusion

David Gauthier's concept of constrained maximization is a path-breaking attempt to solve the compliance problem, "the profoundest problem in ethics." Constrained maximizers are discriminating; they cooperate with and only with the similarly disposed. But it is not clear how similar a disposition it is rational and moral to demand. Other agents may be more, less, or exactly as cooperative as oneself. In each case, we have seen that Gauthier's preferred disposition is problematic. Constrained maximizers' agents cooperate with niave unconditional cooperators. I argued that this is not rational and that allowing others to exploit these innocent agents is also not moral. The third section showed that the problem of coordinating with agents very similar to oneself requires more procedural specification than Gauthier provides.

I conclude that reciprocal cooperation is more rational and no less moral than constrained maximization. Thus, reciprocal cooperation tentatively closes the compliance dilemma in the two-player Prisoner's Dilemma. This is a crucial testing ground for rational morality, but it is not the only test. Indeed, in retrospect, the Prisoner's Dilemma appears ideally suited for the combination of openness and opportunistic adaptation that enable reciprocal cooperators to prevail. Other situations, like Chicken and many-player games, may prove resistant to these techniques. For this reason, I have tried not only to specify a decision procedure that solves the compliance problem in the PD, but also to develop methods to generate and test new candidates for rational morality in other situations. We have seen that it is often hard to imagine new alternatives and difficult to test them due to strategic complexities. Both problems have their analogues in the field of artificial intelligence. I conjecture that artificial morality will prove to be a fruitful way to develop and test the seminal ideas of *Morals by Agreement*.

17 Rational constraint: Some last words

David Gauthier

The view ex post differs from the view ex ante. Critical response and further reflection would yield a different book. Despite the best efforts of some of my critics to convince me otherwise, I still think that most, and the most important, of the particular arguments that appear in *Morals by Agreement* (henceforth *MbA*) are sound. But when I wrote *MbA* I did not fully grasp the structure of the theory of which the particular arguments are the parts. I shall therefore take the opportunity afforded to me here of having (for the moment) the last word to say something about this structure.

I treat morality as involving *constraint*. I introduce this idea in the opening pages of *MbA*, claiming "to defend the traditional conception of morality as a rational constraint on the pursuit of individual interest" (p. 2). This formulation is unfortunately misleading insofar as it suggests that morality merely constrains egoism; I want to defend morality as a rational constraint on the pursuit of one's aims or objectives, whether or not these objectives have any connection with one's interest, or one's personal well-being.[1] Yet, of course, I also want to insist that one acts rationally in pursuing one's aims or objectives; the formal aim of the rational individual is the maximum realization of her substantive aims.

---

[1] Not only my reference to interest, but my insistence on nontuism, is misleading. Christopher Morris discusses some of the problems with nontuism in "The Relation between Self-Interest and Justice in Contractarian Ethics," in *The New Social Contract: Essays on Gauthier*, edited by E. F. Paul, F. D. Miller, Jr., and J. Paul (Oxford: Blackwell, 1988), pp. 154–72 (the contents of this volume appear also as *Social Philosophy and Policy* 5 [1988], with the same pagination); see my reply in "Morality, Rational Choice, and Semantic Representation: A Reply to My Critics," in the same volume, pp. 213–17. See also Christopher Morris, "Moral Standing and Rational Choice-Contractarianism," and Peter Vallentyne, "Contractarianism and the Assumption of Mutual Unconcern," Chapters 6 and 5, respectively, in this volume.

How then can a constraint on the pursuit of one's aims be rational? And if such a constraint is rational, is it therefore moral?

In *MbA*, I appeal to the structure of interaction made explicit in the Prisoner's Dilemma (henceforth PD) to show how constraint can be rational and how rational constraint can be moral. In a PD, each person has a strongly dominant action or strategy – that is, an action that is her best response (in terms of maximizing the realization of her substantive aims) to whatever be the action or actions of the other(s). Each does best, then, to choose her dominant action. But everyone would do better were each to choose some alternative action, and so to exercise constraint in pursuing the realization of her substantive aims. Each would do worse, of course, from her own constraint, but each would gain more from the constraint of the other or others than she would lose from her own.

Introducing the PD, and noting its ubiquity in interaction, naturally suggests that persons, expecting to face such situations, would do best, individually and collectively, to agree to mutual constraints. No one, seeking the maximum realization of her aims, would rationally undertake to constrain her direct pursuit of that realization unilaterally, but each should rationally agree to constrain herself provided her fellows do the same. We thus show how a constraint on the pursuit of one's aims can be rational. And since a constraint is rational only insofar as it is mutual, so that a rational constraint applies in the same way to everyone, it exhibits the impartiality that, we may suppose, identifies it with morality. Confirmation of this last claim is found if there is a significant overlap between the constraints that would result from the agreement of rational persons and the traditional principles of morality.

I find the argument condensed in the last two paragraphs extremely compelling. And it leads us into the heart of the contractarian understanding of morals and politics. Although we should not suppose that our actual moral practices and social institutions result from agreement, we may nevertheless hold that the appropriate justificatory test for the principles, practices, and institutions that govern and structure human interaction in ways that constrain the individuals involved is whether they would have been accepted by those individuals were they fully rational persons, each concerned to advance his own good (or the realization of his substantive aims), and collectively able to determine ex ante their terms and conditions of interaction by voluntary and unanimous agreement. This test is seen by the contractarian as affording a justification that is at once rational and moral. I defend a specific interpretation of it in *MbA*, claiming that fully rational persons would reach agreement by bargaining on the basis of the principle of minimax relative concession (MRC), and that their agreement would be voluntary and their subsequent interaction fully cooperative provided that none of them bargained from an initial position that violated a revised Lockean Proviso, which essentially prohibits persons from bettering their own position by worsening that of others.

How far my particular account of the contractarian test affords an adequate way of specifying the underlying idea of rational agreement is evidently a matter for debate. I am now convinced that MRC needs at least some modification. Marlies Klemisch-Ahlert has offered a rigorous formulation of the intuitive ideas underlying the principle.[2] As she shows, for the general (n-person) case, MRC should be replaced by a lexicographic principle, which can be formulated as a maximin principle in relative utility gains (relative benefit in my terminology) as she does, or as a minimax principle in relative concessions. I believe that this meets the *formal* inadequacies of MRC for bargaining involving more than two persons. There may be, however, a deeper inadequacy, since both MRC and Klemisch-Ahlert's lexicographic principle ignore the structure of the interactions by which what is distributed in bargaining has been produced. Whether and how to refine either the formulation of MRC, or the way in which it is applied to interactions in order to accommodate this structure, are unresolved issues. My brief discussion in "Moral Artifice," where I am primarily concerned to reply to Jean Hampton's objections to MRC, only sketches some of the dimensions of the problem.[3]

To discuss the other part of the contractarian test – the revised Lockean Proviso – would take me far beyond the bounds of these brief remarks. The formulation of the proviso in *MbA* is at best only a first approximation.[4] But a more adequate formulation would leave unanswered the strong challenges that may be brought against its relevance for both agreement and compliance. Occasionally, I find myself tempted to discharge the proviso from its contractarian employment, giving it a strong letter of recommendation to rights theorists seeking a principled basis for their position. But then I find myself once more convinced that it is exactly that power of the proviso – to convert, as it were, a Hobbesian state of nature into a Lockean one – that is needed in a full contractarian moral theory. Hoping to clarify these matters in my unwritten paper (tentatively titled "Rational Choice and the Lockean Proviso"), I pass on to the principal theme of these comments.

Important as the contractarian test is, I have come to realize that it is not the central theme of *MbA*. Morality, as I have said, involves *constraint*,

---

[2] See Wulf Gaertner and Marlies Klemisch-Ahlert, "Gauthier's Approach to Distributive Justice and Other Bargaining Solutions," Chapter 11 in this volume.

[3] See Jean Hampton, "Equalizing Concessions in the Pursuit of Justice: A Discussion of Gauthier's Bargaining Solution," Chapter 10 in this volume, and my "Moral Artifice," *Canadian Journal of Philosophy* 18 (1988): 395–8.

[4] See the critique by Don Hubin and Mark B. Lambeth in "Providing for Rights," Chapter 8 in this volume.

but constraint is not in itself a moral concept. It is, however, the key concept of my theory, and it should be understood prior to introducing morality. This is not best done by relating it solely to the basis afforded by the PD for rational agreement. In *MbA*, I do, of course, recognize that to show the rationality of agreeing to mutual constraints is not to show the rationality of actually complying with or adhering to those constraints. I follow the familiar progression of Hobbes's argument in *Leviathan*, recognizing that agreement (the theme of his second law of nature) is distinct from compliance (the theme of his third law), and that the Foole's objections to the third law must be answered. But this progression obscures as much as it reveals, and I have come to the view that whatever may be the links between agreement and compliance (and I remain convinced that there are such links), the fundamental argument for the rationality of accepting and complying with certain constraints on the direct pursuit of one's substantive aims does not depend on supposing either that others will comply with them, or that it would be rational to accept them if and only if others agree to accept them as well.

The argument for the rationality of compliance is best understood if we recognize that it has no essential connection with the PD, and is simply an instance of a more general argument for the rationality of accepting certain constraints. And this more general argument has no direct connection with morality; the constraints it justifies need be neither mutual nor impartial. Consider a story quite different from that of the prisoners. You and I have been engaged in some clandestine activity, and each of us is now considering whether to reveal our involvement. Each of us knows that if either of us talks, he will represent the other's involvement unfavorably. Therefore, neither of us wants the other to talk. But if the other does talk, neither of us wants to have remained silent. I don't want my involvement revealed; I strongly prefer that we both be silent. You, however, would like best to tell your story, if you could do so before I tell mine. The situation has this structure:

	You talk	You remain silent
I talk	mutual second worst	my second best, your worst
I remain silent	my worst, your best	my best, your second best

You have a dominant strategy: talk. If I know your preferences, I know this, and I have a best response: talk. The outcome is, as in the PD, the mutual second worst. But if I could count on you to remain silent, then my best response would be to remain silent, and we should both do better. If you know my preferences, you know this, and so you want to convince me that you will remain silent – even if the price of convincing me is the cost of actually remaining silent. To be sure, you would prefer to deceive me. But you may believe, and be correct to believe, that your prospect of deceiving me is slim. Unless you are sincerely committed to remaining silent, I shall not trust you and shall talk.

Suppose you believe that, if you are committed to remaining silent, you will be able to communicate your commitment to me, so that there is a high probability that I shall remain silent. And you believe that if you are not committed to remaining silent, then there is a high probability that I shall talk. Suppose you prefer a high probability of mutual silence with the alternative that I alone talk to a high probability of mutual talking with the alternative that you alone talk. Then it is rational for you to commit yourself to the constraint of remaining silent. And this commitment is independent of any expectation you have about my willingness to accept any constraints.

In *MbA* I defend *conditional compliance* in PD-type situations. I argue that if you are confronted with a PD, it is rational for you agree to act in a way that is mutually advantageous rather than individually maximal, and to comply with this agreement given that you expect the other person to comply (or, in the case of several others, given that you expect sufficient compliance). It might seem, from this argument, that only conditional compliance is rational. It might be supposed, therefore, that constraint, to be rational, must be mutual. By treating morality as a matter of mutual constraint, it might seem that all rational constraint is moral. But the example we have just considered shows that this would be mistaken. In some situations, it is rational for an individual to accept a unilateral constraint on his efforts to maximize the realization of his aims.

I emphasize this, not only to remove the temptation to equate rational constraint with morality, but also to correct possible misinterpretations of my defense of conditional compliance in *MbA*. Some persons want to argue that it is rational to act in a mutually advantageous way in PD situations, provided others do so as well, because one gains more from their constraint than one loses from one's own. This is a bad argument, which I totally reject. However, in focusing on mutual constraint in *MbA*, my rejection of it may be less clear than it should be. It is rational to act in a mutually advantageous way in PD situations, if one gains more from one's own disposition to constraint, than one loses from one's actual exercise of constraint. This is a good argument; it is the argument of *MbA*; and it has nothing to do with mutuality.

I cannot embark here on the task of constructing a theory of rational constraint. I explore some relevant ideas in a recent paper.[5] The key idea might be expressed as *opportunity maximization*. The rational individual

---

[5] See "In the Neighbourhood of the Newcomb-Predictor (Reflections on Rationality)," *Proceedings of the Aristotelian Society* 89 (1989): 179–94.

develops those dispositions, forms those intentions, and adopts those plans that afford him the most favorable opportunities, even though they may require him to act in ways that do not maximize the realization of his aims. In his interactions, others are led, through knowledge or belief about his dispositions, intentions, and plans, to behave in ways that enable him to do better, even though he does not maximize, than he could expect to do were he believed to be disposed to perform only maximizing acts. Thus, in our example, believing that you intend to keep silent, I keep silent; you then do better, keeping silent, than you could expect to do were I, believing that you would always maximize and so talk, myself to talk.

Prominent among the issues that a theory of rational constraint must face is the way in which constraint is to be characterized. Some, influenced by the view that the agent's aims are revealed in her choices, would insist that one cannot, literally, choose a nonmaximizing act. Wishing to assure me of your silence, you do not commit yourself to an act that would not best realize your aims, but rather you change your aims, coming to prefer silence to talk. Instead of treating your aims simply as exogenously given, we allow them to be endogenously revisable. You exhibit what, from the standpoint of your original aims, would seem to be constraint, but in fact you act so as best to fulfill your revised aims.[6]

Others, willing to admit that an agent can choose a nonmaximizing act, nevertheless deny that such a choice can be truly rational. Wishing to assure me of your silence, you commit yourself, quite rationally, to an act that itself is irrational. Constraint is an instance of rational irrationality.[7]

I reject both of these interpretations, holding that an agent can choose a nonmaximizing act and can do so with full rationality. You choose to keep silent, and your reason for so choosing is found in your belief that, had you not been committed so to choose, you would be less favorably placed and would be realizing your aims to a lesser extent than you are actually doing. But I cannot debate the possible interpretations of constraint here. I mention them simply to emphasize their importance on the agenda set by the idea of rational constraint.

In a revised presentation of the ideas of *MbA*, I should establish the rationality of certain forms of constraint before introducing the PD as revealing a structure of interaction calling for mutual constraints. And I should then focus on the interpretation of mutuality. In *MbA*, I treat mutuality as requiring *conditional* cooperation; a rational person should

[6] The position mentioned in this paragraph is suggested by Edward F. McClennen in "Constrained Maximization and Resolute Choice," *The New Social Contract*, pp. 108–18.
[7] The position mentioned in this paragraph is suggested by Derek Parfit, *Reasons and Persons* (Oxford: Clarendon Press, 1984), pp. 1–23.

constrain her behavior in interactions with persons who, she expects, will exercise constraint themselves. Peter Danielson has argued that I should treat mutuality as requiring *reciprocal* cooperation; a rational person should constrain her behavior in interactions with persons who, she expects, exercise constraint in interaction with, and only with, those who, they expect, exercise constraint.[8] I take the issues raised by Danielson to be important and unresolved. His book, *Artificial Morality: How to Make Morality Rational,* will be a major contribution to advancing our understanding of the form that mutual constraint should take.

Only after addressing mutuality, would I introduce morality in my hypothetically rewritten *MbA.* I should appeal to the structure of the PD to show how the general argument for the rationality of certain constraints may be applied to the subclass of mutual constraints. And I should then characterize morality as a set of dispositions, both practical and affective, that enables agents who have the capacity for constraint to exercise that capacity so that they may engage in cooperative ventures for mutual advantage (to adapt, as I so often do, Rawls' useful phrase). In this way, we may reach a contractarian understanding of the *form* of morality. Note that this understanding makes no explicit reference to agreement; the contractarian element is provided entirely by the requirement of mutuality. And it leaves the content of morality quite unspecified; the dispositions that are considered moral virtues and the principles that establish moral obligations have yet to be rationally determined.

Is there a problem in determining them? It may seem that we need only consider which of those constraints that are generally accepted an individual should rationally follow. If morality consists in constraints that are both rational and mutual, what else could be relevant? Here is the point in a contractarian moral theory at which the idea of agreement is needed. As I noted near the beginning of these comments, in recognizing the benefits of mutual constraints, we are naturally led to consider them as possible objects of rational agreement. Each person must find it rational to agree with her fellows to constrain her behavior in certain determinate ways, provided she may expect others to do so as well. And it is the constraints that individuals would find it rational to agree to, rather than the ones that they actually find it rational to accept, that provide the content of contractarian morality.

The actual principles and practices that most persons accept and comply with need have little to do with realizing mutual benefit. Given that most persons accept them, and expect others to do so as well, a particular

[8] See "Closing the Compliance Dilemma: How It's Rational to be Moral in a Lamarckian World," Chapter 16 in this volume, and "The Visible Hand of Morality," *Canadian Journal of Philosophy* 18 (1988): 376–83. I discuss this matter, briefly and quite inadequately, in "Moral Artifice," *Canadian Journal of Philosophy* 18 (1988): 399–402.

individual may find it rational to accept them herself. Now from a descriptive standpoint, we may say that these principles and practices constitute the morality of those who follow them. But a morality in this sense need have no rational foundation or justification. The only rationale for complying with it is that such compliance is expected. And, of course, once this is recognized, the morality is undermined. Only if the principles and practices would be agreed to, by persons seeking the fullest realization of their aims, would there be any substantive rationale for compliance. Recognition of such a rationale sustains morality, and the constraints it imposes.

Agreement thus enters the contractarian characterization of morality, bringing rationality into the specification of its contents, so that we may determine the particular principles, practices, and institutions with which each person would find it rational to commit herself to comply, could she expect general compliance. Here then is the place for the argument that I sketched at the very outset of these comments in support of the contractarian test, as a standard for both the morality and the rationality of constraint. But note that this argument idealizes the appeal to agreement, by treating the contractarian test, not as a matter of what persons would agree to given their actual social circumstances, but rather as a matter of what persons would agree to were they to choose ex ante their social circumstances. I defend this idealization by arguing that moral structures that satisfy the contractarian test may be expected to have a stability lacking in principles and practices that depend for their rationale on the particular structure of an actual society.[9] The test appeals to an agreement among persons for whom the usual social contingencies of bargaining are altogether irrelevant, and who lack any power to coerce each other. Thus, in reaching such an agreement, each may exercise only his own rationality, addressed to the equal rationality of his fellows. The constraints that the test endorses are, therefore, rationally salient. This salience both facilitates convergence on them as a basis for interaction and inhibits departures from that basis.

The conclusion of the contractarian argument is not that rational persons, whatever their actual circumstances, must comply with the constraints of morality. No argument could show that morality is rational in that sense. What the contractarian argument does show is that rational persons will recognize a role for constraints, both unilateral and mutual, in their choices and decisions, that rational persons would agree ex ante on certain mutual constraints were they able to do so, and that rational persons will frequently comply with those mutual constraints in their interactions. I claim no more in *MbA*, and I remain convinced that I am entitled to claim no less.

---

[9] See "Why Contractarianism?" Chapter 2 in this volume, and "Morality, Rational Choice, and Semantic Representation: A Reply to My Critics," *The New Social Contract*, pp. 177–90.

Bibliography

Note: Only works closely related to Gauthier's work are included here.

Arneson, Richard J. "Locke versus Hobbes in Gauthier's Ethics." *Inquiry* 30 (1987): 295–316.

Baier, Annette. "Pilgrim's Progress." *Canadian Journal of Philosophy* 18 (1988): 315–30.

Baier, Kurt. *The Moral Point of View: A Rational Basis of Ethics.* New York: Random House, 1965.

Baier, Kurt. "Rationality, Value and Preference." *Social Philosophy and Policy* 5 (1988): 17–45.

Barnett, Philip M. "Rational Behavior in Bargaining Situations." *Noûs* 17 (1983): 621–36.

Braybrooke, David. "Inequalities Not Conceded Yet: A Rejoinder to Gauthier's Reply." *Dialogue* (Canada) 21 (1982): 445–8.

Braybrooke, David. "The Maximum Claims of Gauthier's Bargainers: Are the Fixed Social Inequalities Acceptable?" *Dialogue* (Canada) 21 (1982): 411–29.

Braybrooke, David. "Social Contract Theory's Fanciest Flight." *Ethics* 97 (1987): 750–64.

Buchanan, James M. *The Limits of Liberty: Between Anarchy and Leviathan.* Chicago: The University of Chicago Press, 1975.

Buchanan, James M. "The Gauthier Enterprise." *Social Philosophy and Policy* 5 (1988): 75–94.

Campbell, Richmond, ed. *Paradoxes of Rationality and Cooperation.* Vancouver: University of British Columbia Press, 1985.

Campbell, Richmond. "Gauthier's Theory of Morals by Agreement." *Philosophical Quarterly* 38 (1988): 343–64.

Copp, David, and David Zimmerman, eds. *Morality, Reason, and Truth: New Essays on the Foundations of Ethics.* Totowa, NJ: Rowman and Allanheld, 1984.

Danielson, Peter. "The Visible Hand of Morality." *The Canadian Journal of Philosophy* 18 (1988): 357–84.

Danielson, Peter. *Artifical Morality.* London: Routledge, in press.

Darwall, Stephen. "Kantian Practical Reason Defended." *Ethics* 96 (1985): 89–99.

Darwall, Stephen. "Rational Agent, Rational Act." *Philosophical Topics* 14 (1986): 33–57.

Farrell, Daniel M. "Comments on Gauthier's 'Hobbes' Social Contract.' " *Noûs* 22 (1988): 83–4.

Fishkin, James S. "Bargaining, Justice, and Justification: Towards Reconstruction." *Social Philosophy and Policy* 5 (1988): 46–64.

Gauthier, David. *Practical Reasoning: The Structure and Foundation of Prudential and Moral Arguments and Their Exemplification in Discourse.* Oxford: Clarendon Press, 1963.

Gauthier, David. "The Philosophy of Revolution." *The University of Toronto Quarterly* 32 (1963): 126–41.

Gauthier, David. "Rule Utilitarianism and Randomization." *Analysis* 25 (1966): 68–9.

Gauthier, David. "The Role of Inheritence in Locke's Political Theory." *Canadian Journal of Economics and Political Science* 32 (1966): 38–45.

Gauthier, David. "How Decisions Are Caused." *Journal of Philosophy* 64 (1967): 147–51.

Gauthier, David. "Moore's Naturalistic Fallacy." *American Philosophical Quarterly* 4 (1967): 315–20.

Gauthier, David. "Morality and Advantage." *Philosophical Review* 76 (1967): 460–75.

Gauthier, David. "Progress and Happiness: A Utilitarian Reconsideration."*Ethics* 78 (1967): 77–82.

Gauthier, David. "Hare's Debtors." *Mind* 77 (1968): 400–05.

Gauthier, David. "How Decisions Are Caused (but Not Predicted)." *Journal of Philosophy* 65 (1968): 170–1.

Gauthier, David. "The Unity of Wisdom and Temperance." *Journal of the History of Philosophy* 6 (1968): 157–9.

Gauthier, David. *The Logic of Leviathan: The Moral and Political Theory of Thomas Hobbes.* Oxford: Clarendon Press, 1969.

Gauthier, David. "Yet Another Hobbes." *Inquiry* 12 (1969): 449–65.

Gauthier, David, ed. *Morality and Rational Self-Interest.* Englewood Cliffs, NJ: Prentice-Hall, 1970.

Gauthier, David. Comments on R. M. Hare, "Wanting: Some Pitfalls," in *Agent, Action, and Reason,* edited by R. Binkley, R. Bronaugh, and A. Marras, 98–108. Toronto: University of Toronto Press, 1971.

Gauthier, David. "Moral Action and Moral Education," in *Moral Education: Interdisciplinary Approaches,* edited by C. M. Beck, B. S. Crittenden, and E. V. Sullivan, 138–46. Toronto: University of Toronto Press, 1971.

Gauthier, David. "Justice and Natural Endowment: Toward a Critique of Rawls' Ideological Framework." *Social Theory and Practice* 3 (1974): 3–26.

Gauthier, David. "Rational Cooperation." *Noûs* 8 (1974): 53–65.

Gauthier, David. "The Impossibility of Rational Egoism." *Journal of Philosophy* 71 (1974): 439–65.

Gauthier, David. "Coordination." *Dialogue* 14 (1975): 195–221.

Gauthier, David. "Critical notice of Arthur C. Danto, *Analytical Philosophy of History.*" *Canadian Journal of Philosophy* 5 (1975): 463–71.

Gauthier, David. "Reason and Maximization." *Canadian Journal of Philosophy* 4 (1975): 411–33.

Gauthier, David. "Critical Notice of Stephen Korner (ed.), *Practical Reason*." *Dialogue* 16 (1977): 510–18.

Gauthier, David. "The Social Contract as Ideology." *Philosophy and Public Affairs* 6 (1977): 130–64.

Gauthier, David. "Why Ought One Obey God? Reflections on Hobbes and Locke." *Canadian Journal of Philosophy* 7 (1977): 425–46.

Gauthier, David. "Critical Notice of John C. Harsanyi, *Essays on Ethics*," *Social Behavior, and Scientific Explanation*. *Dialogue* 17 (1978): 696–706.

Gauthier, David. "Economic Rationality and Moral Constraints." *Midwest Studies in Philosophy* 3 (1978): 75–96.

Gauthier, David. "Social Choice and Distributive Justice." *Philosophia* 7 (1978): 239–53.

Gauthier, David. "The Social Contract: Individual Decision or Collective Bargain?" In *Foundations and Applications of Decision Theory*, Vol. 2, edited by Cliff Hooker, Jim Leach, and Edward McClennen, 47–67. Dordrecht, Holland: D. Reidel, 1978.

Gauthier, David. "Bargaining Our Way Into Morality: A Do-It-Yourself Primer." *Philosophical Exchange* (2) (1979): 15–27.

Gauthier, David. "Confederation, Contract, and Constitution." In *Philosophers Look at Canadian Confederation = La confederation canadienne: qu'en pensent les philosophes?* edited by S. G. French, 193–9. Montreal: Canadian Philosophical Association, 1979.

Gauthier, David. "David Hume: Contractarian." *Philosophical Review* 88 (1979): 3–38.

Gauthier, David. "Thomas Hobbes: Moral Theorist." *The Journal of Philosophy* 76 (1979): 547–59.

Gauthier, David. "The Irrationality of Choosing Egoism – A Reply to Eshelman." *Canadian Journal of Philosophy* 10 (1980): 179–87.

Gauthier, David. "The Politics of Redemption?" In *Trent Rousseau Papers*, edited by J. MacAdam, M. Neumann, and G. LaFrance, *Revue de l'Universite d'Ottawa* 49 (1980): 329–56.

Gauthier, David. "Justified Inequality?" *Dialogue* 21 (1982): 431–43.

Gauthier, David. "No Need For Morality: The Case of the Competitive Market." *Philosophical Exchange* 3 (1982): 41–54.

Gauthier, David. "On the Refutation of Utilitarianism." In *The Limits of Utilitarianism*, edited by Harlan Miller and William H. Williams, 144–63. Minneapolis: University of Minnesota Press, 1982.

Gauthier, David. "Three Against Justice: The Foole, the Sensible Knave, and the Lydian Shepherd." *Midwest Studies in Philosophy* 7 (1982): 11–29.

Gauthier, David. "Critical Notice of Jon Elster's *Ulysses and the Sirens: Studies in Rationality and Irrationality*." *Canadian Journal of Philosophy* 13 (1983): 133–40.

Gauthier, David. "Unequal Need: A Problem of Equity in Access to Health Care." In *Securing Access to Health Care: The Ethical Implications of Differences in the Availability of Health Services*, vol. 2, *President's Commission for the Study of Ethical Problems in Medicine and Biomedical and Behavioral Research*, 179–205. Washington, DC: U.S. Government Printing Office, 1983.

Gauthier, David. "Deterrence, Maximization, and Rationality." *Ethics* 94 (1984):

474–95. And in *The Security Gamble: Deterrence Dilemmas in the Nuclear Age*, edited by Douglas MacLean, 101–22, with "Afterthoughts," 159–61. Totowa, NJ: Rowman and Allanheld, 1984.

Gauthier, David. "Justice as Social Choice." In *Morality, Reason, and Truth*, edited by David Copp and David Zimmerman, 251–69. Totowa, NJ: Rowman and Allanheld, 1984.

Gauthier, David. "The Incompleat Egoist." In *The Tanner Lectures, on Human Values*, Vol. 5, edited by Sterling M. McMurrin, 67–119. Cambridge: Cambridge University Press, 1984.

Gauthier, David. "Bargaining and Justice." *Social Philosophy and Policy* 2 (1985): 29–47.

Gauthier, David. "Maximization Constrained: The Rationality of Cooperation." In *Paradoxes of Rationality and Cooperation: Prisoner's Dilemma and Newcomb's Problem*, edited by R. Campbell and L. Sowden, 75–93. Vancouver: University of British Columbia Press, 1985. (From *Morals by Agreement* by David Gauthier, chap. 6, sec. 2 and 3, with revisions by David Gauthier.)

Gauthier, David. "The Unity of Reason: A Subversive Reinterpretation of Kant." *Ethics* 96 (1985): 74–88.

Gauthier, David. *Morals by Agreement*. Oxford: Oxford University Press, 1986.

Gauthier, David. "Reason to be Moral?" *Synthese* 72 (1987): 5–27.

Gauthier, David. "Reply to Wolfram." *Philosophical Books* 18 (1987): 134–9.

Gauthier, David. "Taming Leviathan" (Critical Notice of Jean Hampton, *Hobbes and the Social Contract Tradition*, and Gregory S. Kavka, *Hobbesian Moral and Political Theory*). *Philosophy and Public Affairs* 16 (1987): 280–98.

Gauthier, David. "George Grant's Justice." *Dialogue* 27 (1988): 121–34.

Gauthier, David. "Hobbes' Social Contract." *Noûs* 22 (1988): 71–82. And in *Perspectives on Thomas Hobbes*, edited by G. A. J. Rogers and Alan Ryan, 125–52. Oxford: Clarendon Press, 1988.

Gauthier, David. "Moral Artifice." *Canadian Journal of Philosophy* 18 (1988): 385–418.

Gauthier, David. "Morality, Rational Choice, and Semantic Representation: A Reply to My Critics." *Social Philosophy and Policy* 5 (1988): 173–221. And in *The New Social Contract: Essays on Gauthier*, edited by E. F. Paul, F. D. Miller, and J. Paul, 173–221. Oxford: Blackwell, 1988.

Gauthier, David. "War and Nuclear Deterrence." In *Problems of Internation Justice*, edited by Steve Luper-Foy, 205–21. Boulder, CO: Westview Press, 1988.

Griffin, Nicholas. "Aboriginal Rights: Gauthier's Arguments for Despoilation." *Dialogue* (Canada) 20 (1981): 690–6.

Habermas, Jürgen. *Legitimation Crisis*. Boston: Beacon Press, 1975.

Haji, Ishtiyaque. "The Compliance Problem." *Pacific Philosophical Quarterly* 70 (1989): 105–21.

Hampton, Jean. *Hobbes and the Social Contract Tradition*. New York: Cambridge University Press, 1986.

Hampton, Jean. "Can We Agree on Morals?" *Canadian Journal of Philosophy* 18 (1988): 331–56.

Hampton, Jean. "Comments on Gauthier's 'Hobbes' Social Contract.' " *Noûs* 22 (1988): 85–6.

Hannaford, R. V. "Gauthier, Hobbes, and Hobbesians." *International Journal of Moral and Social Studies* 3 (1988): 239–54.

Hardin, Russell. "Bargaining for Justice." *Social Philosophy and Policy* 5 (1988): 65–74.

Harman, Gilbert. "Justice and Bargaining." *Social Philosophy and Policy* 1 (1983): 114–31.

Harman, Gilbert. "Rationality in Agreement: A Commentary on Gauthier's *Morals by Agreement.*" *Social Philosophy and Policy* 5 (1988): 1–16.

Herbert, Gary B. "The Issue of Validity in Hobbes's Moral and Political Philosophy." *Philosophy Research Archives* 1(1020) (1975): 1–9.

Hubin, Don, and Mark Lambeth. "Providing for Rights." *Dialogue* 27(3) (1988): 489–502. Reprinted in this volume, Chapter 8.

Jolley, Nicholas. "Hobbes' Dagger in the Heart." *Canadian Journal of Philosophy* 17 (1987): 855–73.

Kalai, Ehud. "Solutions to the bargaining problem," in *Social Goals and Social Organization: Essays in Memory of Elisha Pazner,* edited by Leonid Hurwicz, David Schmeidler, and Jugo Sonnenschein. Cambridge: Cambridge University Press, 1985.

Kalai, Ehud, and Meir Smordinsky. "Other Solutions to Nash's Bargaining Problem." *Econometrica* 43 (1975): 513–8.

Kavka, Gregory. *Hobbesian Moral and Political Theory.* Princeton: Princeton University Press, 1986.

Kavka, Gregory. "Morals by Agreement." *Mind* 96 (1987): 117–21.

Kraus, Jody S., and Jules L. Coleman. "Morality and the Theory of Rational Choice." *Ethics* 97 (1987): 715–49. Reprinted in this volume, Chapter 15.

Lomasky, Loren. "Agreeable Morality?" *Critical Review* 2 (1988): 36–49.

MacIntosh, Duncan. "Libertarian Agency and Rational Morality: Action-Theoretic Objections to Gauthier's Dispositional Solutions of the Compliance Problem." *Southern Journal of Philosophy* 26 (1988): 499–525.

McClennen, Edward F. "Constrained Maximization and Resolute Choice." *Social Philosophy and Policy* 5 (1988): 95–118.

McGray, James. "Classical Utilitarianism and the Analogy Argument." *Southern Journal of Philosophy* 22 (1984): 389–402.

MacIntosh, Duncan. "Two Gauthiers?" *Dialogue* (Canada) 28 (1989): 43–61.

McNeilly, F.S. "Pre-Emptive Violence: A Reply to Gauthier." *Inquiry* 15 (1972): 330–41.

Mendola, Joseph. "Gauthier's 'Morals by Agreement' and Two Kinds of Rationality." *Ethics* 97 (1987): 765–74.

Morris, Bertram. "Gauthier on Hobbes' Moral and Political Philosophy." *Philosophy and Phenomenological Research* 33 (1973): 387–92.

Morris, Christopher. "The Relation Between Self-Interest and Justice in Contractarian Ethics." *Social Philosophy and Policy* 5 (1988): 119–53.

Narveson, Jan. (1984). "Reason in Ethics – or Reason versus Ethics." In *Morality, Reason, and Truth,* edited by David Copp and David Zimmerman, 228–50. Totowa, NJ: Rowman and Allanheld, 1984.

Narveson, Jan. "McDonald and McDougal, Pride and Gain and Justice: Comment on a Criticism of Gauthier." *Dialogue* (Canada) 27 (1988): 503–6.

Nelson, Allan. "Economic Rationality and Morality." *Philosophy and Public Affairs* 17 (1988): 149–66.

Nelson, William. "Justice and Rational Cooperation." *Southern Journal of Philosophy* 14 (1976): 303–12.

Paul, Ellen Frankel, Fred D. Miller, and Jeffrey Paul, eds. *The New Social Contract: Essays on Gauthier.* New York: Blackwell, 1988.

Pence, Gregory. "Recent Work on Virtue." *American Philosophical Quarterly* 21 (1984): 281–98.

Perkins, Michael, and Donald C. Hubin. "Self-subverting Principles of Choice." *Canadian Journal of Philosophy* 16 (1986): 1–10.

Provis, C. "Gauthier on Coordination." *Dialogue* (Canada) 16 (1977): 507–9.

Rawls, John. *A Theory of Justice.* Cambridge: Harvard University Press, 1971.

Ripstein, Arthur. "Gauthier's Liberal Individual." *Dialogue* (Canada) 28 (1989): 63–76.

Roemer, John. "The Mismarriage of Bargaining Theory and Distributive Justice." *Ethics* 97 (1986): 88–110.

Sayre-McCord, Geoffrey. "Deceptions and Reasons to Be Moral." *American Philosophical Quarterly* 26 (1989): 113–122. Reprinted in this volume, Chapter 12.

Scanlon, T. M., Jr. "Contractualism and Utilitarianism." In *Utilitarianism and Beyond,* edited by Amartya Sen and Bernard Williams. Cambridge: Cambridge University Press, 1982.

Scanlon, T. M., Jr. "Equality of Resources and Equality of Welfare: A Forced Marriage." *Ethics* 97 (1985): 111–18.

Sobel, J. H. "Interaction Problems for Utility Maximizers." *Canadian Journal of Philosophy* 4 (1975): 677–88.

Sobel, J. H. "Maximizing, Optimizing, and Prospering." *Dialogue* (Canada) 27 (1988): 233–62.

Summer, L. W. "Justice Contracted." *Dialogue* (Canada) 26 (1987): 523–48.

Thomas, Laurence. "Rationality and Affectivity: The Metaphysics of the Moral Self." *Social Philosophy and Policy* 5 (1988): 154–72.

Vallentyne, Peter. "Gauthier on Rationality and Morality." *Edios* 5 (1986): 79–95.

Vallentyne, Peter. "Contractarianism and the Assumption of Mutual Unconcern." *Philosophical Studies* 54 (1988): 73–8. Reprinted in this volume, Chapter 5.

Vorbej, Mark. "Gauthier on Deterrence." *Dialogue* (Canada) 25 (1986): 471–6.

Webster, Michael. "Minimax Concession." *Edios* 5 (1986): 47–64.

Wein, Sheldon. "Plato and the Social Contract." *Philosophy Research Archives* 12 (1986): 67–77.

Weirich, Paul. "Hierarchial Maximization of Two Kinds of Utility." *Philosophy of Science* 55 (1988): 560–82.

Index